Mao's Generals Remember Korea

Mao's Generals Remember Korea

Translated and edited by

Xiaobing Li
Allan R. Millett
Bin Yu

University Press of Kansas

Published by the University Press of Kansas (Lawrence, Kansas 66049), which was
organized by the Kansas Board of Regents and is operated and funded by Emporia
State University, Fort Hays State University, Kansas State University, Pittsburg State
University, the University of Kansas, and Wichita State University.

Library of Congress Cataloging-in-Publication Data

Mao's generals remember Korea / translated and edited by Xiaobing Li, Allan R. Millet,
Bin Yu.
    p.   cm. — (Modern war studies)
  Translated from individually written Chinese originals.
  Includes bibliographical references and index.
  ISBN 0-7006-1095-2 (cloth : alk. paper)
    1. Korean War, 1950-1953—China. 2. Korean War, 1950-1953—Participation, Chinese.
I. Li, Xiaobing, 1954- II. Millett, Allan Reed. III. Yu, Bin. IV. Series.

DS919.5 .M36 2001
951.904'2351—dc21   2001017737

British Library Cataloguing in Publication Data is available.

Printed in the United States of America

10 9 8 7 6 5 4 3 2 1

Contents

Acknowledgments

Many people from several institutions have helped us with this book. The first note of appreciation is addressed to Professor Shuguang Zhang of the University of Maryland, who helped with the selection of chapters and with approaches to critical issues in the early stages of our project.

Special thanks go to many individuals at the University of Central Oklahoma. Dr. T. H. Baughman, dean of the College of Liberal Arts, and Dr. Kenny Brown, chairman of the Department of History and Geography, have been very supportive throughout the past years. Dr. John Osburn reproduced the photographs, and Joanete Randell provided secretarial assistance.

We also want to thank our Ohio State University and Wittenberg University colleagues and collaborators, especially Charles Finfrock, Witttenberg University, and Maj. James C. Fischer, U.S. Army, for their cartographic assistance, and Beth Russell of the Mershon Center, Ohio State University.

At various times, Donald M. Bishop, former deputy public affairs officer, U.S. Embassy, Beijing, 1997–2000, and Dr. Song Zhongyue of the China Society for Strategy and Management Research, Beijing, People's Republic of China, encouraged us in our research and provided essential information.

In evaluating and editing the memoirs of Gen. Chai Chengwen, we received invaluable advice from important surviving members of the United Nations Command negotiating team at Panmunjom: Col. Howard S. Levie, JAG, USA (Ret.), the staff counsel; Col. James C. Murray, USMC (Ret.), senior liaison officer; Lt. Col. Kenneth Wu, USA (Ret.), Chinese interpreter; and Richard F. Underwood and Dr. Horace G. Underwood, Korean language interpreters.

Any remaining errors of fact, language usage, and interpretation are ours.

A Note on Transliteration

The pinyin romanization system is applied to Chinese names of persons, places, and terms. The transliteration is also used for the titles of Chinese publications. Some popular names have traditional Wade-Giles spellings appearing in parentheses after the first use of the pinyin. The appendix contains a list of selected Chinese leaders' and CPVF commanders' names in both pinyin and Wade-Giles.

Abbreviations

CCP	Chinese Communist Party
CIA	Central Intelligence Agency
CINC FECOM	Commander in Chief, Far East Command
CINC UNC	Commander in Chief, United Nations Command
CMC	Central Military Commission
CPVF	Chinese People's Volunteers Force
DMZ	Demilitarized Zone
DPRK	Democratic People's Republic of Korea
FEAF	Far East Air Force (U.S.)
FRUS	*Foreign Relations of the United States*
GMD	Guomindang
JCS	Joint Chiefs of Staff
KMT	Kuomintang
KWP	Korean Workers' Party (North Korea)
NATO	North Atlantic Treaty Organization
NEBDA	Northeast Border Defense Army
NEMR	Northeast Military Region
NKPA	North Korean People's Army
NSC	National Security Council (U.S.)
PLA	People's Liberation Army
POW	Prisoner of War
PRC	People's Republic of China
ROC	Republic of China
ROK	Republic of Korea
UN	United Nations
UNC	United Nations Command

UNF	United Nations Force
U.S.	United States
USA	U.S. Army
USAF	U.S. Air Force
USMC	U.S. Marine Corps
USN	U.S. Navy
USNR	U.S. Navy Reserve
USSR	Union of Soviet Socialist Republics

Introduction

Xiaobing Li, Allan R. Millett, Bin Yu

One hot afternoon in late July 1988 several retired People's Liberation Army (PLA) generals gathered for a tea party. The host was retired Maj. Gen. Chai Chengwen, former head of the People's Republic of China's (PRC) military mission to Pyongyang in 1950 and chief administrative officer for the Chinese negotiating team at Panmunjom. That day's "idle conversation" [*liaotian*] soon focused on the Chinese intervention in the Korean War as Chai reminded his guests that the next July 27 would be the thirty-fifth anniversary of the signing of the Korean cease-fire agreement. Excited and nostalgic, the generals talked freely about their Korean experience. As Chai prepared to record the conversation, some guests warned that they should remain anonymous, but others insisted that "now that we all are retired and carry no responsibility for any government offices, we shall voice our personal opinions freely" [*changsuo yuyan*].¹ The result of that afternoon's chat—and many others—is the collective memoir, *Banmendian Tanpan* [*Panmunjom negotiations*].

No matter how politically indoctrinated they might have become, the generals were culturally bound to cherish the memory of the past. More important, they had only recently felt comfortable in talking about their past experiences, including Korea, and in allowing their recollections to be recorded, written, and even published. The late 1980s and 1990s brought a considerable number of Korean War memoirs to Chinese readers. Some are in the form of books, some appear as journal and magazine articles, and others are printed as reference studies for restricted circulation only. Almost all of the living high-ranking commanders who participated in the Chinese intervention have contributed to the body of Korean War memoirs in one way or another.

Interestingly, the Chinese generals' counterparts, the senior officers of the U.S. armed forces and the United Nations Command (UNC), published their memoirs long ago. Omar N. Bradley's *A General's Life* (1983), Mark W. Clark's *From the Danube to the Yalu* (1954), J. Lawton Collins's *War in Peacetime* (1969), Douglas

1

MacArthur's *Reminiscences* (1964), and Matthew B. Ridgway's *The Korean War* (1967) have been continually cited by scholars and have enriched the Korean War literature. More interestingly, several of the American generals' memoirs have been translated into Chinese and widely circulated and frequently cited on the mainland.

What have the Chinese generals remembered about their Korean experience? How have they characterized the Chinese intervention? What insights have they provided with regard to Chinese Communist war philosophy, military doctrine, political mobilization, strategy, and tactics? How have they reflected upon their experience retrospectively? English readers now can acquire some answers to these questions from these collective reminiscences of Chinese generals on their Korean War experience. The editors hope that this book will be a unique contribution to the English-language literature on the Korean War since it offers direct testimony by the Chinese generals themselves.

If "forgotten" in the West, the war in Korea is by no means forgotten by the Chinese. Emerging victorious from the civil war in China (1946–1949), the Chinese Communist Party (CCP) founded the People's Republic of China on October 1, 1949, with the new regime's capital in Beijing (Peking). Shortly afterward the CCP leadership undertook a series of foreign policy initiatives. In November 1949, Mao Zedong (Mao Tse-tung) traveled to Moscow for a summit meeting with Soviet leader Joseph Stalin, occasioned by the celebrations for his seventieth birthday. After long and difficult negotiations with Stalin and others, Mao and Stalin signed a Moscow-Beijing alliance in February 1950, which ensured Soviet military assistance if China was invaded by an "imperialist" power—most possibly, the United States or Japan. The Chinese feared that a resurgent Japan would use American forces for its reentry to Manchuria. There seems little doubt that this military alliance marked the beginning of a new stage of the Cold War on the Asian front.

The Cold War situation soon deteriorated in East Asia. A civil war that began on the Korean peninsula in 1948 escalated into an international war on June 25, 1950, when North Korean Communist troops launched a surprise attack on South Korea. The Truman administration immediately responded by sending in armed forces under the UN flag to stop "Communist aggression." The battlefield situation tilted in favor of the South Koreans when Gen. Douglas MacArthur's amphibious envelopment at Inchon and the U.S. Eighth Army's counteroffensive in September caused the North Korean army to disintegrate and the Communist's main line of resistance to collapse. Early in October, the UN Command ordered an all-out offensive northward, first crossing the Thirty-eighth Parallel, the political demarcation line between North and South Korea, and then approaching the Yalu River, a boundary river separating North Korea and Northeast China.

Galvanized by the UN/U.S. intervention in Korea, the Chinese Communists did not sit still with "folded hands." From the beginning of the conflict, Beijing openly supported North Korea's "national liberation" and condemned U.S. "imperialist intervention." Meanwhile, the CCP leadership decided to get psychologically and militarily prepared for a possible war between the United States and China. In

August the CCP Central Military Commission [*Zhongyang Junshi Weiyuanhui*] deployed four infantry armies (the Thirty-eighth, Thirty-ninth, Fortieth, and Forty-second)—among the best PLA combat forces—to Manchuria. In September, a large number of strategic reserve divisions were also placed in North China.

Informed by periodic reports from his military mission to Pyongyang, led by then-colonel Chai Chengwen, an expert on American military forces and a trusted member of the PLA's intelligence directorate, Mao Zedong watched the development of the Korean War with growing dismay. Despite Chinese warnings to the North Korean leadership that the United Nations Command would conduct a major amphibious landing at Inchon, Kim Il Sung's army could not respond rapidly enough to prevent the retake of Seoul by late September 1950. Nor could Kim halt the collapse and retreat of the North Korean People's Army (NKPA) from South Korea and past the prepared defenses along the Thirty-eighth Parallel.

The NKPA's defeat—and the failure of the Soviet Union to undertake air and naval operations against the UNC—forced Mao to face directly the prospect of Chinese military intervention in the war. Mao communicated through Chai Chengwen to Kim Il Sung that such a consideration was under way, probably with the hope that this implied promise of support would stiffen the North Koreans, who still might patch together a new front that would start at Pyongyang on the west and stretch to Wonsan on the east coast. This hope took its first shock when the Republic of Korea's (ROK) Third Division crossed the Thirty-eighth Parallel to stay on October 1, encouraged by Syngman Rhee to unify Korea. Rhee faced no restraint from any American commander, not even from Washington and the commander in chief, Harry S. Truman. In fact, the Truman administration had decided to unify Korea by force and awaited only United Nations approval of this policy to order a general advance northward by the entire Eighth Army. If Mao expected to change the fortunes of war, he had to act swiftly.

Having received direct requests for military intervention from both Stalin and Kim Il Sung, Mao called a meeting of his most influential and important advisers in Beijing on October 1. Most of them were members of the inner council (Politburo) of the CCP Central Committee's Standing Committee, itself an inner elite of the Central Committee. Some of the participants held positions on the CCP Central Military Commission (CMC) as well.

During the meetings that followed, the party leaders received military counsel from Zhu De (Chu Teh, titular commander of the PLA), Nie Rongzhen (Nieh Jung-ch'en, acting chief of the PLA General Staff), and Peng Dehuai (P'eng Teh-h'uai, vice chairman of the Central Commission and commander of the First Field Army, the territorial force in Northwest China). General Lin Biao (Lin Piao), the foremost field army commander of the Chinese civil war, had already expressed deep reservations about any military intervention in the Korean War, and he argued that his perilous health (a complex set of circulatory problems aggravated by malaria and the stress of unpleasant assignments) prevented him from postponing an immediate medical trip to Russia. Lin's departure was not a good omen, but his reluctance also found persuasive expression in two other colleagues, Zhou Enlai (Chou En-lai) and Gao Gang (Kao Kang), two of the most influential members of Mao's inner circle. Mao had probably made up his mind by October 1 that China had no alternative to military intervention. He actually drafted a message to Stalin pledging military aid to North Korea. He did not, however, enjoy full support from his colleagues, and his actual message to Stalin was that Chinese intervention did not look promising *at that moment*. Mao reported that "a final decision has not been taken." For two weeks the future of the People's Republic hung in the balance.

Stripping away the secondary issues of Chinese domestic politics and the international attempt to neutralize the American war effort through pressure from other postcolonial nations, especially India, the Chinese dilemma was quite simple: if the Chinese army entered the war, what kind of direct support could it count on from the Soviet Union? The Sino-Soviet Treaty of Friendship and Alliance (1950) pledged "all-out" assistance in the case that either party was attacked by a third party, but such an attack had not yet taken place. The treaty contained no specifics on just what sort of military assistance would be provided or whether the recipient thus assumed an obligation to pay for the assistance in some way.

The Chinese position, communicated through Zhou Enlai during an emergency trip to Moscow (October 8–18, 1950), emphasized aid that would open the gravest risk to the Soviet Union of war with the United States: direct offensive air support for the Chinese troops during their operations within North Korea. Such operations might include attacks on American air bases within Korea itself, but not attacks on the bases in Japan. It is unlikely that the Chinese raised the issue of air attacks on Anglo-American carrier task forces, although Soviet naval aviation units based at Vladivostok and Port Arthur might have carried them out, even coordinated them with Soviet submarine attacks. The Chinese, however, had been quite professional in identifying UNC air attacks as their most serious operational problem.

The nature of Soviet air support dominated Zhou Enlai's negotiations with Stalin, and these talks, interpreted for Mao by Zhou in a series of messages to Beijing, almost brought a halt to Chinese military intervention. Stalin promised to provide interceptors, a ground-based air intercept radar system, and several regiments of antiaircraft artillery for the defense of Manchuria, including the air space above the Yalu River; but he would not provide air cover for the Chinese divisions fighting within Korea itself. He promised to accelerate the creation of the PLA air force, already under way in the training of Chinese to fly MiG-15s and Soviet jet light bombers. Stalin held out the possibility that the PLA air force might be able to provide offensive air support for the Chinese troops within Korea, along with the reconstituted North Korean air force. Not only would the Russians provide aircraft, but they also would provide the ground-support material to establish Communist air bases within Korea. The Chinese had other requirements for waging war in Korea: the modernization and standardization of PLA weapons from small arms to heavy artillery and the transfer of thousands of trucks (and some trained Russian drivers) to the PLA for logistical operations on both sides of the Yalu River.

There was no serious disagreement on this type of assistance, although its scope and cost remained open for further negotiations.

Dismayed by the qualified nature of Stalin's commitment of air support, Zhou Enlai (with the pro-Soviet Lin Biao at his side for military advice) warned Mao on October 12 by telegram that the Russians might not provide the air support the Chinese required, which included air superiority operations to protect the Chinese at a minimum and offensive air operations against the UNC within Korea at a maximum. Just how alarmed Mao really was remains debatable, but he certainly told Peng Dehuai and Gao Gang, his senior military and civilian representatives in Manchuria, to stop the last-minute military preparations for invasion. The news of the pause—which might become permanent—went directly to Stalin, who would not be moved from his position on the limitations of air support.

In the crisis Mao conferred with his inner circle on October 12 and 13, and on October 14 he issued orders that the preparations for intervention should continue. This decision meant that Chinese support units would cross the Yalu and create supply depots for the fighting armies of the Chinese People's Volunteers Force (CPVF), 260,000 strong, still massed north of the river. Through Peng Dehuai, the commanders of the CPVF conveyed their worries about the UNC air threat, but Mao would not be moved. On the night of October 19–20 the advance guard of the CPVF's Fortieth Army crossed the Yalu over the Andong-Sinuiju bridge by train and then marched south to meet forward elements of the U.S. I Corps.[2]

From its first successful encounter with three South Korean divisions and the U.S. First Cavalry Division in the battle of Unsan-Onjong, October 25–November 6, 1950, the Chinese army entered two and a half years of war within Korea that ended with a military armistice on July 27, 1953. The cease-fire brought an opportunity for the United Nations Command and the Chinese People's Volunteers Force to redeploy their forces to other areas. After five major offensives in 1950 and 1951 and two minor offensives in autumn 1952 and in July 1953, Mao Zedong conceded that the CPVF could not reunify Korea by force of arms or continue the war for any useful purpose that justified the sacrifice of additional Chinese lives.[3]

But China did not withdraw its forces from Korea until 1958. The Chinese People's Volunteers Force had been in Korea for eight years since its first entry in October 1950—two years and nine months of actual combat, and five years and three months of peacetime duties. The People's Republic of China had paid a huge price for its military intervention. As many as twenty-five infantry armies (73 percent of the PLA infantry forces), sixteen artillery divisions (67 percent of the artillery forces), ten armored divisions (100 percent), twelve air force divisions (52 percent), and six security guard divisions fought in Korea along with hundreds of thousands of logistical personnel and laborers.

According to Chinese statistics, a total of 2.3 million combatant troops entered Korea and engaged in the war. In addition, twelve air force divisions had 672 pilots and 59,000 ground-service personnel participating in the war. China had also mobilized a large number of laborers for the war, totaling 600,000 men. As part of the

Chinese Volunteers, they entered Korea and worked in logistical supply and support services such as warehouse keeping, manpower transportation, and railroad and highway construction. Thus, a total of 3 million Chinese Volunteers eventually participated in the Korean War. Observers had every reason to believe that, although the PRC government did not declare war on any foreign country and the Chinese forces entered Korea in the name of the Volunteers, this war, in fact, was the largest foreign war in Chinese military history.

From October 19, 1950 to July 27, 1953, the Chinese casualties in the Korean War totaled 1,010,700 men, including 152,000 dead, 383,000 wounded, 450,000 hospitalized, 21,700 prisoners of war, and 4,000 missing in action.[4] China had spent a total of about 10 billion yuan in Renminbi (equal to $3.3 billion according to the exchange rate at that time).[5] In terms of the war materials and supplies, the Chinese force consumed a total of 5.6 million tons of goods and supplies during its intervention, including the loss of 399 airplanes and 12,916 vehicles.[6]

Why did the Chinese Communists intervene in Korea? How did the Chinese Communist forces fight the war? What lessons, if any, did the Chinese learn from their combat experiences? These questions must be addressed if one is to arrive at a keen understanding of what had caused the first "limited war" fought by the United Nations under its provisions for collective security and the first "international war" fought by the Chinese Communist regime to halt counterrevolution. This collection of reminiscences of the Chinese generals will certainly help one to come to grips with such issues.

These collective reminiscences offer an important source of information for concerned scholars and learned readers of Korean War history who do not read Chinese. This book contains new and reliable materials on the Chinese intervention. Each of the generals offers special, personal insight into specific aspects of the war, including combat operations, logistics, political control, field command, and communications. It is important to point out that, in writing their memoirs, most of these high-ranking officials relied not only on their personal papers but also on still classified archives. Moreover, they have constantly cited from such important documents as *Mao Zedong Junshi Wenxuan—Neibuban* [*Selected military works of Mao Zedong—internal edition*] (1981), *Jianguo Yilai Mao Zedong Wengao* [*Mao Zedong's manuscripts since the founding of the PRC*] (1987–1993), *Peng Dehuai Junshi Wenxuan* [*Selected military works of Peng Dehuai*] (1988), *Nie Rongzhen Junshi Wenxuan* [*Selected military writings of Nie Rongzhen*] (1992), *Zhongguo Renmin Zhiyuanjun Kangmei Yuanchao Zhanshi* [*The history of the Chinese People's Volunteers Force in the War to Resist America and Aid Korea*] (1988), *Kangmei Yuanchao Zhanzheng* [*China Today series: The War to Resist America and Aid Korea*] (1990), four volumes of *Kangmei Yuanchao Zhanzheng Houqin Jingyan Zongjie* [*A summary of the CPVF's logistical service experience in the War to Resist America and Aid Korea*] (1986–1987), and two volumes of *Zhongguo Renmin Zhiyuanjun Kangmei Yuanchao Zhanzheng Zhengzhi Gongzuo Zongjie* [*A summary of the CPVF's political work in the War to Resist America and Aid*

Korea] (1985 and 1989). There can be little doubt that the official accounts attempt to glorify the Chinese intervention. Given the sources referred to, however, much of the information found there is insightful and cannot be found elsewhere.

This book also provides insights so important that no serious scholar could afford to neglect them. As the commander in chief and political commissar of both the CPVF and the Chinese–North Korean Allied Forces in Korea, Marshal Peng Dehuai gives detailed information and personal accounts of the major battles he commanded, important decisions made on the front, daily intensive communication between him and Mao Zedong, cooperation with Kim Il Sung, his visit to Moscow with Stalin, and his meetings with American generals at the Panmunjom peace negotiations. Peng wrote his autobiographies as a dismissed marshal during the decade when he was put under house arrest by Mao, so his recollections were not part of China's propaganda for its "glorious war" in Korea. Peng's name was even excluded from the literature of the Korean War for more than two decades, and his memoirs were not allowed to be published until 1981. The excerpts from them provide the fullest account of his military experience and political concerns during the Korean War.

Acting Chief of Staff and Marshal Nie Rongzhen's account of how the top CCP leadership debated and then decided on the intervention in Korea is invaluable. In charge of the war mobilization from 1950 to 1952, Nie in particular recalled the difficulties the new regime faced in financing the Chinese intervention. Chief of Staff and Marshal Xu Xiangqian (Hsu Hsiang-ch'ian), who resumed the leadership of the PLA Headquarters of the General Staff late in 1952 after a two-year sick leave, wrote about the subtle and sometimes difficult PRC–USSR relationships; his vivid description of his trip to Moscow for more material assistance in 1952 enhances one's understanding of that "special relationship." Excerpts from General Yang Dezhi's memoirs, *Weile Heping* [*For the sake of peace*] (1987), reveal the secrets of Chinese Communist military strategy and tactics. As a deputy commander of the CPVF responsible for combat operations from early 1951 to the end of the war in July 1953, Yang discussed in great detail how the CPVF Command designed and organized each battle, offensive and defensive alike. The CPVF faced a stiffened UNF, richly endowed with heavy field artillery and offensive aviation. Another deputy commander of the CPVF, General Hong Xuezhi, who took charge of the CPVF logistics during the war, provides a comprehensive account of CPVF rear service problems and performance. It was only during the Korean War, Hong explained, that the Chinese Communist forces began to realize the importance of a standardized and efficient logistics system.

An answer to how the CPVF survived a war in the rear—i.e., battling the air raids on Chinese supply lines—lies in Hong's narrative. A no less significant account is CPVF Political Department director and general Du Ping's reflection on the CPVF political task. Political mobilization and indoctrination were an integral part of the Chinese Communist military tradition. Du addressed such issues as new challenges to CPVF political control, new tactics employed, and new lessons learned in Korea. General Chai Chengwen applied his knowledge of Western military forces and political affairs to provide an especially useful account of the armistice negotiations that finally produced a cease-fire agreement in 1953.

Further, this book is meant to be readable. Although individually written, the generals' accounts are largely issue-oriented, focusing on matters such as decision making, operation plans, battle commands, field communication, combat organizations, political mobilization, logistical service, and truce negotiations. A special effort is made to avoid unnecessary repetition. Emphasis is also placed on memories, description, and interpretations of the generals' personal experiences in the war. However, the language—especially the technical terms—remains a formidable obstacle. As a revolutionary and largely irregular force, the Chinese Communist army developed its own rhetorical and conceptual frameworks on military affairs, which are largely alien to Western readers. To solve this problem, commonly used Western military terms are included to help define the equivalent CCP political and military terms.

The memoirs of the Chinese generals are important source materials for Western readers. For a more comprehensive understanding of the PRC's conduct of the Korean War, however, a summary account by Bin Yu on the CPVF in the Korean War is included as chapter 1. Originally published in the *Journal of Strategic Review* in 1998 and thoroughly revised here, it is the most updated short history in English, based on Chinese sources, dealing with the CPVF's operations. As an essential part of the book, it may provide the means to place the translated excerpts in context and perspective. It also demonstrates that the PRC has drawn, and is continuing to draw, military, diplomatic, and strategic lessons from the war it fought fifty years ago with the world's most powerful military.

One more unique feature of this book is the inclusion of a series of photos and illustrations depicting various aspects of the CPVF's Korean experience, such as the battlefield landscape; its defensive works, including tunnels and bunkers; individual officers and soldiers; settings for political meetings; and logistical efforts. Used with the permission of the PLA Military Museum in Beijing, these illustrations for the most part have never appeared in English-language books.

Why did the Chinese intervene in Korea? How did the Chinese People's Volunteers fight the war? To help readers understand these questions and to trace the story of the Chinese intervention in the language of the senior Chinese commanders, this book offers Westerners a unique introduction to the Chinese experience in the Korean War.

1

What China Learned from Its "Forgotten War" in Korea

Bin Yu

INTRODUCTION

China's decision to intervene in the Korean War (1950–1953) has been extensively documented in the West,[1] though not necessarily completely. Recent Russian and Chinese literature on the origins of the Korean War points to an emerging, certainly revisionist, interpretation that Stalin's decision to allow North Korea to unify the country by force was primarily because of his concern about China, not the United States.[2]

While the scholarly focus has been on China's decision to intervene in Korea, much less is known about how the Chinese People's Volunteers Force actually confronted the U.S. military during the war.[3] Ever since the 1990s, this three-year war has become one of the most discussed subjects in China. Aside from veterans' nostalgia, historians' curiosity, and the public's new thirst for any information about this "forgotten war," an unspoken reason for the recent proliferation of Korean War literature is related to the shift in the People's Liberation Army's strategic thinking since the mid-1980s. The PLA has turned its attention from preparing to fight a total war to dealing with wars limited and localized in scope.

With the Soviet empire having vanished almost overnight, the potential threat to China's security now seems to come only from the United States, the lone military superpower. Although this "automatic upgrading" of the United States as the number-one potential enemy has yet to become a reality, the PLA must prepare for a variety of scenarios, ranging from a crisis across the Taiwan Straits to the defense of its territorial claims in the South China Sea, which could involve one or more major powers. Again, the Korean War is the only meaningful reference point for sustained PLA contingency operations beyond China's border.[4] The Korean War is also the only real experience, no matter how outdated, that the PLA has had operating against the U.S. ground forces.

Despite China's renewed interest in the lessons of the Korean War, current Western scholarship tends to dismiss it as a useful experience for China, except for "highly dubious lessons."[5] Such an attitude by the PRC is said to be determined by its persistent Communist ideology[6] or by a highly romantic and certainly irresponsible view on the threat and use of force.[7] These arguments also challenge the long-held realist interpretation that China intervened because of a heightened security concern.[8] To argue that China has security concerns like any other power is even politically incorrect, as recent scholarship suggests, in that it is "sympathetic" to Beijing's position.[9]

These "ideological" and "cultural" arguments, however, tell us little about the timing and manner with which the PRC and PLA made and executed strategic and tactical decisions. Nor can they explain the PRC's policy adaptation and changes both during and after the war. A cursory look at the Chinese literature suggests that a learning curve by the CPVF and the PRC did occur in both tactical and strategic terms. Such a curve is not linear but twisted and is not without extended delays. The dynamic bargaining process—between China and its allies and between top political elites and field commanders—certainly sheds new light on the behavior of China's foreign and defense policies as well as on its civil-military relations. To dismiss entirely China's security and strategic concerns in the Korean peninsula as purely ideological or cultural, therefore, will run the risk of misperceiving China again, particularly at a time when the situation in Korea anticipates radical and far-reaching changes and when the Taiwan Straits situation has entered a more conflictual phase, with the proindependence Democratic Progressive Party's (DPP) victory over the 100-plus-year-old Nationalist Party (KMT) in the presidential election of 2000.

Given this risk, the question now is what lessons did the PLA learn from the war? How did the CPVF conduct its operations, given its recognition of superior American power? What was the learning curve, forming the right or the wrong lessons, for the CPVF in a new and unfamiliar situation like Korea? To what extent do the lessons of the war affect China's conflict and diplomatic behavior in the past, present, and future, particularly in policies toward the Korean peninsula? How have these lessons influenced the PLA's current modernization and professionalization?

One of the keys to understanding how the CPVF acquitted itself can be found in the assessments Chinese leaders made of the UN forces and in how they prepared the CPVF. The most crucial period for China's learning occurred during the first eight months after its intervention in October 1950 when the CPVF engaged in what it called "five campaigns." After this, the war settled into a more conventional pattern of trench warfare along the Thirty-eighth Parallel. The CPVF's first two campaigns caused considerable losses among the UN forces because of the impact of the former's surprise intervention. Their initial victories, however, led to some unrealistic expectations by the PRC leaders regarding the CPVF's capability; hence, a series of strategic and tactical mistakes resulted in considerable losses to the CPVF in the next two campaigns. These developments forced the PRC leaders to scale down significantly their war aims—from driving the UN forces out of Korea to a more realistic goal of protecting China's security and reaching a negotiated solution to the war.

Readers of this book will be able to probe into official accounts of the Korean War and into many new unofficial publications that are beginning to offer a more objective and comprehensive assessment of the CPVF's conduct of the war. Interviews conducted during trips to China in the past few years add significantly to that perspective.

PREWAR ASSESSMENT AND PREPARATION

The outbreak of the Korean War on June 25, 1950, came as quite a surprise to Mao, who was not informed by either the North Koreans or the Russians with regard to specific war plans and strategy.[10] Nor did the Chinese anticipate any direct involvement in the early stage of the war.[11] It was not until early August when the North Korean military offense was stalled at Pusan that Mao and others started to take a serious look at the war.[12]

The possibility of engaging the U.S. military, nonetheless, was a profound challenge to the doctrines and capabilities of the PLA. From the beginning, top political and military leaders realized that this conflict was going to be very different from others in PLA history. In fact, most of them opposed an intervention in Korea,[13] since they were well aware of the superior firepower of the U.S. military. Lin Biao, for example, strongly opposed military intervention, both before and after Mao's October 2, 1950, decision to intervene. He even declined to command the CPVF. As a result, Mao had to turn to his second choice, Peng Dehuai, though Lin clearly had been the most capable PLA field commander during the Chinese civil war (1946–1949). Lin had argued that the firepower of an American division was perhaps ten to twenty times more powerful than its Chinese equivalent. He and others who opposed China's intervention also pointed to the huge gap between Chinese and American war-sustaining capabilities as well as the possibility that the war might destroy China's industrial base and indefinitely postpone its modernization.[14]

Mao, however, was more focused on geopolitical and historical considerations. After all, Korea had been a convenient invasion route to continental Asia. Japan had launched several invasions against China through the Korean peninsula between the 1868 Meiji period and World War II. Mao also reasoned that China might have to confront the United States if Korea fell under UN control. He was therefore more willing to trade the tactical disadvantage facing the CPVF for the future safety of the Chinese state by engaging UN forces outside China.[15] That said, Mao also was acutely aware of the difficulties China would face in confronting UN forces. His cable to Stalin on October 2, 1950, reflected his concerns:

According to our intelligence to date, an American corps (composed of two infantry divisions and a mechanized division) has 1,500 guns of 70mm to 240mm caliber, including tank cannons and anti-aircraft guns. In comparison, each of our armies (composed of three divisions) has only 36 such guns. The enemy dominates the air. By comparison, we have only just started training pilots. We shall not be able to employ more than 300 aircraft in combat until February 1951. Accordingly, we do not now have any certainty of success in annihilating a single American corps in one blow. . . . For the purpose of eliminating completely one enemy corps with a certainty of success, we should in such a situation assemble four times as many troops as the enemy (employing four field armies to deal with one enemy corps) and firepower from one-and-a-half times to twice as heavy as the enemy's (using 2,200 to 3,000 guns of more than 70mm caliber to deal with 1,500 enemy guns of the same caliber).

The lack of modern equipment clearly constrained the CPVF's deployment. In the same telegram to Stalin, Mao also outlined his rather conservative and cautious tactical approach: "At the initial stage, they [CPVF] will merely engage in defensive warfare to wipe out small detachments of enemy troops and ascertain the enemy's situation; on the other hand, they will wait for the delivery of Soviet weapons. Once they are [well] equipped, they will cooperate with the Korean comrades in counterattacks to annihilate American troops."[16] Although this part of the cable may have been intended to "blackmail" the Soviet leader by implying "no weapons, no action,"[17] it also reflected genuine concern about engaging the world's most powerful country. Thus, Mao intended to limit the scale of the conflict as much as possible. For example, he was toying with the idea of how to put the PLA's regulars into Korea without giving the United States an excuse to expand the war into China at a later date.

Mao consulted with some noncommunist elites regarding how to intervene without a formal declaration of war against or by the United States. Huang Yan-pei, then a noncommunist vice premier of the Administrative Council (Zhengwu Yuan), suggested that the term "volunteers" would indicate the "unofficial nature" of the Chinese military in Korea.[18] Mao quickly accepted the term. On the eve of China's entrance, Peng even briefed CPVF commanders that "we at present do not want to fight a major war. Nor do we intend to declare war on America, but only to assist [the] Korean revolutionary war in the name of People's Volunteers."[19]

Concern for the possibility of high casualties for the CPVF without air cover almost reversed Mao's October 2 decision in the next few days after Stalin refused to honor his earlier agreement to provide it.[20] Peng, who was about to enter Korea for consultation with North Korean leader Kim Il Sung, was immediately recalled on October 12 to attend an emergency meeting of the Politburo in order to reconsider the earlier decision to intervene. Meanwhile, the deployment of 200,000 first-line troops of the Thirteenth Army Group was halted.[21] Mao's final decision to intervene came the next day on the grounds that although intervention meant tactical disadvantage and anticipated heavy casualties for the PLA, such a move would be translated into the strategic advantage of engaging the enemy outside China before it could pose a direct and permanent threat to the vital areas of the country's industry. Meanwhile, PRC leaders understood that even a limited intervention meant a high price tag for the PLA. Specifically, the Chinese military expected some 200,000 casualties in the first year of its fighting in Korea. Logistical arrangements were being organized for such an expected outcome.[22]

Preparation for the CPVF's intervention was at best inadequate. In fact, its entrance into the war was hastened by the unexpectedly rapid advance of UN forces toward the Yalu River. Although Mao and other top leaders correctly anticipated events unfolding in Korea, including MacArthur's Inchon landing,[23] the PLA had barely three months to become combat ready (early August to late October). The immediate problem was its limited knowledge regarding the structure, tactics, equipment, and strategies of the enemy. One limited source of information about the U.S. military was from those individuals who had previously served in the Nationalist military and later joined the PLA. Some of them had worked with U.S. military personnel during the Burma operation in World War II.[24]

Psychologically, too, the PLA was not yet attuned to its new mission of fighting Americans on foreign soil. According to Gen. Du Ping, political commissar of the Thirteenth Army Group, by mid-August 1950 only half the Thirteenth (260,000 strong) was "actively supporting" the intervention, and about 40 percent only "passively" accepted orders from above. The remaining 10 percent opposed intervention due to concern about U.S. firepower and atomic weapons. The situation improved somewhat after intensive political and psychological preparations during the two months leading up to the intervention.[25]

Another pressing problem was the lack of weapons standardization among CPVF units. Because almost all the PLA's equipment was captured from either Japanese or Nationalist forces, the CPVF's weapons inventory included a wide range of makes, calibers, and capabilities. Because of the limited capacity of China's military-related industry, it could not keep up with the diverse requirements of the various weapons systems. In fact, the backward and war-ruined Chinese industry was able to produce only several thousand tons of ammunition a year, in contrast to the million-ton annual capacity of the United States.[26]

Finally, the main source of the CPVF's military equipment, the Soviet Union, had yet to ensure delivery of more weapons. This delay created a logistics nightmare for the CPVF. To simplify efforts, the CPVF tried to standardize weapon systems by swapping weapons between units. For example, both the Thirty-eighth and the Fortieth Army originally had a mix of Japanese rifles and American rifles captured from the Nationalists. The Thirty-eighth then traded its American arms to the Fortieth for their Japanese rifles.[27]

While the PLA field commanders proceeded to implement Mao's order with a minimal materiel base and insufficient knowledge about the U.S. military, they repeatedly requested better equipment and a possible delay of the intervention. As early as August 31, the commanders of the Thirteenth Army Group suggested in a joint letter to Zhu De, the PLA's commander in chief, that adequate air cover, antiaircraft guns, and logistic supplies were key to a possible victory in Korea. After Mao's final decision to intervene on October 13, the same commanders made a final appeal to Peng for a two-to-three month delay so that new equipment, along with air cover and antiaircraft capability, could be secured. Peng, however, rejected the appeal and ordered them to proceed.[28]

The CPVF's hasty intervention proved to be timely for its armies on the western front that halted the UN's advance but fatal for the other armies on the eastern front that were underprepared to fight the U.S. X Corps.

THE FIRST AND SECOND CAMPAIGNS: OLD TACTICS IN A NEW ENVIRONMENT

Before Korea, the PLA's most recent combat experience had been in fighting the Nationalists during the civil war, in which the PLA claimed to have annihilated 8 million Nationalist troops in four years. Some of the familiar and successful tactics of the PLA included outnumbering the enemy whenever the situation permitted in order to wipe out entire enemy units (battalions, regiments, divisions), instead of simply repelling them; engaging the enemy in mobile operations (*yundong zhan*) and avoiding trench warfare; and achieving surprise whenever possible (for example, through night operations and close-range engagements) in order to avoid the usually superior enemy firepower.

In the First Campaign (October 25 to November 8, 1950), the CPVF employed all these familiar tactics: surprise, numerical superiority, and mobile operations. By maneuvering at night and resting during the day, some 300,000 CPVF troops deployed south of the Yalu River and remained undetected for one week, ready to engage the frontline Republic of Korea units. Although U.S. intelligence officers did detect large-scale military movement and deployment to North Korea, they failed to convince top U.S. military and civilian leaders that a major intervention by China was either imminent or possible. Meanwhile, the CPVF learned of the whereabouts of the UN forces and their plans by listening to American commercial broadcasting and military transmissions.[29]

Mao instructed the CPVF to engage the ROK troops first in order to gain some experience before dealing with the more powerful U.S. units.[30] Between October 25 and November 1, the CPVF dealt heavy blows to the ROK's First, Sixth, Seventh, and Eighth Divisions by destroying many of their scattered regiments or sending them into hasty retreat. The CPVF also found that ROK troops, once attacked, were quick to abandon their equipment and scatter into the woods. It was therefore difficult to wipe out those units unless the Volunteers had the time and manpower to block and comb the surrounding areas.[31]

The CPVF's first encounter with an American unit was accidental. Indeed, some CPVF units even tried to avoid U.S. troops.[32] The Thirty-ninth Army attacked Unsan on the night of November 1, believing the town was held by ROK units. Only after sighting a much taller and heavier enemy did the CPVF realize that it was engaging the Americans (the Eighth Regiment of the First Cavalry Division, which was taking over the defense of Unsan from the ROK Fifteenth Regiment). The Americans were caught completely off guard, to the point that they believed the approaching forces were ROK units and tried to shake hands with some of them. The Thirty-ninth Army opened fire at close range, overrunning one battalion and defeating another two of the Eighth Cavalry Regiment.[33]

After this first encounter with Americans, many observers in the CPVF believed that the advantage the U.S. forces had was also a disadvantage. Although these mechanized units had tremendous firepower and mobility, they also depended considerably on roads, air and artillery cover, and uninterrupted supplies. The U.S. troops also were afraid of night and close-range engagement. They tended not to move too far away from the road and were not flexible enough to occupy more advantageous terrain, thus providing the CPVF with opportunities to cut them into smaller pieces.

Thus, for the first time since the UN Inchon landing in mid-September, the CPVF's First Campaign managed to stabilize the situation for the North Koreans, providing valuable breathing space by pushing the front line south of the Chongchon River. The First Campaign also revealed some major problems in the CPVF, however. One was its inadequate firepower, which was so weak that a much larger CPVF unit was often unable to overcome a small enemy unit (battalion level) in a hastily built defensive position. The CPVF was also unable to pursue retreating UN forces because of its unmotorized infantry and lack of supplies. These difficulties were therefore one of the main reasons for its "disappearance," which has been widely interpreted by Western analysts as part of the CPVF's strategic plan after the initial engagement with the UN forces. For these reasons, Peng turned down the North Koreans' request to pursue the retreating UN forces.[34] The First Campaign, then, managed to drive UN forces south of the Chongchon River, but it fell short of the original plan of annihilating three enemy divisions.[35]

The initial contact between the CPVF and the UN forces surprised MacArthur, but he continued to believe that the Chinese force was symbolic and insufficient to halt his final campaign to unify Korea. Meanwhile, the CPVF was resupplied and reinforced. Peng suggested to Mao that UN forces be lured into preset "traps" as far north as possible so that individual UN units would be extended with longer supply lines and thus be more easily isolated and destroyed. Mao quickly approved the plan. Peng instructed that each CPVF army would withdraw its main force farther north but leave one division "to conduct mobile and guerrilla warfare . . . to wipe out small enemy units while engaging and luring larger enemy units to the trap." The CPVF tried to create the false perception of a disorderly retreat from the advancing UN forces. Some CPVF units even reduced the duration of each rearprotecting effort so that UN forces would assume that the CPVF's combat capability was diminishing. As a last effort to keep MacArthur on the hook, the CPVF also released some 100 POWs (including 27 Americans), who were deliberately told that they were being released because the Volunteers had to return to China because of supply difficulties.[36]

On November 24 MacArthur launched his "home-by-Christmas" offensive, but there was a huge gap between his Eighth Army on the western front and X Corps on the eastern front. The CPVF waited until dusk the next day to launch its counterattack (the Second Campaign), when all the major UN units were in the anticipated places to be encircled and attacked. While four CPVF armies (the Thirty-ninth, Fortieth, Fiftieth, and Sixty-sixth) launched a frontal attack on the Eighth Army, the Thirty-eighth made a flanking move through the gap between the ROK Seventh and Eighth Divisions in Tokchon. The 113th Division of the Thirty-eighth Army advanced 72.5 kilometers in fourteen hours and occupied the strategic points of Samso-ri on November 28 and Karhyon-dong the next morning, right behind the U.S. Second Division, threatening to trap part of the Eighth Army through this encirclement from the south. During the next two days, the U.S. Second Infantry Division and the First Cavalry Division, with heavy air and artillery cover, tried to attack the CPVF's 113th Division from both the north and south in order to establish contact. They remained separated, however, by less than one kilometer.[37] Although abandoning some of its heavy equipment, most of the IX U.S. Corps was able to flee along a coastal highway but lost 3,000 POWs, the largest such group captured by the CPVF during the war.[38] On the whole, the Second Campaign was a major victory for the CPVF, thanks to careful planning and execution and not just the result of "sheer good luck," as some scholars have argued.[39] In only nine days, the CPVF dealt heavy blows to the UN forces, pushed the battle line to the Thirty-eighth Parallel, and recaptured Pyongyang.[40]

But the Second Campaign also revealed more CPVF shortcomings. On the eastern front, the 150,000-strong Ninth Army Group (the Twentieth, Twenty-sixth, and Twenty-seventh Armies) was not adequately prepared for the subzero Korean winter. It was hastily thrown into combat against the First Marine Division and the U.S. Seventh Infantry Division. Although the Ninth Army Group scored the CPVF's only major victory during the three-year war in Korea when it wiped out an entire regiment of the U.S. military (the Thirty-second Regiment of the Seventh Division), it suffered a terrible toll from the Korean winter. More than 30,000 officers and men, some 22 percent of the entire Ninth Army Group, were disabled by severe frostbite, and some 1,000 died. Following this experience, the entire Ninth Army Group became a giant field hospital for three months as the men recovered from frostbite, the most serious incidence in the PLA's history. The Ninth Army Group, therefore, was incapable of annihilating a much smaller enemy force, as originally planned.[41]

Another problem during the Second Campaign was again the CPVF's weak firepower. Even when it was able to trap a large number of enemy forces and cut them into smaller pieces, it was unable to destroy them. In a number of instances, UN forces were able to hold their ground, thanks to their superior firepower and air cover, exhausting the CPVF's repeated attempts to annihilate them. The CPVF was particularly impressed by the First Marine Division on the eastern front and ranked it as the best among the American units. According to one account,

> Attacking the divided and surrounded enemy forces turned out to be extremely difficult. According to the experience of the CPVF, the 1st Marine Division was indeed the toughest fighting unit among the American forces. (The division was famous for its fierce battle with the Japanese in the battle of Guadalcanal during the Pacific War.) After being divided and surrounded, the 1st Marine Division immediately formed defense perimeters at three places with the help of 200 tanks.[42] It also constructed a makeshift airstrip for resupply of ammunition and winter equipment, as well as for shipping out its casualties. . . . The CPVF's 20th and 27th Armies, which were some 100,000 strong, had to depend primarily upon their infantry weaponry to break the enemies' strong defense line. With only 8 to 9 rocket launchers for each regiment, the 20th and 27th Armies were unable to finish the job, even though they repeatedly broke some enemy positions at night.[43]

The Second Campaign was also affected considerably by the CPVF's logistical constraints, imposed by UN airpower as well as by the lack of transportation assets and bad road conditions. CPVF units had supplies for one week at best. Originally, CPVF Headquarters planned a double encirclement by two armies and two divisions. However, food shortages forced the Volunteers to forego the extra two divisions; otherwise, they would have been more successful.[44]

The Second Campaign represented the peak of CPVF performance in the Korean War. As it began to strike south, however, the tactics it had successfully used to that point began to lose effectiveness as UN and U.S. forces rapidly adjusted to them. And, as the CPVF's supply line became extended, UN airpower began to cause heavier damage to its primitive logistical efforts. Furthermore, the CPVF and top Chinese leaders, particularly Mao himself, encouraged by China's initial gains, began to pursue goals that were far beyond the force's capabilities.

TO SEOUL AND BACK: THE BURDEN OF INITIAL SUCCESS

Following the Second Campaign, the CPVF was exhausted. The Ninth Army Group was virtually disabled due to frostbite. CPVF units on the western front had fewer than 300 trucks for almost 300,000 troops and a supply line that was now twice as long. Because the UN air forces had destroyed much of the CPVF's winter clothing supply, many men had inadequate protection from the cold. Accordingly, on December 8, 1950, Peng requested a pause of a few months until the next spring and wanted to confine the forthcoming campaign to areas north of the Thirty-eighth Parallel. He rejected a suggestion by the Soviet ambassador to North Korea that the CPVF pursue UN forces farther down the peninsula. Peng believed that the CPVF was not yet ready to fight a more fortified enemy along the Thirty-eighth Parallel. If his troops could not deal heavy blows to the UN forces, it did not make much sense for them to cross the Thirty-eighth Parallel and capture Seoul. Besides, an immediate crossing would make supplying his troops even more difficult.[45]

Mao, however, was more concerned about the political implications of a stalemate at the Thirty-eighth Parallel. A cease-fire there, which had been suggested by the United Nations, was viewed as a trick to halt the CPVF's advance. Meanwhile, the initial success had led Mao to believe that the American forces were even weaker than the Nationalist forces had been during the Chinese civil war. In his December 13 cable to Peng, Mao insisted that "our troops must cross the 38th Parallel [now]," arguing that if the CPVF ceased operations for the entire winter, rumors would run rampant in the capitalist world and there might even be skepticism among friendly countries. He therefore demanded that the next campaign be launched in early January (a month and a half ahead of Peng's request) in order to boost the morale of the Socialist countries.[46]

The CPVF commanders questioned Mao's judgment. Some even raised the question of how far political considerations should dictate military operations. But sensing that Mao's orders could not be reversed, the commanders planned a Third Campaign to cross the Thirty-eighth Parallel. Peng, however, continued to scale down Mao's ambitious plans and demanded greater flexibility. In his December 19 cable to Mao, Peng noted "a rise of unrealistic optimism for quicker victory from various parts" and suggested a more prudent advance. He warned that although the CPVF would not suffer a defeat in the coming campaign, there was a possibility that its advance would be blocked or that the success would be modest. Mao eventually agreed (December 21) to Peng's more conservative plan and granted him the tactical flexibility to disengage and stop the operation whenever necessary. He nonetheless also instructed that "political agitation work be stepped up, and the CPVF won't be withdrawn from Korea until all enemy forces are destroyed."[47] The latter statement was clearly an unattainable goal, as the CPVF soon found out.

The decision-making process for the Third Campaign thus reveals a unique bargaining process between Mao and his field commanders. From that point until the end of the Fifth Campaign, political goals defined by Mao tended to go beyond CPVF capability. Rarely could field commanders ignore or refuse these often unattainable goals. They nevertheless always argued for tactical flexibility so the goals could be pursued within some range of realism or with lower expectations. The final outcome of this bargaining, explicit or implicit, tended to be a compromise between political desirability and tactical feasibility.[48]

On New Year's Eve 1950, while still undersupplied and with home-supplied food meeting only one-quarter of its minimum needs, the CPVF launched its Third Campaign across the Thirty-eighth Parallel against UN forces entrenched across the entire peninsula, an operation very different from its earlier practice. The campaign did achieve tactical surprise, however, since it was conducted on New Year's Eve. In a matter of eight days, the Volunteers crossed the Thirty-eighth Parallel, recaptured Seoul, and pushed UN forces to the thirty-seventh parallel. For their part, the UN forces conducted an orderly retreat, and most American forces suffered few casualties. In contrast, CPVF units were exhausted after days of constant fighting, walking, and staying on high alert.[49]

Pressure urging the CPVF toward more ambitious goals for the next phase of war, however, came from both the top and the rank and file, as well as from allies. Because of the three relatively successful campaigns, many in the CPVF became more confident and questioned Peng's decision not to pursue the retreating UN forces following the capture of Seoul. Some felt that an earlier victory would bring the troops back home. Peng had a hard time convincing CPVF "adventurists" that despite initial successes, they could not ignore the UN's superior firepower. The CPVF also faced mounting problems, including poor supply of food and ammunition, extreme fatigue, lack of a coastal defense, poor rear-area security, and a delay in getting reinforcements. As a result, at this point it had only 280,000 poorly supplied and very exhausted troops facing 230,000 well-equipped UN and ROK forces. A more cautious strategy was therefore necessary after the Third Campaign.[50]

The Soviets were also pressuring the CPVF to launch the next operation immediately so that the UN forces would be driven out of Korea as soon as possible. Immediately after the CPVF stopped pursuing the retreating UN forces, the Soviet ambassador to Pyongyang once again urged Peng to go after the enemy. "No commander would stop pursuing the fleeing enemy," he said, while also complaining to Stalin and Kim Il Sung about the CPVF's decision. Peng was furious. "I am the commander-in-chief of the CPVF," Peng reportedly cabled Mao, who later sent Peng's cable to Stalin. Sensing the tension between the Soviet ambassador and Peng, Stalin ordered the ambassador to keep quiet and later transferred him home.[51]

Likewise, Kim Il Sung questioned the sudden end of the CPVF's Third Campaign. Shortly after Peng's argument with the Soviet ambassador, Kim visited Peng and insisted that the CPVF resume its pursuit. Peng disagreed, explaining that the UN forces were not really defeated but had deliberately evacuated Seoul in order to lure the CPVF farther south so they could then strike back with another amphibious attack. The CPVF had suffered considerable losses and was worn out after three months of almost nonstop operations; a pause of three or four months was therefore necessary. Peng's explanation was countered by North Korean Foreign Minister Pak Hon Yong, who cited opinions of his "Soviet comrades" calling for an immediate drive south to force UN troops from the peninsula. Peng categorically refused. Sensing that a hot pursuit of retreating UN forces was impossible, Kim Il Sung instead pushed for a pause of only a month. Peng disagreed and insisted that the CPVF's just finished Third Campaign was conducted with considerable difficulty and for "political considerations" only. He would not launch the next campaign without adequate rest and resupply for his troops. After some hard bargaining, Peng compromised on a two-month pause.[52]

Far away in Beijing, public rallies were held to celebrate the CPVF's capture of Seoul on January 4, 1951. An editorial in the *People's Daily,* the official party organ in China, urged the CPVF to advance farther and "drive the U.S. invasion army down to the sea." These activities reflected in part Mao's more optimistic view of the battlefield situation. Peng, however, became upset when he learned of these things and posed a question: what would happen if Seoul were retaken by the UN forces at a later date?[53] But Mao's view prevailed, and he made what a Chinese military historian later called "strategic misjudgments" at this point.[54] In a cable of January 14, 1951, to Peng and others, Mao anticipated that the UN forces would eventually withdraw from Korea only under two circumstances: at best, they would pull out with minimum resistance if they knew that the CPVF was well prepared, and at worst, they would dig in along the Taegu-Pusan line and withdraw when they were unable to fight the CPVF any longer. Two weeks later, Mao cabled Peng again with more specific directives:

Our forces must immediately prepare to launch the 4th Campaign with the purpose of wiping out 20 to 30 thousand enemy forces and advancing to the Taejon-Andong line. This can be really difficult because our troops have not been re-supplied. However, if we concentrate our forces . . . , it is possible to annihilate part of the American forces and four or five South Korean divisions. Please explain this to other commanders.

Following Mao's directive, the CPVF prepared for the next operation, designed to drive the UN forces farther down and off the peninsula if possible.[55]

The CPVF commanders were under tremendous pressure from the political leaders of China, Russia, and North Korea to strive for a quick victory. The gap between political goals and tactical reality thus became wider at the end of each campaign. It appeared that although Peng was able to fine-tune the execution of each campaign, he was nonetheless unable to define their timing, scope, and goals according to battlefield reality. Civilian leaders, who were far away from the battlefield, tended to dominate in the major decisions. And the battlefield reality, for its part, was changing fast.

On January 25, 1951, only seventeen days after the CPVF stopped its pursuit, UN forces launched counterattacks to retake Seoul. It came at the very time CPVF and North Korean commanders were meeting to plan their next move. Although the CPVF managed to organize some delaying actions, it was forced to abandon Seoul on March 14, 1951, and withdraw its forces north of the Thirty-eighth Parallel. Thus, the front line at the thirty-seventh parallel established at the end of the Third Campaign was the southernmost line the CPVF ever reached. Years later, some CPVF veterans and military historians noted that if it had tried to consolidate along this line and translate its military gains into a political compromise, instead of planning a more ambitious operation, the war might have ended much more favorably for the CPVF and North Korea.[56]

According to Chinese accounts, the UN counterattack succeeded for several reasons. First, U.S. troops were better equipped and organized, and they took the lead in the operation instead of being deployed behind ROK forces, as had been the case in the first three CPVF campaigns. Second, UN forces had become more familiar with CPVF tactics and adjusted their own accordingly. One successful tactic of the UN forces, according to CPVF accounts, was the so-called "magnet," which was based on the "one-week" operational limit imposed on the CPVF because of poor supply. Small UN units sought constantly to engage CPVF units until they became exhausted. UN forces also abandoned the fast-advance strategy along highways and tried to advance in close formations so that their flanks would not be exposed. The more disciplined tactics allowed them to take advantage of superior firepower. U.S. observation aircraft also increased considerably the accuracy of U.S. artillery fire.[57]

As a result of these adaptations by UN forces, the CPVF decided to pull back before the Han-gang River melted. Although it was able to organize some successful efforts, such as the Hongchon Operation (February 11, 1951), other operations revealed further weaknesses. The failed attempt to attack and destroy UN forces around Chipyong-ni (February 13–16, 1951), for example, exposed the inherent weakness of the CPVF units and convinced UN commanders that they now had the upper hand.[58]

Overwhelming UN firepower, in turn, forced the CPVF to change its tactics. In the first twenty days after the UN began its counterattack (January 25 to February 16, 1951), the CPVF managed to hold its position south of the Han River, but only after taking heavy losses. As a result, it adopted the so-called mobile defense. It would deploy its forces lightly at the front while reserving the main units at greater depth. This helped to reduce casualties from UN fire and allowed it to maintain some flexibility for mobile operations. In essence, Peng was trying to trade space for time—the two to three months he needed before reinforcements would arrive.[59]

However, the CPVF's situation continued to worsen under steady pressure from UN forces. Lacking even minimum supply and reinforcement, Peng sensed that the CPVF's earlier gains were slipping away. Worse, Peng believed that top leaders in Beijing had an inadequate perception of how bad the battlefield situation had become for the CPVF. In late February 1951, Peng hurried back to Beijing to tell Mao that the Korean War was entirely different from the Chinese civil war. He cited the inability of the CPVF to be reinforced quickly after taking losses; the impossibility of using captured materiel, given the UN's use of airpower and his own lack of personnel trained to handle the equipment; and the constant food shortages. In general, UN air operations exacerbated each of these problems. In light of these facts, Mao finally realized that the war in Korea could not be won quickly; he nonetheless continued to urge Peng to win as quickly as possible.[60]

It was not until after the CPVF's Fifth Campaign (April to June 1951) that Mao came to the conclusion that the goal of driving the UN forces out of Korea was unattainable. In early April preparations for the Fifth Campaign were in high gear. One of Peng's main concerns was the possibility that UN forces would attempt another amphibious landing in the rear. According to the official history:

> Various sources of intelligence indicated that enemy forces would continue to strike north after recapturing the 38th Parallel Line, and it was highly likely that there would be another amphibious landing to assist [the] enemy's frontal assault. It was believed that the possible sites for amphibious landing would be Wonsan and Tongchon-ni on the east coast. . . . If the enemy could amass a bigger force (say, 60,000), it was capable and likely to carry out amphibious assaults from both the east and west coasts. . . . The main goal of the enemy was to occupy the 39th Parallel Line. If this scheme of the enemy succeeds, our supply lines would be cut off and our forces would be in grave danger.

The UN forces had increased their harassment, intelligence, and redeployment activities along the Korean coastal areas. These actions prompted Peng to launch the Fifth Campaign before the UNF could be reinforced and proceed with an amphibious landing.[61]

Considerable disagreements, however, existed among CPVF officers over how to execute the campaign. In fact, most of its top commanders disagreed with Peng's idea of striking south. They preferred an "in-house" operation, engaging UN forces after luring them into areas occupied by the Volunteers. Such an approach would shorten their supply line and allow them to engage the enemy by using mobile operations in terrain familiar to their unseasoned units. Despite these arguments, Peng was determined to launch the Fifth Campaign and seize the initiative after months of being pressed by the UN forces. Mao approved Peng's plan on April 14, 1951.[62]

The CPVF's Fifth Campaign was its largest of the war. Together with the North Koreans it deployed some 700,000 troops against 340,000 UN forces, and the two sides fought for some forty days. But the results were disappointing for the CPVF. In fact, the campaign failed to achieve its goal of destroying five enemy divisions (including three American ones). At the same time, CPVF units suffered heavy losses from UN firepower. In fact, the CPVF's 180th Division was completely destroyed by quick UN counterattacks. Additionally, 17,000 POWs were taken by UN forces, representing some 80 percent of the total CPVF POWs during the entire war. More important, the front line was pushed farther north. Peng later admitted that the Fifth Campaign was one of only four mistakes he made during his entire military career.[63]

THE CPVF'S ASSESSMENT OF ITS OPPONENTS

These five campaigns in eight months were of tremendous importance in terms of the PLA's understanding of modern military operations. Not only did the war fully explore the PLA's potential in modern warfare, but it also revealed many strategic and tactical problems.

Changing Assessment of the U.S. Military

Chinese civilian and military leaders gradually changed their perceptions of U.S. military tactical capabilities. Many CPVF field commanders began the war with great apprehension about the U.S. troops. They became more confident after their successes in the first two campaigns, concluding that the U.S. military was strong in firepower but weak in morale. This assessment, however, cost the CPVF dearly when it failed to anticipate the UN forces' sudden counterattack on January 25, 1951. From that point, the CPVF treated the U.S. military as a much more formidable adversary, especially given its ability to adapt its tactics. During the second half of the Fifth Campaign, for example, many CPVF units were completely surprised by the blitzkrieg-style U.S. counterattacks and encirclement operations, tactics that were very different from their cautious movements during the Fourth Campaign. CPVF units were particularly impressed by the U.S. military's excellent coordination of air, artillery, and infantry units, which improved steadily and significantly during the course of the war. Indeed, the longer the war dragged on, the harder it became for the CPVF to confront the U.S. military.

U.S. Firepower

According to the CPVF, the strength of the U.S. military lay specifically in its superior firepower, which was capable of disabling the CPVF's frontline units, particularly during the daytime. As a result, these units had to conduct most operations at night.[64] As a more stable front line emerged after the Third Campaign, the superior firepower of UN forces rendered obsolete most of the PLA's traditional tactics, such as deep flanking. On many occasions, CPVF units were able to surround UN forces and cut them into smaller groups; yet they were unable to destroy these forces, even during night operations. On the political front, CPVF commanders could not convince Mao until after the Fifth Campaign that the old tactics were outdated and that it was almost impossible to annihilate a regimental enemy unit in a single operation.[65]

U.S. Airpower Versus CPVF Logistics

The UN's firepower, particularly its airpower, caused heavy damage to CPVF supply lines, greatly reducing its sustainability. This was particularly true during the Fourth and Fifth Campaigns when its supply lines were several hundred kilometers long. According to the CPVF, UN forces dropped some 690,000 tons of bombs during the Korean War, four times more than were dropped on Japan during World War II, some five tons for every square kilometer in North Korea. As a result, almost all bridges twenty meters or longer were destroyed by UN air strikes. During the first two campaigns, CPVF logisticians were able to supply only one-quarter of the food needs of their frontline troops; the rest was obtained by foraging.

Because of UN air operations, all CPVF trucks had to operate at night without lights on badly damaged roads. Although its logistics units had some 2,000 trucks at the beginning of the Third Campaign, most could travel only thirty to forty kilometers a night. As a result, frontline troops received only 30 to 40 percent of their minimum needs, and almost all CPVF operations were seriously constrained by inadequate supplies. The logistical constraints were also the main reason for the ubiquitous malnutrition and health problems within the CPVF, problems that had reduced these forces by 13 percent during the Fifth Campaign. UN airpower was also responsible for the deaths of about 20 percent of CPVF truck drivers during the campaigns, which was twice the percentage of frontline troops thus killed. This was the first time in PLA history that casualties among logistical personnel were proportionally higher than those of frontline troops.[66]

Though the CPVF captured large numbers of UN heavy equipment and vehicles during many of its operations, most were destroyed immediately by UN airpower. The CPVF had neither adequate air cover nor enough trained drivers to take the captured equipment away.[67] This outcome was the opposite of the PLA's experience during the Chinese civil war, when its main supplies consisted of captured enemy goods.

LESSONS FOR CHINA

The course of the war was never the same once China intervened. Contrary to the claim recently made by some observers that PRC and CPVF leaders failed to learn from the war,[68] the lessons gained from the five military campaigns substantially transformed the perceptions of Chinese civilian and military leaders with respect to strategic and operational goals. At the outset, the CPVF's operations and tactics were based on the traditional approach of annihilating complete enemy units on the battlefield. But gradually, Chinese leaders realized that this practice was not valid in Korea, where the CPVF faced a more formidable enemy. In a limited war, it was difficult if not impossible for either side to overpower its opponent completely, in contrast to the situation in both world wars and the Chinese civil war. In fact, the failure of the Fifth Campaign led Chinese leaders to change their goal from wiping out UN forces in Korea to a more modest one of defending the security of China and ending the war with a peace/truce agreement.[69]

From the conclusion of the Fifth Campaign until the end of the war, the CPVF adopted more cautious and realistic strategies, including maintaining a relatively stable front line; increasing CPVF air force, artillery, and tank units; and beefing up logistical supplies. Indeed, it increasingly became a mirror image of its American counterpart in its calculations and operations. Ultimately, the CPVF emphasized professionalism, the role of firepower, improving logistics capability, and seeking a negotiated and realistic end to the war. In this respect, the United States turned out to be a "useful adversary" in the Korean War.[70]

In an effort to end the war earlier, the CPVF even tried to "communicate" with its opponents through measured and carefully orchestrated operations. For example, its last operation, which took place around the Kumsong-Kumwha area prior to the truce, was specifically planned to avoid U.S. positions and to attack only ROK units. By doing so, the CPVF hoped that the ROK would become more willing to negotiate a peaceful end to the war. In this respect, the operation was a success.[71]

The CPVF's operational behavior also provides some insight into Chinese civil-military relations. Mao played a dominant role in both the preintervention decisions and in the detailed execution of CPVF operations. He was clearly more willing than his top military commanders to intervene in Korea. He also constantly pushed the CPVF beyond its limits by setting higher strategic, political, and operational goals as well as by demanding earlier starts to each successive operation (except for the Fifth Campaign). By basing his decisions on his experience during the Chinese civil war, Mao was responsible for some early successes of the CPVF, but in the end, for some major setbacks also. It would be wrong, however, to suggest that today's political leaders would play a similarly dominant role with respect to military operations. Mao could act decisively because he and his colleagues belonged to a generation of leaders who were experienced in both civil and military affairs. That may not be the case with China's current civilian and military leadership. As the PLA becomes increasingly professionalized and modernized, the future operational behavior of the PRC's armed forces will perhaps be more like those of their Western counterparts, whose operational calculus tends to be based on tangible rather than intangible factors.

Field commanders of the CPVF proved to be realistic and prudent. At least they adapted relatively quickly to the battlefield reality. Although they questioned Mao's judgment and requested more cautious moves, Mao always managed to convince them to aim higher. As a result, the failure of the Fifth Campaign was by no means Peng's sole responsibility but the logical end of a series of extremely exhausting operations. The CPVF did manage to stabilize the front around the Thirty-eighth Parallel during the Fourth and Fifth Campaigns, but it paid a heavy price and was never able to regain the thirty-seventh parallel line it had established by the end of the Third Campaign.

In general, the Korean War was the first time the PLA engaged in a large-scale operation outside China. Despite the disguised title "volunteer," the Chinese military went all out in engaging the best military in the world. The three-year war cost China 6.2 billion yuan.[72] Half of that amount involved loans for Soviet weapons. Between 1950 and 1953, China's defense spending was 41.4, 43, 32.9, and 34.2 percent of its total governmental annual expenditure. Right after the war, Mao demanded this be reduced to below 30 percent.[73]

The valuable lessons of this limited war, however, were not adequately studied by the PLA in the following decades because of a series of domestic upheavals. Peng Dehuai did preside over the PLA's modernization and professionalization between 1953 and 1959. But he was among the first of the top Chinese leaders to be purged by Mao in 1959 because of his opposition to the latter's unrealistic domestic economic programs. The PLA's shift to "spiritual refinement" during the 1960s under Lin Biao further postponed its chance to digest fully the lessons learned in Korea. The subsequent Sino-Soviet conflict also convinced Chinese leaders that another all-out—not limited—war was pending. From a tactical perspective, then, the Korean War became China's own version of the "forgotten war."

It was not until the 1980s that the PLA finally reverted in its thinking to a "limited and localized" strategy, partially as a result of its 1979 border war with Vietnam, which serves as a painful reminder of its outdated strategy and tactics. As a result, the Korean War is being seriously studied anew for its potential lessons. The rediscovery of this war comes at a time when the senior echelons of the PLA are filled with its veterans. Their first, if not the last, experience of modern warfare with the world's strongest military is in many respects a lasting reminder of the PLA's weakness, both then and now, relative to China's enemies and potential adversaries. Thus the recent emphasis on military modernization and professionalization reflects to some extent the lessons learned from China's five campaigns during the Korean War. In the foreseeable future, the PLA still has to prepare for asymmetric warfare because the technology gap between China and other major powers is even bigger today.

Perhaps the most important lesson that China learned from its engagement in the Korean War is to avoid or prevent such a war in the future, or both. Although it fought the war into a stalemate with the most powerful military in the world, Beijing paid a tremendous price economically, diplomatically, and strategically, including sowing the seeds of its discontent with Moscow. Indeed, the war tested the limits of China's cooperation with both Russia and North Korea.[74] Chinese leaders (Hu Yaobang, for instance) later reportedly vowed that China would never again be drawn into such a conflict in the Korean peninsula.[75] As a result of the lessons of the war, political/diplomatic means to resolve the conflict, real or potential in the peninsula, have always dominated the PRC's policies toward Korea. The rather neutral stand of China's foreign policy in the immediate post–Korean War period, as exemplified by the "Bandung spirit" of 1955, and China's low-profile and covert involvement in the Vietnam War, are cases in point. In the Korean peninsula, Beijing has tried to maintain the delicate equilibrium and stability at any cost, and this was true even during Mao's time.[76]

During the reform decades, China's approach to the Korean issue was further adjusted to a more balanced posture. It quietly but significantly changed its thirty-year official version regarding the start of the Korean War. By redefining it from one that was started by the United States and its "puppet" state South Korea to one of "Korean civil war," Beijing actually implicitly blamed North Korea for the three-year war.[77] Ever since the early 1980s, China has made clear, publicly and privately, that it supported only "peaceful" and "reasonable" means on the issue of Korean reunification.[78] Beijing continues to support the North publicly, but this support is not unconditional. For example, China chose not to condemn North Korea publicly in the 1983 Rangoon explosion and the 1987 bombing of a South Korean airliner, which drew strong international outcries and destabilized the sensitive Korean peninsula. But neither did China defend the North's behavior. Meanwhile, China also worked for medium and long-term goals so that the North would eventually find its own way to have normal relations with the outside world. Thus, North Korean leaders have been carefully provided with opportunities to get acquainted with China's economic reform and other domestic changes. China even intermediated a series of U.S.–North Korean diplomatic meetings at the councillor level in Beijing during the late 1980s.

Until the most recent breakthroughs in both intra-Korean politics and in the North's relations with Russia and America, Beijing was the only major power that enjoyed friendly relations with both Seoul and Pyongyang, a pivotal position regarding the future of the peninsula. In the 1990s it normalized relations with Seoul, supported "dual entry" of the two Koreas into the United Nations, cooperated with other powers in the resolution of the North Korean nuclear weapons issue, publicly opposed disturbances to the stability of the peninsula from any direction, participated in a quadripartite talk for a peace treaty in Korea, supplied food to the North, and worked with the South to ease its financial crisis. During the height of the Korean nuclear and missile crises, Beijing acted as a "constructive broker" between the Koreas and other major powers. Unlike the U.S. attempted surgical strike against North Korea's nuclear sites in 1994 and Japan's subsequent temptation later by its own air force,[79] Beijing urged patience and prudence, insisting that the Korean problem is more political than military. Major powers, therefore, should aim at long-term goals but not short-term returns.

These policies stabilize the peninsula and serve the interests of all major powers in the region. At the onset of the new millennium, PRC policies, together with efforts by other powers as well as the two Korean governments,[80] have led to the historical summit between North and South Korea in June 2000. For the first time in history, the two Koreas seem embarked on the path toward national reconciliation and eventual unification.

THEORIES AND REALITY: IMPLICATIONS FOR REGIONAL SECURITY

The dynamics of the PRC's learning process regarding the Korean War in both strategic and tactical terms, however, seem to be either ignored or misinterpreted, particularly by some revisionist historians. One of the key issues involved is how to generalize or theorize this complex process of PRC decision making and implementation during conflict/crises. This is not merely a methodological question but is crucial for comprehending the foreign and defense policies of the PRC, a rising economic and possibly military power. Ideological and cultural arguments, though convenient politically and academically, do not lead to a more refined and nuanced understanding of the PRC's conflict behavior. Theories are to distill, not distort, the reality. There are, therefore, limits on how much one can and should generalize. Those monocausal factors may function at best as a background but certainly not as the only factor(s). Much of this excessive generalization also relates, curiously, to an opposite trend, that is, the endless quest for details, as the Cold War archives become more available. With increasingly opened archives in the PRC, some scholars are preoccupied with trees and even leaves but apparently lose sight of the forest. In treating the rapidly proliferating Korean War literature in China, scholars should identify and analyze the real implications from many self-glorifying sources for public consumption. Publicly articulated views by top leaders therefore should be interpreted with great care. Assuming that those published views reflect their true beliefs[81] simply cannot explain many policy changes and adaptations by the PRC and PLA during and after the war.

China's rekindled interests in the Korean War are therefore of considerable significance for the United States and other powers in both strategic and operational perspectives. Although Chinese leaders may have later regretted China's hasty entrance into the conflict, Mao's fateful decision in 1950 indicates that the Korean peninsula constitutes a vital part of China's security. Such a consideration goes far beyond the Cold War setting, Communist ideology, cultural traits, and certain leaders' idiosyncrasies; rather, it is largely based on China's concern for major-power balance. This concern is reinforced by a historical fact of life: the peninsula has served as a major springboard to the conquest of continental Asia, particularly by Japan. Of the fourteen wars Japan waged between its 1868 Meiji Restoration and its defeat in World War II, ten targeted China and most often through the Korean peninsula. Japan's conquest of China's northeastern provinces (Manchuria) from 1931 to 1945 resulted in the longest occupation and colonization carried out during World War II.[82] Japanese military activities during that war directly caused the deaths of 35 million Chinese and China's economic loss of $100 billion (based on 1937 Chinese currency). China's indirect economic loss was about $500 billion.[83] Any major disturbance to the peninsula's delicate stability will therefore lead to serious concern, regardless of the capability of the PRC's and the PLA's power and the nature of China's domestic political system.

In this regard, much of the ongoing "China threat" debate[84] misses the point. While the "threat" school points to an upcoming or present threat from China, more cautious assessments insist that it will be a threat only in the future when the PLA is substantially modernized. The U.S. encounter with the Chinese military in Korea, however, demonstrates that a much weaker China would resort to the use of force if it views the security of its environment as sharply deteriorating. This trend in the PRC's foreign/defense policy is also evident in the more recent cases of China's show of force in the 1996 Taiwan Straits crisis and in the PRC's coercive diplomacy toward Taiwan beginning early in 2000. The key to understanding China's behavior, therefore, lies more in its strategic calculus.

A more relevant and perhaps more pressing issue of this "forgotten war" in Korea for both China and other powers[85] relates to the unification of the two

Koreas, much anticipated by the West, either as a result of North Korea's economic difficulties in the late 1990s or from the sudden surge of optimism radiating from the June 2000 summit between the two Kims. Partially because of this, the postunification security arrangements on the peninsula suddenly appear on the agenda of foreign and defense policy makers of all major powers in this part of the world. In any case, Washington has made clear its intention to continue the U.S. military presence in a unified Korea and possibly the entire peninsula, even if the target for such a presence will have disappeared.

Although the process of unification is yet to be substantiated, China hopes it will be gradual and peaceful and believes it should be managed by the Koreans themselves. With the presence of the U.S. forces still in the peninsula, and there to stay, Beijing will be more likely to react strongly to a scenario in which the U.S. forces move north of the Thirty-eighth Parallel. In a general sense, any direct military intervention by other major powers without China's acquiescence will be of grave concern to Beijing. A largely neutral unified Korea and a less militarily oriented Korea–U.S. alliance will be in the interest of China. In this regard, the lessons and impact of the Korean War, which occurred half a century ago, are still relevant today and into the foreseeable future.

2

My Story of the Korean War

Marshal Peng Dehuai

Editors' Note: Peng Dehuai was the CPVF commander and political commissar and the commander in chief and political commissar of the Chinese–North Korean Allied Forces during the Korean War. As the top Chinese military leader in Korea between 1950 and 1953, Peng commanded all major operations, made most of the important decisions at the front, communicated with Mao Zedong in Beijing intensively every day, worked with Kim Il Sung and other top North Korean leaders, and visited Stalin in Moscow to discuss Korea's situation and the peace talks. He became a marshal of the People's Liberation Army and one of the most powerful and revered military leaders of the revolution.[1]

Born in Xiangtan County, Hunan Province, in 1898, Peng joined the Chinese Communist Party in 1928 and then commanded the Fifth Army of the Chinese Red Army, which led the vanguard of the Long March. He had attended Hunan Military Academy and served briefly as a Nationalist officer, becoming a brigade commander before defecting. His revolutionary fervor and military aggressiveness gained Mao Zedong's attention and favor by 1930. In the Chinese civil war, he was the commander of the Eighteenth Field Army, the Northwestern Field Army, commander and political commissar of the First Field Army, deputy commander in chief of the People's Liberation Army, and the first secretary of the Northwestern Bureau of the Chinese Communist Party. After the founding of the People's Republic of China, he served as the vice chairman of the Revolutionary Military Committee of the Central Government, chairman of the Northwestern Military and Political Committee, commander of the PLA Northwest Military Region, first secretary of the CCP Northwestern Bureau, defense minister, and vice premier. With Zhu De and Lin Biao, he was one of the PRC's most dedicated and experienced generals.

In 1959 Mao Zedong accused Marshal Peng of forming a "right opportunist clique" and conducting "unprincipled factional activity," charges that often meant pro-Soviet political positions, and removed him from his post as minister of defense. He lived thereafter under virtual house arrest. Peng then wrote many long, personal letters to Mao and the CCP Central Committee, appealing for pardon until he died in 1974. In December 1978 the Central Committee announced his rehabilitation. In 1981 the CCP Central Military Commission organized an editorial team to review Peng's papers and records and published one of his autobiographies, written in 1970. This book provided the fullest account of his life and career. Translated into English, Japanese, Russian, and Korean, it sold about 3 million copies. In these excerpts from Peng Dehuai Zishu [Autobiography of Peng Dehuai] *(Beijing: People's Press, 1981), he discusses the top Chinese leaders' decision to enter the Korean War, the major military operations during the five campaigns of 1950 and 1951, and China's goals in Korea. The following chapters are selected, abridged, and translated from Peng's book with translators' and editors' notes and with our own annotations.*

DISPATCHING TROOPS TO AID KOREA

It was after the National Day of October 1, 1950.[2] Around noon on October 4, Beijing sent an airplane [to Xi'an] and asked me to board immediately and come to Beijing for an urgent meeting without even one minute's delay; I arrived at Zhongnanhai around four o'clock that afternoon.[3] The Central Committee was holding a meeting [at Zhongnanhai], discussing the issues regarding sending our troops to aid Korea. A comrade at the meeting told me that [before I arrived] Chairman Mao had asked the participants to focus their discussions on the disadvantages for China in sending its troops to Korea. After all had expressed their opinions, the chairman said, "All you said sounds reasonable and logical. When we, however, are standing on the side, just watching other people undergoing a national crisis, we feel terrible inside, no matter what." I did not say anything since I had just arrived there. I, however, said to myself that we ought to send our forces to rescue Korea.

After the [afternoon] meeting, comrades from the Administrative Bureau of the Central Committee took me to the Beijing Hotel. I could not get any sleep that night. I thought it was because of the soft bed, which I could not enjoy. But after I moved to the floor, I still could not sleep. I kept thinking and thinking about the war situation in Korea. America occupied Korea across the [Yalu] River, threatening Northeast China. It also controlled Taiwan, threatening Shanghai and East China. It could launch a war to invade China with any excuse anytime it wanted. The tiger always eats people, and the time when it wants to eat depends on its appetite. It is impossible to make any concessions to a tiger. Since America came to invade us, we had to resist its invasion. It would be very difficult for us to build up our Socialist country without challenging the American imperialists. If the Americans decided to fight against us, a quick war would be favorable to them, but a protracted one to us; regular warfare would be favorable to them but the methods [of guerrilla warfare] that we had used to deal with the Japanese [in World War II] would be favorable to us. In comparison to our situation during the War to Resist Japan, the current situation was much more favorable to us since we had political authority over China, plus Soviet assistance.

Moreover, we should send our troops [to Korea] in consideration of the future of our nation's reconstruction. It was always said that our Socialist camp, headed by the Soviet Union, was much stronger than the capitalist camp. How could [we] show our power and strength if we did not send our forces to aid and save Korea? Our forces ought to be dispatched also in order to encourage the peoples of colonial and semicolonial countries to carry on their nationalist and democratic revolutions against the imperialists and invasions. Our forces ought to be dispatched in order to extend the influence of the Socialist camp. I repeatedly read the chairman's sentences in my heart a couple of dozen times: "All that you said sounds reasonable and logical. When we, however, are standing on the side, just watching other people who are undergoing a national crisis, we still feel terrible inside no matter what we may pretend." I understood Chairman Mao's instructions, which combined internationalism [to save Korea] with patriotism [to defend China]. Mao's first sentence, "All you said sounds reasonable and logical," obviously related to nationalism. [But these comrades were] not being internationalists if they thought [merely about China itself and not about] the crisis situation in Korea. I therefore believed that sending our forces to assist Korea was an absolutely correct decision. It was not only because of its necessity but also because of its brilliance and urgency. I had become convinced and fully supported this wise decision by the chairman. Mao needed a willing military commander since his first choice, Lin Biao, clearly was reluctant to take the assignment.

The Central Committee continued the discussion at the Yinian Hall [in Zhongnanhai] the next afternoon. After other participants spoke, I expressed [my opinion] in few words: "Sending the troops to aid Korea is necessary. If we lose, it means nothing more than a couple of years delay in liberating China. If the American military places itself along the Yalu River and in Taiwan, it could find an excuse anytime it wants to launch an invasion." The chairman decided to ask me to go to Korea. I did not decline. After the meeting, one of the participants said to me [as we walked along] Nanhai Lake, "It seems that age does not diminish you."

THE FIRST CAMPAIGN

At dusk on October 18, 1950, I crossed the Yalu River with the first group of the advance troops of the Chinese People's Volunteers Force.[4] The next morning we reached the power station at Raekosao, and on October 19 we arrived at a small valley northwest of Puckchin. By that time the enemy troops had ridden north in their trucks and tanks. Some advanced enemy units had already reached the Yalu

River.[5] On the morning of October 21, a division of our Fortieth Army met with Syngman Rhee's puppet troops [Seventeenth Regiment, Sixth ROK Division] after the division had just passed Puckchin. The First Campaign was an unexpected or surprise encounter. I immediately changed our operational plan [to move the CPVF's troops to the south]. Having employed the unique flexibility and mobility of our army, we annihilated part of Rhee's puppet troops right there in the Puckchin-Unsan area. Then we successfully resisted the American and puppet armies' pursuit and attacks and gained a firm footing [in North Korea]. By October 25 we ended the First Campaign with a victory.[6] American, British, and puppet troops quickly withdrew to and regrouped at the Chongchon River and Tokchon region with their mechanized transportation and constructed defense works there. Our army did not pursue the enemy because we had eliminated only six or seven puppet battalions and a small unit of the American army.[7] We did not get their main force. Their mechanized troops moved fast and built up defense works quickly. They had already tied together a defense system, especially with their tank units. It was unfavorable to assault the enemy's fortified positions with our technology and equipment. We might even lose.

THE SECOND CAMPAIGN

We thereafter adopted combat tactics to pretend that we were weak so as to let the enemy advance, make them overconfident, and lure them in deep.[8] I used small units to maintain contact with the enemy while our major forces were deployed along the eastern and western areas of Puckchin. Taking advantage of the favorable terrain, our main forces worked on their counterattack positions undercover about thirty kilometers from the starting point where the enemy would launch an attack. One day in mid-November, MacArthur reconnoitered [our positions] by airplane. Then his headquarters broadcast directly to his troops through radios: "You must get ready, drive to the Yalu, and we will be back home for Christmas." We were also well prepared because we figured out that the enemy was about to launch a major offensive.

Around November 20, the enemy launched a fierce attack on our positions.[9] According to our plans, our small units resisted at every step so as to lure them into continuing their attack. We waited until the enemy reached the Unsan-Kusong line, which we chose as the front for our counterattack positions. That evening, when the enemy was tired after daylong attacks and unable to consolidate, part of our troops cut into their rear. With well-prepared and properly organized manpower and firepower, our troops overwhelmed their positions. We used grenades and bayonets and fought hand-to-hand combat. The enemy could not employ their superior firing power in the battle. The Chinese Volunteers fought bravely and pushed forward so that the enemy was forced into complete disarray. Unexpected and unprepared for our attack, the enemy troops had never experienced this kind of battle before. Surprise is the combat tactic that guaranteed our victory in the Second Campaign. There was no better way to win it.

The Second Campaign was a big victory. We captured more than 6,000 enemy vehicles, about 1,000 tanks, and artillery pieces.[10] Most of these vehicles and weapons, however, were burned and destroyed by the enemy himself with a large number of incendiary devices. We could keep only a small part of them. After this battle, the enemy troops fled in desperation, giving up Pyongyang and retreating to the Thirty-eighth Parallel. This campaign recovered the entire territory of the Democratic People's Republic of Korea and laid a firm foundation for our victory in the War to Resist America and Aid Korea.

THE THIRD CAMPAIGN

Having won the Second Campaign, we continued our triumphant advance.[11] By mid-December, we moved undercover near the Thirty-eighth Parallel. After conducting detailed reconnaissance, our troops prepared an all-front attack. On New Year's Eve 1951 (the evening of December 31, 1950), we broke the [enemy] defense line along the Thirty-eighth Parallel, took over Seoul, crossed the Han River, and recovered Inchon Harbor, thus pushing the enemy back to the thirty-seventh parallel.

The enemy changed strategy, transferring additional troops from Japan and America and their veterans from Europe, totaling about four divisions, to the Naktong River to work on a new defense line.[12] They were joined by troops from the Hamhung area along the eastern front. Their mechanized units were pulling back about thirty kilometers per day. It was exactly the mileage our army could move forward [by foot] in one night. These moves showed that the enemy was leading us into [the trap of] assaulting their well-defended positions. When our army was exhausted, they would launch a frontal counterattack as well as conduct a flank landing so as to cut our retreat route.

After entering Korea, the Chinese People's Volunteers Force had fought three big, continual campaigns for three months. It was in the middle of the cold winter. We did not have any air support and lacked the protection of antiaircraft artillery. Enemy airplanes raided us every day, and their long-range guns shelled us day and night. We could not move at all during the daytime. Our troops did not have even a one-day break. You can imagine how tired they were. As our transportation lines were getting longer and longer, it became extremely difficult to get supplies to the front. By that time, our troops had lost almost half their men because of combat and noncombat losses.[13] They badly needed a rest and to resupply in order to be ready for the next battle. At that moment, three of our armies had already entered the area south of the Han River and were close to the thirty-seventh parallel. Our main strength was regrouping and resting in the region north of the

Han River along the Thirty-eighth Parallel and in some areas south of it. While waiting for battle opportunities, they constructed defense works so as to be prepared for a possible enemy counterattack and for a prolonged war.

THE FOURTH CAMPAIGN

Thus we stopped our attacks when our troops reached the thirty-seventh parallel [along the Suwon line].[14] The enemy failed to lure us in deeply enough to its well-prepared, heavily fortified positions along the Naktong River. Having realized that this plan had not worked, they launched a counterattack in late January.[15] We concentrated five armies to meet the assault. This campaign eliminated about two enemy divisions, Rhee's puppet troops; the rest were French, Belgian, and Luxembourgian, a total of 2,000 men. The American army lost only one battalion. At any rate, we repulsed the enemy's counterattack.[16]

Between February and March 1951, I returned to Beijing and spent a couple of days there [seven days for the entire trip]. During my short visit, I reported to the chairman [Mao] about the military situation in Korea and asked for his strategic guidance. I pointed out that the Korean War could not be a quick victory. We must pull back our Fiftieth Army, which had its back to the river, from the southern to the northern side of the Han River before February 15. During our meeting, the chairman gave very clear instructions for our war: "Win [a] quick victory if possible; or at least win some advantage instead." Thus, thereafter, we had a clear and flexible principle.

THE FIFTH CAMPAIGN

After the enemy failed to lure our army to the Naktong River, they launched a large-scale, northward offensive campaign in mid-February.[17] We fought defensive actions at every step and had many tough battles. After about forty days of fighting, the enemy pushed forward to the Thirty-eighth Parallel along the western front [in April 1951]. Then we had a counteroffensive there and drove the enemy back to the area near Seoul. The enemy, however, did not give up Seoul this time. This was the first phase of the Fifth Campaign. On the eastern front, the enemy troops also advanced to the Thirty-eighth Parallel. They did not withdraw either; instead they deployed their troops in a stair-step [echelon] pattern toward Seoul. The Chinese Volunteers and a unit of the North Korean People's Army joined forces so as to fight the enemy back along the eastern front. One of our armies, however, moved too far south (close to the thirty-seventh parallel) and could not receive supplies. The soldiers had a big problem with food and became extremely exhausted, so they withdrew. And one of the divisions of the Sixtieth Army lost about 3,000 men. The division did not have a carefully designed operational plan, so it was surrounded and attacked by an enemy mechanized army corps and enemy airplanes during its movements. These were the casualties we had during the second phase of the Fifth Campaign, and also the first [large number of] casualties we had during the entire War to Resist America and Aid Korea.

The scale of the Fifth Campaign was so large that we employed about 1 million troops, and so did the enemy.[18] We, however, were unable to eliminate even one regiment of American forces. Our troops had destroyed whole [American] battalions in only six or seven locations and had wiped out only one entire puppet division [again the ROK Sixth Division, which disintegrated, then reformed]. The rest of the enemy troops we had eliminated were merely parts of their units. It would take us two days to annihilate an entire American regiment if we could surround it. The problems were that our army's technology and equipment were so backward and that enemy air and mechanized forces tried so hard to save their troops. Only once during the Second Campaign did we annihilate an entire American regiment, and no single enemy soldier could escape.[19] In most battles we usually attacked enemy units of battalion size. In many cases, if we surrounded enemy troops but could not annihilate them the same night, they would be rescued one way or another the next day. Then Chairman Mao sent a telegram instructing us that our mouths should not open too wide when fighting the American forces. We must adopt the tactic of "eating sticky candy"—bite by bite. This was a good tactic. However, we still needed to find a way to consolidate our positions so as to adapt [to the new tactic]. Without a consolidated position, we could not bite the other side.

After two months of intense fighting, from the Fourth Campaign to the end of the Fifth Campaign, the enemy was exhausted. Our [defense] positions began to take shape and gradually consolidated. Our surface defense warfare had transformed itself into an underground, tenacious defense warfare. The actual operations included constructing step by step more underground tunnel fortifications in depth along the Thirty-eighth Parallel. Because of our consolidated tunnel defense system, the enemy was unable to break through our positions (our defense of Pork Chop Hill was a good example). And the enemy's repeated assaults on our positions were frustrated.

Meanwhile, we could concentrate our forces, prepare our attacks, and select [its weak point] in order to break enemy positions. Thus, we had learned not only how to use the tunnel systems as a cover to conduct defense but also how to use them for offense. With the consolidating and stabilizing of our trench warfare by summer and fall 1951, we began to carry out the chairman's tactic of "biting sticky candy," that is, concentrating available manpower and firepower, constructing covert offense launching positions, and then attacking and eliminating one small unit of the enemy forces [each time], generally a battalion unit. We conducted quite a few of these operations, about four or five times a month. The cumulative effect was quite impressive. Moreover, we had also truly learned how to break into heavily fortified positions. Our last attack on enemy positions took place on the eve of the cease-fire [of the Korean War in late July 1953]. Four of our armies broke through the enemy's defense works about twenty-five kilometers wide and twenty-five kilometers deep. In this battle, we eliminated most of four puppet divisions and one American heavy artillery regiment.[20] Thus, we developed a whole new set of tactics for active defense in trench warfare. Even with inferior equipment and technology, we could defend our positions when the enemy was attacking. Having been able to conduct both offensive and defensive operations we had the initiative in our hands on the battleground. Our success reflected the integrity of our revolutionary army's superior political and military qualities and created favorable conditions for our protracted positional warfare in Korea.

Our victories forced Gen. [Mark W.] Clark, commander in chief of the UN forces, to request that the Korean Armistice be signed immediately. Clark told his subordinates, "This is the first time in American history that an American general signs an armistice for a no-win war." When I signed the armistice, I was thinking that we had already created a precedent for many others that would exist for years to come. This [cease-fire] sounded laudable to the peoples [of the world]. I, however, felt a bit disappointed because we had just become so well organized for combat. We had not fully used our might to deliver bigger blows to the enemy.

Our experiences in the War to Resist America and Aid Korea are rich and valuable. The logistical experiences, supplying the front without any air support, are also significant. We gained much valuable experience from antibacterial warfare as well.

On the Korean battlefield, the Chinese People's Volunteers Force and the North Korean People's Army fought side by side, helping each other like brothers. Through the three-year struggle for our common cause, our army had greatly enhanced our friendship, sealed in blood with the Korean people and their army, thus creating a deeper internationalist feeling between the two countries.

3

Beijing's Decision to Intervene

Marshal Nie Rongzhen

Editors' Note: Nie Rongzhen was the acting chief of the PLA General Staff and vice chairman of the CCP Central Military Commission and the People's Revolutionary Military Committee during the Korean War. As one of the top military commanders and Mao Zedong's senior aide in Beijing, he took part in high command decision making, planned major military operations, and shared the responsibility of war mobilization. In 1955 he became one of the ten marshals in China.[1]

Born in Jiangjin County, Sichuan Province, in 1899, Nie became a Chinese student activist when he studied in Paris in 1919, and he joined the Chinese Communist Party in 1922. He went to the Soviet Union for further education in the military and defense industry in 1924 and 1925. On his return to China, he served as secretary and instructor in Huangpu (Whampoa) Military Academy's Political Department, where Zhou Enlai was the director. He was appointed military commissioner of the CCP Guangdong (Canton) Provisional Committee in 1926 and then secretary of the Military Commission of Hubei Provisional Party Committee. During the armed revolt on August 1, 1927, now celebrated as the PLA's founding day, he was the CCP representative to the Eleventh Army.

With his organizational skills and Soviet military training, Nie became a deputy director of the Political Department in the Chinese Red Army Command in the late 1920s and political commissar of the Red Army's First Army Group in the Long March of 1934–1935. During the Anti-Japanese War (1937–1945), he was the political commissar of the 115th Division of the Eighth Route Army Group and commander and political commissar of the North China Military Region.

During the Chinese civil war (1946–1949), Nie served as the second secretary of the CCP's Northern China Bureau and commanded the PLA's Northern Military Region. In 1948 and 1949 he worked closely with Mao Zedong on a daily basis after the Communist leadership moved from Yan'an (Yan-an), the remote Communist capital in the northwest, to North China, closer to the civil war bat-

tlegrounds. Nie successfully protected the CCP Headquarters and PLA high command by defeating the Nationalist attacks and personally saved Mao's life once in an air raid when Mao refused to leave his bedroom for a shelter. Nie's efforts enabled Mao to achieve his military and political success throughout the war, and Nie became one of Mao's closest working colleagues and trusted generals.

When Mao founded the People's Republic of China in Beijing in 1949, Nie was appointed mayor of Beijing, commander of Beijing-Tianjin (Tienjin) Garrison Command, and deputy chief of the PLA General Staff. He ran the General Staff because Zhou, as its chief, was preoccupied as the PRC's premier and foreign minister and because the entire General Staff was Nie's former Northern Military Region Staff, people who had worked with Mao in the war and then moved into Beijing with him. Nie became acting chief of the General Staff in 1950, vice chairman of the CMC and the Chinese People's Revolutionary Military Committee in 1951, and after 1954 was one of the party's eleven top national leaders as a member of the Standing Committee of the CCP Politburo. During the 1958 Taiwan Straits crisis, the Chinese leadership decided to build their own atomic bombs. Nie then headed China's nuclear and missile programs as director of the National Science and Technology Commission from 1958 to 1967 and served as chairman of the National Defense Science and Technology Committee and director of the CCP Central Committee's Science Commission. He also served as vice premier from 1959 to 1966. Nie died in 1992.

Marshal Nie published his recollections in two volumes, Nie Rongzhen Huiyilu [Memoir of Nie Rongzhen] *(Beijing: PLA Press, 1984). Excerpts describing how the top CCP leadership debated over and decided on the intervention in Korea prove invaluable. In charge of the war mobilization from 1950 to 1952, Nie in particular recalled the difficulties the new regime faced in financing the Chinese intervention. His account also reveals how Beijing directed its operations in Korea through a unique civil-military bureaucratic system. The following chapters are selected and translated from Nie's book with translators' and editors' notes.*

CHAIRMAN MAO'S CALCULATIONS

After the founding of the People's Republic of China, we badly needed a lasting international peace to heal the wounds of the civil war and to develop our national economy.[2] Historical evolution, however, has its own objective rule that is independent of our subjective desire.

In June 1950 the American imperialists invaded Korea. At the same time, the United States occupied Taiwan as well, a territory of our country.[3] That November, the American invading forces outrageously crossed the Thirty-eighth Parallel and launched an all-out, fierce offensive against the Democratic People's Republic of Korea. Then they pressed on toward the Yalu and Tumen Rivers, our northeastern borders joining North Korea. Meanwhile, the American air forces invaded and raided our northeastern region. Thus, the American imperialists forced a war on the Chinese people.

As to a war against the United States in Korea, it was not at all easy for us to decide whether to fight or not. In the end, the CCP Central Committee and Comrade Mao Zedong decided to intervene. After three years of fighting, we won a great victory in the Korean War. Having suffered heavy casualties, the American imperialists, who considered themselves unexcelled in the world at that time, were forced into truce negotiations and ended their invasion of Korea. The victory showed again the invincible power that our party, army, and people have. The victory proved once again the great and unusual courage and resourcefulness of Comrade Mao Zedong as a proletarian revolutionary.

Before the American army crossed the Thirty-eighth Parallel, the CMC had decided to take precautionary measures. We ordered the PLA strategic reserve forces [with three armies], commanded by Comrade Deng Hua, plus the Forty-second Army, to move from Henan Province [Central China] to the Yalu River [Northeast China], the Sino-Korean border areas.

Meanwhile, we stepped up our offshore attacks on some islands along the southeastern coast, occupied by the remnants of the Guomindang [GMD, or Kuomintang, KMT: the Nationalist] troops. Before we entered the Korean War, we had liberated all the offshore islands except Taiwan, Penghu (the Pescadores), Jinmen (Quemoy), and Mazu (Matsu). These offshore operations created important and favorable conditions that gave us a free hand in conducting our War to Resist America and Aid Korea.

By August 1950 the North Korean People's Army had reached the Naktong River through its counteroffensive campaigns. The NKPA troops had liberated a large part of their country and were pressing on toward Taegu and Pusan. Calculating [the war situation], Comrade Mao Zedong and the Central Committee believed that the American imperialists would never resign themselves to defeat. With naval and air superiority, the Americans would possibly launch a counteroffensive to retrieve lost ground. The NKPA had penetrated deep into South Korea, and its rear areas were vulnerable. North Korea would very likely experience a setback and some complications in the war.

Thus, according to the CMC's decision, I telegraphed an order to the strategic reserve forces on August 5: "Complete all the necessary preparations within this month. Be ready for the order of new movement and engagement." Since their preparation tasks were extremely arduous and urgent, it was difficult for them to get everything ready that month. On August 18 I cabled Deng Hua again: "Please step up your supervision of the preparations. Finish all the preparation tasks before September 30."[4]

As anticipated, the American army landed at Inchon on September 15 and then launched an all-out counteroffensive northward. The American army was pressing on fast toward the Sino-Korean border areas. Since our army had already been prepared, the Chinese People's Volunteers Force troops were able to move quickly toward the border areas and expeditiously enter Korea in October. Our quick response prevented the American imperialists from occupying the whole of Korea and invading China. We could have been caught unprepared and bungled the chance of winning the Korean War had Comrade Mao Zedong and the CCP Central Committee not predicted the possible complications of the situation and organized our strategic reserve forces on time.

Certainly, many psychological problems needed to be resolved. As we publicly criticized the American imperialists' invasion, some of our comrades were scared. They believed that it would be disastrous if we fought a war against the United States, the strongest imperialist nation in the world. Their mental state stabilized after our timely education and various forms of persuasion.

At the same time, some dissenting opinions emerged among our leading party members. They mainly argued that, having fought wars for so many years, we had an urgent need to recuperate and rebuild. Our new republic had just been founded in the previous year and was facing many difficulties and challenges. It would be better not to fight this war as long as it was not absolutely necessary.

Comrade Mao Zedong had been pondering whether or not to fight [in Korea]. He remained undecided even when our forces reached the Yalu River and Deng Hua's advance troops were poised to cross it and enter Korea. Mao asked me to send a telegram to Deng, asking him again to slow down [the troops' movement] and wait for a while. After careful consideration, Mao finally made the decision. He had racked his brains and indeed thought about this many times before he made up his mind. Mao did not like war, but the Americans had already brought the war to our borders. What could we do without fighting back? We thus decided to fight this war. And we must fight with all our strength to win. Mao could not have made such a great decision of historical importance had he not possessed unusual revolutionary courage, resourcefulness, foresight, and sagacity and had he not had firm confidence in our party, army, and people.

In September 1950 our General Staff Headquarters was working intensively on the operational plans. On September 30 Premier Zhou Enlai announced to the whole world: "The Chinese people can never tolerate any foreign aggression. The Chinese people can neither allow the imperialists wilfully to invade our neighbors, nor can we ignore such provocations."[5]

Since the People's Republic of China and the United States did not have diplomatic relations at that time, Zhou asked the Indian government to pass China's warning to the American government through K. M. Panikkar, the Indian ambassador, whom Zhou summoned. If the American army crossed the Thirty-eighth Parallel, the premier said, China would send its forces there to support Korea.

American president Harry Truman immediately informed [Gen. Douglas] MacArthur of China's warning. The Truman administration then tried to create the impression that the American army would stop at the Thirty-eighth Parallel. In the early morning of October 2, however, we received the information that South Korea had ignored China's warning, and its army had already crossed in large numbers. They were soon followed by American troops.

After several meetings in early October presided over by Mao, the CCP Central Committee decided to send part of our military forces, to be called the Chinese People's Volunteers Force, to Korea to fight the Americans and their running dog Syngman Rhee's troops in order to support our Korean comrades.[6] Mao raised the cry: "Resist America and aid Korea; defend our nation and guard our homeland." This was a clarion call, a perfect slogan, linking the Korean War with our national interests. It clarified the question for the Chinese people all over the country that our involvement was not only to resist America and aid Korea but also to defend our nation and guard our own homeland. This slogan thereby combined internationalism with patriotism.

Lin Biao opposed sending our troops to Korea.[7] At first, Mao had chosen Lin to command the CPVF in Korea, but Lin was so fearful of this task that he gave the excuse of illness and obstinately refused to go to Korea. It was strange to me because I had never seen him so timid in the past when we worked together.

Then Mao decided to select Comrade Peng Dehuai, who was in Xi'an at that time, as our commander in Korea. On October 4 Peng came to Beijing and the next day attended the Politburo's meeting at Zhongnanhai. Peng was well known for his bravery and decisive manner. After the Central Committee had decided that he would command the volunteers, he expressed his resolution to carry out this order. At the Politburo meeting, he firmly supported Mao's proposition to dispatch our troops to Korea. He said that when we fought against the United States, the American army might, in the worst case, invade China, which would result in nothing more than a couple of years' delay in liberating China again. I was very much impressed by Peng's firm stand at the meeting.

On October 8, 1950, Comrade Mao Zedong officially issued *The Order to the Chinese People's Volunteers Force,* which declared, "To support the Korean people's liberation war and resist the American imperialists' and their running dogs' aggression in order to protect the common interests of the Korean people, Chinese people and all the peoples in the East, we order the Chinese People's Volunteers Force to enter Korea immediately. They should assist the Korean comrades, fight the war against the invaders, and strive for the glorious victory."

On the same day, Peng Dehuai was appointed as the CPVF commander in chief and political commissar. He then rushed to the northeastern front. On October 10 he cabled the General Staff, "According to our original plan, two armies and two artillery divisions will enter [Korea] first. But if the Yalu River bridge is bombed and destroyed, [we will] have difficulties in concentrating our large number of forces and [we might] miss the opportunity. So [I] have changed the original plan and decided to move all the troops to the south of the river." Peng's idea was that the eighteen divisions that had assembled along the border must enter Korea at once to achieve numerical superiority. After I reported to Mao, he endorsed Peng's suggestion.

On October 13 Chairman Mao and the Central Committee again reaffirmed the necessity of our entry into the Korean War. Other comrades in the Politburo he had talked to, Mao pointed out, unanimously agreed that it would favor us if our forces entered Korea to fight, and [our intervention] would be extremely advantageous to our country, Korea, the East, and the whole world. It could be disadvantageous to all if we did not send our troops. First, when the enemy reached the bank of the Yalu River, the international and domestic reactionary bluster would surely grow louder. This would not only be disadvantageous to our country, but it would also pose an even bigger threat to Northeast China. The entire Northeastern Border Defense Army would be tied down there, and the electric power plant in South Manchuria would be subject to the enemy's threat. After all, we believed that we should enter the war and that we must participate in it. Our entering the war could be most rewarding; failing to do so would cause great harm.

On October 18 the Central Committee instructed the General Staff to issue an order stating that "the Chinese People's Volunteers Force will begin to cross the Yalu River on October 19." On October 25 the American army had reached Taegwandong, about thirty kilometers from the Yalu River.[8] On the same day, our troops encountered [ROK] enemy forces and then started the First Campaign, which was the prologue to the War to Resist America and Aid Korea.

At that time, the enemy forces deployed a total of ten divisions and one brigade along the front line, more than 130,000 men.[9] We immediately sent eighteen divisions to Korea.[10] If we had first sent six divisions in accordance with our original plan, we could have landed ourselves in a disadvantageous position. Since we enjoyed numerical superiority from the beginning, with our higher morale, better quality, and courageousness and indomitability in battle, our troops won a series of victories after they entered Korea. These successes laid a foundation for our final victory in the war.

In retrospect, the strategic decision to send our troops to Korea at that time was absolutely correct. Comrade Mao Zedong and the members of the Central Committee were indeed brilliant. If the American imperialists' plot had been allowed to succeed in Korea, they would have forced us to have a showdown with them on another battleground [in China]. We could have been pushed into a passive situation. China could never have been what it is today.

Our experience in the War to Resist America and Aid Korea proved that we fought successfully there. Because of our victory, the American imperialists never dared to extend the war into our territory. According to our statistics, which the General Staff compiled after the war, the American army suffered a total combat loss of 390,000 men in thirty-seven months. Their monthly casualties were more than 10,000 men on average.[11]

We fought for thirty-three months in Korea. We had heavy casualties as well, but ours were smaller than the Americans'.[12] Moreover, the war materials that the American military used were several dozen times more than what we used. The war had undermined America's strength to a great degree. Through the War to

Resist America and Aid Korea, our country has become more united, and our people have become more confident in their ability to defeat any foreign invaders.

In contrast, during the war defeatist sentiments among the American ruling classes had developed to an unprecedented extent. They complained and blamed one another. The officials and diplomats in the White House, the State Department, and the Pentagon were extremely worried. Some claimed, "We have been trapped in Korea. Only God knows what is going to happen next." "The Korean War is a bottomless pit," others said. "We have to transfer all of our armed forces from the United States if we want to replenish our combat troops to full strength in Korea."

The American imperialists did not expect China to send its troops to Korea. They assumed that we had not yet finished our civil war and had many economic difficulties so that we dared not go to Korea for a showdown with them. The only preparation the Americans had ever made before we entered Korea was MacArthur's plan to counter our possible attack on Taiwan. Something like this occurred when he maneuvered the American troops for their Inchon landing. The American invaders thereby had made a fatal miscalculation in their strategic thinking, which unavoidably resulted in their disastrous defeat.

OPERATIONAL DECISIONS AND PLANS

After the Chinese People's Volunteers Force began its foreign military operations, the General Staff Headquarters mainly focused on the War to Resist America and Aid Korea.[13] From October 1950 to June 1951, the CPVF and the NKPA conducted five coordinated large-scale counteroffensive campaigns. These operations had forced the enemy to withdraw from the north to south of the Thirty-eighth Parallel, switch to a defensive position, and agree to negotiate on a truce.

During the Korean War, the General Staff often drafted combat operational plans based on battlefield situations, which were then sent to the Central Military Commission and to Comrade Mao Zedong. He carefully read our drafts of telegrams concerning the CPVF's operations. After his cautious changes and approval, these plans were telegraphed to the front.

The First Campaign was an unplanned engagement. From October 25 to November 5, 1950, the CPVF troops had dealt head-on blows one after another to the puppet [ROK] First, Sixth, and Eighth Divisions and the U.S. First Cavalry Division, which had made rash advances. After a twelve-day campaign, our troops on both the eastern and western fronts eliminated a total of 15,000 enemy troops and drove the enemy back to the south bank of the Chongchon River.

Our victory in the First Campaign tremendously enhanced the morale of our troops, who now felt "sure" about the war. The enemy, however, continued to underestimate our strength. At first, they thought that we dared not send our troops to Korea. Then they believed that our troops there were only "symbolic." Taking advantage of the enemy's miscalculation, the CPVF adopted a tactic of pretending weakness, indulging the enemy, and feeding their arrogance. The CPVF troops pulled back in order to lure the enemy father north and to find the opportunity to annihilate it.

The United Nations Force (UNF) commander MacArthur made a mistake again in his calculations. He believed that the Chinese Volunteers in Korea were no more than 50,000 men, not a significant, strong force. He launched an all-out northward offensive along the front so as to "end the war by Christmas."

[The Second Campaign] involved major operations: on the western front, our army lured the enemy into an engagement; some of our best units drove through the enemy lines and cut off their rear; then we started a powerful counteroffensive, destroying three American and puppet divisions.[14] On the eastern front around the Chosin Reservoir area, our army surrounded and inflicted heavy losses on the U.S. Seventh Division and the First Marine Division. This Second Campaign shocked the entire world. It started November 25 and ended December 24, 1950; within one month, we had eliminated a total of 36,000 enemy troops and forced the enemy to withdraw south of the Thirty-eighth Parallel.

After the Second Campaign, Comrade Mao Zedong instructed us to continue our offensive operations in Korea as the Third Campaign in order to support our efforts in the General Assembly of the United Nations. At the assembly meetings, Comrade Wu Xiuquan as the PRC's representative accused the United States of the military invasion and occupation of our territory Taiwan, thus enhancing our political influence in international organizations.

However, Peng Dehuai reported from the front that our troops needed to rest and to be supplied immediately. The troops had been fighting without a break for more than two months. They were exhausted and running out of munitions and food. Moreover, according to our intelligence, our troops then did not have an over-whelming numerical superiority any longer on the front line. (We had only two to five more divisions than the enemy forces at the time.) Thus I also suggested [to Mao] that it would be appropriate for us to postpone the next campaign for two months.

Mao, however, still insisted on his decision to start the Third Campaign imme-diately so as to coordinate with our political struggle [at the UN]. Therefore, on December 31, 1950, the CPVF launched the Third Campaign in the wake of its victory in the Second Campaign. Without allowing the enemy a breathing spell, our army fought nonstop for nine days and liberated Seoul, eliminated 19,000 enemy troops, and drove the enemy south of the thirty-seventh parallel.

From January 27 to April 21, 1951, our army conducted the Fourth Campaign. After our heavy blows in the First, Second, and Third Campaigns, the morale of the American and puppet troops was sinking lower every day. They blamed each other, and their problems became more and more serious. To turn such a disadvantageous situation around, the American imperialists launched a continual offensive for more than eighty days. The American army attacked us on the western front and the pup-pet army on the eastern front. They gathered sixteen divisions, three brigades, and most of their artillery, armor, and air forces. The enemy offensive was focused on the western front. Our troops tenaciously resisted and fought counteroffensive battles, eliminating a total of 78,000 enemy troops. Both the American and puppet armies suffered heavy casualties and could advance only about one and a half kilometers on a daily average.

In mid-April 1951 we repeatedly received information that more American troops were being transported from the United States to Korea. A new army had been established in the United States and was actively preparing a landing attack on the CPVF's side or rear areas.

To crush the Americans' attempt and eliminate the enemy troops in larger numbers, from April 22 to May 21, 1951, our army launched the Fifth Offensive on the enemy, who had already been forced into a defensive posture. After one month of heroic fighting, our army annihilated 80,000 enemy troops and forced the American and puppet forces to retreat again to Seoul and the south. The Americans gave up their plans for landing on our side or rear areas. In July they accepted our suggestion for truce negotiations. During the Fifth Campaign, however, one of our divisions on the eastern front had suffered heavy losses because it lacked effective command and control ability when it was surrounded by the enemy.[15]

After our Fifth Campaign, the CCP Central Committee held a meeting in Beijing to discuss our next step. Most of the committee members considered it proper that our army should stop at the Thirty-eighth Parallel. They agreed that we should begin truce talks while continuing to fight so as to work toward a negotiated settlement. I concurred with the others on this idea. I believed that we had already achieved our political goal, i.e., that the enemy should be driven out of northern Korea. Our pausing at the Thirty-eighth Parallel, in fact, was a return to the prewar status quo. This would be easily accepted by all the parties in the war. We were not afraid of continuing the war, for we would only become stronger in the fighting, though not without difficulties. Presided over by Mao, the meeting reached the final decision to fight while negotiating. Then we carefully carried out this policy for the rest of the war.

After June 1951 the American and puppet armies conducted several so-called "limited offensives" against our positions along the Thirty-eighth Parallel (including their large-scale summer and fall offensives) in order to put more pressure on us in the truce talks so as to get a favorable peace treaty. During this period, our army again annihilated a large number of enemy troops. Through the intense battles to crush the enemy's continual offensives, our army had enriched its combat experience and achieved a better understanding of the nature of war.

Then Mao put forward a timely new strategic principle: "Fight a protracted war, and defend ourselves actively." Under this guideline, the rank-and-file volunteer troops developed their tunnel defense works, which were significant in the Korean War. They constructed an "underground Great Wall" consisting of strong fortifications from the eastern to the western coast. Thereafter, Mao came up with a new tactic—"eating sticky candy bit by bit" [Lingqiao niupitang]—attrition tactics to eliminate enemy troops bit by bit. Our army employed Mao's tactic in combat, concentrating a superior force to fight many small-scale battles of annihilation. During this period, although only one enemy company or even one platoon was eliminated in each battle, the accumulated number of eliminated enemy troops was no less than that of the previous campaigns. By the end of 1951, about a half year later, we had not only defended the Thirty-eighth Parallel but had also eliminated more than 250,000 enemy troops.[16]

During 1952 the American forces used chemical and biological weapons, strategic bombing, and many other criminal kinds of warfare in northern Korea.[17] These criminal activities were crushed by the Chinese and Korean armies and peoples.

By October 1952 the American and puppet armies had not yet resigned themselves to defeat. Gathering a force of more than 60,000 men, they attacked our positions on Osung Mountain more than 900 times within forty-three days. Depending on their dauntless heroism and strong underground fortifications, our defense troops defeated continual enemy attacks. They held their positions and eliminated more than 25,000 enemy troops in the battle of Shangganling, well known both domestically and internationally.[18] This battle proved that our creative defense system, based mainly on tunnels and fortifications, had offset the enemy's superior air and artillery firepower and proved that our army's position was invulnerable to any enemy.

In 1953 our army launched three strong summer offensives to teach the enemy one more lesson after they obstructed the negotiations at Panmunjom without any reason, delaying the truce treaty and dreaming of having a so-called "honorable truce." In the Kumsong counteroffensive, our troops broke through a major enemy defense area about twenty-five kilometers wide and ten kilometers deep in twenty-four hours, delivering a heavy blow to the American and puppet forces. Through those summer offensive actions, our army annihilated 120,000 enemy troops in all and forced the American imperialists to sign the Korean Armistice on July 27.[19] This general narrative records the major steps that the CPVF took in the Korean War to assist the NKPA in their military operations.

My main job at the General Staff during the war was to analyze the military situation and plan the CPVF's operations. I worked intensively and exhaustively day and night during that period. Besides the operational planning, I was also responsible for other tasks concerning the war.

The NKPA had been equipped with Soviet-manufactured weapons, which were more advanced than what the Chinese army had at the time. Their manpower available for military service, however, was limited. South and North Korea had a total population of 30 million, but the north had less than half of that total. North Korea therefore had big problems in conducting a large-scale war in terms of manpower resources.

In January 1950 Comrade Kim Il Sung sent Kim Kwang Hyop and other comrades to China. They asked to transfer into North Korea 14,000 PRC soldiers of Korean origin currently serving in the PLA. Most of these soldiers had joined our army in Northeast China during the Anti-Japanese War and the Chinese civil war.

Then, within the PLA's Fourth Field Army (the former Northeastern Field Army), they had fought in many parts of China.

After Kim Kwang Hyop arrived, the CCP Central Committee instructed me to be in charge of this matter. After our discussions, we agreed that all the Korean national soldiers in the Chinese army would be transferred to the Korean People's Army. Then Kim pointed out that "the Korean army does not have extra weapons and equipment. We have to approach the Soviet Union again for weapons' purchases, after we incorporate those 14,000 soldiers into our army. The communication and negotiations will take a long time. Please consider whether the Chinese comrades can equip those troops." "I understand the Korean comrades' needs," I said; "I will give you our answer after I report to the Central Committee."

Generally speaking, I viewed the Korean comrades' request favorably. But how much equipment we could give them should be decided on the basis of the Fourth Field Army's condition. Along these lines, I wrote a report to the Central Committee on January 21, 1950, which it approved the next day. The Korean comrades were satisfied after the General Staff Headquarters transferred 14,000 Korean national soldiers (with their weapons and equipment) to Korea in accordance with the instructions from the leading members in the CCP Central Committee.

After the Korean War broke out, we had an immediate concern about the protection of the Yalu River bridge.[20] It was the key point of communication and transportation between China and North Korea and thus extremely important to us. As soon as the war broke out, the comrades in Northeast China cabled the General Staff, asking whether we should deploy antiaircraft units south of the bridge within the Korean border to protect it. After I received the telegram, I thought it wise to do so. I reported to Mao and Zhou, explaining the situation and reasons. My report was soon approved. Upon an agreement with the Korean comrades, we protected the Yalu River bridge during the entire war. Although American airplanes bombed it many times, the traffic across the bridge was never interrupted.[21]

One of the problems we pondered quite often was how to reduce our troops' casualties. Confronting an enemy equipped with modern weapons, we tried to find ways our troops could deal with the disadvantage caused by such a weaponry gap so as to minimize their casualties. I believed it extremely important that we should replenish the CPVF troops with seasoned soldiers as the backbone in battle in order to bring our army's strongest asset into full play. Through such replenishment, not only the CPVF troops in Korea would be kept up to their full strength, but the PLA troops in China would have their combat consciousness and morale heightened nationwide after our mobilization.

After Mao approved my plan [on this issue], we began to work on it. At that moment, the CPVF badly needed replacements because of large troop losses after engaging in four campaigns one after another with no break. The arrival of those seasoned PLA troops on the Korean front greatly strengthened CPVF capability, heightened its combat morale, and increased its combat effectiveness. Our approach had a strong impact on the successes in the Fifth Campaign and later battles.

After the Fifth Campaign, the front line stabilized along the Thirty-eighth Parallel. Our logistical work, however, was still difficult. To solve this problem, Mao decided to withdraw part of the CPVF troops from the battleground to ease the heavy burden on our logistics organization.

Mao's idea was to withdraw 300,000 troops to Northeast China as the first step for recuperation, training, and new planning. This was a large-scale operation. I called for a meeting and discussed it with the comrades involved in this task. I worked out a detailed proposal in which I suggested withdrawing 260,000 men, which Mao and Zhou approved. After it was put into effect, the CPVF's supplies in Korea improved a great deal.

According to Mao's instructions, another task of ours was to rotate the PLA units to fight in Korea. Through such a rotation, not only could our troops in China gain experience in combat with the American army, but also our troops already in Korea could come back for needed recuperation. Our rotation program started in fall 1952 and went through two major steps. By spring 1953, about two-thirds of all our troops had been rotated. As our troop rotation started on a large scale, we also organized a group rotation of our officers from various military institutions and bureaus across China. Many of those staff officers thus gained combat experience in Korea. This rotation started in January 1953 and was completed within four months.

Through these two types of rotation, most of the officers and men in the PLA gained new, foreign combat experience in Korea. Our army had previously fought in wars against Japanese imperialists and Jiang Jieshi (Chiang Kai-shek), but we knew little about the American army, which was equipped with modern weapons. Korea became a huge school that offered us combat training. Our troops and officers gained new experience in fighting a modern war in this school and hence further increased combat capability to a great extent. Mao had made a farsighted decision.

We had always paid special attention to our intelligence work, because information was extremely important for decision making. At the General Staff Headquarters, we had to have access to all kinds of information. Only with all the information we needed could we make accurate analyses and correct calculations to provide a reliable basis for the leading comrades of the Central Committee to make decisions and to create favorable conditions for our successful military operations on the front. I therefore required my headquarters' operational planning and intelligence departments to work together during the war. I emphasized that they must try every possible means to obtain timely information on all aspects of the enemy. Generally speaking, given the great efforts of our intelligence agencies and close cooperation with Korean comrades, we did a good job in the war on information gathering. Because we had relatively accurate information about the enemy, we could make quick and correct decisions. One day after the Fifth Campaign, for example, our front sources reported that two enemy warships had appeared offshore near Wonsan. Our troops were alarmed since they thought the enemy might be mounting a new offensive. I held an intelligence department meeting. We analyzed the current situation and, based on our information from various sources, concluded that the enemy troops did not presage any large-scale activities. They might be doing some exercise, or reconnaissance, or even some feinting moves. Later I reported my assessment in writing to Mao. He wrote down a few words in the margin next to the phrase "feinting moves" on my report: "Note: Agree with Nie's [assessment]."

WAR MOBILIZATION AND LOGISTICS TASKS

Strictly speaking, it was during the War to Resist America and Aid Korea that we fully realized the importance of logistics in modern warfare.[22] Modern war is largely a war of manpower and material resources. It would have been impossible for us to defeat an enemy force, especially one like the American army with advanced technology and equipment, if we had failed to provide the minimum material needs for our troops.

After the founding of our People's Republic in 1949, we had done everything we could to speed up the recovery of our national economy. Annual steel production increased from 158,000 tons in 1949 to 600,000 tons in 1950 when the War to Resist America and Aid Korea started. Grain production increased from 216 billion *jins* [one *jin* equals 0.5 kilogram] in 1949 to 249.4 billion *jins* in 1950. Other production sectors also recovered significantly and made great progress. All these changes strengthened our efforts in the war.

The PLA, however, still had big problems in logistics. During the previous half century, China had undergone one war after another, which devastated its economy. [When the Korean War broke out, our soldiers'] weapons were in disarray since our equipment and weapons had been seized mainly from enemies with various makes and models. Our transportation means were backward and primitive. An organized system of logistics had yet to be established. By contrast, the U.S. military was much better equipped than ours and was supported by modern logistics means because the United States was the most developed industrial country in the world. We were facing a powerful opponent and obvious difficulties.

In the Korean War, we had conducted continual campaigns involving huge forces. As a result, we consumed an unprecedented amount of war materiel. During the first two years, we transported from China to Korea a total of 2.6 million tons of more than 9,000 different kinds of war supplies. Every single campaign consumed enormous quantities of war materials. In the summer offensive of 1953, for instance, a twenty-minute artillery barrage consumed more than 1,900 tons of munitions.

Moreover, during the war, our entire logistical service had always been the main target of enemy air raids. We suffered heavy losses of material and equipment. Shortly after the CPVF entered Korea, for example, one of our truck regiments lost seventy-three trucks in one enemy air raid. (At that time, one CPVF truck regiment had only about 100 trucks.) During another air raid on the Sam-dung train station, we lost more than eighty railroad cars loaded with war supplies.[23]

With such heavy costs and losses, our traditional ways of supporting and supplying our army, as in past domestic wars, could no longer meet the demands of this modern war in Korea. In the past, we obtained our supplies locally wherever we fought in China. Our foodstuff was provided entirely by the local Chinese people. Our munitions came from whatever we seized from enemy troops. We never knew that our logistics service would have such enormous problems in the Korean War. Our troops were fighting in a foreign land with limited available local resources. Even though they seized some enemy supplies, most of them were quickly destroyed by enemy air strikes. Thus, the troops depended largely on supplies coming from China. These experiences fully revealed the complexity of and difficulties with our logistics.

At that moment, Comrade Yang Lisan was head of the PLA General Logistics. A veteran in this work, he had been in charge of our logistics since the Red Army period [1927–1935]. Hardworking and intelligent, Yang had developed many different ways of supporting and supplying our troops on the front. Unfortunately, he suffered from cancer and later died in the Soviet Union. During the Korean War, I worked with him a great deal. We analyzed the situation and tried every possible means to meet the needs on the front. The telegrams [from the Korean front to Beijing] regarding logistics were far more numerous than messages on anything else. Every day we received a stack of telegrams on logistics problems.

The entire logistical work in the war was conducted under the leadership of Comrade Zhou Enlai. I reported to him almost everything about our logistics and asked for his instruction. He paid close attention to our work. Shortly before the CPVF was preparing to enter Korea, Zhou had attended many meetings and listened to briefings on our logistical preparations. He gave us detailed instructions about our tasks, such as the supplies of foodstuff, clothes, weapons, and munitions; communication and transportation in Korea; medical sources for the wounded and sick Volunteers; and staffing for the logistics officers.

He set up principles of self-reliance, particularly that we should supply our army from our own resources in China. The first group of the CPVF left for Korea in a great hurry and needed winter clothes immediately. Zhou made many phone calls to the General Logistics Headquarters, asking for the expeditious manufacturing and shipment of winter clothes. During their early combat, the CPVF also encountered a serious problem with its food supply. To deal with this emergency, Zhou asked the State Council to instruct the Northeast, North, and Central [CCP] authorities that all the provincial and metropolitan governments should mobilize the masses to make parched flour for the CPVF. Shortly afterward, almost all the families from northeastern to central China were devoted to the cooking of parched flour. Zhou himself took part in the cooking when he visited some governmental offices in Beijing to check their cooking and packing process.

We paid special attention to the northeastern region in terms of the rear services during the war because Northeast China was the CPVF's rear base and our transport post. Despite his busy schedule, Zhou asked us many times to investigate logistical problems there, and he even sent officials to the sites in the Northeast. To solve the logistical problems, he worked out many detailed plans himself. He made it clear that both headquarters—the General Staff and General Logistics—must be completely mobilized to help overcome the difficulties in the northeastern region.

In January 1951 the Northeast Military Region (NEMR) held a meeting to discuss how to improve CPVF supply and support, and Zhou asked me to go with him. We traveled to Shenyang, listened to the reports, and solved a number of urgent problems. The meeting summarized in a timely fashion our experience and lessons from the war. Thereafter, we significantly improved and strengthened our logistics service. Indeed, Zhou devoted a lot of attention and made valuable contributions to the CPVF's logistics.

We gained good experience in our logistical services but only after we paid a high price for it. During the Second Campaign, for example, we originally planned to employ a total of two armies and two divisions in order to outflank the enemy in the west. Because we failed to transport enough foodstuff to the front, however, we had to cut two divisions from the flanking force. This deficit prevented us from achieving better results in the campaign.

Our troops on the eastern front entered Korea in a big hurry. Hardly prepared, they had many logistical problems. The soldiers did not have enough to eat; their winter clothes were too thin against the cold, so they suffered large, nonbattle losses. If there had not been so many great difficulties in the support and supply service and in some other aspects, our troops on the eastern front could have annihilated the U.S. First Marine Division east of the Chosin Reservoir as we had planned. The American radio broadcast had already announced that the First Marine Division had been eliminated; in fact, however, it escaped by sea.

As the front line pushed southward, our transportation lines became longer and longer, and our supply tasks became increasingly difficult. In the Fourth Campaign, our munitions and foodstuff supply became extremely limited. Since our artillery forces were short of shells, for instance, our infantry troops did not have the necessary fire support, thus greatly impairing their combat effectiveness. Since our infantry troops were short of munitions, they sometimes could use only their bayonets against the enemy. During the Fifth Campaign, after our troops broke through the enemy defensive line in the Hyon-ri area, they had to call a halt to their attacks for three days to wait for supplies of munitions and food, consequently losing a good battle opportunity. There were other similar cases in which our troops had surrounded an entire regiment or battalion of enemy troops but because of the shortage of munitions could not defeat them. Moreover, some of our units were even forced to withdraw, due to supply shortages that seriously hamstrung our military operations.

In our mobile warfare, there were many such cases in which the CPVF had to call a halt to attacks or suffer heavier casualties in the battles because they did not get supplies of food and munitions on time. Later, the enemy found out the pattern of the CPVF operations. They knew that our forward offensives depended entirely on the food and munitions carried by the attacking troops themselves. Usually the portable food and munitions could support only a one-week-long operation; indeed, the American army called our charges "one-week attacks." During the first week of our offensives, therefore, the enemy would withdraw its troops under covering fire, not wanting to fight the CPVF recklessly. After one week, believing we had run out of supplies, they began all-out counteroffensives. In the late period of mobile warfare, our army suffered a great deal because of [this logistics problem].

An old Chinese saying states, "Food and fodder should go ahead of troops and horses" [*Bingma weidong, liangcao xianxing*]. Our experience in the War to Resist America and Aid Korea has proved that this is still an important principle in fighting a modern war. Although we predicted the war and prepared to resist America and aid Korea, we had only about two weeks between deciding to intervene and actually entering Korea. We entered the war in haste and were not well prepared. Moreover, we had little combat experience with the American army outside China.

Thus, at certain stages of the Korean War, our logistical services could not meet the demands of our troops, handicapping their military operations and limiting the outcomes of the battles. It is time now to learn the following lessons and to be prepared accordingly: within the limits of our national financial and productive resources, and on the basis of our army's needs in its modernization and military operations, we must strengthen the construction of our logistical services and store necessary war materials in peacetime. In case of a military emergency, therefore, our support and logistical services will be able to play the role of "going before the others" [*xianxing*].

On May 3, 1951, the CPVF Party Committee issued Directives on Logistical Problems, emphasizing that the party committees at all levels must consider the support and supply tasks as the first priority of their routine. The Central Military Commission endorsed the committee's instructions. On May 19 the CMC issued a document accordingly, Decision on Strengthening the CPVF's Logistics. The commission approved the establishment of the CPVF Logistics Department; its command was to direct the rear support services and to organize logistics. Thereafter, the CPVF logistical situation gradually improved.

On the front, the CPVF Logistics Department first abolished all the logistics departments in the army corps in order to simplify administrative structures. It then set up a new system that was aimed at supplying areas rather than units. Specifically, the area branch-headquarters, with a large amount of munitions and foodstuff in each area, was responsible for supplying all the troops stationed within that area. The new system improved the supply capacity at army and divisional levels and increased our troops' combat effectiveness.

With this new supply system, our combat troops did not have to carry all the supplies with them all the time and instead could receive them immediately from whatever place they moved into. This improvement heightened the CPVF troops' fighting effectiveness and mobility. Moreover, to make the logistical service fit into our military operations, each area's supply depots were also co-commanded by the army group command stationed in that area. Thus each service depot would know its area's operational plans ahead of time, receive instructions promptly, and provide what the combat troops needed on time.

In addition to improving our logistics system, the CPVF armies helped to maintain a transportation network in North Korea for the service stations and participated in many construction projects in the rear areas. The rear supply service units were urged to support the Three Carings Movement: caring for war material, caring for vehicles, and caring for the wounded. They were also urged to use available local resources and captured enemy material. These activities had a positive, functional impact on our victory in the war.

Through these efforts, some of the supply problems were solved, and our logistics services were drastically improved. Later, in the battle of Shangganling and the Kumsong counteroffensive, our supply services successfully met our troops' needs in battle, a result of the highly centralized and mobilized logistical system.

Our experience in the war proves that the CPVF initiatives in improving supplies were successful. And it taught us several lessons: to adhere to the principle of close coordination between rear supply services and combat commands; to strengthen unified leadership and organization of the logistics services; to combine the structure between the area supply and the unit supply; and to establish a transportation network connecting all the service stations. Today, we should still pay attention to these lessons and study them carefully.

Many of these major improvements should be attributed to Comrade Hong Xuezhi, who organized the logistical work and carried out specific tasks in Korea. At that time, he was deputy commander of the CPVF and chief of the CPVF Logistics Department. Very thoughtful and resourceful, Hong made a great contribution to the improvement of our logistics service.

The CPVF logistics departments encountered numerous difficulties. What impressed me most was how those services overcame the specific obstacles involved in supplying food, clothes, and, in particular, transportation.

First, we had a big problem feeding our soldiers in the war. Since enemy airplanes bombed us frequently, grain could be transported to the front only with difficulty. Even though some reached the front, our troops could not cook their food. Cooking needed fires, and fires caused smoke, which would surely expose our troops' position and attract enemy air raids. There was almost no way to solve this problem. During our five offensive campaigns, many CPVF troops had to allay their hunger with "one bite parched flour and one bite snow" [*yiba chaomian, yibaxue*]. We should say that the parched flour had played a significant role in our food supply during the mobile warfare period. However, eating parched flour with snow caused diarrhea.

At the end of the Fifth Campaign, the front line tended to stabilize gradually. We had strengthened our organizational work on the rear supply services in China by that time. And all the personnel in the logistics services had made great efforts to improve supplies and transportation in Korea. The food supply also improved. Later, the Volunteer troops could enjoy crackers, egg powder, fried peanuts, and other food; sometimes they could even have canned food. Meanwhile, the CPVF instructed its troops to grow vegetables, raise pigs, and make bean sprouts and *dofu* [tofu, bean-curd paste] themselves. As a result, their food supply was getting better and better. The soldiers became happy with their life in Korea.

Still, I was deeply concerned about the difficulties with the CPVF food supply. I repeatedly told the comrades at the PLA General Logistics Headquarters that we needed to develop our motorized kitchens. The Soviet Red Army had already been equipped with them. In the Soviet army, moreover, each regiment even had a bakery unit. Conveniently storable bread could be kept for a long time without spoilage and was easily digestible. The Soviets' motorized kitchens were able to serve at least one hot dish and one soup for both lunch and supper; sometimes the troops had beef in the soup. In the cold winter, it was ideal for soldiers to have hot soup.

We also needed to manufacture a variety of canned food, which can be kept for a long time. Some cans could be made big enough for a platoon. I recently told the comrades at the General Logistics Headquarters that we needed to improve our food service for the troops in wartime through the development of motorized kitchens, baked bread, and canned food. These developments in fact are not difficult at all. We now are able to do them. After all, food service is a major issue relating to our army's fighting capability. We should pay more attention to it.

Second, we had many problems in clothing our soldiers during the early period of the war. Winter in North Korea was very cold. On entering Korea, the CPVF usually had to fight the enemy in temperatures colder than ten degrees below zero Fahrenheit. Before departing from China, our troops had only a faint idea of the weather conditions in Korea. Many did not bring winter clothes with them, and we then suffered unnecessary losses. Moreover, there were many mountains and forests where our soldiers' clothes were easily torn and wore out fast. Also, intensive enemy air raids—sometimes with napalm bombs—caused heavy losses of our clothes and supplies.

This problem, however, was relatively easier to solve than the difficulties of providing meals. We supplied our CPVF with sufficient clothing, relatively quickly. Our experience in the Korean War suggests that we must make our soldiers' uniforms neither too thin nor too thick; a thick uniform is heavy and will handicap the soldiers' combat capability. In future wars, we cannot neglect the issue of clothing our soldiers. As far as it is compatible with military operations, we should make uniforms as light as possible in order to reduce the troops' load. In short, we must properly solve the problem of clothing in wartime on the basis of available resources and local conditions.

Third, transportation, trains and motorized transport alike, was extremely difficult to provide, if not impossible, throughout the war. The enemy had concentrated its air raids on our communication and transportation lines. In response to these raids, in September 1951 a transportation planning group met in northeastern China. The meeting, chaired by Comrade Lu Zhengcao, focused on finding possible solutions for wartime railroad transportation.

As reported at that meeting, North Korea had suffered a huge, unprecedented flood that year. Since July 1951 the mountain torrents and the UNC's "strangulation warfare" had seriously damaged railroads and highways throughout North Korea. Since repair materials and equipment could not be shipped to the heavily damaged locations on time, the traffic slowed, then stopped. Moreover, most train stations in Korea had only single-track main line and double-terminal siding tracks at that time. And it was hard for one train to find a siding when it met another crossing from the opposite direction. At that time, the front needed supplies so badly that we had to send loaded trains from China to North Korea one after another [on a one-way trip]; as a result, there was a big traffic jam along the railroads. The empty cars could not make timely returns to China, and more than 5,000 lay idle in North Korea.

By fall 1951 the number of trains and cars needed for the war amounted to about 20 percent of our national railroad transportation system. Boxcar requirements numbered 60 percent of the national total. Such a huge demand for railroad transportation became one of the major problems in our rear supply and support services. Wartime transportation was extremely heavy. For instance, between mid-September and the end of October, we needed to send over 12,000 railroad cars of supplies to the front—grain, fuel, munitions, clothes, parts, and equipment for artillery and tank forces; materials and machines for the railroad engineering troops; and supplies for the NKPA. Given our railroad transport capacity at the time, however, even under the best conditions we could dispatch only about 6,000 railroad cars such a long distance within one and a half months. When Zhou became aware of this difficult situation, he instructed us to ship the grain, fuel, and clothes first and the other items later in order to ensure the minimum needs of our troops on the front. Following his instructions, we worked hard to organize emergency repair shops and emergency transportation assets, and eventually we accomplished our tasks.

We had invented many ways to safeguard our transportation from being interrupted by air raids. Our major methods included, for example, deploying more anti-aircraft artillery pieces to key positions, bridges, and transportation hubs. We organized the ground forces along the transportation lines to fire at low-flying enemy planes (mainly with both our light and heavy machine guns). We also sent our fighters to patrol certain areas and to engage invading enemy planes in order to ease the pressure on our ground-transportation lines. We took strict precautions against enemy intelligence agents who might sneak into our rear areas in order to send up their ground–air communications. There were more methods, such as constructing alternative lines of railroads and highways; increasing the number of air-raid shelters along the transportation lines; widely deploying antiaircraft observation posts; overcoming various difficulties in nighttime transportation; storing repair materials ahead of time at the locations that might possibly be bombed; building underwater bridges and alternate bridges in some areas; and taking other measures.

Moreover, we stationed five regiments of the railroad engineering corps at the front. Deployed around key positions, they were to repair bridges and keep communication lines open. Our railroad engineering corps played an important role. After they entered Korea, our engineers made the railroad bridges there "unbreakable." Their slogan was, "The enemy bombs bridges daily, we repair them immediately and reopen them shortly." The troops stored a lot of repair equipment and materials near the bridges. As soon as enemy bombing was over, they would rush to repair the damaged bridge and quickly open it to traffic. In their epic struggles to keep railroad transportation going, many heroes like Yang Liandi emerged.[24]

To improve highway transportation, our truck drivers invented many effective methods to protect their trucks and cargoes from air raids. Our losses drastically declined from 40 percent of the total vehicles at the beginning of the war to below 1 percent later. The drivers did a remarkable job.

We also established the Front Headquarters of Railroad Transportation, its specific mission to improve logistical supplies and transportation. The headquarters unified the command of the military transportation departments, railroad engineering corps, and some antiaircraft artillery forces assigned to protect the railroads. Meanwhile, the CPVF Logistics Department organized a strong motorized transport command, a special transport loading unit, a transportation-line security force, and a communications force—all to keep our transportation and communications going safely and smoothly. The CPVF General Headquarters also selected a group of officers capable and experienced in military command for positions in logistics and transportation, thus strengthening the entire logistics and support services.

The glorious achievement of the CPVF transportation services is one of the major reasons that we won the Korean War. Our experience in Korea has proved that in a modern war the difference between the front and the rear is getting smaller and smaller. The logistics departments must employ the most able officers who have experience in both military operations and support services in order to prepare for combat. We could then effectively cope with various enemy attempts to destroy our rear supply and transportation lines and provide a great deal of supplies to our combat troops on time. All nations' armed forces have paid increasing attention to their logistical needs. Given our firsthand experience in Korea, we too must pay more attention to logistics. Among other important issues in any future war against invasion, the logistics departments still need to organize an active antiaircraft defense task force, using different methods and depending on their own combat adaptability to keep our transportation and communications going.

Fourth, replacing CPVF equipment and weapons was an important issue in our logistics and support services. Before the CPVF entered Korea, some units were armed with Soviet-made weapons, some with captured Japanese-made weapons, but the majority with American-manufactured weapons that had been seized from Jiang Jieshi's troops during the Chinese civil war. Thus, because our weapons were of mixed models and calibers, our munitions supply task turned out to be difficult. Moreover, the war required massive expenditures of munitions, and our national production was bound to fall far behind demand. We had to adopt a number of policies to increase military productivity, such as enlarging the scale of military industries, recycling American and Japanese artillery shells, and other measures. We could provide only about 10 percent of the required munitions for the CPVF in Korea, however. During the first quarter of 1951, for example, the Korean front needed more than 14,100 tons of munitions, but the capacity of our military industry could produce only about 1,500 tons. We had to order the remaining 12,000 tons from foreign countries.

At that time, the only foreign country in the world that would possibly provide us with weapons and munitions was the Soviet Union. Even though we had American and Japanese weapons, we preferred to replace all our weapons and equipment with Soviet ordnance [to simplify our training and ammunition supply]. We therefore had to ask the Soviets for their assistance. They replied by providing us with a loan for arms purchase.

When the situation in Korea intensified, the United States calculated that the Soviet Union might send its forces to Korea. But in fact the Soviet Union did not send any forces except some pilots, fighter planes, and antiaircraft artillery units, which assumed some covering and support duties in the rear areas in northern Korea. Several Soviet antiaircraft artillery regiments were deployed around important railroad sections and key positions in the rear areas. Soviet airplanes were not supposed to cross the Thirty-eighth Parallel. At any rate, the Soviets played an important role in the air defense struggle in cooperation with Chinese and Korean troops. In retrospect, the Soviet Union under the leadership of Stalin supported our War to Resist America and Aid Korea both morally and materially. Why did the Soviet Union not send its ground forces to Korea? It feared a third world war, which might be caused by a direct Russo-American engagement in Korea.

From 1950, we borrowed from the Soviet Union a total of 5.6 billion old rubles (approximately U.S. $1.34 billion at that time), most of which was spent on the war. To replace our equipment and weapons completely, we bought enough Soviet-made weapons to arm 100 Chinese divisions. The first part of our purchase provided the weapons and equipment for thirty-seven Chinese divisions. From this we gave the NKPA some weapons, enough to arm several Korean divisions. After that, we gradually replaced our old weapons with Soviet-made weapons in Korea and set up a series of new military industries in China [which were capable of manufacturing Soviet-type weapons and munitions].

The problems of a disorganized and complex ordnance structure were a legacy from the past. We tried to solve them bit by bit throughout the war. Since it brought such huge expenditures, I believe that in the future our weapons, equipment, and munitions must be standardized. We must rely on ourselves in arms production, and we must stockpile sufficient supplies.

Our experience in the war has also proved that logistics service equipment must match combat troops' needs so that the support services can follow the combat troops closely enough to ensure victory in combat. Otherwise, even though our troops have advanced weapons, they cannot fully exploit combat opportunities. To enhance the all-around fighting capacity of our army, we must work intensively on the standardization and systematizing of our logistics service equipment and machines, including them as an integral development of our army's equipment system. We also need to use the results from science and technology to modernize our logistical services and their headquarters.

Fifth, medical service at the front—transporting the wounded to the rear and treating them appropriately and promptly—posed another major challenge in the war. Our medical personnel displayed dauntless heroism and a self-sacrificing spirit both at the front and in the rear areas. They did a remarkable job and left a legacy of many touching stories and much valuable experience. In the future, although we must emphasize the improvement of our medical service on the front, we should do further research on how to organize the transport of seriously wounded soldiers to rear areas. We also need to pay sufficient attention to the construction of our field hospitals.

The Korean War was the largest modern war since World War II. The enemy dominated both in the air and on the sea. The geographic features of the Korean peninsula were favorable for the enemy to have full play of its air and naval superiority. It was under such conditions that we learned the lessons regarding logistics. Our experience is rich and valuable. I believe that the more modernized weapons and equipment become, the more important the logistical supply and support services will be. Without efficient rear support and supply services, no one can win a modern war. In planning the future of our military development, we should continue our careful research on the Korean War and learn from all the valuable experience that the CPVF gained in its support and logistical services.

In conclusion, the Korean War was one of the largest modern international wars, a conflict the American imperialists forced on us right after the founding of our new republic. Although we paid a huge price, we defeated the strongest nation in the imperialist world because of the wise decisions made by the CCP Central Committee and Comrade Mao Zedong. We assisted our Korean comrades and defended our newborn people's republic as well. And we gained valuable experience in modern warfare and advanced our army's development. The American imperialists had never suffered such a loss until the Korean War. After it, the United States started to decline. As a new republic, our international status and reputation have since increased. In this war of great disparity in weaponry between us and the enemy, the Chinese People's Volunteers Force—the best of our people—has made magnificent contributions under the command of Comrade Peng Dehuai. Its great contributions are immortal.

The CCP Central Committee had thought about the question of how to end the Korean War from the very beginning. When the CPVF intervened, the committee had already intended to resolve the Korean issues justly and in accordance with the people's will. On November 4, 1950, the CCP and all the democratic parties in China issued a joint statement: "It is only through our resistance that the imperialists can possibly learn a lesson and that we can possibly solve the problems of independence and liberation in Korea and in many other countries in accordance with their own people's will."

War is a kind of total competition. Victory and defeat are conditioned by many factors. We can win a war only wherever objective conditions permit. It is impossible for us to strike for a victory in war beyond the limits set by objective conditions. Korea is a long, narrow peninsula. The United States had absolute air and naval dominance. If we had pushed southward too far, there could have been another Inchon landing. Meanwhile, it was hard for us to maintain our supply lines for such a long distance under fierce enemy air raids. If our troops had fought mainly in South Korea, supplying them would have been very difficult. In the late period of the war, we firmly defended the Thirty-eighth Parallel and won victories in many tough battles, for example, at Shangganling and in the Kumsong counteroffensive. We proved that the American army could not break through our defense line; indeed, we could possibly make further breakthroughs of their defensive line. By then, the United States agreed to end the war as did North and South Korea; therefore, all the parties ceased fire along the Thirty-eighth Parallel.

At the beginning of the war, MacArthur was arrogant beyond reason. He always contemplated crossing the Yalu River. As a capitalist, he owned some factories in South Korea.[25] Even after the CPVF dealt several direct blows to his forces, MacArthur refused to admit defeat. He did his utmost to bring the flame of the war into China. The ruling class in America, however, did not want to take any more risks after they met with some hard rebuffs. As a result, President Truman fired MacArthur and replaced him with Matthew Ridgway. Around 2:00 A.M. on April 11, 1951, the radio stations in Tokyo broadcast the news that MacArthur had been dismissed from his four commands. At that moment, MacArthur himself did not even know about it. Later, he went before the U.S. Congress and insulted those who fired him.

MacArthur's story has revealed that serious debates over the Korean War had been going on at high levels inside the United States. Truman was worried that if the war extended into China, the American army could be engulfed in the boundless ocean of a people's war there just as the Japanese invading army had been. Another important element was that the United States had neither domestic nor international support for its actions in Korea. Eisenhower won the presidential election of 1952 partly because he had promised in his campaign that he would end the Korean War if he became the next president.[26] We had analyzed the situation at the time and considered it possible to limit the war to Korea. History has proven that our CCP Central Committee's and Comrade Mao Zedong's calculations and decisions were correct.

4

Political Mobilization and Control

Lieutenant General (Ret.) Du Ping

Editors' Note: Du Ping was the director of the political departments in the CPVF General Headquarters and the Western Coast Headquarters and the party committee's chairman of the Chinese Delegation to the Korean Armistice Negotiations during the Korean War. His missions ranged from organizing the Volunteers to participating in the truce talks, mostly the CPVF's political tasks. As one of the top CPVF officers, he spent three and a half years in Korea. In 1955 he was given the rank of lieutenant general.[1]

Born in Wanzai County, Jiangxi Province in 1908, General Du joined the CCP and the Chinese Red Army in 1930. During the Chinese civil war, he served as the director of the organization departments in the Northeast Field Army and then the Fourth Field Army. After the founding of the People's Republic of China, he was director of the political departments in the Thirteenth Army Group, Northeast Military Region, Shenyang Regional Command, and Nanjing Regional Command. He was also the vice political commissar of the Shenyang Regional Command.

After his retirement, at eighty, Du wrote his recollections of the Korean War, Zai Zhiyuanjun Zongbu: Du Ping Huiyilu [At the CPVF General Headquarters: Memoirs of Du Ping] (Beijing: PLA Press, 1989). The following chapters, excerpted and translated, with editors' notes, give a significant account of Du's reflections on the CPVF's political work. Political mobilization and indoctrination are an integral part of Chinese Communist military tradition. Du addresses such issues as new challenges to the CPVF's political control, new tactics employed, and new lessons learned in the Korean War.

POLITICAL MOBILIZATION BEFORE INTERVENTION

The Shenyang Meeting

Train wheels clanged against the rails.[2] The iron torrent surged forward. All the forces of the newly established Northeastern Border Defense Army (NEBDA), originating from the Thirteenth Army Group, began to move northward by train in successive waves around mid-July [1950].[3] Arriving in Northeast China one after another before the end of the month, the armies assembled and awaited further orders.

The Thirty-eighth Army came to Fengcheng on July 24 and then moved to the Kaiyuan-Tieling area in August. The Thirty-ninth Army had been stationed at Liaoyang and Haicheng since July 25. The Fortieth Army reached the strategically important city of Andong (now known as Dandong) on the Yalu River by July 26. Meanwhile, under the [CMC's] orders, the Forty-second Army had ceased all farming work and aligned itself with NEBDA. It was stationed at Ji An, pending new orders.

By this time, NEBDA had four armies composed of twelve infantry divisions, three artillery divisions (the First, Second, and Eighth), three antiaircraft artillery regiments, three truck transportation regiments, one defense artillery regiment, one tank regiment, one engineering regiment, and one cavalry regiment under its command. Totaling 260,000 strong, the army became a bastion of iron—an impregnable fortress along the banks of the Yalu.

Our calendar turns to August 5. An urgent cable from the Central Military Commission had arrived, requesting that the Border Defense Army become fully combat ready by early September. The war in Korea seemed most imminent. Our preparations had to be intensified.

On August 13 the Northeast Military Region (NEMR) held a meeting of its commanders at and above the division level in Shenyang. It was chaired by Gao Gang, commander and political commissar of NEMR.[4] Comrades Xiao Jinguang and Xiao Hua made a special trip from Beijing to attend.[5] Gao delivered a speech about the current war situation and NEBDA's tasks. Then Comrade Deng Hua talked about military tactics in possible battles against the American armed forces.

The meeting focused on such general questions as how to ensure our national defense and how to defend the northeastern borders. Through a rather lively discussion, all attending commanders believed that if imperialist America occupied all of Korea, it would retrace imperialist Japan's old path to invade our Northeast and North China. Therefore, was it actually acceptable for us to allow America to take Korea and then invade China, where we would then have to resist? Or would it be better for us to take the initiative now to assist the NKPA in Korea in order to preserve ourselves?

The discussion was animated, with diverse views. Most of the commanders argued that we should take the initiative, since the enemy had not yet established a foothold in Korea. We could assist the NKPA and press on without letup until we completely crushed the enemy's dream of aggression in Asia. Some of the comrades, however, worried about whether we could achieve a victory in a war with the U.S. Army. The enemy had modern weapons and technology, many times more artillery pieces than we did, and they enjoyed air and naval superiority. They also possessed nuclear bombs. Engaging such an enemy would be a totally different situation from all previous wars fought by [the Communists in] China. We could not underestimate them. In the end, the discussion led to a heightened sense of confidence among most of the comrades to fight against American troops, chiefly because we analyzed particularly the conditions favoring us by which we could win the war.

First, our forces were superior in numbers; at that time, we estimated a ratio of three to one. The United States itself was short of manpower. Its forces had to be divided between the defense of Western Europe and its homeland. Even though it could send reinforcements, the maximum of American forces in Korea could hardly exceed 500,000 men. We, however, could keep transferring our forces to Korea rather easily from our more than 4 million troops in China.

Second, our forces were superior in political quality. The American forces were being sent to Korea without a clear mission. Their morale was low. Our army would fight to defend our motherland. As the victorious army [in the Chinese civil war], the PLA's fame had spread far and wide, and its morale was extremely high. With its extensive combat experience and, moreover, its ability to bear hardships, perform tough jobs, and brave difficult situations, the Chinese army was imbued with an indomitable spirit to crush all enemies.

Third, the logistics service was to our advantage. Modern war demands huge amounts of logistical supplies. The enemy heavily depended on their overseas shipments from America, which took ten days just to cross the Pacific Ocean and more days for their inland transportation. With nationwide support and an overland connection between Northeast China and Korea, our transport of supplies was much easier, as we calculated at the meeting. Later, our operative experience proved that our logistics service was not secured at all without control of the air. In fact, we never gained a strong grip on the supply problem.

Fourth, justice was on our side. Popular support all over the world was with us. The enemy was in an unfavorable position as far as international opinion was concerned.

We then explicitly assessed the factor of nuclear weapons and concluded that it was men, not one or two atomic bombs, that determined the outcome of war. And an atomic bomb used on the battlefield would inflict damage not only on the enemy's side but also on friendly forces. Furthermore, the people of the world opposed the use of nuclear weapons; the United States would have to think twice before dropping them.

When the meeting was nearing an end, I saw Xiao Hua, who sat at the front, turn around and give a signal to Liu Xiyuan, political commissar of the Thirty-eighth Army, who sat behind him. It seemed to me that Xiao was pressing Liu to take the lead in clarifying the commanders' position. One of the youngest army political commissars in the PLA, Liu was just thirty years old. Then he stood up and spoke out: "There is no need to say more about it. We will firmly carry out every order from the party's Central Committee and CMC. I still keep the same words: death under the shield is just facing the sky; survival is coming back to face a new life. Whenever the Central Committee calls upon us to act, we will act right away, and will guarantee to fulfill the tasks without losing face for our motherland and people." Then Wu Xinquan, commander of the Thirty-ninth Army, raised his voice: "Damn the fears! American devils do not have three heads and six arms. It is no more difficult to beat a paper tiger than to beat a real tiger. We will show the people of the world that we can beat American troops."

After the Shenyang meeting, Comrade Xiao Jinguang returned to Beijing and reported to Chairman Mao Zedong in person about NEBDA's meeting. Xiao also talked to Mao about the army's difficulties, including the shortage of military equipment and medical personnel. Basing his action on an earlier decision made by the CMC, Nie Rongzhen, acting chief of the PLA General Staff, had already cabled NEBDA on August 5, instructing the army to finish its preparations within the month and to await new orders regarding future deployment. Taking notice of those problems, and since the Shenyang meeting had considered it difficult for the army to accomplish its preparations on time, Acting Chief Nie sent another cable on August 18 extending the army's deadline for the completion of preparations until the end of September.

When the CMC's second cable arrived at NEBDA Headquarters, I had left Shenyang for Zhenjiang Mountain in Andong. The mountain, one of Andong's commanding heights, was one of northeastern China's Big Eight Scenic Areas at that time. A radar station sat on its top. Arriving there, I lived in an old-fashioned apartment building at the foot of the hill, as did the staff of the Thirteenth Army Group's Political Department.

One night, Deng Hua, Hong Xuezhi, Xie Fang, and I carefully studied a newly received CMC cable.[6] We felt the situation was getting increasingly serious in Korea and that the war could possibly come upon us earlier than we had expected. Our preparations had to speed up. Although we talked about accelerating preparations, it was too late for us to resolve so many problems, especially regarding the rear logistics and support services. There just was not sufficient time. Most important, the transportation system was terribly poor. Hong calculated that we needed at least 700 transport trucks; otherwise, we could not move our troops [to the front]. NEMR could not solve this problem, given its limited resources. Also important was the severe shortage of both truck drivers and medical staff. For example, it was estimated that we were short of the latter by more than 1,000 persons.

Xie was familiar with operational planning and able to make combat plans quickly. He insisted that at present our troops were badly in need of antitank weapons. The few antitank guns our troops had were left with local PLA units when they were departing for Northeast China. Other problems included surface-to-air communication, operational equipment, and standardized regulations—all of which had to be attended to by the CMC.

As a cautious individual, Deng compared the conditions of enemy troops, our own forces, and friendly forces and assessed the Korean terrain in great detail. He believed that the enemy might have two plans. First, its forces might land at a couple of coastal points in northern Korea to attack the rear of the NKPA. These forces would attempt to harass and pin down the North Koreans while the main enemy force would advance from its current position and drive from south to north along the major railroads and highways. The second option involved a small frontal assault against the NKPA around its present positions to be followed by a massive enemy landing attack on its rear areas (close to Pyongyang or Seoul). The NKPA's front and rear would then be attacked simultaneously, putting it in a tough situation.

The most opportune and advantageous moment for us to enter Korea and join the war, Deng believed, would be after the enemy reached the areas north of the Thirty-eighth Parallel. The right timing would bring us not only political benefits but also military advantages. Our purpose was to eliminate enemy forces in Korea. It would then be favorable for us to put an end to the war quickly.

Deng, Hong, and Xie submitted a joint report on August 31 to Zhu De, PLA commander in chief. They summarized their points of view and gave three suggestions on how to achieve the goal of "fighting a quick war to force a quick determination." Their first suggestion was to make every effort to engage the PLA air force on a large scale, a critical means to realize our ends. If the Soviet Red Army could help us with its air force, or its aviation technology and equipment to a greater extent, our goal would be materially ensured. If our air force was not ready for operations, we might as well postpone its participation. Their second suggestion was to employ two more army groups for the war and strengthen our troops with various heavy artillery pieces, tanks, and other necessary equipment. Of most concern to the commanders was the lack of antiaircraft weapons. They suggested adding an antiaircraft artillery battalion to each army. (This battalion could be organized into an artillery regiment together with each army's rocket-gun battalion and antitank artillery battalion.) Each division should have an antiaircraft artillery company. Their third suggestion was to strengthen the rear support service system. Meanwhile, the support service offices should begin to prepare food, ammunition, transportation, service stations, and hospitals. But first they should send their competent officers to Korea to study the situation and to learn from the North Koreans' transportation and supply experience.

As was predicted, more than 70,000 American and ROK troops, covered by a host of 260 ships and 500 airplanes, landed at Inchon on the western coast of Korea on September 15.[7] The next day, as soon as I walked into the headquarters' office, I heard my comrades' loud discussion, with everybody eager to put in a word: "The American forces have landed at Inchon. What are we going to do?" I did not answer their question but said to myself that we were not too far away from the day we would enter the war.

At that moment, I had a deep understanding of the CCP Central Committee's brilliant foresight about the situation in Korea and of its incomparable correctness in taking relevant military measures. Had the Central Committee not organized NEBDA earlier, had it not moved the armies to the northeastern border for combat preparation, had it not ordered the armies to complete all their preparations before September 30, had we delayed our preparations until the American forces landed at Inchon on September 15, we would possibly have lost an advantageous military opportunity and would have left ourselves in a passive position both politically and militarily.

Arrow on the Bowstring

Our troops seemed to have made two sharp turns, as if they were following an S-shaped course.[8] We had turned abruptly from civil war to peacetime reconstruction; then we were suddenly forced to make the transformation from peacetime to preparations for a foreign war.[9] The first curve [from civil war to peacetime] was relatively smooth and fast because we had paid careful attention to our troops' mental preparation from the very beginning. Nevertheless, we encountered a problem because we had not been able to avoid submerging ourselves in economic activities during peacetime reconstruction. Tactical drills and combat consciousness had been weakened. How could we do a better job of shifting the mind-set of our troops this time?

After the meeting of August 13, I called for an army group's political affairs meeting to discuss these issues. We first analyzed the psychological condition of the soldiers who were preparing for the war, dividing them into different categories.

The first consisted of those troops, approximately 50 percent, with a positive attitude toward participating in the Korean War. Those soldiers came from a reliable group with high political awareness. Seasoned during the civil war, most of them had fought well and without any hesitation about sacrificing themselves in the battles. Facing the outrages of American intervention in Korea, they were filled with indignation. They even submitted written statements asking to fight the American troops and to help the Korean people.

The next category, the intermediate elements, made up about 40 percent of our troops. Their attitude was that they could fight as ordered but it did not matter to them if there was a war or not.

The last 10 percent consisted of those soldiers who were in an unsettled state of mind. Generally, they were the liberated soldiers who came from the GMD's troops, or the young soldiers who joined the PLA from newly liberated regions. They lacked sufficient recognition of the great significance in resisting America and aiding Korea. Reluctant to leave their peacetime life behind, they were afraid of hardship and war. Scared of American troops and nuclear weapons, they were greatly worried about fighting against the imperialist forces. A few of them even named the Yalu's bridge the "gate of hell," complaining that "to resist America and aid Korea is like poking our nose into other people's business" or "to draw fire against ourselves."

Moreover, at that time, there existed numerous rumors, as the troops could look at Korea from their camps on the other side of the Yalu River. One rumor underestimated the enemy by claiming that the American soldiers were spoiled boys. They had to lie down on their carpets before they could shoot and could not bear hardships and casualties. Another rumor, however, was that the American forces were formidable. They had many airplanes and big guns. One of their artillery shells could kill an entire company of ours.

As the director of the Thirteenth Army Group's Political Department, I realized the current political task was to guarantee the successful transformation of each soldier's mind-set from peacetime reconstruction to combat-ready preparations. We had to work exceptionally hard on the third category of soldiers so that they would not be tossed out of railway cars while the historical train was running at full speed. Instead, they could become part of a driving force to push the train forward. Therefore, after our political affairs meeting, the whole army group launched a campaign of ideological education emphasizing patriotism, internationalism, and revolutionary heroism. The campaign helped our troops answer most of their questions about "whether or not we should fight" and "whether or not we can fight."

First, our effort emphasized the "must-fight" argument by explaining the necessity and righteousness of resisting America and aiding Korea. Through an educational approach, we reviewed historical facts about American imperialist aggression in China so as to arouse hatred against the invading troops. According to my memory, the Political Department edited and printed a history booklet for this program. It started with the year 1839 [1840–1843] when U.S. Navy Commodore Lawrence Kearny led the East India Squadron that sailed arrogantly all over the China Sea. Then the booklet moved to 1857 when America forced the Qing [Ch'ing Dynasty] government to sign the unfair Sino-American Tianjin Treaty. Next it covered the history from America's participation in the Eight-Power Allied Forces' invasion of China in 1900 to its support of Jiang Jieshi, who waged a civil war against the Communists and the people. The booklet listed all the historical facts, one after another, about the U.S. armed forces' invasions of China within the past 100 years.

Our booklet also focused on the interpretation that America's military invasion of Korea was the beginning of its plan to follow in the steps of imperialist Japan's invasion of China. After their occupation of Korea, American troops would aim at us as their next target. Their aggressive forces had already invaded our country's territory, Taiwan. They were continually sending their airplanes to raid and bomb our cities and villages along our northeastern borders and sending their naval warships to shell our commercial ships on the high seas. American imperialists had already provided us with indisputable proof, through countless deeds of their aggression, that America was the most dangerous enemy of the Chinese people.

Meanwhile, in the campaign, we repeatedly referred to the traditional friendship and geographical relations between China and Korea, explaining that we were fraternal neighbors as closely related as lips and teeth. If the lips [China's neighbors] were gone, the teeth [China itself] would get cold. To help the neighbor was to help ourselves. We did not set fire to ourselves, but it was the enemy who had already set flames of war on our doorway. This war must be fought; the American imperialists were forcing us. We had to take care of the problem, which was by no means other people's business.

Then we moved on toward a "dare-to-fight" and "can-fight" argument for the purpose of enhancing the confidence and courage of the rank and file. We emphasized an exploration of the American imperialist "paper tiger" nature and its strategic weaknesses. Even though the U.S. military had modern weapons, the American troops were fighting an unjust war and suffering from low morale. They were short of manpower, and their rear support was distant. Our army was dedicated to a just cause. As a victorious army, we had the brilliant leadership of the Communist Party and Chairman Mao and the full support of our people, the Korean people, and peace-loving peoples all over the world. Our weapons were not as advanced as the enemy's, but we enjoyed a numerical advantage. And our troops had valuable experience in beating a superior enemy with our inferior weapons. Moreover, mountainous operations in Korea would help our troops bring their advantageous skills of close combat and night combat into full play. We were capable of defeating the invading American forces. To overcome some soldiers' psychological fears of Americans, we invited some liberated GMD soldiers, who had once fought together with the American troops in Burma during World War II, to talk about the latter's conditions and characteristics. These arguments proved that American troops were not invincible but were absolutely defeatable.

In dealing with the questions of "whether or not we should fight" and "whether or not we can fight," we also taught the troops to discipline themselves strictly in their relations with the local people. We stressed the need to unite the Korean people and the friendly forces. We required our troops to care for and love the Korean people's interests in all respects. We must care for every Korean hill, river, flower, and tree as much as we love our own motherland. We must not give ourselves the airs of a big nation or make any excuse not to respect the Korean people.

We also invited the troops to discuss the possible difficulties that our operations in a foreign land would entail. We asked them to be psychologically prepared for these situations, such as frequent raids by enemy airplanes, cold weather, supply shortages, language barriers, and different lifestyles. In retrospect, this part of the education campaign was insufficient. Arriving in Korea, our troops faced difficulties much more serious than what we had discussed. Many new psychological problems emerged because of insufficient mental and material preparation. Had we had a fuller discussion about the possible difficulties before we entered the war, in addition to stressing favorable conditions and "can-fight" and "must-win" confidence, our troops' situation might have been much better.

During this period, we had to make many preparations besides focusing on ideological education. We were terribly busy. The Political Department was small in number but efficient. Despite being an army group's political department, there were fewer than thirty people working there, including the director and all officers. Most of them, however, were experienced officers of the former Political Department of the Fourth Field Army, and we worked together well. Hardly anyone was seen in the departmental offices except the persons on duty because most of the officers were with the troops. The Political Department seldom requested reports from the lower levels; the information was brought back by our own staff, who visited there. If I needed to report to the higher levels, I drafted the reports myself.

The two-month effort at prewar ideological education brought about a remarkable effect. The intense psychological education stimulated strong [revolutionary] class consciousness among our commanders and soldiers. The rank and file clearly saw the aggressive nature of the American imperialists, understood the close relationship between the Chinese and Korean peoples, and came to believe that to assist in the Korean people's liberation war was to defend our own country. It was a righteous action. Our troops basically cleared up the "fear-of-America" attitude and established a "dare-to-fight" and a "must-win" faith. Thereafter, a popular movement for joining the CPVF swept the troops.[10] Everybody wanted to help our friendly neighbor and participate in the Korean War.

After the education campaign, a soldier from the Fortieth Army wrote a verse:

The American imperialist is a ball of fire,
It will burn China after burning through Korea;
China the neighbor rushes to put out the fire,
China can be saved by helping Korea.

This poet vividly illustrates the understanding of the relationships between resisting America and aiding Korea and between safeguarding homes and defending the country. He also reveals that the soldiers' political and ideological awareness had been improved after the educational movement. Among other soldiers was Chen Dehui from the Sixth Company of the 357th Regiment. He submitted to the company's commanders a written request for a battle assignment in an earnest tone:

Report to my superior in a hurry. I cannot wait any longer. I am unable to endure the new hatred piled on old. My mother was hounded by the landlord. My father worked for the landlord as a farm laborer to his death. I pastured the landlord's pigs since I was twelve. I had been whipped and abused until sixteen, when I was drafted by the GMD into military service. Isn't it the American devils who supported Jiang Jieshi so that we the working people lived in misery and suffered disasters? After our liberation, can we watch the Korean people suffer the same fate without lending them a hand? The poor all over the world belong to one family. I am requesting to go to the Korean front to kill American devils!

I still have a long-lasting impression of an expedition poem written by Ma Fuyao, political instructor of the Fifth Company, Twenty-sixth Regiment, First Artillery Division: "Valiantly and spiritedly, we cross the Yalu River. / To defend peace and the motherland is to save my home." This poem expressed the desire among the broad ranks of CPVF officers and men, and it spread fast. After being polished and set to music by composer Zhou Weichi, it became the "Battle Song of the CPVF," an excellent fighting song. Everybody in the army loved it, learned to sing it, and was inspired by it.

The accusations against the American imperialists were everywhere among our troops, and urgent requests for entering the Korean War were widespread in the CPVF. The whole army was just like a dry haystack soaked with gasoline; it might become a raging flame ignited by a single spark. In early September, all the armies held "hero and model representatives" meetings, one after another, where representatives were elected to attend the [PLA] National Combat Hero Representatives Conference in Beijing. This poured more gasoline on the fire, which was burning inside our soldiers' hearts.

During the same period, combat and logistics preparations were also intensive. Although preoccupied by this, Deng Hua, Hong Xuezhi, Han Xianchu, and Xie Fang found time to study the situation in Korea and to work out some battle plans.[11] Lights in their rooms were on all night, night after night. One night, the army group's commanders gathered for a briefing regarding the CPVF logistical supplies from NEMR. The briefing officer, due to a minor mechanical problem with his car, was a bit late and discovered all the leading commanders sleeping at the meeting table like logs. They were too tired!

During this period, the armies were reorganized and replenished in accordance with the CMC's plans for wartime buildup. The Thirty-ninth Army, for example, organized a six-barrel rocket-artillery battalion and an antitank artillery battalion. Its logistics and medical sections were combined into the army's logistics section. The section also set up its rear support office and an accelerated middle school. The support office organized the army's families, female comrades, recuperating personnel, and the old and weak. Each division of the Thirty-ninth Army established a security battalion, an antiaircraft artillery battalion, and a medical battalion. Each regiment organized its own medical company. So did the other armies.

The armies had two phases of drills before going into battles. Completed by mid-September, the first phase focused on the exercises of small-group combat tactics, including shooting, throwing grenades, demolition, antiaircraft training, and nighttime anti–air raid practice. The second phase stressed courses of group-attack tactics for platoons, companies, and battalions. These exercises were aimed at the demolition of enemy defense works under enemy fire. The second phase of the drill continued till the troops entered Korea.

Meanwhile, each army assembled its officers at and above the battalion level for ten or fifteen days of training. They studied geographic conditions in Korea,

American military tactics, coordination between our artillery and infantry troops, antiaircraft tactics, and problems involving attack, defense, and nighttime combat in mountainous areas. They grasped the primary characteristics of American military tactics and definitely understood our operative principles. Because Americans employed tanks frequently in battles, all the armies offered classes in antitank training, brought in skilled antitank personnel, and prepared to fight enemy tanks.

Among other important political tasks to be done before we went into Korea was strengthening ideological control. During our training on "whether or not we dare to fight" and "whether or not we can fight," we had pointed out emphatically that the key was to build "dare-to-fight" courage as well as a "can-fight" capacity. During mobilization, the rank and file channeled their hatred of the enemy into active practice in combat training in order to master the skills necessary to destroy it.

Moreover, during this period, we sent political cadres right to the drill fields to work with the troops during their training. Many of these individuals performed outstanding deeds during combat training, and these were publicized. The CPVF therefore was able to maintain its high morale in drilling, strengthening its training quality and combat capacity.

To overcome the difficulty of the language barrier in operating abroad, NEMR mobilized more than 2,000 young Sino-Koreans as interpreters for our army to serve as liaisons. Half were members of the CCP and the Chinese Communist Youth League, and most of them had been local civilian cadres with good political standing. Because there was no designated institution in the CPVF for enemy affairs, those comrades reported to the army group's security department and civil transportation department. After a ten-day training session on their specific responsibilities, they were assigned to units. Given the need for those interpreters, however, the Army Group Command, Political Department, and Logistics Department were given priority. After that, two interpreters were assigned to each unit. There were a couple of interpreters who came to our political department. Because of the urgency of operations in Korea, a special schedule was set up for them to teach us Korean. We started by learning simple vocabulary and basic conversation to cover our immediate needs after we entered Korea.

When our military had been redirected from war to peacetime activities after the founding of the PRC, many forces had eliminated their logistics offices. Thus, preparations in that service began with reestablishment of its departments (or offices) at the army and division levels. Thereafter, based on combat needs, those new support services started to stockpile military materials, replenish and repair technical equipment, and recruit rear support service cadres and technical personnel. They did a tremendous job.

After two months of preparations, all the troops had been changed from loose, peacetime-reconstruction units into taut, combat-ready formations. As an arrow on the bowstring, the 260,000 combat soldiers stationed along the Yalu River were waiting for the order from the CMC.

THE CPVF'S POLITICAL TASKS IN THE KOREAN WAR

Political Mobilization Order

When the CPVF General Headquarters was stationed at Taeyudong [in North Korea], the offices of the Political Department were quartered at the bottom of a valley about a half mile away.[12] I lived together with the other leading commanders at the headquarters, so it was convenient to communicate with one another.

After dinner one evening, I began to draft the Political Mobilization Order, designed to help us strive to win the first battle after entering Korea. In it I emphasized that after the CPVF troops had left our country, the people in China and all over the world would be watching us and wishing us victories. We had acquired both the resolve and confidence to fight for a big victory in the first battle. At this point, our First Campaign was about to start. It had an extremely important bearing on future developments in the war and on our army's prestige in the world. The enemy was chiefly afraid of our ability to fight in man-to-man combat. We should boldly cut off its route of retreat and penetrate its rear. The closer we approached, the more scared their troops would be and the less useful their planes and guns.

When I finished drafting the order, it was already late. I first asked Comrade Hong Xuezhi, who shared the room with me, for his comments and suggestions. Hong had extensive experience in political work because he had once held the posts of battalion political commissar, director of a regimental political section, and director of division and army political departments in the Chinese Red Army during the Agrarian Revolutionary War.[13] Considering the time pressure, Hong did not read it but suggested that it was probably better to send it to Commander Peng Dehuai immediately for approval.

As soon as he picked up the Political Mobilization Order, Peng deleted several slogans and then removed "Peng Dehui, Commander in Chief and Political Commissar," substituting "Du Ping, Director of Political Department," as the signatory. Putting down his writing brush, Commander Peng chatted with me. "This 'Political Mobilization Order' should be issued," he told me. "Our slogan is to put up a good fight in the first battle after entering Korea. Our purpose is to achieve a victory in this initial battle. In drafting the 'Political Mobilization Order,' we should pay attention to and proceed from the actual conditions of both us and the enemy, clearly explaining favorable and unfavorable conditions in the light of facts, and fully showing our army's determination for an inevitable victory. Try not to use exaggerated words."

"Chief Peng," I suggested, "you are the commander and the political commissar. It is better to use your name as the signatory. I feel inadequate to sign my name."

"For a political mobilization order," he said, "it is all right to use the name of the political department's director. You will be in charge of all the political matters from now on. Do your work as aggressively as possible. Don't be afraid of confronting any problems."

Nevertheless, I still changed the signature. Instead of using my own name, I put "CPVF Political Department" when I wrote the final draft.

When I walked out of Peng's wooden cabin, the Taeyudong area was bathed in the dim light of night as if in a foggy mist. Mining workers' sheds at the bottom of the hill were in a haze, the moonlight blending the sheds and hill together. Even a superb, skillful pilot could hardly discover that this was a hiding place for dragons and tigers.

Given Peng's corrections on the Political Mobilization Order and his instructions for our political work, I felt I had already grasped one of his requirements. The word was "pragmatism." I had regarded the Political Mobilization Order as merely propaganda at the beginning. Some of the facts had been previously discussed, so I had written the "order" in a slogan style. Peng's changes were innovative for me. From then on, I knew that not only the political mobilization orders should be free of slogans and big talk but also that the entire project must stress practical results, like shooting arrows at the target, and strictly avoid the tendency to indulge in empty talk.

Peng's changes in the order made me respect him even more. He was not as frightening as others said and was not at all what he often said about himself at meetings, "a terrible person." Philosophers are right when they say that the unity of opposites is a universal phenomenon. Personal character has different aspects; some contrasting features can be unified in one person. Commander Peng was that kind of person. He had one aspect of toughness (as some people said), as well as another side of kindness (as he worked on the draft of that order). His instructions, especially on our political work, were concise and explicit, which made us like and respect him.

Harboring my admiration for him, I remembered what Peng had said—I would be in charge of all future CPVF political work. Realizing he was really shouldering heavy responsibilities, I wanted to share a little of the burden with him. Since I was not sure about whether I could do so, I made up my mind that I would not bother him with routine business and would simply report to him and ask for his decisions only on important matters.

The Taeyudong Meeting

On November 13, 1950, at Taeyudong, the CPVF held its first expanded party committee meeting since entering the Korean War.[14] The First Campaign in Korea was summarized, and we discussed guiding principles for the next operation.

The CPVF Party Committee was founded in accordance with the CCP Central Committee's decision of October 25; among the members of its Standing Committee were Peng Dehuai, Deng Hua (deputy commander and vice political commissar), Hong Xuezhi (deputy commander), Han Xianchu (deputy commander), Xie Fang (chief of staff), and Du Ping (director of the Political Department). Peng was appointed as secretary; Deng Hua was the deputy secretary.

According to the same instruction from the CCP Central Committee, the Thirteenth Army Group's Headquarters and Political Department were reorganized into the CPVF's Headquarters and Political Department, which together formed the CPVF General Headquarters. Its staff was small in number but capable and flexible. There were only seven sections and one office in the Commanding Headquarters, operations, intelligence, communication, internal affairs, telegraph encoding, headquarters attached units' affairs, administration, and the headquarters coordinating office. The head of the Operations Section was Ding Ganru from NEMR. The deputy of the Intelligence Section was Cui Xingnong, a member of an advance team composed of Zhang Mingyuan, deputy chief of the NEMR Logistics Department, and five other officers; they had conducted a previous field survey of the battleground situation in Korea.

The Political Department consisted of only five divisions. The chief of the Secretariat Division was Wang Jian. The acting chief of the Organization Division was Ren Rong, and the deputy chief was Cao Delian. The chief of the Propaganda Division was Zhuo Ming, and the deputy chief was Li Weiyi. The chief of the Security Division was Yang Lin, and the Civilian Mobilization Division was headed by Yang Wenhan.

The CPVF had yet to form its own logistics department since all the supplies were provided by the NEMR Logistics Department. To accompany the CPVF Headquarters, a frontal logistics command was established by the NEMR Logistics Department and led by Zhang Mingyuan, deputy chief of the department, and Du Zheheng, chief of the Agriculture Department of the Northeast People's Government. The Medical Division of the NEMR Logistics Department also set up its front command post for field operations.

The comrades attending the CPVF's party meeting recognized that our First Campaign had caused more than 15,000 enemy casualties and had driven the enemy from the Yalu back to the Chongchon River. Significantly, the campaign stabilized the military situation in Korea and enhanced the reputation of our action as a just war. Moreover, the CPVF got a firm foothold in northern Korea. It had basically grasped both the enemy's strong and weak points and had strengthened its confidence in victory.

Yet it was pointed out that although the First Campaign had achieved a great victory, it had annihilated fewer enemy troops than previously expected. A major reason was that some of our armies did not have effective political mobilization. They had overrated the American troops and thus had not dared to penetrate into the enemy's rear and flanks to cut off its path of retreat. Commander Peng criticized the Thirty-eighth Army at the meeting and called for opposition to such pessimistic thinking. Peng's criticism both shocked and inspired the entire CPVF.

At the meeting, it was decided that our army would still follow the principle of employing a combination of mobile, positional, and guerrilla warfare and of defensive and offensive operations before we would receive adequate support from the air, artillery, and armored forces. Our next campaign would be an in-house operation aimed to lure the enemy into a deep trap, where their troops could be encircled and eliminated one by one. The committee urged each army to find ways to destroy one or two enemy regiments in the next campaign. Participants from various armies stated that they would convey the spirit of the meeting to all party members and would mobilize the rank and file to fight one more campaign before the end of the year. It was understood that our next campaign would aim at anni- hilating at least six or seven enemy regiments, pushing the front forward to the Pyongyang-Wonsan region and forcing the enemy to switch from offense to defense. Thus the next campaign would create favorable conditions for our future large-scale counterattack.

After the meeting, our political department held a political-task workshop involving the directors from the army's political departments. We exchanged views about political effectiveness during the First Campaign and discussed how to achieve better political mobilization in order to guarantee a greater victory in the next cam- paign. I still have a vivid memory about this workshop and some of the issues we discussed because it was the first one of its kind since we had entered Korea.

First, ideological education must connect with the current military situation, our operational tasks, and the psychological state of our troops. Such education must be continuous. The victory of the First Campaign indicated the achievements resulting from our two-month political education and mental mobilization cam- paign before the troops left the country. Our slogan of "winning the first battle in Korea" greatly inspired the troops. They fought bravely and performed well in many operations that became models for others. The questions of "whether or not we can fight" and "whether or not we dare to fight" had been primarily answered during our educational campaign.

Two problems, however, were evident: first, the commanders had not been edu- cated as much as the soldiers. Some of the former overestimated the enemy's strength, and as a result they moved slowly and missed the opportunity to engage enemy troops. Some unit commanders even recoiled in fear during battle. Second, our indoctrination stressed favorable conditions but did not prepare the troops for unfavorable conditions. Thus, they lacked the mental stamina for a long-term, tough war. A soldier's verse revealed that problem: "From the North to the South, / one wave ends the war, / wiping out the enemy, / going home for the New Year." Our soldiers were told during mobilization that the enemy had airplanes but that we did also. And they complained in the First Campaign, "How come we never see any air- plane of ours in the battles?"

At the task workshop, we requested that all the armies pay attention to these two problems, which had already appeared during our political work. We required each army to follow the guiding principles formulated at the expanded meeting of the CPVF Party Committee and to inform their troops about the reality of the enemy forces, such as their strengths and weaknesses, as well as the truth about ours. Through organized discussions, the troops' confidence in victory should be founded on an ideological basis for fighting a protracted war and for bearing severe hardships.

As for the commanders, we should pay attention to overcoming their "overly cautious tendency." We could compare successful cases, involving close-quarters combat, night combat, or breaking up and surrounding enemy units and annihilating enemy troops, with cases in which hesitant and delayed moves caused the loss of battle opportunities. The comparison would show that although the American forces had modern equipment, technology, and air superiority, they depended too heavily on these advantages and lacked aggressiveness. Certainly we could defeat them, as long as we fought bravely and skillfully. Our workshop required each army to educate the troops through different approaches so that the rank and file would better understand the glory in participating in this great war to defend our motherland and world peace as an internationalist soldier.

A second issue at the workshop was our battle honor system in a new tactical situation. Fighting abroad created a special environment for rendering outstanding service. The appearance of the first group of heroes who fought the enemy and won honors heightened morale. Some of the units, however, complained that fighting abroad did not receive the same recognition as fighting at home. Medals, certificates of merit, and certificates for meritorious service had yet to be issued. The discussion at the meeting led to criticism of our work, but it also improved our efforts. Taking notice of the new situation of fighting in a foreign land, we established new requirements for winning honors, which were aimed at guiding our troops' efforts in a new direction.

Conditions in Korea were different from those in the civil wars we had fought in the past. The enemy's airplanes attacked everywhere, and their bombing operations were furious. At the beginning, our troops were anxious about how to achieve success in battle under such circumstances. After the initial battles, our attacking troops had come to believe that they had felt the enemy out, and their tactics enabled them to deal effectively with it.

Our defending troops, however, contended with enemy gunfire so fierce that it was not easy for them to hold their positions. In postbattle appraisals of merit in accordance with our new requirements, our defending troops paid a lot of attention to those units and individuals who firmly held their positions and eliminated large numbers of enemy troops but suffered relatively small casualties. Their particular defense tactics were popularized and lauded. Our troops thus suggested that although it was necessary to praise meritorious performances during battles to increase morale, it was thought to be more effective to have widespread commendations after the battles and to enumerate acts of bravery and brilliance. The commanders should immediately announce commendations and issue awards after the battle, wherever time permitted.

Third, workshop participants emphasized that the format of our political efforts should meet the new demands of the war as it progressed. The impression was widespread that the political efforts during the First Campaign were not active enough. The precampaign mobilization was insufficient and the battlefield motivation not timely. During the battle of Unsan, when our troops returned after having successfully pursued the enemy forces, some of our soldiers actually thought they had lost the battle.[15] Our troops complained that it was a "confusing campaign" with "puzzling battles." There were some objective reasons for this, such as hasty engagement, severe enemy air raids, our troops' dispersion, and continuous fighting. The major subjective reason was that the format of our political efforts had not been adjusted and had not caught up with the new combat environment. Most political instructors at the company level were oriented to prepare troops politically for positional offensives—storming the enemy's heavily fortified positions. They followed prescribed ways of doing their jobs and could not cope with the mobile campaign, which was executed in haste. Neither could political officers in higher level headquarters. In most cases at the division level, only directors of the political sections went with the divisions' commanding headquarters. A few political officers followed the troops' movements, and most of the political cadres were left behind, not doing that much on the battleground during this campaign.

At the workshop we found that under the new circumstances of severe enemy air raids and our mobile operations, our political tasks should assume a new format that would stress decentralized, small activities and make good use of time. The political cadres should operate anywhere and at any time, focusing on the activities at group and squadron levels. They should also be dispersed to lower levels. One of the political instructors from the First Artillery Division had learned a method for political instruction from the Red Army—talking with soldiers during troop marches. To have conversations with his soldiers on the march, the instructor would start at the head of the column, then gradually move to the rear. Thus he learned about the condition of his troops and assigned tasks to the squads as he passed through them. When he reached the end of the column, he had fulfilled his mission. His methods were acknowledged approvingly at our meeting. The experience of the Forty-second Army was also introduced to the participants at this meeting. It sent its political cadres to each regiment before battle to collect information and assist in regimental operations. The cadres traveled to the army's forward positions all the time, assigning tasks, dispensing propaganda, and galvanizing the soldiers.

Fourth, according to the discussions at the workshop, destroying the cohesion of the enemy forces was very important. Fighting in Korea, our troops gradually recognized that it was possible to rout the enemy troops but difficult to capture them. A main problem was that our policy toward prisoners of war (POWs) had not been made known to the enemy, and the language barrier made it more difficult [to persuade the enemy troops to surrender].

Not incorrigibly obstinate, the enemy troops might have laid down their arms if they had known we did not kill POWs. After the Thirty-eighth Army penetrated their positions, the panic-stricken enemy troops showed a willingness to surrender, but they were afraid of being killed. One of our soldiers gestured to the enemy troops, "Lay down your arms, we will spare your lives," and they did surrender their weapons immediately. In one of the battles, the Thirty-ninth Army caught an American soldier who could speak Chinese. He asked, "Are you Koreans?" "No, we are Chinese," our soldiers answered. He said he had been in China before. Our soldiers told him that they would spare his life if he laid down his arms. He surrendered his weapon right away and called up dozens of American soldiers to surrender as well.

The Fortieth Army attacked the Sixth Division of the puppet forces at Kutoudong, and the enemy soldiers scattered. The next morning, our troops combed the area and surrounded the enemy remnants in a valley, but they did not dare to come out or lay down their arms. Later, one of their battalion commanders was captured. Having explained to him our policy of lenient treatment toward prisoners of war, our troops asked him to gather his men. He called more than eighty soldiers out of the valley to surrender.

However, our psychological warfare did not work well, being largely handicapped by language barriers. Before we entered Korea, none of our troops had had a chance to learn some simple Korean or English. We did not print any propaganda materials in foreign languages. Thus, at our workshop we concluded that psychological warfare had already become part of our agenda of political work and needed to be strengthened.

As we found out at this meeting, our policy toward the prisoners was carried out during the First Campaign. Our army had a great tradition of treating POWs leniently in the past. Before entering Korea, we had conducted a widespread educational program about our policy toward them. Generally speaking, our soldiers would not search POWs' pockets, nor would they take POWs' personal belongings. The 115th Division held a POW who had eight gold rings on his fingers, and he did not lose any of them. He admired our policy and discipline. Among the American prisoners captured by the Fortieth Army was an officer who had graduated from the U.S. Military Academy. Although he had a reactionary attitude, he did appreciate the fact that we did not search our prisoners' pockets. "There is no other army in this world that does not take away prisoners' property," he said. "You are fighting bravely, and not searching your prisoners' pockets. You would have no match in the world if you had airplanes and large artillery." A few commanders were interested in the prisoners' pens and watches; they wanted to have that "foreign-made stuff." As soon as the thefts were discovered, the men were criticized and ordered to return the prisoners' belongings.

Finally, our workshop emphasized that our troops should genuinely respect and learn from the Korean Workers' Party, government, people, and the NKPA. Commander Peng called upon the rank and file of the CPVF troops not to behave like a big-country donor. He in particular talked about this at the CPVF's Party Committee meeting. "As for the Korean comrades, we must look at their strengths and learn their good points. If we want to find out some weak points, we have some ourselves at home, so why do we bother coming abroad to look for them?"

The First Release of Prisoners

The comrades in the CPVF Political Department had prepared extensively for how political work would ensure success in the coming campaign.[16] On November 8, 1950, the department issued the pamphlet "Propaganda and Education Guideline to Achieving Counterattack Victory in Northern Korea" to the CPVF troops. While underscoring our victory in the First Campaign and its significance, it explained that the Korean War was so arduous that we should not underestimate the enemy. We could not give way to impatience, expecting victory by a fluke or lowering our guard. The guideline prepared our troops psychologically for the Second Campaign.

Then, on November 24, on the eve of the Second Campaign, we issued "Order of Political Mobilization [for the Second Campaign]" by telegram to all the troops. It pointed out that the enemy was closing in on us on both eastern and western fronts. We already had a well-conceived plan to lure them deep into a trap. We hoped that all our comrades would be brave and smart in this campaign so as not to miss any opportunity to annihilate the enemy. The troops should implement their plan of eliminating enemy soldiers and compete for battle honor. Our order enhanced the troops' morale. And among all the preparations, release of the POWs was most influential and had a direct effect on the war.

As early as the Jinggangshan period, Chairman Mao Zedong had made our army's policy toward prisoners of war one of lenient treatment.[17] For many years, this policy had always been one of the most important elements in our army's political work. During the prolonged civil wars and the Anti-Japanese War, our POW policy was well known and appreciated by enemy forces. During our First Campaign in the Korean War, it was said that enemy troops were easily beaten but rarely captured. That meant the American and puppet soldiers apparently did not yet know our policy.

We had to expose the enemy's false propaganda by which they slandered us, stating that the Chinese troops killed all prisoners, even gouged out their eyes and cut off their noses. We also had to advertise our policy among the enemy troops to break them down psychologically. Learning from the experience of the First Campaign, we needed to employ more practical and effective propaganda measures to spread word of our policy.

On November 17 I reported to Commander Peng the result of our workshop on political tasks and especially the problems with the POW policy and psychological warfare. After my report, Peng asked, "Is it workable to select some prisoners for release?"

"I am afraid there will not be much impact if we release only a few," I replied, and then asked him, "Can we release a large number of them?"

"Excellent!" Peng said. "We can release a large number of them, if possible."

During the civil wars in the past, we had routinely released prisoners; there was no need to report to higher command for permission. Now we were in a war in a foreign country, and the situation was different; there was no precedent to be followed in our military history. In Korea, we were fighting not only a military but also a political battle. Releasing prisoners might affect international opinion in different ways. What were we going to do about prisoner exchange later? Considering the current situation in terms of military operations, however, we had to release some of the POWs as soon as possible in order to make enemy troops understand our lenient policy.

I thought about this over and over but still could not figure out a satisfactory solution. So I suggested to Commander Peng: "Since this matter is imminently important, we may need to make a special report."

Mulling it over for a while, Peng agreed. "You think about it in more detail Then draft a telegram to report to the Central Military Commission. You take good care of this matter."

I drafted a telegram the same day. Approved by Peng, it was sent to the CMC:

Military Commission:
We are proposing to release 100 American and puppet Rhee's prisoners before the next campaign (including 30 Americans and 70 puppet prisoners). Our main objective is to publicize our lenient treatment policy toward POWs in order to overcome the enemy troops' fear of being murdered once captured. We plan to send those prisoners back through the frontline positions during the night of the 19th. Please instruct us immediately whether it is all right.
Peng Dehuai, Deng Hua, and Du Ping
November 17, 1950—0900 Hours

The next morning, we received Chairman Mao's reply: "You are right in releasing a group of POWs. [They] should be released immediately. Henceforth release [the POWs] in groups, and no need for our instructions."

After reading the telegram, Peng told me, "Do not wait until tomorrow. Do it tonight. The sooner, the better."

"Tonight?"

"Yes! Now we are racing against time," Peng said firmly. "Have you ever thought about this? When you entered Korea on the 23rd of the last month, the Military Commission and Chairman Mao telegraphed us that all the long-distance scouting teams dispatched by different units of our armies must be disguised as members of the Korean People's Army, so as not to be referred to as the Chinese People's Volunteers. Why did we do this? To confuse the enemy!"

I understood Peng's intentions. The release of the POWs was to be used to confuse the enemy. Peng explained this trick with a sense of humor. "We can tell the prisoners that we are short of food supplies, that we are starving, and probably are going to withdraw back to China. Didn't the American officers say that the Chinese Volunteers entering Korea were merely tearing down and removing equipment from Korea's Yalu Power Plant to 'reap a big profit'? Didn't they say that their air force was so strong that our rear communication and transportation totally collapsed? We want to play right into the Americans' hands and beat them at their own game." I looked at Peng with a smile of understanding.

At that moment, the U.S. Air Force, carrying out MacArthur's orders, was conducting "the two-week, largest scale bombing of the war." Countless American planes spread out over North Korea every day for reconnaissance and raids, with roads and highways as their major targets. To avoid unnecessary casualties from the air raids, we had prohibited personnel and traffic on the roads during the daytime.

When Commander Peng said "we release the prisoners tonight," it meant that our comrades who carried out this order had to rush to the front during the daytime. To ensure success, I selected Si Dongchu, sectional chief of the Organization Division, and Wang Dahai, a driver at the CPVF Political Department, to carry out this mission.

Si Dongchu originally was a commander of the Ninth Group, Third Brigade of the Northeast Military–Political University. In July 1947 he was transferred to the Political Department of our Northeastern Democratic Allied Forces. (Later the Northeastern Allied Forces became the Northeastern Field Army, then the Fourth Field Army.) During the Liao-Shen and the Ping-Jin campaigns, Si had worked with me at the Front Headquarters.[18] I had assigned him to escort some important GMD prisoners of war, such as Fan Hanjie, deputy commander in chief of the GMD Army's Northeastern General Headquarters for Extermination of the Communists, and Chen Changjie, commander of the Tianjin Defense Forces. Si did an excellent job. Our first release of Korean War POWs was of such grave significance that I thought of him again. It was proper to assign him to this urgent and important mission since he had a strong sense of responsibility and also understood English.

Wang Dahai was the best driver in our Political Department. He and Li Dianrui had been my drivers since the War of Liberation. Li drove a compact jeep, and Wang drove a midsize one. Wang was not only a skillful and brave driver but also a careful and thoughtful person. He had accomplished many critical assignments, and I trusted him for this one.

I sent for a guard so that I could assign Si and Wang this mission face to face. Meeting with them, I stressed the urgency of the task and the potential danger of daytime driving:

> Comrade Si Dongchu, you must pay attention not only to your own safety but also to the prisoners' safety. Please note that you should pick out some prisoners who had been lightly wounded but now are almost recovered after our medical treatment. It may be better to hold a send-off ceremony for the released prisoners. Then you may take these prisoners to the Unsan front in trucks in good condition. I will contact our unit over there by phone shortly, asking them to choose the spot for the release. You must take care of this mission to its completion. Only return after you see the prisoners being released. I believe that you will accomplish this mission successfully.

On the afternoon of November 18, dark clouds covered the sky. The cold wind of the early winter spattered drizzle, and blowing trees shook and rustled. At this moment, the battlefields were deadly quiet. There was only the sound of Wang Dahai's jeep running on the road toward the Unsan region. Si Dongchu told me about their trip later. "Dahai did a great job," he said. "We were racing all the way at full speed. We were occasionally delayed by enemy airplanes. Wang contended with them quickly and smartly. When Wang saw the airplanes beginning to dive, he made a sudden stop, or a fast turn, leaving the airplanes behind. The enemy planes attacked us a couple of times. Their machine guns continuously and fiercely strafed us. Their bullets whizzed past us and hit the ground around us. Their bombs landed nearby. But they could not get at us."

Arriving at the post where the prisoners were detained, Si selected 103, including 27 Americans (1 from the First Cavalry Division's Fifth Regiment, 21 from its Eighth Regiment, 4 from the Twenty-fourth [Infantry] Division, and 1 from a chemical [4.2 inch] mortar company) and 76 South Koreans (54 from the Sixth Division and 22 from the Eighth Division).

After the prisoners had attended a brief educational session, the CPVF soldiers at the POW retaining post gave them haircuts, showers, new clothes, and some travel money. At the dinner, they were served extra dishes. There was also a send-off party attended by all prisoners, including those who would not be released.

That evening trucks loaded with the prisoners reached our forward position south of Unsan after having avoided American air raids. With the help of our interpreters, Si told the prisoners, "In case you cannot pass through the American troops' defensive line, you can come back. You will be welcomed again by the Volunteers." Many of the prisoners held up their thumbs and yelled, "OK!" Some of them were moved to tears by our actions and thanked the CPVF for saving their lives. They swore, "We will never forget the Volunteers' tremendous consideration. We will never fight against the Volunteers!" They came to our soldiers and shook their hands and gave them hugs, saying "Thanks!" and "Good-bye!"

Later that night, Comrades Si Dongchu and Wang Dahai rushed back to General Headquarters to report to me. In recognizing the merit of Wang's accomplishment, the CPVF Political Department awarded him a Citation for Merit, First Class.

The release of the POWs had an immediate and strong impact on international opinion. Reporters White and [?]Bowles from the Associated Press reported on November 23 that the released American prisoners said that the Chinese Volunteers "treated them very well." They had the same foods as the Volunteers, who also shared their limited medical equipment in treating the wounded prisoners. "The Chinese did not search American soldiers' pockets, and allowed them to keep their own cigarettes, gold watches, and other private valuables."

Such reports about the released Americans made public our army's lenient treatment of POWs. Those news stories caused great panic among the American military authorities. They hurriedly blocked the information and started to monitor closely the released POWs. The Associated Press reported, "The representatives of the press are neither allowed to visit the released prisoners, nor take their pictures. All officers were under orders not to leak the information about the release but are referring to it as 'top secret.' " The AFP [Agence France-Presse] also reported that the release of the prisoners "made many officers under MacArthur extremely nervous. The American Army, in fact, withheld the information for 38 hours. And the U.S. Information Agency even asked to prevent the publication of the most important detailed information [about the releases]. The leaders of the American wire services tried hard to downplay this as a small matter. . . . Meanwhile, wherever those 27 American prisoners went, there were always an American general and three colonels with them, as if they took good care of those ex-prisoners." Apparently, the former-prisoners' freedom had been taken away just because they had told the truth after their return.

Trying to block the news, the American military soon sent the released prisoners back to the States. The story of our army's POW policy nevertheless spread widely and quickly among the American troops. The result came much faster than we had anticipated.

During the Second Campaign, we actively conducted psychological warfare together with our military pressure. We began to have frontline talks with enemy troops. This led to two occasions, each of which involved more than 100 American soldiers surrendering their arms in a large group. One of these surrenders occurred during a battle at Konchakae where our Ninth Army Group attacked the enemy positions. The Ninth took advantage of the opportunity when the enemy troops suffered heavy casualties, their leading commanders were wounded, and they had no hope of breaking out of our encirclement. The enemy troops were in terrible panic, and the political officers used American prisoners to call for a group surrender. The Ninth Army Group thereby created a model for our armies to break down the enemy's morale on the front lines.[19] It was on the evening of November 30; a cold wind was blowing hard. About 400 American and puppet officers and soldiers with seventy-five trucks and tanks were surrounded by our Ninth Army Group. There was no way for the enemy troops to escape south, and there were no reinforcements for them. Under our psychological pressure, they sent over four officers to negotiate with us for their surrender. Among the four was a puppet officer, who served as the interpreter for the negotiations. The talks were conducted with the help of handwriting and hand gestures. They asked for four conditions: a guarantee for their safety, and no executions; a promise to release them in the future; food and permission to rest; and permission to write to their families soon.

Through the patient explanation of our policy and an agreement to send them home after the war, our commanders cleared up their suspicions and fears, and they surrendered their arms. Among the surrendering troops was a lieutenant colonel of the U.S. First Marine Division, 2 of its majors, and 179 American, British, and Turkish officers and soldiers.[20] Moreover, there were 53 of Rhee's puppet troops, 3 Japanese, 2 of Jiang's Chinese Nationalist agents, and a number of trucks and tanks. Among the others was a group of American soldiers coming to surrender.

They marched over to our line in good order as in a drill, with their hands up and empty pistol holsters on their waists. Our soldiers said with a smile, "The American soldiers have also been well trained for surrendering."

The second case involved the surrender of an engineering company, composed of 120 black American soldiers.[21] These two examples eminently demonstrated that although the American imperialist invading troops were well equipped and seemingly strong, they had "too much iron but not enough spirit." They could be broken down, despite the language difficulties.

Our first release of the POWs was welcomed by Chairman Mao. He pointed out in his telegram of November 24: "Your release of the American war prisoners has received a great response from the international community. Please prepare another release of a large group, for instance, about 300 to 400 men, after this campaign."

Following Mao's instruction, we strengthened our psychological warfare campaign with a new office for it established in the CPVF Political Department. (Originally it was the Section for Psychological Warfare under the Propaganda Division; then it was extended to the Division of Psychological Warfare.) The new office issued orders for the strict enforcement of lenient treatment of POWs and selected the units and individuals who had a good performance record in carrying out our policy.

The new office also dealt with those Volunteers who violated our policy, patiently educating them and persuading them to improve. Some of the violators, especially the severe cases, were punished according to the seriousness of their offenses. Through our propaganda and education, which sought to distinguish right from wrong, advantage and disadvantage, and reward and punishment, the CPVF rank and file saw to it that there were no beatings, insults, murders, abuses, or unlawful searches. Our troops abided by their promises in their own words: "No envious eyes, nor itching hands, respect the rights of prisoners."

Our efforts increased our influence among the American soldiers. The U.S. Army's Propaganda Division had to recognize that our propaganda "had sapped the [American] soldiers' fighting will." "The Communists knew how to do brainwashing." American soldiers' attitudes shifted from a fear of capture at the beginning to a belief later that "it is safer being a prisoner than a fighter." In the prison camps, many captured American soldiers and officers said,

> We hurt the Volunteers in the battlefields because we did not understand your humane lenient policy toward all the war prisoners. After being captured, we know that you are really peace-loving people. Particularly, you are the best regarding morality in war. As your prisoners, we were not killed; instead, we are treated as good friends of yours, sleeping on the hot "*kang*,"[22] smoking cigarettes, getting candies, reading newspapers, and receiving medical treatment. . . . Especially, sometimes, under difficult conditions, when you only had one meal a day yourselves with corn or potatoes, you still saved the rice

for us. Your spirit of humanity is the best and the most humane in the world. We forget we are prisoners.

After the first release of prisoners during the Second Campaign, our Political Department carried out Mao's and Peng's instructions and released prisoners several more times during later campaigns; these had great effects.

I remember that we released the second group of prisoners at the Han River's front line, a total of 132 men, including 41 Americans, 5 British, 3 Australians, and 83 puppet soldiers. Before the release, the office of the CPVF's prisoners administration held a special dinner and a send-off party for them. The prisoners said there was a sharp contrast between the Volunteers' lenient treatment and the American and ROK's crimes. The Volunteers did not kill or abuse prisoners, or search their pockets. Instead, they treated prisoners humanely every day and gave them medical care. The American troops and Rhee's puppet forces slaughtered the prisoners and committed war crimes. The [soon-to-be-released] prisoners said they would never again be cannon fodder for Wall Street's big shots and for Syngman Rhee after their return. Those stories reveal that the policy of lenient treatment of POWs and the disintegration of enemy morale worked effectively not only in the domestic wars but also in foreign battles against imperialist forces.

A Problem at the CPVF General Headquarters

The Second Campaign was just about to begin.[23] Commander Peng's office and all the CPVF General Headquarters' departments appeared extremely tense and busy. The comrades at the headquarters seemed hurried in everything they did, talking, walking, and even dining.

According to Comrade Zhang Yangwu, the establishment of Peng's office was announced to him by Commander Peng himself. Peng appointed Comrade Xie Fang as the secretary general of the office, Zhang as the deputy secretary general and office director, and Comrade Yang Fengan as the deputy director. Cheng Pu was a staff member; Mao Anying, the secretary;[24] Jin Changxun, the Korean interpreter; and Guo Fengguang, the bodyguard.

When the General Headquarters moved to Taeyudong, all the comrades lived in mountain caves, sleeping on the ground and eating parched flour and hardtack. They drafted orders and telegrams by candlelight. The housing conditions were bad, and it was difficult to get food supplies. Peng lived under the same conditions as the others. Even under such tough circumstances, he worked day and night and stayed up all night quite often. Sometimes he just closed his eyes and took a nap instead of sleeping at night. Although the comrades worried about his health, they admired his spirit.

Generally speaking, in the PLA's history, safety was never a problem for the General Headquarters, nor was it a problem for the headquarters at the army and division levels during the domestic wars. But during the War to Resist America and Aid Korea, especially during its early stages, all the Volunteers faced the same situation of life and death. This was true not only for those working at the army and division headquarters but also for those working at the General Headquarters and even those working for Peng. Since our army had no air superiority, we could not separate the front lines from the rear or safety from danger.

During the early period of the Korean War, the CPVF Headquarters had prohibited all troops from firing at American airplanes with light weapons, lest they reveal to the enemy that our main strength had entered Korea. As a result, American planes flew with unusual freedom and abandon. They shaved the treetops and the roofs of houses, even penetrating deep into the narrow valleys to seek targets. Whenever the American planes saw anything at all—a person, a wagon, a haystack, a cow, a dog, or even a chicken—they fired on it or bombed it. They even fired at a wisp of smoke.

In the first month after the CPVF Headquarters had moved to Taeyudong, American planes raided it numerous times in a short period. The same morning that the second group of our headquarters officers arrived, American planes bombed both the headquarters and nearby areas. Several trucks parked at the foot of the hill were destroyed. Given these experiences, we knew that some antiaircraft measures, including a lookout to detect enemy planes, would be necessary. Later there were several air raids on the headquarters, but there were no personnel casualties or serious property damage.

Despite facing wanton and indiscriminate bombing by American planes, most of the comrades in the General Headquarters kept their spirits up. They did not fear bombing, death, hardships, or fatigue. They stood fast at their posts and performed their individual duties. This was especially true of those female comrades, including secretaries, telephone operators, doctors, nurses, and interpreters, who had just been transferred from civil service to military duty. They did their jobs very well and faced danger fearlessly. Because all the comrades worked together with one mind, sticking to their posts like screws, the main engine, or General Headquarters, functioned normally in its role as the nerve center.

The Political Directive

Before the CPVF entered Korea, our troops had been taught that they were to take good care of its land, mountains, rivers, and people.[25] Our troops, for the most part, kept up our army's glorious tradition during the war, showing a high level of political consciousness and internationalist spirit. Food supply was extremely difficult. Our troops endured the torments of hunger while battling the enemy. However, they encouraged each other and took pride in not taking the Korean people's food and in not violating rules regarding respect for the land and its people.

During the war, the Korean Workers' Party, government, and people supported and cared for the Chinese Volunteers as if they were members of their own families. Their support further enhanced our army's conscious care for the land and the people, and we formed a special discipline and rules regarding relations with the Koreans. During the first two months after the CPVF had entered Korea, there were many cases where our volunteers committed exemplary deeds to succor the people, which were widely acclaimed and helped ensure our army's two victories during the first two campaigns.

Some of our comrades, however, did not realize the importance of discipline in our relationship to the people. They thought only about fighting and believed that violation of discipline did not matter as long as they fought well. Moreover, some of our commanders either tolerated or ignored such violations, especially under the conditions of supply shortages and overcrowding, which gradually led to more violations.

A few deserters, in particular, considered themselves so above the law that no one would dare check on them, and they left their units and acted wildly in defiance of regulations. Some of them rummaged through chests and cupboards, ate food without paying for it, and beat or abused the Koreans. A few lawless soldiers even insulted [raped] Korean women. If we had not determinedly corrected the situation and had allowed it to continue, our reputation as a highly disciplined army would have been jeopardized, along with damaging the friendship between our two countries. Allowing such behavior would have dishonored the sacrifice of blood and lives of our men and placed our army in a disadvantageous situation.

Thus, the CPVF General Headquarters adopted two measures. Initially, it issued a Political Directive in the names of Peng Dehuai, Deng Hua, and Du Ping that reemphasized the importance of observing the rules of discipline regarding relations with the masses. Issued on December 14, 1950, the Political Directive set up six definite requirements for the CPVF troops.

First, we required that all the units must continue and strengthen education on observing discipline regarding relations with the masses, stressing the love and the care of the Korean people's land, mountains, rivers, and trees, which had to be actively and genuinely practiced.

Second, each unit must make observation of discipline a practice with popular participation and clearly defined regulations so that people would encourage and check on one another, and follow such discipline conscientiously.

Third, we required our troops to teach the Korean people how to safeguard against air raids in combat zones. They must help the people store up grain and cover their property to prevent it from being bombed and destroyed. If some of our troops needed to borrow food, they must not take everything; they had to leave the people enough. If our troops had to borrow certain things from abandoned homes, such as firewood and hay, they must leave some paperwork and not take advantage of such an occasion to abuse those households.

Fourth, if any violation of discipline was detected, the unit(s) must investigate immediately, dealing with infractions in a timely way and publicizing it among all the troops. For those who refused to mend their ways despite repeated admonitions, we had to mete out punishment when necessary.

Fifth, all the civil affairs offices must closely observe and supervise discipline. All the companies must resume the tasks of their civil affairs teams. Under the supervision of the company's political instructor, each team must take the responsibilities of enforcing their company's discipline, conduct public relations affairs with the Korean residents around their station area, and check on discipline regarding relations with the masses.

Sixth, after receiving this directive, all party committees and political offices of the army, divisions, and regiments must make their decisions on how to observe discipline and how to conduct a large-scale inspection regarding relations with the masses. All the officers should help their soldiers solve particular problems and overcome their difficulties as much as possible. They must help their troops to avoid committing the slightest offense against the civilians and establish a close relationship with the Korean people.

After the Political Directive was issued, all the CPVF units made regulations in accordance with their own conditions. The CPVF troops on the western front considered implementing the Political Directive as part of their operating methods. They took three days out just for the inspections. They organized their security detachments and assigned them widely to the major towns and important lines of communication. Working with the Korean people closely, these detachments maintained our army's reputation and kept social order in rear areas.

The second measure that Headquarters adopted was to establish the CPVF Military Law Enforcement Office, which was to punish by military criminal code those who had seriously violated military law. I held a concurrent post as the chief of this office.

Given that those who seriously broke our military law were usually the deserters, I drafted the first declaration of the Military Law Enforcement Office, and it was posted at the intersections of major traffic lines. I also assigned Comrade Ren Rong, chief of the Organizational Division in the CPVF Political Department, to be in charge of dealing with violations of discipline. Leading a task team, he traveled all over the rear areas to check on infractions, a tough job. However, Ren, as usual, never compromised or even mentioned the difficulties. He displayed a good grasp of our policies, educating the majority, punishing a few, and ordering capital punishment only for a very few bad men who had sneaked into our army and were steeped in evil. These actions were favorably received by the local people and helped maintain the CPVF's reputation, friendship, and unity with the Korean people.

While strengthening discipline, we also paid special attention to the political education of our troops. The Volunteers' morale was high at that time. Their psychological condition was generally stable because of successful campaigns.

There were, however, some unhealthy attitudes that deserved our special attention. We called it war-weariness fatigue at the time, caused by continual fighting, a shortage of supplies, and the heavy casualties some units had suffered. For example, many soldiers had washed their faces only two or three times during more than two months after they had entered Korea; this in particular indicated such fatigue. Even when it was possible, many soldiers still did not want to wash their feet, or take off their shoes when they slept, or make toilet pits, or boil water before they drank it. Although those who suffered this kind of emotional fatigue were in the minority, it could damage our troops more than physical fatigue.

To solve this problem, on December 23 the CPVF Party Committee sent out a Letter to All Party Members from the Volunteers' Party Committee, calling for all CCP members to take the lead in preventing and overcoming war weariness. The letter pointed out that during all the battles of the great War to Resist America and Aid Korea, our troops had defeated the well-equipped invading American army without the assistance of a single airplane or large artillery guns—all because we had countless staunch Communist Party members in our troops. They influenced and united all the [nonparty member] soldiers. But it was by no means an easy task to defeat the American imperialists completely. The question lay in whether or not we could bear hardships; if we could bear and even overcome these, it was possible for us to accomplish this task. Commander Peng said that in order to overcome difficulties, we should have some small-scale recreational activities in various forms, suitable for the current situation. These could put everybody in a positive frame of mind and body. We should realize that the more difficult the situation was, the more friendship, caring, and kindness the troops needed; the tougher the task was, the more united we had to become.

After receiving the letter, all the party branches organized discussions at both group and individual levels and developed small recreational activities. As a result, a gratifying situation emerged—the more difficult the situation was, the more optimistic our troops became.

POLITICAL EDUCATION AND PROPAGANDA

The Volunteers Newspaper

We had achieved three victories in three offensive campaigns.[26] The Third Campaign quickly broke through the Thirty-eighth Parallel defenses and liberated Seoul, bringing tremendous enjoyment to all the CPVF rank and file. As happy as the others, I composed a poem with pleasure, "Three Campaigns, Three Victories":

> Three blows to the invading foe,
> Three victories for high morale;
> Nothing stops the just allies,
> Of the victorious Sino-Korean force.

The victories brought both happiness and new psychological problems—the tendency to underestimate the enemy, a growing belief in a quick victory, and disagreements over certain strategic policies. The old question about why there was no forward push in the wake of victory after the First and Second Campaigns now became more prominent in the New Year offense. Some of the comrades said that whenever the enemy withdrew quickly, we should advance even faster. We had never had this sort of battle without following up a victory with hot pursuit, they complained. Some said that the Americans already intended to withdraw from Korea and that we should exploit our victory by throwing them into the Pacific Ocean.

Commander Peng paid special attention to these disagreements on strategy, immediately reporting them to Chairman Mao. Meanwhile, Peng asked us to reflect carefully on our experience, which proved that "no pursuit of the enemy was to be one of our victorious strategies" during the Third Campaign. In Peng's calculation, the CPVF faced more difficulties than ever in the New Year campaign, when we were charging the enemy's defensive lines. After our offensive unfolded, the enemy retreated step by step while maintaining contact. Originally, we had not expected that our army could so quickly break through the Thirty-eighth Parallel, occupy Seoul, and cross the Han River. Peng, however, ordered the troops to cease continuous and deep pursuit. I remember that he gave us three reasons.

First, the enemy rapidly escaped (their motorized troops were not interested in engagement with the enemies). It was hard for us to eliminate them while we pursued their trucks on foot. After we had broken their in-depth defensive line along the Thirty-eighth Parallel in the New Year campaign, the Fiftieth Army, one division of the Forty-second Army, and North Korea's Second and Fifth Corps had once chased the enemy for fifty to seventy kilometers. Our armies, however, failed to catch up with and annihilate them.

Second, our army had yet to be resupplied after those three campaigns. Our material support was short at the time since our transportation lines were overextended and wrecked by enemy airplanes. Our search for food was difficult since all the Korean people in the newly occupied areas had evacuated. These factors made it impossible for us to pursue and eliminate more enemy troops. Moreover, our strategic reserve forces could not participate in the campaign immediately after they entered Korea.

Third, Korea has unique geographic circumstances. It is a long and narrow peninsula with mountains of great length and breadth and with seaports along a long coastal line. Enemy troops could land at any port on both eastern and western coasts. If our army had driven straight and deep, the enemy could have repeated its Inchon landing by exploiting our vulnerability in the rear areas. We could have fallen into the enemy's trap just as the NKPA had done.

Commander Peng did not believe at the moment that America intended to withdraw from Korea. In his opinion, if it gave up Korea now, it would face a big disadvantage in the imperialist camp. Britain and France had not asked American imperialists to withdraw. After having suffered one or two more setbacks and losing two or three more divisions, the enemy might retreat into some enclaves but would not entirely withdraw from Korea anytime soon.

The leading commanders of the CPVF General Headquarters—all of us—shared Peng's opinion with no dissent. Thus, in the publicity for the Third Campaign, we not only underscored victory but also talked about the protracted and arduous nature of the war to prevent or overcome wishful thinking about a quick victory.

The CPVF Political Department issued the Propaganda and Education Guidelines for the Third Campaign's Victory in early January 1951. Primarily, it pointed out that this campaign had great significance. We had wiped out the enemy's effective strength, destroyed its strategy to gain a respite, and had further foiled its aggressive arrogance. But we emphasized at the same time that the invading American army would not willingly quit Korea. It still had considerable strength and would put up a last-ditch struggle. We must guard against relying only on good fortune, underestimating the enemy, and giving way to impatience. We had to strengthen our determination to fight until we destroyed the invading American forces.

At that time, our new propaganda medium—*Zhiyuanjun Bao* [Volunteers Newspaper]—was born. I was happy to see that we had a new weapon for our political work in the Korean War. Issued by the CPVF's General Headquarters and the Political Department, our newspaper started publication on January 15, 1951, when we publicized our victory of the Third Campaign and removed any belief in a quick victory.

In the first issue of *Zhiyuanjun Bao,* I published an article, "Three Campaigns, Three Victories," explaining the strategy. To further inspire our army's morale, the article began with a comprehensive description of our experience, military achievements, and the great significance of the three victorious campaigns. Then I stressed that despite our success, we should not underestimate the enemy. We must know that the American imperialists were the most ferocious of the reactionary camp and equipped with modern weapons. In fact, the invading troops fighting today were armed to the teeth. Each of them had a helmet, was supported by air cover, and moved by trucks and tanks. They also had deployed a great deal of naval and airpower in the war. By the heavy blows of our three campaigns, the enemy's effective strength had been seriously weakened. Nevertheless, it had not yet been dealt a deadly blow. We must by no means underestimate it.

Zhiyuanjun Bao, just like the CPVF's fighting in Korea, made its progress gradually, by overcoming countless difficulties. After the first campaigns, the CPVF troops had widespread complaints about the lack of Chinese newspapers, radios, and information about national or international events. They did not even know how the other CPVF troops had fought, calling the conflict "the silent war." The morale of the troops was neither high nor spirited. Some of the comrades suggested that the New China News Agency should send special dispatches to the CPVF in Korea; others suggested that the CPVF have its own newspapers.

After discussing these suggestions, the comrades in the Political Department agreed to run a newspaper. Comrade Li Weiyi, deputy chief of the Propaganda Division, was its strongest advocate. He immediately began to work with his divisional comrades on preparations and put forth a detailed proposal.

The name of the newspaper was to be *Zhiyuanjun Bao*. They would ask Commander Peng to inscribe its title. Its tasks were to carry out the leadership's policy objectives of the CPVF Party Committee, Commanding Headquarters, and Political Department. It would summarize combat experiences and achievements, announce them among all the armies, publicize heroes as models, inspire enthusiasm for battles, and expose shortcomings that needed to be corrected. The newspaper would also report the suggestions and needs of the rank and file.

Its principles were to strengthen both patriotism and internationalism in order to heighten our troop's awareness and affirm their determination for battle. It would disseminate ideas of hatred, spite, and condescension toward the American imperialists so as to strengthen our soldiers' confidence in winning the war. Our newspaper was to explore the nature of war and publicize successful strategies and tactics so that our troops would be inspired to fight for victory. It would spread stories of revolutionary heroism to heighten morale. To improve our jobs, the newspaper would introduce working experience, fighting skills, and various technologies from military, political, and logistics units. It would educate the troops on our policies and discipline so that they would become more conscientious in observing rules. The newspaper would also entertain troops on the front lines and enliven their daily activities.

As proposed, the staff of the newspaper would include a full-time managing editor and twelve part-time editors and reporters. For the time being, we did not appoint the formal editor in chief and assistant editor in chief; the chiefs of the Propaganda Division were concurrently in charge of those duties.

The Propaganda Division's distribution section would be responsible for the newspaper's circulation, and the CPVF General Headquarters and the Political Department would be responsible for its publication. We also sent our proposal to the General Headquarters of the Korean People's Army for approval.

Endorsing the proposal, the CPVF Party Committee made its official decision to publish *Zhiyuanjun Bao* on January 14, 1951. Commander Peng was happy to inscribe the title. In its decision, the committee clearly outlined the newspaper's principles and major tasks, its goal to be extensive news reporting and correspondence. The committee also requested military commanders and political officers from all ranks to write articles or news for *Zhiyuanjun Bao,* all of which had to be examined and checked. As one of the routine tasks of political education units, political offices and cadres at all levels were requested to organize newspaper readings for the troops.

The first issue of *Zhiyuanjun Bao* had four pages in tabloid size. However, our plan for two issues per week was not easily put into practice. Without a professional editorial department, we could not receive news and reports from the troops on a regular basis, nor could we guarantee the printing of the newspaper. The CPVF Political Department had a small printing shop consisting of only a dozen people when we left for Korea, which moved, along with the General Headquarters, with heavy printing machines and type. Because of frequent moves between different locations, it was difficult for the printing shop to set up its machines and work on schedule. When the first issue of *Zhiyuanjun Bao* was published, we had to send a special mission by car, driving all the way back to China to have the newspaper printed in Andong. After the newspapers were shipped back to us in Korea, our Propaganda Division then distributed the papers to the armies. After that, they were sent to companies throughout the military mailing offices by liaison personnel. Most of the troops complained that they could not read *Zhiyuanjun Bao* on time because they were in high-risk combat situations and because their communications were hampered, due to the damaged roads and bridges bombed by American airplanes.

As the war stabilized, a formal editorial department was established. With support from the CPVF officers and soldiers, we would receive over 1,000 news reports, articles, and letters every month. Meanwhile, we built a special printing shop for the newspaper, which became ever more closely related to the troops and the CPVF's current tasks. The troops called the newspaper "a good battle companion of ours" and an indispensable "food for the mind." Celebrating the first anniversary of the War to Resist America and Aid Korea, both Commander Peng and Prime Minister Kim Il Sung wrote a few words of encouragement for *Zhiyuanjun Bao,* further increasing its prestige. Peng wrote, "Our army will grow stronger with the fighting, the enemy is getting weaker in the war. We will win, the enemy will lose." Kim wrote in exquisite Chinese, "Consolidate a united strength of Korean and Chinese peoples, and fight for a final victory in the War to Resist America."

Zhiyuanjun Bao published its 100th issue on August 20, 1952. By that time it had made some progress as a politically mature and journalistically vigorous newspaper, with growing mass appeal and entertainment value. It had been enlarged from $8\frac{1}{2} \times 11$ inches to 11×15 inches in size. In contrast to its first issue, the newspaper now looked more professional. Nevertheless, it still had a long way to go compared to the PLA regional newspapers at home and the demands of the Volunteers.

For further improvement, the newspaper solicited opinions from more than 30,000 of its readers and carefully analyzed the responses. I was in Beijing at the time for the PLA's national sports competition. The editors of *Zhiyuanjun Bao* wrote to me about this project, asking me to make some suggestions for the newspaper in the form of writing a dedication.

I believed that as a newspaper published in a combat situation and serving the needs of the grassroots level, it was imperative to sharpen its journalistic edge. This should be achieved by focusing on reality, serving the needs of the grassroot units and the rank and file. Therefore, for the 100th issue of *Zhiyuanjun Bao* I wrote, "Strengthen links with the masses, make the whole army run the newspaper, publicize stories of heroic deeds of the Volunteers, educate the masses, heighten morale, and defeat the enemy." Later, I read in the newspaper that CPVF Acting Commander and Acting Political Commissar Deng Hua, Deputy Commander Song Shilun, and Vice Political Commissar Gan Siqi had also written instructions for the newspaper. Deng Hua in particular put forth new tasks for both *Zhiyuanjun Bao* and its readers. "Improve our troops' modern tactical skills and their ideological understanding. Do a better job, fight better battles, and eliminate more enemy forces. Strive for peace in Korea and the world."

Supporting the Government and Cherishing the People

On December 22, 1950, we received a telegram from Beijing, in which the Ministry of Internal Affairs of the Central Government and the People's Revolutionary Military Committee issued a joint notice to launch a movement [for the PLA and the CPVF] to support the governments and cherish the peoples [*yongzheng aimin*], and [for the Chinese and Korean peoples] to support the armies and give preferential treatment to families of soldiers and martyrs [*yongjun youshu*] during the 1951 Chinese New Year.[27] The notice emphasized that "the people's armies must link the masses very closely at all times and protect their interests. Without its people's active support, the army could not have possibly achieved today's victory and would not achieve new victories over the war to resist America's aggression and defend our country."

"This telegram is so timely!" I told myself. Gaining the support of the Korean people would prove decisive regarding whether or not the War to Resist America and Aid Korea could continue over a long period of time. At that time, most comrades of the CPVF Political Department went to all the armies to assist the troops in their preparations for the New Year offensive campaign. I asked my secretary Fang Hong to convey immediately by telephone to our department's comrades the gist of the notice and my instructions. They were to check the progress for implementing the CPVF Headquarters' Political Directive of December 14 about maintaining a good relationship with the Korean masses. I also wanted them to seek out good examples and identify existing problems in our public relations. The information might help us to improve our wartime work with the masses and to establish a closer relationship with the Korean people.

The 1951 [Chinese] New Year brought a scene of great joy. All our troops celebrated, toasting our victory with snow instead of wine, making jokes about what utterly nauseating characters America's and South Korea's soldiers were, and wishing the best for one another. While sharing the gaiety of the festival with our troops, section and division heads of the CPVF Political Department, who had been sent on fact-finding missions at lower levels, submitted a series of written reports during the New Year campaign. Using these, I made many entries in my working diary on a series of stories about how the Korean people supported the Chinese army and how the Chinese army cared about the Koreans.

One of those stories was from the Fortieth Army. After the New Year campaign started, one of its companies advanced to Sangpaeri in Yangju County. Sangpaeri was a little mountainous village with only a dozen households. When our company got there, the village had been reduced to ashes by American airplanes' devastating raids. Babies were screaming, and the elders were crying for help. Our soldiers were outraged when they saw such a terrifying scene. They voluntarily donated all the Korean money they had for relieving the victims, about 14,700 Korean dollars [won]. Although not a huge amount, the money represented the hearts of our soldiers! The victims stopped crying and gathered close around our men. One old man said with tears on his face, "You are indeed a Buddhist salvation army who helps the needy and relieves the distressed!"

Another story was reported from the Fiftieth Army. The brave Korean people used the Chinese leaders' names like "Mao Zedong" and "Zhu De" as honorable titles for their guerrilla units, which were fighting behind the enemy's lines. Wherever the Volunteers arrived, the Korean people welcomed them as if they were their own family members. With their strong Korean accent, men and women, old and young, warmly cheered, "China, Mao Zedong!" To welcome the Volunteers, they dug out all their stored items, such as foodstuff, tobacco leaves, candy and cakes, and brown rice wine, which they had hidden underground around their houses. When the Volunteers politely declined their offers, the Koreans said from the bottom of their hearts, "You are fighting Americans side by side with us. You are the members of our families. If you do not accept our food, you consider yourselves as outsiders instead of our family members."

Problems had also been reported from the lower levels, however, which bothered me. The problems resulted mainly from a self-assumed role as a "temporary helper" by a few Volunteers. They did not realize how serious it would be to violate rules guiding relations with the Korean people. "Isn't it for the Korean people that we come to Korea to fight and suffer hunger and cold weather? What's wrong in eating or drinking some of their stuff?" Without the people's permission, those Volunteers took away the doors and windows from the houses for their antiaircraft shelters. They forced the Koreans to sell pigs and chickens. Abusing them and eating their food arbitrarily, they rummaged through the Koreans' property. Not leaving even daily essentials and seeds for planting, they forcibly "borrowed" the Koreans' grains and foodstuff and never paid them, damaging their property without compensation.

Moved by the Koreans' loving care and profound concern for our Volunteers, I was really worried by those offenses against their interests. I was even more worried when a few commanders in the CPVF became arrogant and cocky after our three victorious campaigns. They looked down on their Korean comrades, gossiping about their weaknesses and problems behind their backs, much too arrogant and self-important because of the victories. After reading these findings of our working teams, I sent a factual report to the CMC and the PLA General Political Department.

On January 19, 1951, Chairman Mao issued an important directive to the CPVF, requiring all the Chinese Volunteers to take good care of everything and everybody in Korea. He gave a clear answer to the questions I raised in my report:

The Chinese and Korean comrades should unite together as close as brothers. Bound by a common cause and undertaking a life and death struggle together, we must fight to the end for a final victory over our common enemies. The Chinese comrades must take care of Korean comrades' problems as our own problems. We must educate our commanders and soldiers to take good care of Korea's hills, rivers, trees, and flowers. We must not take away a single needle nor a piece of thread from the Korean people. We must think and do everything in Korea the same as we do in China. This is the political basis for our victory. As long as we are able to follow this line, we are going to win the final victory.

The CPVF implemented Mao's directive immediately and earnestly. The CPVF Party Committee considered it as one of the most important agenda items for its forthcoming [CPVF–NKPA] joint high-ranking officers' meeting. Scheduled in late January, it would be a good opportunity to implement Mao's directive by learning from the Korean comrades so as to forge closer ties with their army and people. The CPVF in Korea carried forward our glorious tradition of "supporting the government and cherishing the people." Shortly after the meeting, the CPVF troops were committed to a widespread movement of supporting the Korean Workers' Party and government and cherishing the Korean people.

At the joint meeting, Commander Peng passed on Mao's instruction. In particular he pointed out that the three CPVF–NKPA victories resulted from full support of the Korean and the Chinese peoples and from assistance from the peoples all over the world. Without them, it was impossible for us to achieve any victory in Korea. He asked the Chinese Volunteers to learn with sincere interest from their Korean comrades.

Aware that the CPVF rules guiding relations with the Korean people had not been strictly maintained, Peng wanted the Volunteers to overcome such problems. All the CPVF troops, Peng continued, should begin a movement to appraise discipline. One method was to set up model units that best observed our traditional Three Main Rules of Discipline and the Eight Points for Attention [*Sanda Jilui Baxiang Zhuyi*].[28] Each company must organize a discipline inspection team that would pay special attention to education for its reconnaissance units, purchasing units, and other support service units. Those Volunteers who fell behind their troops must be rounded up. Koreans suffering from property damage [caused by our troops] must be compensated. Meanwhile, Peng added, we should redouble our efforts in our propaganda and organizational works among the rank and file. Thus, we should convince the Chinese Volunteers of the Korean people's upcoming victory and should explain to our troops the policies of the Korean Workers Party and the North Korean government and expose enemy lies.

At the joint high-ranking officers meeting, I gave a talk about the issue of discipline and its implication for our wartime relations with the Korean people. I described some successful working experiences with the Koreans by our Fortieth Army's 118th Division and the Thirty-ninth Army's 116th and 117th Divisions. I also introduced the Forty-second Army's specific regulations for its companies. While praising good examples of observing the guidelines in relations with the local masses, I also criticized, with supporting evidence, some individuals and units that had violated our discipline. I concluded that our experience showed that good discipline in our troops lay in a good relationship with the Korean masses around our stationing areas. Our officers at all levels, I recommended, should help the troops solve problems in their daily lives as much as possible and at the same time request them to observe discipline strictly.

To help our troops establish a better relationship with the Korean masses on a day-to-day basis, the CPVF Political Department put together some of our good experiences in public relations and issued Task Instructions for Units to Establish Good Relations with the Korean People. These required that all CPVF units, large or small in size, must make great efforts in public relations with the Koreans wherever they were stationed or moved to. If one area had multiple units, the political departments at divisional and regimental levels should coordinate the different troops and divide the tasks through an integrated channel. When there was a half-day break, the Volunteers should work on public relations, now to be considered as set regulations and which consisted of several specific elements.

First, as instructed, whenever dealing with the Korean people, the CPVF troops should publicize our military achievements and the significance of the three victorious campaigns with various means. They should explain our goals, policies, discipline, and tasks in the war, and why and how we needed to borrow food from them.

Second, we should organize the Korean people by *ri* or *dong* to work together with us.[29] Based on their own situation, the CPVF troops ought to organize them into support teams for the front. They would help us collect foodstuff, be our guides, and take care of our wounded. They also could be organized into local security teams, guarding the villages against bandits, enemy agents, and possible fires; constructing antiaircraft shelters; and coping with deserted enemy soldiers and reactionary landlords' militia, which resisted our troops.

Third, we should assist the Korean people in their household work. If possible, the Volunteers should help them fetch water, clean yards, and do other jobs around their houses.

Finally, our troops must leave the Korean people with a good impression after they passed through each village, no matter how large or small. The political departments or sections at all levels, especially the civil relations offices within the departments or sections, should pay special attention to this task. Units and individuals who established good relations with the people should receive awards. Our tasks thus would become a new movement among all the CPVF rank and file.

To implement our instructions, the Thirty-eighth Army issued to its units ten specific regulations to enforce exemplary behavior:

1. Respect the Korean people. Treat them like our own fathers, mothers, brothers, and sisters; neither take liberties with or abuse women.

2. Observe Korea's tradition and customs. Take off shoes before entering Korean houses; speak politely; dig toilet holes frequently; do not urinate or defecate just anywhere; do not spit anywhere inside their rooms; keep clean and tidy both inside and outside Korean houses.

3. Ask for permission before moving into Korean houses. Leave enough space for the owner and his family; never use force or occupy the entire house; do not monopolize the kitchen area; take good care of the Koreans' household and possessions, and keep houses in good shape, whether the owners are home or not.

4. Take good care of borrowed furniture, wooden materials, and bedding hay. Return them before leaving the village; compensate at a reasonable price in case of damage; and apologize for any damage before leaving.

5. Pay Korean guides and laborers in accordance with our regulations. Treat them nicely; do not hit or swear at them or press the people into service arbitrarily.

6. Respect the Korean people's property. Do not break a single blade of grass or a tree; do not take away a single needle or a piece of thread; never eat their food without permission or step on a single young plant in the rice fields.

7. Follow the regulations and write down the people's names before borrowing any grain and hay from them. Pay them in full with our grain and hay coupons; do not ransack boxes and chests or clear off everything in the house or "fish in troubled waters."

8. Pay a fair price for everything we buy. Do not force the people to sell anything; do not pay a low, unreasonable price or use credit or ask the people to make donations or contributions; do not eat their cows or their young pigs under seventy pounds.

9. Educate the Korean people. Persuade them to return to their homes; hold mass meetings propagating our victories and exposing the American and South Korean armies' crimes in order to enhance their awareness of the war situation and [to encourage their] cooperation with us; spare time to help them do their housework in order to unite the masses through our daily cherishing activities.

10. Share the Korean people's hardship and help them by all means. Introduce them to our antiaircraft methods; assist them actively in hiding their grain and other possessions; guard against careless cooking and heating to avoid setting their houses on fire; do not play with guns carelessly to avoid accidents.

I believed that these were fine, practical regulations. I signed them and also had them published in *Zhiyuanjun Bao*.

During the New Year campaign, we broke the enemy line and chased the fleeing troops day and night. An increasing number of our soldiers fell behind their units during exploitation operations. To prevent these stragglers (those separated from their units) from violating our discipline and regulations, the CPVF Political Department instructed the troops to organize the task of collecting them. The department also notified all Korean local authorities that they had the power to arrest and interrogate the Volunteers who had been found violating the laws or regulations. Those arrested were sent to nearby CPVF units for punishment. Our directive included three specific requirements.

First, the CPVF frontal logistics depots, large or small at army or divisional levels, must set up guest houses for those Volunteers who fell behind their own units due to sickness, wounds, or weakness, no matter which unit they belonged to. The guest houses should inform the soldiers' units and arrange for their return. Besides collecting the stragglers, the guest houses must also host our personnel who traveled on duties or business so that they would not arbitrarily ask the Korean people for food and drink.

Second, every Volunteer on duty trips must travel with his pass issued by an office above the army level. Without a valid pass, he could be detained. All traveling personnel must bring grain and hay coupons with them.

Third, all armies should immediately dispatch officers to the rear areas to close their service offices there or combine them with nearby service depots. Those offices should be placed under the unified control of and supplied by local logistic depots or departments.

On March 5 Commander Peng came back from Beijing. Passing through Andong, he sent a telegram to Deng Hua and me about what he had heard from the leading commanders of the Liaodong Provincial Military Command [in Northeast China]. The provincial commanders complained that some CPVF deserters had appeared around the Chinese-Korean border areas. In small groups and with arms, they even occasionally robbed the Chinese villagers. In the city of Andong alone, the provincial command had collected as many as several hundred CPVF deserters. Peng believed that other areas along the border must have the same problem and asked us to notify all the provincial military commands and local governments in Northeast China to collect these deserters.

For some serious cases, Peng pointed out that the local authorities in the northeastern region must conduct public criminal trials on the spot and the criminals be penalized according to the CPVF laws. After having the deserters collected and educated, the local governments ought to inform each one's army, which should send officers to pick them up and return them to their units. The army should treat deserting as shameful behavior. Crimes, Peng continued, like robbery and extortion had damaged the unity between the army and the people and between China and Korea. More important, such crimes would damage the great prestige of the Chinese Volunteers. We must organize all CPVF party branches and the rank and file to fight against any violation of the CPVF discipline and rules. We must call for mass meetings at the squad, platoon, company, or battalion levels, to criticize these violators seriously and at the same time to allow them to perform services to atone for their crimes. If party members violated the rules, Peng emphasized, they must be expelled.

Around the Chinese New Year, the CPVF General Headquarters sent officers with 500,000 pounds of grain to help relieve the Korean people in the war disaster areas. The officers also brought with them a large number of letters expressing our sympathy and solicitude. They visited five counties in North Korea, including Unsan, Pakchon, Taechon, Nyongbyon, and Kaechon. Bombed, slaughtered, and looted by the enemy troops, the people in these areas lost an average of 40 percent of their population. Most of their homes had burned down as a result of the enemy's air raids.

The local people truly appreciated the Chinese Volunteers' sympathy and relief efforts. "All of us know that the Volunteers are fighting valiantly on the front and hardly hesitate to sacrifice their own blood and lives," said the chairman of the People's Committee of Songil-ri, Pakchon County. "Without enough food for themselves, the Volunteers still have saved grain to relieve our Korean victims. We and our children will never forget such a spirit of internationalist loving care."

Seeing many Koreans thinly clothed and most without blankets, our officers reported to the CPVF General Headquarters and Commander Peng; on March 18 our Political Department then sent a notice to all the CPVF armies. The General Headquarters had decided that our Volunteers' cotton-padded clothes and comforters with cotton wadding should be disassembled and converted into lined clothes and lined quilts. Each CPVF unit would collect and deliver the removed padding or wadding, packed and free of charge, to the needy Korean people. It would be gathered together by each company and then collected by each regimental political office. No unit would be permitted to give away its cotton without its regiment's approval, or trade it for the Korean people's products, or sell it in any sort of disguised form. Before delivery, all the regimental political officers should have joint discussions with Korean committees at either *ri* or *jun* levels around their stationing areas about the location and apportioning of the distributions. The officers should distribute the materials to as many Koreans as possible. Priority should be given to the members of martyrs' families, the NKPA's families, and poor families, in order to honor and benefit them in a practical way.

The comrades working in the CPVF General Headquarters were active in our efforts to support the Korean government and care for its people during the Chinese New Year. As a result, they were enthusiastic about learning the language. One day my security guard Hou Yulin asked me, "Director, why is it so difficult to learn Korean words? I can't even remember the word for 'thanks.'" Before I could answer his question, there came a messenger from the Civil Relations Department. "It is not too difficult to learn, Little Hou," he said. "Listen, there is a tall horse. How high is it? '*Simida*' [four meters in Chinese]. That is '*Gaoma Simida*'! [Thanks in Korean; the tall horse is four meters high in Chinese.] You see, it is easy to remember, isn't it?" He made all of us laugh.

February 8 was the third anniversary of the NKPA, and Commander Peng talked with me about attending the celebration. Given that few of our leading commanders could be there, Peng instructed me to send a congratulatory telegram to Gen. Kim Il Sung, NKPA supreme commander, in the name of the CPVF rank and file. Peng also asked me to organize a delegation for the celebration ceremony.

The first delegate who came to mind was Comrade Yang Wenhan, chief of the Public Relations Division in our Political Department. My age, Yang was a senior secretary of the district party committee in North China. He had been working on public relations for many years since he joined the revolution. Transferred to the Fourth Field Army during the Jinzhou campaign [in the Chinese civil war], he became the chief of the Public Relations Division of the Thirteenth Army Group when it was founded at Zhengzhou. Capable and vigorous, Yang had already participated in the Koreans' celebration of Pyongyang's liberation on the CPVF's behalf.

Consulting with Yang Wenhan about the NKPA celebration ceremony, I asked for his nomination of our delegates. Yang said, "If possible, Wang Jian, chief of the Secretariat Division in my department, could join me. And Comrade Zhang Zhimin in my division, who can speak Korean, also ought to go with me. We guarantee accomplishing this mission." After they returned, they told me that the celebration ceremony, held in a cave, was successful. Kim attended the ceremony and he proposed a toast for our delegation at the reception afterward.

Through the movement of supporting the government and caring for the people, the CPVF troops' relations with the Korean masses was strengthened a great deal. Our Volunteers showed care and admiration for the mountains, rivers, trees, and flowers, not because they had to observe regulations but because they regarded their loving care as a conscious demonstration of their internationalism. Commander Peng in particular described the loving care of one role model Volunteer in his own words: "The model of martyr Luo Shengjiao is the indicator of the internationalist consciousness of our entire army."

Here then is the story of Luo Shengjiao. The date was January 2, 1952. The reconnaissance company of the 141st Division had just finished its morning drill around Sokjon-ri, a small village in Songchon County, where the company was stationed. The company's secretary, Luo Shengjiao, was washing his face when he heard somebody crying for help from the river outside the village. Luo rushed to the river and saw a Korean teenager, Choi Young, struggling in an ice hole. Skating with some other children on the ice, Choi had fallen into the river when the thin ice in the middle broke. In spite of the twenty degrees below zero weather, Luo jumped into the ice hole and looked for the Korean girl. He found her in the river and lifted her out of the water several times. But she fell into the water again and again because the ice around the hole was too thin to support her body. Finally, Luo pushed her out of the ice hole with his head. Choi was saved, but Comrade Luo Shengjiao drowned. He sacrificed himself with glory.

After his martyr's death, the Korean folks in the village cried their hearts out. Holding the most grand funeral ritual in the Korean tradition, they buried Luo in a newly built mountainside grave. They renamed the river the Luo Shengjiao River, the mountain where he was buried the Luo Shengjiao Mountain. They changed the name of their village where Choi Young lives to Luo Shengjiao Dong.

A wooden tablet with a written record was set on the bank of the Luo Shengjiao River: "All the people who are born and grow up in the one-thousand-mile land of Korea should always bear in mind the great friend of ours—Comrade

Luo Shengjiao. We must learn from his great spirit of internationalism. To remember him forever, we specially name this river the Luo Shengjiao River. Founded by the people of Sokjon-ri, Sangryong Myon, Songchon, on March 20, 1952."

On the hill of the Luo Shengjiao Mountain, a monument and a memorial tower for Luo Shengjiao, martyr, was built. On the front of the memorial tower, four big Korean characters were written in horizontal calligraphy, "Leaving a Reputation Forever." The inscription by Kim Il Sung was carved on the monument: "The internationalist spirit of martyr Luo Shengjiao lives with the Korean people forever!" On the other side of the monument, an elegiac couplet by the CPVF General Headquarters and Political Department was also carved: "Eternal life to the glorious internationalist soldier—martyr Luo Shengjiao!"

Comrade Luo Shengjiao was born in Xinhua County, Hunan Province. As an exemplary member of the Chinese New-Democratic Youth League, he had the high aspiration of sacrificing himself to the cause of the Korean people after he joined the CPVF in April 1951. Luo had composed a short poem:

When I should fall by invaders' bullets,
I wish you not to stop by my body;
Continue to march bravely forward
To avenge thousands of Korean people and our comrades in a heroic death!

On receiving the report from the Forty-seventh Army about Luo's story, the CPVF Political Department was convinced that his heroic death suggested the high quality of great internationalism and revolutionary heroism of the Chinese Volunteers. The heroism carried forward the fine tradition of the Chinese people's revolutions and further enhanced the unity between the Chinese and Korean peoples. Thus, the Political Department made a special decision that martyr Luo should be awarded posthumously a special-class merit citation and have conferred upon him the glorious title, First-Class Model of Cherishing the Korean People.

To commend the spirit of great patriotism and internationalism that Luo displayed in sacrificing his life to save a Korean child, the Central Committee of the Chinese New-Democratic Youth League decided to award him posthumously the certificate of merit, honoring him as a model member of the Youth League. The Central Committee also edited and printed Luo's heroic story in a book to educate all the members of the Youth League and the mass of youth all over China.

During this time, the Korean people under the leadership of the Korean Workers' Party and Kim Il Sung actively supported the Chinese Volunteers' operations. In various forms they assisted our troops in collecting and preparing foodstuff, constructing and repairing bridges and roads, transporting supplies, rescuing the wounded Volunteers, and guiding our troops.

Countless heroic, model Koreans and their outstanding deeds emerged one after another. For example, Comrade Pak Jae Gun, known as Korea's Luo Shengjiao, covered a wounded Volunteer with his own body during an enemy air raid. Pak died but saved the Chinese Volunteer's life. Such events encouraged our troops to love and care more about the Korean people and their property, inspiring our troops to respect the principles of Korea's independence, its party, and its government conscientiously. Our troops now were willing to observe Korea's laws, policies, customs, and values. The entire movement strengthened our great friendship and military unity, which was cemented with the blood of the Chinese army and the Korean people.

Returning to Beijing with Glory

Early on the morning of September 26, 1951, I boarded the train, leaving Shenyang where I had attended a CPVF security meeting, and traveled to Beijing in great haste.[30] Looking outside, I saw that the northeastern plains were permeated with a harvest beauty in the late autumn. Inside the train, ninety-eight combat heroes selected from the CPVF troops as the Volunteers' representatives were getting more excited as they got closer and closer to Beijing. I had been thinking a lot about this trip.

One morning in early September, a rosy cloud of dawn was beginning to blossom. Red rays gilded the hills and valleys around Kongsa-dong where the CPVF General Headquarters was located. I got up very early that morning and took a walk outside the cave where we lived. Boxed inside the cave for a whole night, I felt very comfortable walking around the valley in the fresh air. At that moment, American night bombers had gone back to their lairs, and daytime bombers had not yet flown from their nest. Indeed, morning was the golden moment for us.

Wei Jilie, head of the Communication and Security Division, came to me hurriedly. "Director Du, here is a telegram from Beijing, sent by the CCP Central Committee." I took the telegram and read it right away. The committee asked the CPVF Headquarters to organize a delegation of their combat heroes in Korea to attend a grand ceremony of the National Day celebration in Beijing.

I reported to Commander Peng about Beijing's notice during breakfast. Peng read the telegram and then said, "It is a great honor and political reputation the Central Committee has granted us. Your political department may issue a circular to all armies and request them to carefully consider and select their representatives." A moment later, Peng added, "I think you ought to be the head of this delegation to return home and visit Beijing for the National Day celebration."

Struck dumb, I could not respond. I asked myself what I had accomplished to deserve such a big honor. "Commander Peng, this is a delegation of our combat heroes; how can I take the lead of it?"

"Why not?" He looked at me and said, "The honor is not only yours, but also belongs to all our comrades of the Volunteers."

At that time, Deng Hua and Xie Fang were in Kaesong;[31] Hong Xuezhi headed the CPVF Logistics Department, Han Xianchu was working at the Front Command, Chen Geng had just arrived, and Gan Siqi had just come to the General Headquarters around August. Among the leading commanders still at headquarters who had entered Korea at the very beginning were only Commander Peng and myself; thus Peng assigned me to the job. The other leading commanders agreed with Peng and also thought it appropriate for me to lead the CPVF delegation to Beijing.

"It is our decision that you should lead the delegation," Peng continued. "You have participated in all the operations during our five campaigns. You know all the situations we have experienced on the Korean battleground. You are familiar with our combat heroes. There is one other reason: all of our leading comrades at the headquarters have visited Beijing since we entered Korea, but only you have not yet done so. You should go back to pay a visit."

I was deeply moved by Peng's consideration and decision. Since coming to Korea last October, I had been too busy to return to visit China. The situation in Korea was tense, my duty for political tasks was heavy, and I did not even have a deputy director in our political department. One year had passed before I realized this. I increasingly missed my comrades-in-arms and old-time leaders in Beijing. Naturally, I was very happy for such a chance. Moreover, the movement to resist America and assist Korea was gaining momentum all over China at that time. Even though I had read a lot about it in newspapers and documents, I needed to have a better impression through my own observation. I could do a better political job after I returned.

At last I was really on the train going to Beijing. Realizing my dream was coming true, how could I not be excited? In fact, I was overexcited; I felt as if the train was overspeeding and approaching Beijing before I could realize it.

The train was slowly reaching the platform. I saw a sea of flags, flowers, and people outside. My ears filled with deafening sounds of gongs and drums, fire-crackers, and cheers. Among the more than 3,000 people who came to the train station to welcome us were Chen Shutong, vice president of the Chinese People's General Committee to Resist America and Aid Korea; Liao Chenzhi, president of the General Committee of the China National Democratic Youth; and representatives from all the democratic parties and all the people's organizations. The representatives of the PLA army, navy, and air force and the PLA combat heroes' delegates who had come to Beijing from all over the country for the National Day celebration also came to the station to welcome us.

Vice President Chen Shutong was waiting for me outside my compartment. As soon as I stepped down, he came up to me and said, "Welcome! I welcome you as our most beloved person on behalf of the people in the capital." I saluted him and said, "We really appreciate the Central Committee's and Chairman Mao's loving care of us Volunteers! We appreciate our people's loving care of us!" Before I could finish my words, I had already been lifted up on the shoulders of a group of young students, who were dancing and cheering with joy. I looked back and saw that the ninety representatives of the CPVF combat heroes also had been lifted up and carried on the shoulders of the happy crowd. What kind of award could I ever have had that would match such glory? I could not help but blush with embarrassment.

Then, a grand ceremony to welcome the CPVF delegation was held at the square of the Beijing train station. Chen gave a warm and ebullient welcoming speech: "You come here to celebrate the joyous festival of our National Day. The National Day festival is your victorious fruit. Participating in the National Day celebration, you will see the great victories and achievements you have made under the brilliant leadership of Chairman Mao and Commander in Chief Zhu."

As I listened to Chen's speech, my mind had already returned to Korea's battleground. Our valiant Volunteers were now fighting a bloody war against the American army and Syngman Rhee's puppet troops in Korea. It was the Volunteers who were defending this glorious National Day with their lives and coloring this flame-red festival with their blood.

After Chen's welcoming speech, I responded. More than 3,000 people welcomed my speech with their thunderous applause. My heart beat so fast. Although I had given many speeches in front of thousands of troops, there was not one like that day's speech. I was more excited than I had ever been before. Today I was here representing all the CPVF comrades on the Korean front and reporting to the people from all over our motherland. I stood before the microphone and spoke loudly:

Our delegation is representing all the comrades of the Volunteers on the Korean front. We come here to attend the grand ceremony of our National Day. We are celebrating our nation's increasing prosperity and strength. Every comrade fighting the war in Korea loves our country very much. Every comrade perfectly understands that our current military mission of resisting America and assisting Korea is at the same time defending our country. We can only protect our national security and economic development by resolutely defeating the invaders. Thus, every Volunteer is firmly carrying on his glorious task which our people have assigned to him.

In my speech, I also talked about the delegation's plans. Our first task, mandated by the CPVF rank and file, was to give a firsthand report to the entire country of the Volunteers' victories and the situation on the Korean front for the past eleven months. The Chinese people should know how their own army had valiantly and bravely beaten the American invading forces. The second task was to bring back to the CPVF's commanders and soldiers on the Korean front what we had witnessed concerning the state of our motherland. We saw with our own eyes the prosperous scene of our country's development and production. We felt the people's strong enthusiasm for the war through their active donations of money to obtain more airplanes and big guns in order to supply the front. These efforts would convince the Volunteers that they had strong support from their motherland and that they would win the war.

After the welcoming ceremony, many young students surged toward us. They held our representatives' hands and asked for our autographs. They came up group after group and overwhelmed our hosts. The masses had a sincere feeling for the Volunteers. We were surrounded and cheered by enthusiastic people all the way to our hotel.

5

The CPVF's Combat and Logistics

General (Ret.) Hong Xuezhi

Editors' Note: Hong Xuezhi was the deputy commander of the Chinese People's Volunteers Force and chief of the CPVF Logistics Department during the Korean War. He was one of the leading commanders who participated in the entire war, from establishing the CPVF in 1950 to negotiating the Korean Armistice in 1953. He was made general in 1955.

Born in Jinzhai County, Anhui Province in 1913, Hong joined the CCP and the Chinese Red Army in 1929. During the Chinese civil war, he served as the commander of the Heilongjiang Provincial Military District, the Sixth Army of the Northeastern Field Army, the Forty-third Army of the Fourth Field Army, and the deputy commander of the Liaoxi Provincial Military District. After the founding of the People's Republic of China, he became the deputy commander and chief of staff of the Fifteenth Army Group, chief and political commissar of the PLA General Logistics Headquarters, director of the National Defense Industry of the PRC State Council, and deputy secretary-general of the CCP Central Military Commission.

General Hong later published his memoirs, Kangmei Yuanchao Zhanzheng Huiyi [Recollections of the War to Resist America and Aid Korea] *(Beijing: PLA Literature Press, 1990). His book was reprinted as a second edition in 1991. The following chapters are selected and translated from this second edition, with editors' notes. The excerpts from Hong's memoirs provide a comprehensive account of the CPVF's rear service problems and performance. It was only during the Korean War, Hong explained, that the Chinese Communist forces began to realize the importance of a standard and efficient logistical system. An answer to how the CPVF survived a war in the rear—battling the United Nations Command air raids against Chinese supply lines—may be found in Hong's personal account.*

UNPREPARED FOR THE INTERVENTION

At dawn on June 25, 1950, the Korean War broke out.[1]

Two days later Truman issued an order that American air and naval forces would provide South Korean troops with support. Truman also ordered the Seventh Fleet of the U.S. Navy to intervene in our Taiwan Straits. Meanwhile, the American government started to put together an armed force from more than a dozen countries to invade Korea in the name of the United Nations. Three days later the U.S. Eighth Army engaged the NKPA directly on the Korean battleground.[2] War flames suddenly wrapped the Korean peninsula, and the situation was worsening on a daily basis.

On June 28 Chairman Mao Zedong made a speech at the Eighth Committee Meeting of the Chinese People's Central Government. Mao condemned the United States for invading both Korea and our territory, Taiwan. He pointed out that "the internal affairs of each country are supposed to be taken care of by its own people. It is not America's business to intervene in another country's affairs. . . . The sympathy of all the Chinese people should go to the invaded side." On the same day, Zhou Enlai, PRC premier and foreign minister, made a public statement: "Truman's announcement on the 27th [of military support for South Korea] and the American Navy's operations are military aggression toward Chinese territory and a total violation of the UN Charter. . . . The American government has instigated South Korea's troops under Syngman Rhee to attack the Democratic People's Republic of Korea. It is America's long-cherished plot and a new move of American imperialists intervening in Asian affairs."

Anything can be accomplished if prepared for in advance; anything will fail if unprepared. Chairman Mao and the CCP Central Military Commission then made an important strategic decision. They immediately moved the PLA's Thirteenth Army Group to Northeast China to augment the defensive strength along the Chinese-Korean borders. In retrospect, this decision was just in time and absolutely correct. It reflected the foresight and sagacity of our top military commanding headquarters.

On July 7 and 10, Zhou, then also vice chairman of the CMC, held two successive national security meetings to discuss which armies should be employed to strengthen the country's northeastern defense. After careful consideration, the members decided to employ the troops of the Fourth Field Army. Consisting of a large number of soldiers who were natives of Northeast China, it had been fighting in the northeastern theater throughout the Liberation War. The troops were familiar with the weather and the geographic situation there.

At that time, the Thirteenth Army Group, including the Thirty-eighth, Thirty-ninth, and Fortieth Armies, was the main strength of the Fourth Field Army. This army group was stationed in Henan Province [Central China] as the CMC's strategic reserve forces, with the Thirty-eighth Army stationed in Xinyang, the Thirty-ninth in Luohe, and the Fortieth in Luoyang. These major armies were concentrated in Central China because it was convenient for the CMC to deploy them to the south, north, east, or west. They could move easily to wherever needed. Thus, the CMC decided after careful discussions that the Thirteenth Army Group would immediately move to Northeast China. Later, the CMC also decided that the Forty-second Army, which already was in the northeastern region, would be incorporated into the Thirteenth Army Group.

During this period, the CMC made several other decisions. Deng Hua, commander of the Fifteenth Army Group, was appointed as the new commander of the Thirteenth Army Group. Lai Chuanzhu, political commissar of the Fifteenth Army Group, was transferred to the Thirteenth Army Group as its new political commissar. Huang Yongsheng, commander of the Thirteenth Army Group, became the commander of the Fifteenth Army Group. As a result of these decisions, there was an exchange of the commanding headquarters between the two army groups, the headquarters of the Thirteenth becoming the headquarters of the Fifteenth. Led by Huang Yongsheng, the new headquarters of the Fifteenth Army Group moved to Guangzhou [South China]. The former headquarters of the Fifteenth Army Group was now changed into the headquarters of the Thirteenth; led by Deng Hua, it moved to Northeast China.

As the former deputy commander and the chief of staff of the Fifteenth Army Group, I was then the only commander at Guangzhou with the new headquarters. The Fifteenth Army Group had already combined with the Guangdong Military Region by then. The commander and the political commissar of the Guangdong Regional Command was Ye Jianying (Ye Ch'ien-ying), whom we used to call Chief Ye. Ye trusted me with most of the daily operating matters of the regional command. Being the deputy commander of the Fifteenth, I was also named the deputy commander of the Guangdong Military Region and the commander of the Defense Force of the Zhujiang River. And I was in charge of suppressing bandits. Thus I had to stay in South China when the Fifteenth Army Group Headquarters and other commanding officers were transferred to the Thirteenth Army Group and moved to Northeast China.

In early August 1950, I received an order from Chief Ye. He asked me to present a report to the CMC about some specific problems regarding the merging of the Fifteenth Army Group and the Guangdong Regional Command. I left Guangzhou by train and arrived in Beijing on August 9.

Beijing's train station was then located at Qianmen. Our train arrived around noon in the middle of summer. The sun was blazing like a ball of fire. The station was as hot as an oven, and my face was bathed in sweat. It had taken a couple of days for me to travel from Guangzhou to Beijing, and I had developed skin ulcers all over my body because of traveling in the hot weather with no water for a bath on the train. At the train station, I was itching, with painful boils on my body and sores running with pus. When I cleaned my face at the platform, I suddenly heard somebody calling me loudly, "*Laoge* [old brother, an idiom in Hunan Province]!" I looked up. It was Deng Hua.

Deng was a longtime comrade and friend of mine. During the Liberation War, we had worked together in the Liaobei Military District, where he was the commander and I was his deputy. After the Northeastern Field Army was established, I became the commander of the Sixth Column [later the Forty-third Army], and Deng was the commander of the Seventh Column [later the Forty-fourth Army]. We had met at meetings and coordinated military operations quite often. Then the Fourth Field Army was organized in Northeast China. When it had fought its way from North to South China, it established the Fifteenth Army Group at Nanchang, Jiangxi Province; Deng was its commander and I was first deputy commander and chief of staff. After that, we were together day and night and on intimate terms with each other. In early July, however, the CMC transferred Deng to the Thirteenth Army Group to be its new commander. He was supposed to have left for Northeast China a couple of days earlier.

When I thought about his transfer, I felt puzzled and could not help but ask him, "Hi, brother! You have gone to the Northeast, haven't you? How come you are still loafing in Beijing?"

Blinking and smiling, Deng answered, "I have not left yet."

"How could you stay here? Wasn't it said that the mission was urgent?"

"I did not go because there is an interesting situation here [in Beijing]."

"Did you come to the train station to pick me up?" I asked.

"You are right. It is perfect for you to come now," Deng said mysteriously. "You come at a perfect time!"

I felt at a loss and asked, "What is going on here?"

Deng told me, "There are some very important matters. Later Vice Chairman Lin [Biao] will talk to you." At that time, Lin Biao had already been transferred from [the post as commander in chief of] the Fourth Field Army to the CMC [as its vice chairman].

"What kind of matter will he talk to me about?" I asked.

"I cannot disclose the secret now," Deng answered me with a smile.

I kept asking him, "How did you know I would arrive in Beijing today?"

Deng said, "I have a mouth under my nose. Can't I ask? That is enough, old brother. Do not ask questions without an end. Let's go to my car."

We walked out of the train station and got into his American-made jeep.

The jeep ran along Beijing's streets and turned repeatedly into small alleys. We got to Lin Biao's residence before too long. Since I was not familiar with the city, I felt at a total loss. I still cannot tell today where Lin Biao lived at that time.

It was a little bit after noontime when we got to Lin's house. Lunch was already on the table—steamed rice and several dishes.

Lin Biao smiled when he saw me and said, "You have arrived. That is good. Let's eat first."

We sat down together. While we were eating our lunch, Lin turned to me: "Comrade Hong Xuezhi, the defense task of the Northeast needs you. It has been decided that you [will] go to the Northeast."

"Me?" When I heard this, I was in a daze. I asked Lin, "What kind of role can I have over there?"

He continued: "To send you there means that we want you to play your role in the Northeast. Today, Comrade Deng Hua is leaving for Korea to find out the situation over there. Currently the armies of the Thirteenth Army Group have already been deployed for defense along the Yalu River. When Comrade Deng Hua is in Korea, many things will need to be taken care of for those troops. These armies are the veterans of the Fourth Field Army. You know them well. So you must go to the Northeast immediately to command and manage those troops. Your train ticket is ready. As soon as you finish your lunch here, you will leave for the Northeast!"

"These are the reasons why I stayed in Beijing," Deng added. "The first is that the party's Central Committee has decided to send me to Korea to find out the situation there. I have been working on the organization of my team and the methods for our information gathering. The second is to wait for your transfer and arrival so that you can command our armies."

I asked, "Why does the commander needed there have to be me?"

Deng responded by asking me, "Why do you have to go? All of those armies in the Thirteenth Army Group are our troops in the Fourth Field Army. And the headquarters of the Thirteenth Army Group has our former staff from the headquarters of the Fifteenth Army Group. You know both commanding bodies and troops very well. If you do not go, who else can go? Let's finish our lunch, friend. We will leave together."

I was worried when I heard that I had to go to Northeast China immediately. It was Chief Ye who had ordered me to come to Beijing. The purpose of my trip was to ask the CMC for approval not to merge the Fifteenth Army Group with the regional command. Chief Ye believed that the army group should command the field forces and serve as the nation's defense force; the military region should command local forces and cope with all the public security problems. Chief Ye had also asked me to report to the CMC some other problems as well. He was expecting me to bring back the [CMC's] answers!

Since I was worried about Ye's order, I said to Lin Biao, "I am a Communist Party member. I must obey orders if the party leadership needs me to go to the Northeast. But what are we going to do with the order I took from Chief Ye? Is it possible for me to go back to Guangzhou to fulfill the mission first and then leave for the Northeast from there?"

"No. It's impossible," Lin said. "We do not have the time. The situation in the Korean War now is getting tense. It is urgent for us to strengthen the border defense in the Northeast. Regarding the mission Commander Ye assigned to you, you can either call or write to him explaining the situation and ask him to find somebody else to take over your job in Guangzhou."

I did not give up but continued, "I do not have any preparation at all. I did not even bring any change of clothes with me. Don't I have time to go to Guangzhou to get some clothes? And I also have skin ulcers all over my body. I probably have to go back there for a treatment." My purpose behind the words was in fact that I wanted to go back to report to Commander Ye first and then leave for Northeast China.

Lin seemed able to read my mind and said, "These are not big deals. You can find some clothes in the Northeast and also get treatment for your skin ulcers up there."

Deng smiled and agreed with Lin. "Don't let him go back. If he runs away and does not return, what are we going to do?"

"I won't do that," I said. "It won't happen like that."

Deng then said, "You can promise. How about Chief Ye? He could say that you cannot leave the job and can force you to stay. What can we do?" Deng continued, "Anyway, do not think about going back since you are already here. So much for the excuses. Play no tricks, and go to the Northeast with me."

After lunch, I called Chief Ye. I told him, "I have already reported to Vice Chairman Lin Biao the matters you asked me to report. But the CMC has decided that I must go to the Northeast and I ask you to find somebody else to take over my job in Guangzhou."

Chief Ye had not waited for me to finish before he got upset. "What is going on? Did you ask for it?"

"No, I did not," I answered. "It appears that the CMC had made the decision before I got here."

Ye said, "I do not have enough people here. You come back first and then we [will] talk."

"I am not allowed to return to Guangzhou. They asked me to go to the Northeast today. It is hard to explain the detailed situation over the telephone. I will write to you."

Then Chief Ye said, "Well, since the CMC has already made its decision, you just go ahead." He paused for a while and continued, "I would never have sent you to Beijing if I had known this before."

"I did not know it either before I got here," I said. Hanging up the phone, I wrote a letter to Chief Ye immediately.

Around one o'clock that afternoon, Deng Hua and I boarded the train for Northeast China. I did not realize at that moment that this trip would start my four-year career in the War to Resist America and Aid Korea.

Deng was a heavy smoker and a Peking Opera fan; in the train he kept smoking while humming Peking Opera songs to himself. I told him I felt sleepy and lay down on the sleeper myself. However, I could not sleep at all because, even though the CMC's decision was a big surprise for me, I was happy with it. I was so excited that I could not help but ponder some possible reasons behind this decision.

Deng seemed able to read my mind and told me, "Big brother, do not make wild guesses. It is I who suggested to the CMC and Chairman Mao that you go to the Northeast."

"So it is you!" I said. "I did not think about you."

"How couldn't you think about this?" Deng explained: "Isn't it obvious? Our army group had three commanding officers. When the CMC issued the order, Lai Chuanzhu and I were transferred to the Northeast, and you were kept at Guangzhou. I went to the Northeast in such a big hurry that I brought with me only a few officers from the commanding section. Our troops now are already in the Northeast, but Commissar Lai is still at Guangzhou, and I am about to leave for Korea to find out the situation over there. If you do not go to the Northeast, who commands our troops? So I made the suggestion to the CMC to transfer you there. Both Chairman Mao and Vice Chairman Zhou thought my suggestion reasonable and indeed necessary. They approved it really fast. Then Commissar Lai called me from Guangzhou at the very moment that you were on the way to Beijing. He said you would deliver yourself to Beijing." When he told the story, we could not help but laugh together. We talked and talked until both of us were completely exhausted, then fell asleep on the thundering train.

I got to know more about my transfer many years later. On the same day I had left Beijing, Lin Biao wrote a letter to Acting Chief of General Staff Nie Rongzhen about my transfer to the Northeast:

August 9

Chief Nie:
Today I have had a discussion with Comrade Tan Zheng over the telephone. He has no problem with Hong Xuezhi's transfer to the Northeast, as long as Hong agrees himself. Hong has agreed to go to the Northeast as the deputy commander of the 13th Army Group, and he will leave with Deng Hua tonight for a meeting in the Northeast. We must now request the CMC to officially appoint Hong to the position (of the first deputy commander of the 13th Army Group), and appoint Fang Qiang to take over Hong Xuezhi's positions as the deputy commander of the Guangdong Regional Military Command and the commander of the South Sea Fleet. Please ask the General Office of the CMC to issue those appointments by cable. And ask Fang Qiang to come to Beijing immediately for a naval meeting.

Lin Biao

It was late night when we awoke. The train arrived in Shenyang, the first stop on our trip. We needed to meet with Gao Gang, commander and political commissar of NEMR, because the CCP Central Committee had decided that he would supervise all the issues regarding the northeastern defense. Thus we had to stop at Shenyang and talk to him about the many specific problems we had.

We were taken to the Dahe Hotel, a former Japanese accommodation center (it is now the Liaoning Hotel). First I took a shower and changed my clothes. Since the weather in Shenyang is much cooler than the areas south of the Great Wall, I felt immediately that my skin ulcers were getting much better.

During that evening, Gao Gang and He Jinnian, deputy commander of NEMR, came to the hotel to visit us. I had known Gao in the past when I worked in the northeastern region. He Jinnian was the former deputy commander of the Fifteenth Army Group and had recently transferred to NEMR [and I knew him as well].

We attended two meetings at Shenyang. The first was held around 9:00 A.M. as a meeting of the Standing Committee of the CCP Central Committee's Northeastern Bureau. There were only a few members attending; Deng Hua was asked to participate. He told me about the discussions at the meeting and said that they also decided to call a meeting of NEMR's commanders and officers above the divisional level about further mobilization. On August 13 this second meeting was held. There were several dozen participants; Gao, Xiao Jinguang, Xiao Hua, Deng, and He gave presentations. After that meeting, Deng and I among others had discussions about how to deploy our armies in Northeast China, for example, how many troops to send to Andong and how many to Tonghua; how to conduct political and ideological mobilization; how to secure the logistics service and supply transportation; and many other issues.

We stayed in Shenyang for about four or five days. Meanwhile, Political Commissar Lai Chuanzhu led the Thirteenth Army Group's Headquarters and the units directly under it to Andong. As soon as our meetings in Shenyang were over, Deng and I also went there.

Andong was then a small town. Famous for its scenic beauty, it faces the Yalu River and has a mountain behind it. The river runs more than 100 meters wide before the city. The mountain was called Zhenjiang [now Jinjiang Mountain]. After arriving, we stayed at the foot of the mountain.

There were four small but beautiful and delicate buildings at the foot of Zhenjiang Mountain. It was unknown whether the Japanese or some Chinese bourgeoisie had built them. The two buildings in the front were of one style, and the other two in the back of another. Deng lived in one of the buildings in the back; Lai and I lived in the two buildings in the front. One more building was available in the back, which Commander Peng Dehuai moved into later.

There were also several rows of one-story houses between the front and rear buildings, which the army group's chief of staff, Xie Peiran (Xie Fang), and the commanding headquarters occupied. Director of the Political Department Du Ping and his departmental members lived on the other side of the mountain. Xie was former chief of staff of the Twelfth Army Group; Du was former head of the Organization Division of the Political Department in the Fourth Field Army.

The Thirty-ninth and Fortieth Armies were stationed along the Andong-Kuandian areas and the Thirty-eighth Army at Tonghua. The Forty-second Army was stationed at Ji'an and later was joined by the Fiftieth Army. At that time the other armies of the Fourth Field Army could not come to Northeast China because they were suppressing bandits in Southwest China. Nevertheless, our force was pretty strong. We had those major armies plus the First, Second, and Eighth Artillery Divisions and two engineering regiments.

According to the original plan, Deng would go to Korea to learn the NKPA's situation in its battles against the American army. But after we arrived at Andong, the situation changed. Deng did not make that trip.

The situation in the Korean War changed from minute to minute. When the NKPA fought its way to the Naktong River region, it deadlocked with the enemy. At that time, our CCP Central Committee clearly indicated the increasing possibility that the Korean War would turn into a protracted war and that the American imperialists would expand it. The Chinese people had to be prepared in order to avoid fighting in haste.

In late August, the American air force, which had already invaded Korean air space, began to invade our territorial sky in Northeast China continually. The Amer ican planes bombed and raided our towns and villages in Andong, Ji'an, and other regions.[3]

On September 15 American invading forces landed successfully at Inchon, a middle point on the Korean peninsula. Thereafter, the NKPA was attacked by the enemy both front and rear. The situation grew serious. Under these circumstances, North Korean Prime Minister Kim Il Sung sent Pak Il U, North Korea's minister of the interior and the general second in command below Kim, to Andong. Pak had worked in China and spoke fluent Chinese.[4]

After Pak arrived, we asked him to describe in detail the situation in Korea. He told us about the experience and lessons the NKPA had had in fighting the American and puppet troops. However, he indicated that the situation had changed drastically and was deteriorating quickly since the American forces had landed at Inchon. He could give us only some general information because the war was out of the NKPA's control. Currently, the enemy was advancing rapidly northward along the main railroads and highways. Their planes bombed savagely so that the rest of the railroads and highways had been destroyed. The NKPA's troops had to withdraw northward along the passes in the mountains. Moreover, many intact NKPA divisions were still in the south and could not be contacted. In concluding, Pak, on behalf of Korea's party and government, earnestly asked the Chinese to send military forces to Korea for support.

After Pak's talk, we understood that the Koreans were in a difficult situation. We told him, "We will certainly report your situation and your request to our party's Central Committee. As soon as our Central Committee issues an order, we will send our troops to support you. Please tell our Korean comrades to trust us."

Pak stayed only one night in Andong, returning to Korea the next day.[5] After he left, we wrote a detailed report and sent it immediately to Chairman Mao and the Central Committee about what Pak had said and asked for. Then we held a meeting that included Deng, Lai, Xie, Du, and me. Han Xianchu, who was also appointed as the deputy commander of the Thirteenth Army Group, had not yet arrived.

At the meeting we carefully discussed the current situation of the war and the deployments of the American forces in Korea. We believed that the American army would not stop at where they were after they landed in central Korea. They would carry on their invasion into northern Korea to extend the war to the Yalu River. This would pose a direct threat to our national security. If our Central Committee decided to dispatch troops to Korea to support the people's war against invasion, it was surely we who would take on this task. So we further analyzed the American army's strength and problems and compared our troops with theirs. We also discussed the preparations necessary before our engagement in the Korean War. We wanted to be ready to enter Korea as soon as Beijing issued an order.

Nevertheless, we did not know the American forces very well at that point. We had only some general information about their landing campaign at Normandy and their operations in Western Europe during World War II. We also knew something about their military operations against the Japanese in the Pacific. Their recent successful landing at Inchon had made the American troops arrogant for a time as if nobody on earth could beat them. They intended to occupy the entire Korean peninsula and thereafter invade the Chinese mainland.

Our analysis concluded that the American ground troops had certain advantages, such as modern weapons, high maneuverability, and strong ground firepower. Moreover, both their air and naval forces had absolute predominance.

In contrast to the American army's, our army's weapons and equipment were obviously inferior. Our infantry troops had only a few mortars. Our few heavier artillery pieces were mostly captured from the GMD army. Drawn by horses, they were difficult to move and conceal. Our troops still depended on rifles and hand grenades.

Our army, however, had many advantages the American army could not match. First, our troops would fight in an antiaggressive war for internationalism. They were troops representing a just cause and fighting for a good reason. They would receive popular support from the Chinese masses and peace-loving peoples all over the world. Both commanders and soldiers in our army had a strong political consciousness and high morale. So we had absolute political superiority. The American troops, on the other hand, fought in an aggressive, unjust war. Sent to Korea without a just cause, they were totally unsupported by the American people and the peace-loving peoples of the world. Their morale was low, and they suffered absolute political inferiority.

Second, our troops had rich combat experience. During the past several decades, our army had always defeated well-equipped enemies with our poor arms. Our troops were skillful in close fighting, night combat, mountain operations, and bayonet charges. Even though the American army had modern weapons and advanced equipment, its commanders and soldiers were not familiar with close fighting, night combat, and bayonet charges. Our army was superior in these areas.

Third, our troops were mobile and flexible in combat. They knew how to outflank the enemy and proceed to its sides and rear. They were good at dispersal along a front and at concealing themselves before launching an attack. The American army operated by books and regulations. It was inflexible and mechanical in combat.

Fourth, our soldiers were brave and able to fight. They were not scared to shed their blood and lay down their lives on the battleground. They could bear hardships and stand hard work. The American soldiers could not endure hardships in Korea. Even their drinking water had to be transported from Japan. The NKPA told us that the American soldiers had an allergy to the water in Korea, suffering dysenteric diarrhea after they drank the local water.[6] The American troops depended totally on their fire superiority. If our army could fight them in close and night combat, their firepower would not have full play and their combat effectiveness would be reduced significantly.

Fifth, we had our motherland right behind us while fighting in Korea. Conveniently close to its rear areas, our army could organize its logistical system easily. The American army was on a cross oceanic expedition. Many of its war supplies had to be shipped from the North American continent to Korea. Even though some of its war materials could be transported from Japan, its transportation lines were much longer than ours. Thus it had problems in logistical supply and manpower replenishment. Moreover, its modern weapons and equipment expended a lot of resources. The more trucks, airplanes, and big guns they had, the more fuel and munitions they would need. We had so few advanced weapons, vehicles, and big artillery pieces that our operations would cost much less in fuel and munitions than the Americans'.

After these detailed analyses, we recognized that our weapons and equipment were inferior to the enemy's and that our army would have some new difficulties in the war. Therefore we needed to be fully prepared and clearly aware of the enemy's strong and weak points. We should avoid its strong points and fully exploit our advantages. We believed that as long as we could exploit the enemy's weaknesses by using our strengths, our army would certainly defeat the well-equipped enemy even with our inferior-quality weapons.

Applying this analysis, we formulated some principles to guard our operations in the Korean War. In terms of strategy, our army must adhere to protracted warfare. In terms of operational concepts, it must always concentrate its troops to maintain its numerical superiority. In order to avoid the enemy's strengths, it must employ its traditional combat tactics, such as close combat, night operations, fighting quick and decisive battles, thrusting deep into the enemy, outflanking them, and cutting up their forces.

Enemy airplanes, for example, bombed heavily and raided frequently in the daytime, which created difficulty for our operations. Thus our troops should be dispersed and concealed during the daytime so as to escape the enemy's raids and bombings. At night, when the air raids were limited, our army should fully exploit our superiority in night operations and attack the enemy in the darkness.

The enemy had heavy artillery pieces and strong firepower. We should thus avoid being locked into a lengthy seesaw battle. Our army must take advantage of its skills in close combat and mobility so as to engage the enemy quickly by surprise. Should we be able to do so, the enemy's artillery and air forces could not make full use of their superior firepower.

The enemy bombed and destroyed railroads and highways in North Korea; however, we could move our troops without them. Our soldiers depended on their feet in combat. Their movement could not compete with the enemy's motorized movement, but it was hard to detect and easy to conceal. Again, our weakness could become a strength. We could bring this capability into full play if we boldly penetrated and outflanked the enemy troops, thrust deep into their positions, and fully used the power of our hand grenades. Isn't the enemy wildly and arrogantly marching toward the north? We could set up defensive positions and wait at our ease for the approaching exhausted enemy troops.

After our discussions we called for several meetings of army and division commanders of the Thirteenth Army Group, asking them to report their troops' condition, preparedness, and operational plans. Among these were Thirty-eighth Army Commander Liang Xingchu and Political Commissar Liu Xiyuan, Thirty-ninth Army Commander Wu Xinquan and Political Commissar Xu Binzhou, Fortieth Army Commander Wen Yucheng and Political Commissar Yuan Shengping, and Forty-second Army Commander Wu Ruilin and Political Commissar Zhou Biao. All of them had been toughened through many revolutionary wars in the past and had rich experience in commanding armies in battle. At these meetings, we repeatedly emphasized that all the army and division commanders must do a good job in their troops' mental preparation, combat training, weapons and equipment replenishment, and logistical service preparations.

These armies [except the Forty-second] had been stationed in Henan Province [before they moved to Northeast China]. The CMC had originally decided that the armies should take part in the nation's economic reconstruction [after the Chinese civil war ended]. The armies had started building their own houses and engaging in farming. Many of their commanders and soldiers, however, had not adjusted at first to this sudden transition from wartime combat to peacetime farming. After a while, however, the armies had done a great deal toward making this physical and psychological transition. But shortly after they had made this successful adjustment, they were ordered to move to Northeast China to prepare for battle in Korea, and once again they were facing another sudden physical and psychological change.

Nevertheless, a psychological transition was quickly completed after our mental mobilization and education efforts. Our commanders and soldiers had been tempered in past wars. They had been fighting for many years, so war was their only profession. It had been only one year since the civil war had ended, and they had not farmed for a long period. Having heard that they would soon fight in battle again, they made the mental transition more successfully and rapidly than they had before. Now they had chances to carry out their ideals and skills. Our heroes now had a place to display their prowess. Our commanders and soldiers were excited as soon as they heard they would be in combat.

After those meetings, Deng, Han, Xie, Du, and I frequently inspected our troops to check and supervise their mental education, combat training, and weapons and equipment replenishment. We also discussed our logistical needs with the comrades of NEMR. It was late fall, and winter would come soon. We needed to prepare our winter clothes, shoes, and other materials ahead of time.

THE DEATH OF MAO ANYING

After the CPVF General Headquarters moved into Taeyudong in late October 1950, it had been bombed many times by American airplanes.[7] The CCP Central Committee sent us several telegrams instructing us to pay more attention to our antiaircraft work and to the headquarters' safety.

In charge of the headquarters' routine work, I took care of its antiaircraft defenses. At that time, I thought Commander Peng's safety so critical that I discussed with Deng the possibility of building an antiaircraft shelter for him. We decided to dig an antiaircraft cave for him outside the valley about a dozen meters from his house. In case of an air raid, we could ask Peng to take shelter inside the cave.

I ordered an engineering company to come to the headquarters to dig the antiaircraft cave. Its construction made a lot of noise because of the use of explosives, and one night Peng was awakened by its blasting. Displeased with the construction, he asked the company to pack up and go. I was not there when this happened. Later I wondered why the company had stopped its work, and I asked its captain to come see me.

He told me the story: "Commander Peng said that this antiaircraft shelter was useless. He stopped our work and asked us to leave."

"You should continue your work regardless of what he does," I answered.

"What can we say if Commander Peng asks us why we came back again?"

"You can tell him that Deputy Commander Hong asked you to come back. You could dig several blasting holes without a break. Then make one big explosion all at once. Before your blasting is in progress, you should tell Commander Peng's security guards. His guards can tell him ahead of time so that he will be prepared. After all, the antiaircraft cave must be built."

After our talk, the captain took his company back to work on the cave again. Peng saw them coming back and asked them angrily, "Who told you to come back?"

"It is Deputy Commander Hong who asked us to come back."

"Stop your work immediately."

"Deputy Commander Hong will not let us stop," the captain insisted.

Seeing that the engineering captain would not listen to him, Peng asked his guards to look for me. As soon as he saw me, Peng yelled loudly, "Why are you messing about up the hill? Don't you have anything to do?"

"We are neither messing about nor doing nothing. We are digging an antiaircraft shelter to protect the headquarters and to secure your safety!"

"That kind of thing does not help."

"Why not? Antiaircraft shelters work. If we do not build it now, we won't be able to build it when enemy airplanes come to raid."

"My antiaircraft matter is my business. It's none of your business." Peng was getting angry.

"Commander Peng," I smiled and said, "it is not the right thing to talk like that. The Central Committee gave the order to place me in charge of this matter."

Peng was quiet after I said this. The engineering company made the best use of its time, digging the cave day and night. Soon it was finished. Then the company dug another, bigger cave near the crest of the hill, about a couple of dozen meters away from the small one. We used the bigger cave for our command operations.

On the afternoon of November 24, four enemy airplanes came to raid Taeyudong twice. They dropped bombs and destroyed the electric power substation on the hill. That evening an enemy reconnaissance airplane, called by Americans a Mustang [F-51 fighter-bomber], came to Taeyudong to circle around a couple of times and then flew away.

The reconnaissance airplane's visit worried me. Since enemy airplanes raided us quite often, we had some experience and knew that if an enemy reconnaissance plane visited a place one day, bombers and fighters must come to raid it the next. Moreover, we had received information that enemy airplanes had been looking for the CPVF Headquarters. So I found Deng and said, "I feel something wrong. Enemy airplanes will very likely come to bomb our headquarters tomorrow. Don't we need to discuss some measures to handle it?"

Deng agreed with me: "Yes, we need to talk about our antiaircraft measures." Then he smiled and said, "But you have to figure out a way to make Commander Peng join us. You should talk him into coming. As soon as Peng comes, we can start our discussion."

I knew what Deng meant by this. Peng was the kind of person who never thought about his own safety while working. I went to Peng's place and talked to him about it. It happened just as I had thought. He said, "I am not afraid of American airplanes. I do not want to hide in the cave. And I do not have time for your meeting."

Deng, Xie, Du, and I had a headquarters' security meeting and discussed some antiaircraft measures for the next day. We decided on three: first, we required all the officers and soldiers in the headquarters to finish eating for the whole day before dawn. Second, no cooking smoke was allowed after dawn. Third, everybody must be evacuated from their offices or living quarters in the morning.

According to our original schedule for that morning, Peng and other leading commanders would meet and discuss our next operational plan since the military situation had changed. Peng had decided to hold the meeting in his small shed. At the security meeting, we thought it not safe at all to have a commanders' meeting in Peng's place because enemy airplanes had raided us several times recently and had just destroyed the electric power substation the day before. We believed it safer to hold the meeting in the antiaircraft cave outside the valley. Thus at our security meeting we decided to change the meeting place and prepare everything for the commanders' meeting in the cave the night before. The leading commanders also agreed to have their meal around 5:00 A.M. After the meal, they would come to the cave to discuss the next operational plan.

After the security meeting, Xie made some arrangements with all the offices in the headquarters. To ensure their safety, I asked the engineering company's captain to double-check the two antiaircraft caves. Peng heard about this and asked me to come to see him. He asked me seriously, "Why do you start this thing again?"

"Commander, please do not worry about it," I answered.

Peng liked to look at military maps. He spent a lot of time day and night, with his hands behind his back, standing in front of his wall map. He could not live without a map in his room. To make him leave his shed and go to the antiaircraft cave the next day, I took his military command map away from his room after he slept and hung it up in the cave.

After 5:00 A.M. the next day, we finished our meal and went to the cave; everybody was there except Peng. We sent security guards and staff to ask him to come several times, but he refused. We discussed having one of the leading commanders go to Peng to persuade him to come to the cave. Deng, Xie, and Du were afraid of Peng's losing his temper and said, "Old Hong makes jokes with Commander Peng all the time. Old Hong should go to persuade him." I was in charge of the headquarters' routine and, most important, I worried about Peng's safety. "OK, I can go," I said.

When I walked into Peng's room, he sat there angrily. He asked me immediately, "Big Hong, where did you hide my planning map?"

I said, "Chief Commander, I took it to the antiaircraft cave. The map is hung up, the cave is warmed up, and everybody is there ready for the discussion of the next operational plan. Everybody is waiting for you!"

"Who told you to have the meeting over there? Why not here?"

"Chief Commander, it is not safe here. The commanders discussed this and decided to move the meeting into the cave because of aircraft concerns."

Peng had a very bad temper. He did not move at all. I kept trying: "Chief Commander, let us leave here immediately. It is dangerous here."

"You are afraid of danger, so you can go. I am not afraid. I see nothing wrong here. I will stay here."

"You have to go. If you do not leave and something happens to you, it will be too late." I knew that he missed his 1:50,000 operations map on which he spent so much time marking, drawing, and studying. He was familiar with everything on that map. "Your map is already there in the cave," I added. "Everything is ready. Everybody is waiting for you to chair the meeting."

"Who wanted you to bother about other people's business?"

"It is not other people's business. This is my business," I insisted.

Finally, Peng stopped resisting. I more or less pushed and pulled him out of his shed.

After we walked out the door, I told the security guards behind us, "Fold up Chief Commander's comforter. Take it to the cave."

"Don't do that. It is all right to leave it there," Peng said loudly.

"We will take it back for you later if everything is all right," I said, taking the comforter.

Thus Peng walked out of his shed reluctantly. I pulled him all the way up the hill and into the larger cave. Peng's security guards did not follow us to the cave, however, but stayed in the basement under his shed. In Peng's room, there were two staff on duty, Gao Ruixin and Cheng Pu, who were not evacuated.

Everybody had eaten early that morning. After the meal, Mao Anying, Chairman Mao Zedong's oldest son, withdrew to the hill with us. Later, I did not know why, he returned to Peng's shed.

Not too long after Peng and I got into the cave, several enemy airplanes came and raided Taeyudong. Without even circling, they bombed Peng's shed directly and heavily. Some of the napalm bombs hit the shed, and at once it was on fire. From the cave, we saw a big fire flaming up. The napalm bombs had intense burning power, able even to melt metals. In only one or two minutes Peng's shed was burned to the ground. Cheng Pu, one of the staff who had stayed in the shed, was able to get out with a little burn on his face. Mao Anying and Gao Ruixin, however, could not make it and both died in the fire.[8]

After the airplanes left, Peng came back to the site. He looked at the two burned bodies with a heavy heart.

Peng's shed was totally destroyed. Yet several of his security guards who stayed in the basement during the air raid were not hurt at all. Peng did not speak a word during that whole day. He sat quietly in the antiaircraft cave. By evening, he still had said nothing but sat in the cave, staring blankly. I walked to him and said, "Commander Peng, it is dinner time."

He grasped my hands and said to me, "Big Hong, I think you are a good person."

"I am a good guy, not a bad guy."

"I would be history if you had not been here today."

"That is right. This morning I asked your guards to bring your comforter. You still tried to stop them doing that and said it was all right. If you had not taken the comforter with you, you would have nothing to cover you tonight."

"You saved the old man's life today."

"So now you won't yell at us when we are doing antiaircraft shelter construction."

Again, Peng was buried quietly in thought. After quite a while, he sighed and said, "Why did Anying have to be killed by the bombing?" Mao Anying had been Peng's secretary and Russian language translator. Supremely gifted, smart, and capable, he was only twenty-eight years old when he died. His death was terribly unfortunate.

MEETINGS WITH PREMIER ZHOU

After the Fourth Campaign started in late January 1951, our logistical supplies to the front became extremely limited.[9] Li Juikui, chief of the NEMR Logistics Department, was in charge of the CPVF's rear supply and support services based in China. At that difficult time, Li came to Korea and visited the CPVF General Headquarters at Kumhwa. His mission was to identify the problems and look for possible solutions.

The NEMR Logistics Department was far away from the Korean front. The department established only a small office at the front headed by Zhang Mingyuan and Du Zheheng. They had a small staff and a transceiver, moving with the CPVF Headquarters. The small staff could hardly meet the huge demands of large-scale, modern warfare.

Li Juikui had been a senior commander in the PLA logistics service for many years, and he was also the key officer in the NEMR Logistics Department. After Li arrived in Korea, Commander Peng discussed with me that he wanted to keep Li at the CPVF Headquarters on the front in order to strengthen its logistical command and service.

A few days after Li arrived at the front, however, he injured his back. On that particular day, Li had gone to a field survey by car. The roads had been bombed by enemy airplanes, and his car struck a bomb crater so hard that he sprained his back and could not move. We had to send him back to Northeast China. Otherwise, we could have carried out our decision to keep Li at the front. Before this accident, Commander Peng talked with me several times about his idea that our own logistics headquarters would be set up in Korea for the Chinese Volunteers. The fact that Li could not stay at the front finally impelled Peng to decide to establish the CPVF Logistics Department on our own.

One day in late April 1951, toward the end of the first period in the Fifth Campaign, Peng phoned me while I was supervising preparations for a frontal supply delivery at the second depot in Namjongri. He asked me to return to the General Headquarters in Kongsudong immediately. After hanging up the phone, I rushed back, but it was almost evening before I got there. As soon as I walked into his cave, Peng said to me loudly, "Old Hong, you must make a trip back to China immediately."

"Go back now?" I asked, certainly surprised.

Peng walked around the cave with his hands behind his back. The candlelight threw the shadow of his body onto the walls. "Our party's Central Committee, the CMC, and our State Council are deeply concerned about the Volunteers' logistical supply and support service." Peng turned around and looked at me with sparkling eyes: "You must make a trip back to Beijing and report to Vice Chairman Zhou about the CPVF logistical situation."

Indeed, it was absolutely necessary, I said to myself, to let the CCP Central Committee and the CMC know the real situation of the logistics service at the front.

In the Korean War, the American army clearly relied on its air superiority. Its air force bombed all important targets to the point of ruin in northern Korea, including cities, villages, factories, train stations, and bridges. Many small groups of its fighter-bombers attacked around the clock. The airplanes flew at very low altitudes along the roads and valleys, searching and raiding day and night without missing one person, a single vehicle, or even a wisp of cooking smoke.

North Korea has many mountains and rivers. Its railroad lines were built mostly along the coastal lines with very few tracks in the central regions. The highways in North Korea were built mostly in a north-south direction, with a few east-west ones. They ran along the mountains across the rivers with many sharp curves and steep hills. Moreover, most of the highways ran parallel with the railroads. Throughout the Korean War, when one transportation point was raided, both railroad and highway systems were devastated. The road systems in North Korea did not suit wartime transportation at all.

The Chinese expeditionary force's supply transportation largely depended on trucks. The Americans knew this and therefore exploited it as one of our weak points. Destroying CPVF rear transportation lines became one of their important military operations in the war. As a result, our logistical transportation system encountered extreme difficulties. For example, when the Fourth Transportation Regiment of the Third Logistics Depot entered Korea, the officers and truck drivers were inexperienced. All their trucks bunched together during one air raid, causing seventy-three trucks to be destroyed by enemy planes.

The war in Korea was complicated and constantly changing. Our troops advanced fast. In the First Campaign, we fought southward all the way to the Chongchon River. Then we reached the Thirty-eighth Parallel during our Second Campaign. The Third Campaign moved our front line south to the thirty-seventh parallel. Thus, our transportation lines rapidly became longer and longer. After the Fourth and during the Fifth Campaign, our frontline troops were doubled and redoubled. Thus our logistical supply and rear support services to the front became more and more difficult to operate.

Facing such serious difficulties, the CPVF Party Committee explored all kinds of possible measures. The committee kept enlarging the size of the CPVF logistical forces. It also adjusted the organizational network in order to be able to supply the front. The new supply network consisted of a chain of frontal service depots. Because of our experience with the frontal service depots' chain during the Liberation War, new depots were established right away wherever our troops moved. Meanwhile, the CPVF logistical service units at all levels shifted their major operations from daytime to nighttime in order to gain efficiency and reduce the losses under enemy airplanes' wanton and indiscriminate bombings. But whatever we tried, our logistical system was still extremely difficult to maintain because of our quick and deep advances and the enemy's savage air raids.

Now [in late April 1951] Peng asked me to go back to Beijing and report the CPVF logistics situation to Vice Chairman Zhou. This was a timely decision indeed. We needed to let our top leaders in the Central Committee have firsthand information about the front. We needed, most urgently, to have a nationwide mobilization of manpower, materiel, and finance.

Peng interrupted my thinking and continued, "During your stay in Beijing, you need to report to Premier Zhou our reasoning in establishing the CPVF Logistics Department."

"Yes," I answered, "I understand."

After packing only a few things for the trip, I left the CPVF Headquarters by jeep that night with my security guard. There was always heavy traffic at night during the war. That night our jeep moved slowly, stopped many times by traffic jams. Because of the darkness, narrow roads, and no headlights, our jeep almost turned over into a ditch. At dawn, the enemy airplanes came to raid the road. Some of them dived, firing on our jeep. Thanks to timely antiaircraft fire from the top of the hill, we passed through safely.

Arriving in Beijing, I was first taken to the CMC's guest house at Shuaifuyuan. Acting Chief of the General Staff Nie Rongzhen met me there and said, "Vice Chairman Zhou is waiting for you. Please go to report to him right away."

At that moment I was wearing the Volunteer uniform and was covered with dust and mud since I had traveled back day and night from the front without halting to rest. But I did not have time to change my clothes and rushed to Zhou's office in Zhongnanhai as soon as possible.

Zhou was waiting for me at the door of his office. I saluted him. He held my hands firmly and said, "Comrade Hong Xuezhi, you must have had a hectic trip!"

"You have been working very hard, Vice Chairman Zhou," I answered.

Zhou was very busy, and he had a weary look at that time. To provide the Volunteers on the front with more parched flour, he kept on participating in preparing it with his staff while fully engaged with his governmental duties. After CPVF commanders and soldiers in Korea heard about this, they were too touched to express their appreciation. When they ate the parched flour, their morale was higher, though.

Zhou let me sit down and asked with concern, "How is the combat situation at the front?"

I briefed him about the frontal situation. Then I emphasized, "After fighting several campaigns, we have the worst situation [yet] because of no air control in Korea. Our army has suffered extremely heavy losses to enemy air raids. The enemy airplanes normally raid us day and night. During the daytime, the fighters and bombers dive and fire whenever and wherever they see a person on the ground. They drop napalm bombs, time bombs, chemical mines, and tire-piercing devices. During nighttime, there are the night bombers, called 'black widows' by our soldiers. They do not circle but drop bombs everywhere, causing big fires to slow down our troops' operations."

Zhou said to me seriously, "The American imperialists bully us into a state of utmost frenzy. But they never expected that regardless of their air and naval predominance, we could fight back all the way to the Thirty-eight Parallel. It is the first time in the world that the American army is being defeated. The Volunteers, however, must work out some methods to deal with enemy air bombings in order to reduce our losses."

"The CPVF Headquarters," I continued, "has already reinforced the antiaircraft artillery troops in Korea with the help of the PLA forces in China. We also increased the number of air-raid warning posts at key points. Our soldiers are now depending on our valiant fighting spirit. For example, when our truck drivers faced an enemy bombing, some of them drove their trucks at full speed. They drove without stopping and raised up a 100-meter-long dust wall to confuse the enemy pilots, who did not know what was going on. The pilots cried on their radio that the Communist army's trucks launched smoke bombs."

Zhou smiled and commented, "The heroic spirit of our soldiers beats the 'America phobia.' Our comrades have contributed their blood and lives. They are educating 400 million Chinese people." He paused for a while and then asked, "Is it possible for the American army to land in China? We are not sure about it right now. However, the bigger the victory we will achieve on the Korean front, the smaller the possibility of an American landing in China. Thus, we must win the war on the Korean front. The CMC is considering sending our airplanes to Korea as soon as possible. Certainly, we do not have many airplanes. A small number of our planes may cause the enemy planes some troubles and boost our troops' morale."

"All the commanders and soldiers at the front are looking forward to seeing our airplanes sent to Korea," I said.

Zhou continued, "China has airplanes. Many countries that are friendly with China have airplanes. But it is not the time for our airplanes to participate in the war. You as the CPVF deputy commander should know it very well."

I agreed with Zhou. Airplanes need fuel. Our present transportation facilities on the front could not meet these needs. Even if we stopped all logistical shipments to deliver fuel, our transportation still could not provide enough for the airplanes. It was true that the transportation, rear supply, and logistics service determined the scale of the war.

Zhou then asked me, "What are some major problems of the CPVF logistical system?"

I reported to him: "Our transportation lines are very long. The Volunteers do not have enough antiaircraft forces. Our road transportation lines are as long as several hundred kilometers. In the Third Campaign, for example, there were 300 or 400 kilometers between our frontal supply stations and rear logistics supply bases. As our long transportation lines were weakly defended, our frontal needs and rear supplies became separated. Moreover, our logistics units are highly decentralized, and they do not have an independent communications network. They quite often lose contact with CPVF combat troops."

Zhou agreed with me and said, "This is why some foreign military experts say that the logistics service is the bottleneck of modern war. We must strengthen the

CPVF logistics service. The CMC is considering attaching more antiaircraft and communication units to the Volunteers' logistical forces."

"The CMC's decision is absolutely correct," I responded. "The major problem currently existing in our logistics is that supplies are not on time. During the past three campaigns, our soldiers defeated the enemy despite their being hungry and freezing. If they had had better supplies, they could have won bigger victories. Our soldiers now have three worries: first, they are worried about no food to eat; second, no bullets to shoot; and third, nobody to take care of them after they are wounded."

Zhou was listening with a serious look, sometimes taking down notes on paper with his pencil.

"At the present," I continued, "enemy airplanes participating in the Korean War have increased from 1,000 to more than 2,000.[10] Their missions have shifted from general to concentrated bombing on our transportation lines. Their napalm bombs are the most destructive to our warehouses and other logistics facilities. The enemy also has sent a large number of spies to our rear areas. They radio their airplanes to direct their bombings. For instance, on April 8, the enemy airplanes dropped many napalm bombs on our storage station at Samdung. During this one bombing, we lost a huge amount of supplies in eighty-four railroad cars that were burned down, including 2,870,000 *jins* of cooked and raw grain, 330,000 *jins* of cooking oil, 408,000 sets of uniforms and shirts, 190,000 pairs of shoes, and large amounts of other supplies. Only 60 to 70 percent of our supplies shipped out from the rear can reach the front. About 30 to 40 percent of our supplies are destroyed by air raids and bombings during transportation between the rear and the front."

Zhou heard about this serious situation with a severe countenance.

"Our Volunteers have adopted many ingenious methods for dealing with these situations," I added.

He looked at me, puzzled.

I explained: "Before we started each battle, first, we would fully load our trucks and horse wagons. Second, we would increase the amount of our soldiers' backpacks. Usually each combat soldier would carry a total of supplies up to sixty or even seventy *jins* [seventy to eighty lbs.]. This is necessary and the only secure way that our frontal troops can survive and fight in the war. They move so fast that our logistics become more and more difficult, and the transportation cannot follow their movements quickly enough."

"Our soldiers have been fighting very hard," Zhou said.

"Though they have to go through hardships," I continued, "they felt more secure carrying supplies on their own backs than waiting for the logistical service to send the supplies from the rear."

"Is it true that the American army often destroys its own logistical materials left behind them?"

"Yes, it is true," I answered. "So it is difficult for us to seize supplies from the enemy on the front. Because of this, we adopted the third method: borrowing grain and food from local Korean people after getting permission from local governments."

"Can this method solve some of the problems?"

"Yes, it can. But it does not work in the areas between the Thirty-eighth and thirty-seventh parallels. These areas were occupied by the enemy for a long time before we took over, and it severely exploited them. The Korean people there did not know anything about the Chinese Volunteers. Thus there was a no-grain area in a 300-*li* wide region.[11] Our method of borrowing local grain and food became very difficult in this no-grain area."

Zhou asked with great anxiety, "Have you taken any measures to cope with the difficulties in the no-grain area?"

"Yes, we have," I continued. "Commander Peng asked us to try everything to solve the problem. Our major method is to improve our transportation. We built up multiple transportation lines. Meanwhile, we broke down our large company-size truck fleet into multiple truck transportation units. Then, our truck drivers divided each road into several parts among themselves. Thus each driver covers only one part, or the same section, of the road every day. He is able to become more familiar with the road conditions and the enemy airplanes' routine in his own section. Moreover, we dug anti–air raid shelters for trucks along the transportation lines in order to reduce our losses."

"Do these methods work well?"

"Yes," I answered. "They have dramatically increased our transportation efficiency."

Zhou said, "The War to Resist America and Aid Korea has raised many new questions for our army's rear supply and support service. You should carefully study the characteristics of the logistics service in modern war. The American imperialists invaded Korea in a bullying manner as if nobody on earth could beat them. They claimed that they would take all of Korea by last Christmas. In fact, however, they are not winning the Korean War. On the contrary, our army fought back to the thirty-seventh parallel. With inferior weapons, we defeat America, which has naval and air dominance and advanced equipment."

He continued, "Our victory in Korea has greatly inspired the peoples in China and all over the world. Our fighting in Korea has tremendously assisted in the anti-imperialist struggles in many countries. During the American Civil War, with inferior weapons, the North defeated the South. My analysis is that America dare not land on China's mainland. Afraid of expanding the war, Britain and France agreed that 'an invasion of China means a strategic failure.' With the Korean people by our side, we must overcome the difficulties and not be afraid of sacrifice. We will certainly defeat the American imperialists, even though they are armed to the teeth."

Then Zhou asked me whether the drivers sent from China adjusted to wartime conditions on the Korean front.

I answered, "Those drivers are very brave. But without knowing much about Korea, they have suffered heavy casualties. So we first gave them appointments as assistant drivers. After they gained some experience in dealing with enemy air raids, we then transferred them to the position of full drivers, step by step."

At this point, Zhou asked, "Do you have some other things to discuss?"

"Yes. Commander Peng asked me to report another important matter to you."

"What matter?"

"About establishing the CPVF's Logistics Department."

"Oh?" Zhou avowed a strong interest. "Tell me about your idea."

"Through the Korean War," I continued, "Commander Peng and other commanders have gradually recognized the important function of the logistics service in modern war. Modern war is often three-dimensional; it is fought in the air, land, and sea at the same time. It is also fought in both the front and the rear at the same time. In a modern war, situations change fast, battlegrounds expand without limit, and the costs of manpower and materiel are extremely high. At present, most European and American forces adopt a strategy of macrologistics: the frontal headquarters takes care of supplies within 50 *lis* of the front; the rear headquarters takes care of everything behind 50 *lis* from the front. Modern war is not only fought at the front but also in the rear.

"The American army now is conducting a total coast-to-coast bombing over our rear areas. It is fighting the Korean War in our rear. This determines not only the scale of the war we fight on the front but also the victory or failure of the battle there. We can secure our frontal victory only when we win the war in the rear. The CPVF logistics must take the challenge of the rear war. We need the CMC to reinforce us with more air defense forces, communications units, railroad engineering troops, and other engineering forces. We are organizing a campaign of combined forces in the rear war. We need to establish the command headquarters— the CPVF Logistics Department—to unify our command of the combined forces in the rear war. We will supply our frontal troops better through our rear combat, and we will win the war in the rear while supplying the front."

The premier nodded his head while listening and said, "Your idea is very good and very important. The CMC will discuss your request and make its decision as soon as possible."

When I finished my report, I stood up and was about to leave.

Zhou said to me, "It will be May 1 very soon. Labor Day. You can prepare yourself and come up to the Tiananmen tower [for the celebration]."

I looked at my old wornout CPVF uniform and said with a smile, "I cannot go to Tiananmen looking so."

"Why not? Your uniform is 'good looking.' You represent the Volunteers."

I smiled, still trying to decline his invitation.

"OK, let us do it this way," Zhou said. "I will tell Yang Lisan to make a new CPVF uniform for you."

On May 1, the people in Beijing held a grand parade to show the unprecedented unity and strength of our nation.

After I arrived at the Tiananmen tower, a staff member informed me, "Chairman Mao Zedong will meet with you."

"When is the meeting going to be?" I asked.

"You wait for a while. I will come to fetch you when it is time."

A little bit later, I was brought to the guest lobby of the Tiananmen tower.

Chairman Mao and other leaders of the CCP Central Committee met me there. I raised my hand in salute when I saw Mao.

Mao told the other leaders, "Comrade Hong Xuezhi is a deputy commander of the Volunteers. He came back from the Korean front and represents the Volunteers here."

Mao asked me, "How is Commander Peng's health?"

"Commander Peng is very well," I answered.

Mao said, "You are beating an enemy who has airplanes, tanks, heavy artillery pieces, and naval superiority. The enemy is armed to the teeth."

Commander in Chief Zhu said, "You are fighting a real modern war."

Mao continued, "You need to carefully learn [from] the experience of each battle." Then he asked, "Did the problems you came back to report have some solutions?"

"I have already reported them to the premier," I said. "The premier has made some arrangements. He will discuss the problems with me again."

Before returning to Korea, I went to see the premier one more time. We discussed the existing problems on the Korean front and possible solutions.

The CMC asked me to return to the Korean front with Chen Geng (Ch'en Geng) and Gan Siqi. Chen was appointed as the CPVF's deputy commander; Gan took appointments as CPVF vice political commissar and director of the Political Department. I left Beijing with Gan for Dalian, where Chen was being treated for his illness. But when we arrived there, Chen had not yet regained his health. I rushed back to Korea with Gan.

Around 6:00 A.M. we arrived at Sipiripo, south of Pyongyang. The sun had just risen, and we planned to have our breakfast there before we continued our trip. After we parked our car next to a bridge, enemy airplanes came to raid. I thought that if the planes destroyed the bridge, we could not cross the river. At that moment, the Korean army's antiaircraft artillery began to fire. After a heavy shellfire, the enemy lost four planes, the rest escaping. The air raid did not cause much damage to the bridge; we rushed to cross it and continued our trip. Back at the General Headquarters, I reported in detail to Commander Peng and members of the standing committee of the CPVF Party Committee about my meetings with Chairman Mao and Premier Zhou in Beijing.

ESTABLISHING THE CPVF LOGISTICS DEPARTMENT

When we were fighting our Fourth and Fifth Campaigns [February–April 1951], we had the most difficult and complicated period with our logistical service in the Korean War.[12] During this time, the Volunteers suffered the heaviest casualties, and many of our commanders and soldiers experienced the worst starvation of the war.

After I went to Beijing and reported these circumstances to Premier Zhou, the CMC gave serious consideration to the situation. During the late phase of the Fifth Campaign, the CMC sent a special group from Beijing to the CPVF General Headquarters, including Chief of the PLA General Logistics Headquarters Yang Lisan, Deputy Chief Zhang Lingbin, Commander of the PLA Air Force Liu Yalou, and Commander of the PLA Artillery Force Chen Xilian. They came to the front to find out the specific problems in the CPVF logistical service, to discuss how to provide more support, and to help the CPVF strengthen this service. With the Fifth Campaign ongoing at that time, we were in the middle of fierce fighting. The enemy was moving up from the south.

Peng emphasized to Yang, Zhang, Liu, and Chen that the most serious problem was with supplies: "The problem is that our troops on the front run out of food and munitions. We have to strengthen our logistical service in order to solve this problem. So our pressing matter of the moment is to establish the CPVF's own logistics department immediately. We cannot solve other problems properly without settling this matter first. I have already asked Hong Xuezhi to report this matter to Premier Zhou in April. I now want to raise this question again."

One may ask why, if the establishment of the CPVF Logistics Department were really important, did we not create it when we entered Korea in October 1950? Why did we raise this question six months later? There are numerous identifiable reasons involving the way the war developed and our own subjective understanding of it, but I shall explain the major reasons.

After [the PLA Thirteenth Army Group] moved to Northeast China [in August 1950], the NEMR Logistics Department took charge of our logistics. In early October the CCP Central Committee made the final decision to dispatch the Chinese Volunteers to Korea. On October 19, we entered Korea. There was only one-half month between Beijing's decision and our engagement in the war. Obviously, we had too little time on such short notice to organize a CPVF logistical department that would have the capacity to supply and support a major force of approximately 300,000 men to engage in a foreign war.

In fact, the NEMR Logistics Department was just established in August 1950. After the Korean War broke out in June, NEMR hastily organized the department in order to secure supplies for NEBDA. From the very beginning, the NEMR Logistics Department was poorly organized and had a serious problem of personnel shortage. At the time when the CPVF was established, the NEMR Logistics Department and its branch headquarters and service stations had a shortage of more than 1,560 managing officers, about 54 percent of their full strength. The CMC then could not solve this serious problem of personnel shortage. The commission apparently did not have the manpower to organize another logistics department for the CPVF in such a short period.

Before the CPVF entered Korea, our anticipated combat area there was very close to China. Then the enemy occupied the Pyongyang area and advanced northward fast from different directions toward the Chinese-Korean borders. With the front lines approaching close to our border, there were no major problems for the NEMR Logistics Department in taking care of the CPVF from its bases in China. It was mainly due to these factors that Chairman Mao made it clear in his order to the CPVF on October 8, 1950, that NEMR should take care of the Volunteers' logistical needs.

To carry out Mao's order, NEMR selected Deputy Chief of Logistics Zhang Mingyuan, Northeastern People's Government's Agriculture Minister Du Zheheng, and a few other officials to organize a front headquarters of the NEMR Logistics Department (called Frontal Logistics). This moved into Korea with the Chinese Volunteers and was in charge of logistical supplies and support services to the frontal areas.

During the first six months [after the CPVF's entry], the war developed and changed fast. The situation gradually convinced us that our logistics system hardly met our wartime demands in Korea.

When the Volunteers entered Korea, the enemy employed 1,100 different airplanes in the war. Most of these were used to raid and bomb our army's rear areas, with only a small number deployed directly to support its combat troops. We had more than 1,300 transportation vehicles when we entered Korea. During the first week after our entry, we lost 217 vehicles, nearly 17 percent of the total. About 82.5 percent of the lost vehicles were destroyed by enemy airplanes.

During the first three campaigns, a massive amount of supplies shipped out by the NEMR Logistics Department could not reach our frontal troops on time. Most were stuck in stockpiles on the banks of the Yalu River or along the railroads because of enemy air raids.

After the Fourth Campaign started, the number of enemy airplanes engaged in the war increased from 1,100 to 1,700. Their main target shifted from our rear areas in general to our key transportation lines. The only three bridges on the Yalu River—Ji'an, Changdian Hekou, and Andong—were bombed, one after another. The major bridges on the Taeryong River, the Chongchon River, and the Taedong River in North Korea were bombed frequently. We repaired the bridges at night only to see them bombed again the next day. We suffered heavy losses of vehicles and logistical supplies. Thus, the advantage of our short supply lines and convenient transportation that we had had earlier disappeared.

After the Third Campaign, the CMC decided to rotate the PLA armies. Before the rotation, it had replenished the CPVF with new Volunteer recruits. Later the commission considered the Korean battleground as a good military school in which all the PLA armies through rotation could be trained and toughened to gain experience in modern warfare. Thus during the Fourth Campaign, a large number of the PLA armies entered Korea to join the CPVF. By mid-April 1951, the CPVF had sixteen infantry armies in Korea totaling forty-eight infantry divisions, plus seven artillery divisions, four antiaircraft artillery divisions, four tank regiments, nine engineering regiments, three railroad engineering divisions, and other supporting troops. The total of the CPVF troops numbered 950,000 men, about three times more than the troops we had deployed when we first entered Korea. As a result, our expenditure of munitions and fuel rocketed upward, especially with the reinforcement of technical and mechanized troops. The NEMR Logistics Department tried hard to manage the supplies for a million-man force, but obviously the job far exceeded its ability.

During the Fourth and Fifth Campaigns, the CPVF troops were mostly engaged within an area about 120 to 150 kilometers wide between the Thirty-eighth and thirty-seventh parallels. Commander Peng pointed out at the fifth expanded meeting of the CPVF Party Committee on April 6, 1951, "It becomes our major problem now: how to overcome difficulties in this 300-*li* no-grain area south of the 38ᵗʰ Parallel." In the second part of the Fifth Campaign, our troops fought mainly defensive battles and seized little enemy materiel. Even though they captured some U.S.–made weapons and equipment, they could not use them because the troops that had recently come to Korea had changed their arms to Soviet-made weapons. Everything they needed on the front depended on the rear logistical supplies.

In the Fifth Campaign, our army's daily expenditures of war materiel increased to 550 tons, but our capacity to supply and transport it could meet only half the needs. As a result, our troops had to stop their attacks in the first and second parts of the campaign because they did not receive food and munitions. In the second part, for example, our troops had to stop their advance after they eliminated the enemy in Hyonri, halting their charge for two days to wait for supplies.

By then we had already sensed that the enemy was not only fighting us on the front but also wanted to extend the war to our rear areas. It became increasingly necessary and urgent for us to establish the Chinese Volunteers' Logistics Department in order to win the Korean War in both the front and the rear.

Yang, Liu, and other comrades from Beijing believed that Peng and other CPVF commanders had good reason to request establishing a CPVF's logistics department. After returning to Beijing, they reported our request to Chairman Mao, Premier Zhou, Chief of General Staff Xu Xiangqian (Hsu Hsiang-ch'ian), Acting Chief Nie Rongzhen, and other leaders in the CMC. The commission accepted our request and made a quick decision. In its order to us, it decided "to organize the Logistics Department of the CPVF General Headquarters between Andong [in China] and the site of the CPVF Headquarters [in North Korea]."

In early May the CPVF Party Committee systematically reviewed the experience and the lessons we had learned in logistics during our strategic counterattack period. Basing its action on this review, the committee issued Directives on the Logistical Supplies Problems on May 3, which I drafted. Fully recognizing the important role of logistics in modern war, the directive pointed out that

> modern war is a competition of manpower and materiel. In the Korean War, especially fighting the American army equipped with advanced technology, we cannot possibly expect a victory over the enemy without minimum logis-

tical supplies. We must realize that our logistics task in the war is extremely difficult and complicated. The enemy has air control. We do not have enough transportation vehicles. All of the war materials, including tanks, big artillery pieces, and engineering equipment which a million-man army needs, must be transported from China to Korea. Merely depending on the efforts of our comrades in the logistical service, we cannot possibly accomplish this kind of arduous task. We need the support for the task from our entire army. Thus, logistics has the first priority in all of our tasks at the present time."

It was a dark evening on May 14. Around 8:00 P.M. we met in the CPVF General Headquarters, a small wooden cabin at the bottom of the hill at Kongsudong, which had many mining caves. Commander Peng called for a standing committee meeting of the CPVF Party Committee; members attending were Peng, Deng, Han, Gan, Xie, Du, and I. We discussed how the CPVF Logistics Department was to be established and how its personnel would be selected.

Peng said at the beginning of the meeting, "There is one thing we need to decide upon first. When the CMC decided to organize the Volunteers' Logistics Department, it required that the department should be operated under the command and instructions of the CPVF General Headquarters. The CMC now sends another telegram to me. It requires that a CPVF deputy commander should hold a concurrent position as the chief of the CPVF Logistics Department. Now let us make a decision first: who is going to hold this concurrent post as the logistics chief?"

After hearing Peng's words, I had a foreboding that it was probably I who would take this post. The Volunteers had three deputy commanders. Since the CPVF had entered Korea, I, as one of them, had been in charge of logistics. Neither of the other two deputy commanders, Deng and Han, had been responsible for logistical work before. If we had to make our choice among the deputy commanders, who else could take the position except me?

But from the bottom of my heart I did not want to take the post, for two reasons: first, I had been a commander for combat operations and political work in our army for a long time. I was very much at ease with both jobs, especially the combat operations, but not with logistics. Second, logistics in the Korean War were so difficult and complicated that I was afraid of being unable to do a good job. If the logistics were bungled, how could I justify myself? I did not want to take the position, but meanwhile I did not feel it proper to ask the other deputy commanders to assume the responsibility. I just sat there quietly.

Although I sat there, the other committee members had a lively discussion. Deng, Han, Xie, and Du gave their suggestions one after another, all saying that "Old Hong" should do this job.

After staying silent for so long, I could not keep from saying, "I cannot take the concurrent position as the chief of the CPVF Logistics Department."

"Why not?" Peng asked.

"You asked me to take charge of logistics before, but I have not done a good job. You now ask me to take the post of logistics commander; I could hardly do it better. I can do anything else except logistics. You'd better find somebody else."

Peng seemed rather unhappy when he heard what I said and asked, "Who will do this job if you don't want it?"

"Comrade Deng Hua may take it," I said. "He is an excellent commander."

"No, I can't," Deng refused immediately. "I am assisting Commander Peng with military operations. I am also the vice political commissar, being concurrently in charge of political work. How can I look after logistics in addition to my main jobs?"

"Well, may we ask Comrade Han Xianchu to be in charge of the logistics?" I said, turning the question to Han.

Han declined my offer right away, saying, "I can't do this either. I always run to the front, checking and supervising the frontal operations. How can I take a job of commanding the logistics in the rear areas?"

I insisted by saying, "Then we can ask somebody to be sent from China."

Peng became more unhappy, knitting his brows, and asked me, "Who can be sent over here?"

"It could be either Comrades Li Jiukui [then NEMR's political commissar] or Zhou Chunquan [chief of the NEMR Logistics Department]."

"No, they can't." Peng shook his head at my suggestion and said, "They are the key figures in charge of the logistical service in China. That is also a tough task."

"We could ask Yang Lisan [chief of the General Logistics Headquarters] to send somebody over. I can be that person's assistant."

"You don't want to do it?" Peng asked loudly, striking the table hard after he saw my obstinacy. "OK, you don't have to do it."

"Who is going to do this job?" I asked him.

"I will!" he said, "You can replace me in commanding our troops!"

Seeing Commander Peng lose his temper, I softened and said, "Chief Peng, you said this [as if it were] an order from the commander. I have to obey it."

"Did I give you an order? Did I challenge you? Or actually are you challenging me?" he asked angrily.

Deng then said to me, "Old Hong, you should do this job. You have been taking care of this business since we entered Korea. If somebody else now takes over, he won't know where to start. It would not be easy for anyone else, don't you agree?"

"Yes, I have been doing this," I answered. "But I did not do a good job."

"Look, don't start this again!" Deng also got angry with me and said loudly, "You did not do a good job; somebody else might not do a good job either."

I came to realize that I could not decline the position any longer and that I would bring this matter to a deadlock if I continued to resist. So I began to bargain with them, saying, "I may take this post as the logistics commander. But I have some conditions. I will do it as long as you agree to my conditions."

Sensing my compromising attitude, Peng softened his tone immediately and asked, "What are your conditions?"

"My conditions are very simple," I said. "First, you must quickly replace me if I am not very successful with this job. Find another comrade fast who is more able than I am. Second, I am a combat commander, and I like military operational jobs better. After the War to Resist America and Aid Korea and after I return to China, I would like to resume a commanding position rather than a logistics one."

Listening with a smile, Peng answered, "Just these conditions? Sure, no problem. I approve your requests. I thought you were going to ask for something else."

Then Peng asked Deng and the others, "Do you agree with these conditions?" They all expressed their agreement.

I told them, "If the Old Chief and the comrades of the [CPVF] party's standing committee all go with my conditions, I agree to take the concurrent position as the logistics commander."

Thus, at this meeting the Volunteers' Party Committee made the final decision to appoint me as the commander of the CPVF Logistics Department. After the meeting, the committee reported its decision to the CMC.

In June 1951 the Chinese Volunteers' Logistics Department was founded on the basis of the former frontal headquarters of the NEMR Logistics Department. At that moment I requested Yang Di, deputy director of the Combat Operations Division in the CPVF Headquarters, to "recommend a couple of cadres who will transfer with me to the CPVF Logistics Department." Yang told me, "Liu Hongzhou and Zhao Nanqi are two very capable staff in our division. I can ask them to go with you." So they did. The CMC approved without any delay the committee's decision and its Directives on the CPVF's Logistics Problems on receiving the report.

On May 19, the CMC issued its Decision on Strengthening the Volunteers' Logistics Tasks:

> The Logistics Department of the Chinese People's Volunteers Force should be established immediately. It will command and manage all the Chinese logistics units and facilities within Korea (including the railroads, highways, and military transportation). The CPVF Logistics Department is under the direct command of the CPVF's leading commanders.
>
> The Logistics Department from now on will take charge of all the CPVF's logistics forces, including supporting troops and rear supply units (such as the engineering corps, artillery units, public security, radio communication, highway transportation, railroad engineering, construction forces, and hospitals). Their operational units, party committees, political organizations, and military commands will all be established under the command of the CPVF Logistics Department. The instructions and supplies to these forces will also be provided by the Logistics Department.

The CMC appointed me as the commander of the department, Zhou Chunquan as the political commissar, Zhang Mingyuan as the deputy commander, Du Zheheng as the vice political commissar, and Qi Yuanwo (later Li Xuesan) as the director of its Political Division. The CMC's decision was important and became a significant document in the historical development of the Volunteers' logistics. Linking theory with practice, the decision identified important functions and the position of logistics in modern war. Having extended our mission's scale and increased logistical authority, the decision indicated a key transition in our logistics from a single service to combined forces.

The Chinese Volunteers badly needed large numbers of weapons and munitions with the rapid development of the war, especially after our second wave of rotating troops entered Korea in large numbers. On May 25, 1951, during the last period of the Fifth Campaign, Chairman Mao sent Chief of General Staff Xu Xiangqian to the Soviet Union to purchase arms. Xu led a delegation to Moscow to talk with the Soviet government about purchasing Soviet-made weapons and equipment to arm sixty Chinese divisions. The talks, which started in early June, lasted until mid-October. Eventually, the delegation reached an agreement with the Soviets. Since the Soviet Union did not have sufficient transportation to deliver the arms at once, it would ship us arms for only sixteen infantry divisions in 1951. About one-third of the arms for the remaining forty-four infantry divisions would be delivered annually until 1954.

During our mobile warfare period, the Chinese Volunteers' logistical supplies were provided in a pattern that we had formulated in the late phase of the Chinese civil war. Following our combat directions, the branch headquarters set up a series of logistical depots. They supplied the CPVF troops through a chain of supply and maintenance points that, following the troops, extended and connected the rear with the front. This system, however, did not work well because the Korean terrain was very narrow, and it was hardly possible to divide responsibilities among the separate logistical services for the army groups, each individual army, and branch headquarters. As a result, administrative organizations overlapped, the logistical services were not systematically arranged, and the rear in a battle [tactical rear area] and one in a campaign were not well structured. Thus, each logistical service depot or department could not play a positive role by itself. And there was even some management confusion, such as depending on others and unnecessarily duplicating supplies.

As we entered the positional warfare period, the CPVF Logistics Department was established. By that time, the troops that this department was to supply increased to seventeen infantry armies, six artillery divisions, four antiaircraft artillery divisions, one tank division, and more than 60,000 horses. Meanwhile, weapons and equipment became more and more sophisticated. The task of our logistical service became even tougher, the problems more prominent. Commander Peng was worried a great deal about this situation, and I certainly felt uneasy, even when eating and sleeping.

What kind of system and methods could we use to improve supply services for the Chinese Volunteers in Korea?

I visited many logistics offices in armies, divisions, and regiments and made trips to the front lines. I reviewed our experience during the mobile warfare period with its service depot chain and branch headquarters' supply points. Then, taking into account our strategy and the military situation in the rear areas, I worked out a plan for our supply system that combined locational supply with each unit's supply.

My plan was based on the consideration of a new development in the war. After we turned to positional warfare, the front line became relatively stable, our branch headquarters were strengthened a great deal, we improved our transportation and communication methods, and the storage of supplies increased with each passing day. I reported my plan to Peng. Accepting that this change was necessary, he ordered the plan to be implemented immediately.

The new pattern of our supply system divided the entire rear region in Korea into two parts: campaign [or strategic] rear base, and battle [or tactical] rear area. Our campaign rear base included areas from Northeast China to each army's logistics depot. Our battle rear covered areas from the army's service depot to the divisional and regimental logistics depot.

The CPVF Logistics Department took charge of supplies for the campaign rear region. On the basis of the CPVF's general war plans, its operational directions, troop deployment, lay of the land, road conditions, and our department's own capacity, the department employed the locational supply system. Accordingly, the campaign rear region was divided into several supply locations with established local service depot lines so as to provide supplies to the armies in the location.

We abolished the army group's logistical service. Instead, each army was mainly responsible for providing supplies in the tactical rear areas. The army's supply service used a different approach—the unit supply system, which was different from the locational supply system. Their supplies were provided from the top to the bottom, along with their unit system, or from armies to divisions and then to regiments.

A combination of two-way supply—locational supply and unit supply— formed a new system for our logistics. Our experience thereafter proved that this new system fit in well with Korea's geography and into our transportation and operational situations, and it clearly showed its usefulness.

The locational supply had its advantage. The American imperialists had absolute air and naval predominance and successful experience in landing operations in both World War II and the Korean War. And Korea is a peninsula. Thus the enemy could land on either or both of the coasts anytime in the war. We might have to fight a two- or even three-front war. The newly adopted locational supply method connected each location with the others. They together formed two supply networks in depth in North Korea: one was from the north to the south, or from the rear to the front; the other was from the east to the west, or from one side to another. These networks could not only secure supplies for the frontal troops in battle but also solve the problems in supplying two- or three-front operations.

Locational supply also provided a relatively stable service. Wherever our troops engaged in combat, they could get supplies in the same location. Wherever they moved, they could receive supplies all along the way. Whenever they advanced into a new area, they could receive timely supplies from one of the nearby local service stations. When the front line extended or shortened, our service depot line would be longer or shorter accordingly. As a result, our combat troops now did not have to carry too many supplies themselves during their operations, thereby becoming more flexible and mobile.

Moreover, the service depots no longer had to follow combat troops everywhere and could maintain their own relative stability in one location. This stability possibly helped them discover the routines and activities of enemy air raids and secret agents in that location and familiarized them with the geographical situation, natural resources, and road conditions in the area. This stability also made it possible for them to concentrate their manpower on some rear constructions, such as warehouses, hospitals, highways, and defense works.

The unit supply had its own advantage. After the abolition of the army group's logistical function, we could deliver supplies directly to the armies. The army's supply services no longer needed local logistical offices. This method avoided the problem of many overlapping logistical organizations on the narrow battleground in Korea. Since each army had its own transportation route, the method also solved heavy traffic problems.

Meanwhile, each army's logistics center changed to a first-level supply service center. All the units below the army level employed the unit supply system. Thus, unity between combat command and logistical service in the army was promoted, helping the troops secure flexibility in their tactical rear areas.

Mao Zedong and Peng Dehuai in Beijing, 1951

The Chinese People's Volunteers Force crosses the Yalu River in October 1950

Peng Dehuai and CPVF commanders visit the Korean front in winter 1950

Peng, Kim Il Sung, and other commanders of the CPVF–NKPA Joint Headquarters in Korea

The CPVF troops charge the wreckage of a U.S. Army convoy, 1950

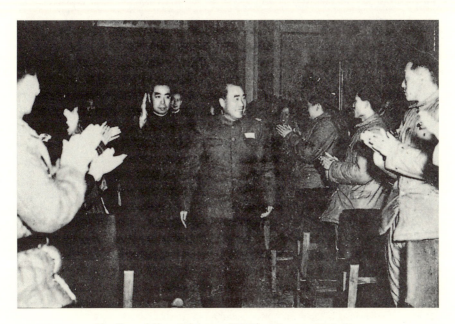

Zhu De and Zhou Enlai meet CPVF logistics representatives

Nie Rongzhen and other marshals in Beijing

A Chinese soldier, 375th Regiment, Forty-second Army, uses a Japanese-made light machine gun to fire at a U.S. airplane in the battle of Ryongduri

The CPVF logistics troops unload supplies from railroad cars

The CPVF troops defend their position

Four American advisers in an ROK division surrender to the troops of the Thirty-ninth Army

Peng and Kim Il Sung at the front

CPVF armored forces cut into the UNC position

A black company, Twenty-fourth Regiment, U.S. Twenty-fifth Infantry Division, surrenders to the 347th Regiment, Thirty-ninth Army

As the advance unit, the 116th Division, Thirty-ninth Army, enters Pyongyang

North Korean women carry munitions on their heads to the CPVF front at night

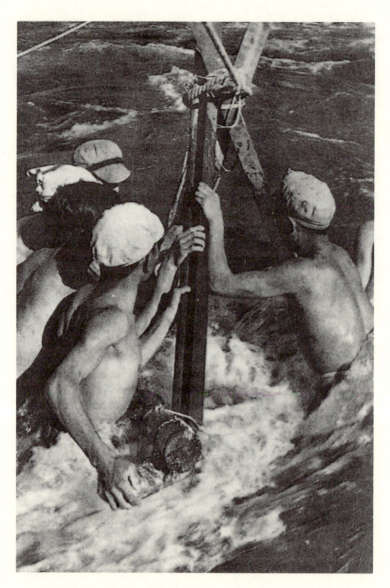

The logistics troops repair a bridge damaged by the UNF air raids

Marshal Xu and the Chinese Arms Purchase Delegation in Moscow

General Yang and his army commanders at the front

The CPVF troops work on tunnel fortifications during trench warfare

The 135th Regiment, Forty-fifth Division, Fifteenth Army, defends Height 597.9 in the battle of Shangganling

The Chinese–North Korean delegation at the Korean truce talks at Kaesong

The POWs of the U.S. Second Infantry Division assemble to march to CPVF/NKPA camps

Peng signs the Korean Armistice agreement at Panmunjom

6

The Purchase of Arms from Moscow

Marshal Xu Xiangqian

Editors' Note: Xu Xiangqian was the chief of the PLA General Staff and vice chairman of the CCP Central Military Commission during the Korean War. In 1951 he made a trip to the Soviet Union to purchase weapons and equipment to arm the Chinese People's Volunteers Force in Korea. In 1955 he became a marshal.

Born in Wutai County, Shanxi Province in 1901, Marshal Xu joined the CCP in 1927 and became one of its military leaders after the party established its own armed forces. During the Chinese civil war, he served as the deputy commander of the Northern Military District and commander and political commissar of the First Army Group. After the founding of the People's Republic of China, he was the chief of the PLA General Staff in 1949, vice chairman of the CMC in 1954, vice chairman of the Chinese People's Revolutionary Military Committee, vice premier in 1965, and defense minister. He died in 1990.

Marshal Xu published his recollections in a combined volume, Lishi de Huigu [History in Retrospect] *(Beijing: PLA Press, 1988). This chapter tells the little-known story of his trip to Moscow during the Korean War after he resumed the leadership of the General Staff, following a two-year sick leave.[1] Xu's recollection reflects the subtle and sometimes difficult PRC–USSR relationships in that period. His vivid description of his trip for more materiel in 1951 will enhance the reader's understanding of that "special relationship."*

MY TRIP TO MOSCOW DURING THE KOREAN WAR

On October 1, 1949, the brightly colored five-starred Red flag slowly rose and fluttered in the breeze over Tiananmen Square.[2] "When the rooster sings, the daylight spreads over the land." The dark rule of old China faced its end, and the Chinese people arose. The birth of the PRC meant that Marxism had won a decisive victory in China, the largest country of the East, with one-quarter of the world's population. This victory had changed the balance of power in the world and ushered in a new era in China's history. Under the leadership of the CCP, the Chinese people felt elated and strode proudly ahead into a great period of their history—the transition from the new democratic revolution to the Socialist revolution and construction.

When the PRC was founded, I was appointed as chief of the PLA General Staff. I was in such poor health, however, that I had to remain a patient at a recuperation center by Qingdao's (Tsing-tao) beach. The Headquarters of the General Staff, in fact, was run by Comrade Nie Rongzhen, its deputy chief. At the time when the new republic was founded, much had to be done, and we were unusually burdened with heavy military tasks. While we were still engaged in the last phase of the Chinese civil war, the PLA's reconstruction was under way. The army was also in charge of maintaining political control and public security for the entire country. Concentrating on suppressing bandits, the PLA proceeded with its own reorganization and reduction of personnel. At the same time, it took a big part in the country's economic reconstruction, supporting the land reforms in the newly liberated areas and assisting in many other local, civil activities. With many tasks to perform, at that time we had an exceptionally heavy responsibility. Nie said that it was the busiest time in his entire life.

The American imperialists, refusing to admit their failure in China, attempted to stage a comeback to strangle the new China in the cradle. In June 1950 they outrageously invaded Korea and sent their Seventh Fleet to the Taiwan Straits to prevent us from liberating Taiwan. The flame of the Korean War soon burned toward the banks of the Yalu River. The next target of the American imperialists' military invasion aimed directly at China's northeastern region.

In October the CCP Central Committee and Comrade Mao Zedong made a wise decision to resist America and to aid Korea in order to defend our country and secure our homeland. [We were determined to] drive back the American imperialists' savage onslaught. Comrade Peng Dehuai was appointed to command the CPVF, which was to enter Korea and engage in the war. The Korean peninsula thereafter became the battleground for a fierce armed rivalry between the Chinese-Korean peoples and the imperialist camp, headed by the United States.

At that time, I had already returned to Beijing from Qingdao. I lived temporarily in a small courtyard at Yiheyuan [the Summer Palace]. Comrades Zhu De, He Long, Luo Ronghuan, Nie Rongzhen, Ye Jianying, and many others came to visit me.[3] Since the war in Korea was of prime importance, we talked about it often. By the next summer [1951], my health had significantly improved. Instructed by the Central Committee, I led a military-industry delegation to the Soviet Union to conduct negotiations to purchase arms.

The War to Resist America and Aid Korea and the modernization of our military demanded massive amounts of new weapons and equipment. Our way of handling this emergency situation was to purchase weaponry from the Soviet Union.

From a long-term point of view, however, there existed an immediate need for us to build up our own military industry.

In February 1950 China and the Soviet Union signed two bilateral agreements, the Sino-Soviet Mutual Assistance and Alliance Treaty and the Agreement on a Soviet Loan to the People's Republic of China. According to these treaties, the two governments would conduct detailed discussions on how and when the Soviets would transfer their military technology to us and help us develop our own military industries. Furthermore, there were specific projects, weapons, and equipment that we badly needed to purchase immediately; thus, China would send a delegation to Moscow to discuss the transfers with the concerned Soviet governmental sections.

In May 1951 Chairman Mao Zedong sent for me to come to his place at Zhongnanhai to give me his personal instructions for the assignment. When I arrived at his residential quarters, Mao was talking with Comrade Li Weihan about the tasks of the united front.[4] Mao asked about my health as soon as he saw me coming in. He was very happy to know that I had recovered and could work now.

Mao gave me a brief analysis of the situation in Korea and then explained the importance of my assignment to negotiate with the Soviet Union. The first part of my mission was to buy weapons and equipment; the second was to obtain more advanced technology so that we could develop our own military production. Now that the imperialists had bullied us so much, he pointed out, we could not survive without our own military industry and without solving our army's weaponry and equipment problems. We had to learn from the Soviet Union and master their advanced technology. Then we could build up a strong national defense army through our own efforts.

Mao suggested that I discuss with Peng and the comrades in the State Council whom to include in the delegation, what projects we were to negotiate, and what problems might emerge during our negotiations. I told him that he could rest easy and that I would do my best to accomplish this mission. After saying good-bye to Mao and Li, I visited Peng at his residence. After our discussions, we worked out a primary list of the delegation members and the negotiating items.

Approved by the PRC State Council and the CCP Central Military Commission, the group was named Arms Delegation of the PRC Central Government; I was its head. Its members included Deputy Commander of the PLA Air Force Wang Bingzhang, Vice Minister of the Heavy Industry Ministry Liu Ding, science and technology expert Qian Zhidao, Chief of Staff of the PLA Artillery Force Jia Tao, Deputy Director of the Operations Planning Bureau of the General Staff Zhang Qinghua, Commercial Counselor of China's Embassy to Moscow Jiang Zemin, and Military Attaché at the Embassy Ji He. In addition, there were three secretaries.

Our delegation had a twofold mission. The first was to purchase Soviet weapons and equipment to arm sixty Chinese infantry divisions. The second was to get Soviet assistance for our construction of ordnance factories, the standardization of our infantry's weaponry system, the transfer of technology, and blueprints to produce various artillery pieces below 152mm in barrel size. Our trip would not be made public.

On May 25, 1951, our delegation left Beijing by train. We traveled north to Manzhouli first, and then passed through Chita, Aumusita, New Siberia, and Kurgan, among other places. After nine days on the train, we arrived in Moscow on June 4. Among those who accompanied us were Lieutenant General Kaldov and his wife. General Kaldov was the military attaché of the Soviet embassy in Beijing and the chief military adviser to China. Kind and honest, they were a nice couple and showed a friendly, internationalist feeling toward the Chinese people. From our conversation I learned that their two sons had unfortunately died in the Antifascist War.[5] They had two daughters who then lived in Moscow.

During our talks in Moscow, General Kaldov usually accompanied us on sightseeing trips and to theaters. Once he invited me to join a family picnic in Moscow's suburbs with his wife and two daughters. The whole family observed strict diplomatic rules. They never talked about official business; certainly we did not try to engage them in such talk. During those days with Kaldov and his family, he made a deep, memorable impression on me and other members of the delegation.

When our delegation arrived in Moscow, Col. Gen. S. M. Shtemenko, chief of General Staff of the Soviet Army, and others greeted us at the train station. After a short conversation, they accompanied us to the Grand Moscow Hotel, where we stayed throughout the negotiations. The next day I returned a visit to General Shtemenko. Noble and dignified, he maintained a high standard of appearance and bearing as a serviceman. During World War II, Shtemenko had served in the Soviet Red Army as the deputy chief of the General Staff, chief of the Operations Planning Bureau, and in some other positions in the Headquarters of the General Staff. He was trusted and highly regarded by Stalin.

During my visit, I explained to General Shtemenko our major goals for the negotiations with the Soviet Union. I hoped that he would fully support us in the talks so that we could reach mutual agreements at an early time. Shtemenko welcomed my visit. He told me that the detailed projects would be discussed first by the experts from both delegations. (The Soviet Union had also organized an eight-member negotiating team.) After these consultations, he continued, we could have talks between the high-ranking delegates. I agreed with his suggestion.

Right after our arrival in Moscow, the Chinese and Soviet experts from both delegations began their negotiations. At that time the Soviet Union was the head of the world Communist and Socialist camp. We Chinese Communists had little experience in modernization of our army or in international diplomacy. As a result, the meeting schedule, negotiating agenda, and almost everything concerning the arms purchase talks were basically determined by the Soviets. At the beginning, we thought the talks would not be very complicated and would not take very long. This turned out to be wishful thinking. A marathon, the negotiations took four months. We started the talks in early June and reached agreements in mid-October.

We had three or four high-ranking negotiating meetings between the Chinese and Soviet chiefs of staff. At first, Shtemenko attended them; later he left on vacation and asked Malynkin to negotiate with us. What Shtemenko said at those meetings left a deep impression on me: Stalin had instructed the Soviet Army's Headquarters of the General Staff to help the Chinese build up a strong army.

To fulfill this task, Shtemenko said that he would do his best. He paid a lot of attention to the structure and components of army units. He emphasized the importance of rational military organization in modern warfare. Drawing on the Soviet experience in World War II he explained the necessity of having a complete logistics system and of establishing divisional corps of infantry, artillery, tank, and cavalry forces. Shtemenko believed that, taking into account the situations in Korea and in China, the Chinese divisions should not have a "unified" or standard structure, nor should they be too large. At present, it was impossible for the Chinese troops to mechanize completely. As a temporary solution, their divisional artillery pieces could be drawn by trucks, but in the regiments or in the smaller units these had to be moved by horses. Forming tank regiments, however, was absolutely necessary, he emphasized. He would rather reduce the number of armies than forego establishing tank regiments in each division.

Regarding our arms purchase, Shtemenko believed that the Soviet Union could deliver to China weapons and equipment for only sixteen infantry divisions during the rest of the year because of limited transportation capacity. One-third of the arms orders for an additional forty-four divisions would be shipped to China within the next two years. The arms delivery would be finished by 1954. Regarding the transfer of technology for weaponry production, Shtemenko said, the first group of technology included seven different types of weapons, such as rifles, submachine guns, light machine guns, and heavy machine guns. The second group would be discussed later. Regarding the Soviet aid to our military industries, Shtemenko avoided talking about it and made no comment at the meetings.

Given this situation, we sent our suggestions from Moscow to the Central Committee and the CMC in Beijing. We suggested that first, Beijing might make a preliminary plan for PLA reorganization according to the Soviet suggestion that we reorganize our infantry divisions so that the delegation could make a comprehensive arrangement for our weapons purchase. Second, the arms orders in this year for sixteen divisions might give priority to some items urgently needed on the Korean front; we might order more antiaircraft and antitank weapons and fewer or no infantry weapons. Third, items to be purchased for the next year and the one following should be based on the outcome of our negotiations for development of our own military production. In principle, we would not order anything that we would be able to produce; we would order only some items that we could not manufacture in sufficient numbers; and we would order all items that we could not produce at all.

In late June the CCP Central Committee sent Gao Gang to Moscow. He brought with him a weapons and equipment purchase order to arm sixty divisions, which our delegation officially passed to the Soviets. The Korean frontline forces urgently needed many items from the Soviet Union. Beijing sent telegrams to us day and night asking to add or change some purchasing orders. We had to talk to the Soviets about the changes all the time, which became a real headache for them. I had a headache, too, because the Soviets did not state their position even after stalling for a long time on our request for aid to our military industry. I was getting worried and kept pressing the Soviets [to clarify their position]. They, however, did not respond at all. That was the Soviet way of dealing with us. Even though greatly worried, I could do nothing. I telegraphed Chairman Mao reporting the situation. In his reply, Mao told me to be patient and wait for whatever might happen; we had to get the technology [for our military industry].

The negotiations virtually stopped for the next two months. The Soviet government arranged a nationwide tour for our delegation. We were invited to the military parade in Moscow on Soviet Aviation Day. We toured the Winter Palace in Leningrad and traveled to Stalingrad, Sverdlovsk, and the Caspian Sea. We visited steel mills, tractor factories, a military manufacturing complex, some military institutes, and army bases.

[Soviet Premier] N. A. Bulganin met with Gao Gang and me in Moscow during this period. When we arrived, [North Korea's] Premier Kim Il Sung was already there. Bulganin made some major points during our conversation, saying that the Soviet Union had been busy working on its own economic reconstruction since the end of the Great Patriotic War. The Soviet government, however, was willing to provide aid to the Chinese and Korean peoples' struggle to resist American aggression and would assist in fighting the Korean War with whatever it could and whatever it should. Still, he implied that the Soviets had their own problems and that it was impossible for them to provide all the military and economic assistance we requested. He wanted us to understand the Soviets' situation.

Shortly after this conversation, the Soviets informed us that our weapons order, which they had agreed to deliver this year, had been cut down from sixteen to ten divisions. I discussed this with Gao and asked him to talk to Bulganin. We insisted on staying with the original agreement for sixteen divisions, but there was no response from the Soviets. In October the government sent our delegation a formal notice that the Soviet Union agreed to transfer to China some technology for our military industry and to help us build some military factories. In the end we reached an agreement regarding this matter.

Generally speaking, the Soviet government treated our arms delegation in a friendly manner and conducted serious negotiations with us. The Soviet leaders respected our victory in the Chinese revolution and supported the Chinese people's engagement in the Korean War. They were willing to provide certain assistance and help us speed up our army's modernization and standardization. The Soviet leaders, however, had their own worries and anxieties. I think that they were afraid of provoking war with the United States. Stalin was also concerned that China could become the second Yugoslavia.[6] Given these concerns, they talked to us with great reserve and were overcautious in considering some of our requests.

The Soviet people are indeed warm and friendly. We understood the difficulties they faced at the time. As everyone knows, during World War II the Soviet people suffered extremely heavy losses in order to defeat the brutal German Fascist invasion. More than 20 million Soviets sacrificed their lives during the war.[7] Most of the major cities and key industries were destroyed. The war had seriously sapped Russian national vitality, and it was only five years after its end that we went to Moscow for the negotiations. The Soviet people were struggling to heal their war wounds, rebuild their economy, and overcome tremendous difficulties resulting from that conflict.

Our political propaganda at home at that time emphasized only how strong and powerful the Soviet Union was but did not mention its difficulties and problems. As Chinese, we could not even imagine these problems had we not gone there to observe them ourselves. In Moscow there were very few new buildings; all the buildings and streets had been built before the war. [We were told that] in the capital, the sex ratio was one male to eight females because so many men had died in the war. The waiters and waitresses in hotels were mostly disabled and handicapped veterans. In Stalingrad, the dilapidated walls and ruined buildings were everywhere. Some industrial business was about to be rebuilt, and there were only a few factories. We saw a shortage of daily goods and empty shelves in every grocery store. The Soviet people had to wait for a long time in lines to buy black bread and other food. In some remote regions like the Far East and New Siberia, the Soviet people lived in even worse poverty than the Chinese people.

It was not easy for the Soviet people to tighten their belts to assist China while healing their own war wounds at the same time. We should understand that sometimes the Soviets were unable to meet our needs. They had been supporting our revolution for a long time and had established a profound, internationalist friendship with the Chinese people. Wherever our delegation visited, we were always welcomed warmly and treated as special guests. We stayed in the best hotels, and our lodging, food, and entertainment were free. The Soviet hosts ate black bread while serving us white bread. They rolled up a small piece of paper with tobacco leaves for smoking while providing us with cigarettes at about seven or eight rubles a pack. When we gave a cigarette to a security guard during our visit to a factory, he expressed a thousand thanks. In some places, when the Soviets knew they would have Chinese guests, they cooked *jiaozi* for us.[8] They made thick pastries filled with meat mixed with butter. [Although that was not the way of making them] we had to eat their *jiaozi* because it was really hard for us to turn down their serious offers. After all, the Chinese and Soviet peoples had built up profound sentiments of friendship in our revolutionary struggles during the long past, a bond so valuable that we should never forget it.

The Soviet Union was the first country in the world to have succeeded in a Socialist revolution. In World War II, it defeated the German Fascists and Japan's Guandong [Kwantung] Army.[9] The country had made great contributions to humanity. Nevertheless, these achievements bloated some Soviets with pride and made them big-nation chauvinists. For example, since we did not know much about Soviet domestic problems, sometimes we inevitably requested a bit too much assistance for some projects during the talks. If the Soviets had patiently explained their own problems in detail, we probably could have reached more agreements.

Some Soviet negotiators, however, often showed signs of extreme impatience. They talked to us in an oversimplified and patronizing way, which we could hardly tolerate. At one meeting, for example, while looking at our purchase list, some Soviets even said that they would have to construct a second trans-Siberian railroad in order to satisfy our requests. They satirized our huge requirements, though in fact we did not intend to obtain those weapons for free; we came to Moscow to buy them and would pay a fair price. At another meeting, Shtemenko asked Wang Bingzhang, deputy commander of the PLA air force, for some information. Wang did not give him the expected answer. Foaming and storming, Shtemenko gave Wang a bad dressing down. I could not argue with Shtemenko at the meeting, but I nearly choked with anger. As we were here for governmental negotiations, what right did they have to dictate to us?

After returning to the hotel, I sent for Kaldov and accused him of failing to pass accurate information to his leaders. I criticized him in sharp language for more than two hours and then asked him to report this conversation to his leaders. Their big-nation chauvinism was not formed overnight, and therefore it was hard to change it right away. Furthermore, after the Soviets delivered the weapons according to our agreements, we found out that most of them were old, used weapons. Some rifle bolts could not be opened, and many rifles shipped to the Korean front would not fire.

Moscow showed signs of winter in late October when our delegation departed for China. We had not brought winter clothes with us [since we did not expect to stay for so long]. After we entered Manzhouli, the heat in our train was turned off. I suddenly caught a cold and then had pleurisy with a high fever. I had to get off the train at Changchun and stayed at the PLA air force hospital. When Premier Zhou was informed of my sickness, he sent over a group of medical experts from Beijing headed by Comrade Fu Lianzhang of the Ministry of Public Health.[10] A couple of days later, Zhou transferred me from Changchun to Beijing for further treatment. I was very ill, and it took a long time for me to recover.

7

Command Experience in Korea

General (Ret.) Yang Dezhi

Editors' Note: Yang Dezhi was the commander of the CPVF Nineteenth Army Group, the CPVF deputy commander in charge of combat operations, and then the CPVF commander during the Korean War. He was given the rank of general in 1955.

Born in Liling County, Hunan Province, in 1910, Yang joined the CCP and the Red Army in 1928. Promoted from a squad, platoon, company, and regiment commander to a division commander, he participated in the Long March of 1934–1935. He became the commander of the 344th Brigade, the 115th Division, and the Second Column of the Eighth Route Army during the Anti-Japanese War, 1937–1945. In the Chinese civil war he served as commander of the PLA's Second and Nineteenth Army Groups in the Northern China Military District. After the founding of the People's Republic of China in 1949, he was the commander of the PLA's Shanxi Military District, Jinan Military Regional Command, Wuhan Military Regional Command, and Kunming Military Regional Command. General Yang was also appointed as the vice minister of the Defense Ministry, chief of the PLA General Staff, and deputy secretary general of the CCP Central Military Commission.

Yang later published his memoirs of the Korean War, Weile Heping *[For the Sake of Peace] (Beijing: Long March Press, 1987), and then his recollection of military experiences in the PLA,* Yang Dezhi Huiyilu *[Memoirs of Yang Dezhi] (Beijing: PLA Press, 1992). Excerpts translated here from* Weile Heping *reveal remarkable insights into Chinese military strategy and tactics during the Korean War. Yang discusses in great detail how the CPVF Commanding Headquarters and army group command designed and organized both offensive and defensive battles. His recollections highlight CPVF command patterns, communication channels, problem-solving approaches, and information gathering. Yang also vividly illustrates and explores the different personalities of CPVF commanders and relations between superiors and inferiors and between officers and soldiers.*

ORGANIZING TRENCH WARFARE

On the Korean battlefield, all the American generals—MacArthur, Ridgway, Clark, Van Fleet, and Taylor—had a blind faith in bombing and shelling.[1] Tons and tons of iron and steel poured down in torrents from the sky upon the ground positions of our army and the land of Korea. Yu Zhen, deputy director of the operational section of the Nineteenth Army Group, had conducted a small experiment at our position in the Rotol Mountains. He randomly chose a piece of land of approximately one square foot and discovered 287 fragments of different sizes.

The operational section also had a survey demonstrating that during the period of the Nineteenth Army Group's defensive combat, the enemy [UN/U.S. forces] dropped more than 7,784,000 shells onto our positions. One would perhaps need at least 51,000 trucks or 4,400 railroad cars to transport so many shells. It was not an exaggeration to say that the bombing ploughed the earth to a depth of three feet, scorching it so that no vegetation survived. The soil became so soft and porous that when our soldiers walked along the positions, they often sank down to their ankles or knees. At that time, our positions were easily detected, being on highly exposed bald mountains and hills. In such circumstances, it was not easy to protect ourselves from the bombing, to maintain our positions, or to decimate the enemy. This type of fighting, in fact, started with a painful experience.

Before the enemy launched the fall offensive [in 1951], the Sixty-fifth Army of the Nineteenth Army Group was deployed 4.5 kilometers in an east-west position in the Kilsu-ri area south of Kaesong, its difficult mission to defend the town. Because of some practical problems faced by the Sixty-fifth's commanders, the party committee of our army group decided that Comrade Li Zhimin and I should join them in order to work out solutions and command the battle together.

It was getting dark when we arrived at the army's headquarters, situated in a bunker located halfway up a hill. On a table made of planks a few candles were lit since the gas lights had just been ignited and were still dim.

At the meeting were the Sixty-fifth Army's Commander Xiao Yintang, Political Commissar Wang Daobang, and Director of the Political Division Chen Yigui. As there was no time for greetings on the battlefield, Xiao told me right away, "Our troops did not fight very well the last couple of days. We had very heavy casualties."

I was aware of it. That was, in fact, why we had come. After moving into the areas around Kaesong, the Sixty-fifth had proposed a motto: "Defend firmly every inch of Kaesong's land." Nothing was wrong with this slogan. However, after the troops were deployed in positions, they were fiercely shelled and continually bombed day and night. Although the positions remained in our hands, the army had lost two battalions in the last two days. Facing the superior iron and steel of the American imperialists, the troops found themselves in a passive position since they had not been fully prepared psychologically for such a tough battle and had not developed contingency plans. A passive posture is what military strategists always seek to avoid. The commanders of the Sixty-fifth Army were meeting to find a way to change the situation.

Even before I came to command this army, Comrades Li Zhimin, Zheng Weishan, and I had talked about their situation. We had reached the consensus that the main mission of the Sixty-fifth was to defend Kaesong, a decision that could not be modified by anyone from either the top to the bottom levels of command. Yet the concept of defense should not be understood as merely clinging to a fixed position.

The concept of mobile warfare, requiring an alternative between offense and defense, had proved effective in our war experience for many years; it was also a major part of the military thinking of Mao Zedong. The Korean War was conducted, of course, on different terrain, and the enemy was different from the one we had faced in China. These differences could provide, nevertheless, an opportunity to enrich our previous combat experience. Moreover, for a military commander, each battle should be a learning experience, an opportunity for progress that should primarily be reflected in his strategic thinking and use of tactics.

Basing my response on this approach, I told Xiao and the other commanders, "I'd maintain the idea of 'defense in mobility and mobility in defense.' That means using mobility as a way to transform the passivity in which we find ourselves. This is, in fact, a matter of our military tradition: I'll not let you hit me when you attack me, but I'll make sure that I strike you dead when I attack you. Here is the real issue: let's first find a way to prevent the enemy from hurting us, then resolve the problem of striking the enemy dead. I hope that you will think and talk more about this point."

We talked quite late into the night. Given that our troops were fighting hard these days with great tenacity, Li Zhimin delivered, in both our names, a telephone speech to those comrades who were in the headquarters at the front:

> Comrade Yang Dezhi and I came here to see you today. We are now at the army headquarters. You are the defenders of Kaesong, which is the focus of the people around the world, because this is where the Korean armistice talks are being held. Thus, to defend Kaesong is, comrades, to defend the armistice talks. That's why your mission is so tough but so glorious! For this reason, we hope that not only can you carry forward the glorious tradition of our army— that is, continuous combat, courageous battle, and fearless sacrifice—but also that we together can figure out, under the new circumstances, new ways to reduce casualties and obtain even bigger victories. Comrade Yang Dezhi and I soon will come to join you. We expect good news from you!

Among the commanders of the Sixty-fifth Army, several had participated in the Shijiazhuang campaign.[2] I invited them to recall what had happened in those battles. The greatest difficulty of that campaign consisted of our primary assaults on fortified positions, in order to capture a major city that was protected by strong defensive fortifications. To overcome this difficulty, we had adopted the tactic of constructing offensive departure fortifications so that masses of troops could easily move forward and through the undetected entrenchments and tunnels, thus ensuring the effectiveness of surprise assaults on the enemy.

My recollection of the Shijiazhuang campaign sparked a vivid interest among the commanders. After a lively discussion, I revealed an idea that had been brewing for a long time in my mind. It stemmed from the beginning of the Anti-Japanese War and surfaced every time we had a defense operation: why not dig a shelter and a couple of holes on a higher earth structure or mound so that we could observe and use snipers against the enemy? If the construction of departure fortifications was an experiment in the Shijiazhuang campaign (they were later called "station holes" on the Korean battlefield), why can't we try even more experiments here in Korea?

Xiao said that he had seen soldiers digging bomb shelters on the rear side of positions to good effect.

"Very good!" I responded. "You should sum up their experience, enhance leadership, and continually stimulate the initiatives of our soldiers. They are always able to make miracles happen." I then proposed to take a look at those bomb shelters.

Xiao seemed somewhat hesitant at my proposal: "The enemy's bombardment has been really fierce these days. If you senior commanders want to go to the front positions, I'd suggest waiting for a while before going."

I smiled and said, "It would be too late if we wait until the armistice takes effect. Let's go now."

Wang Daobang then asked the army's chief of staff to report our action to the CPVF General Headquarters.

"Don't do that!" said I. "Commander Peng won't let us go if he knows about it."

Seven or eight of us took two vehicles; on arriving some 100 meters behind the front positions, we got out and advanced on foot. To reduce our visibility, we divided into two smaller groups. Li and I joined different ones. He joked to me, "Let's split up! That way, if one dies gloriously, the other will survive."

"May neither of us be glorious. It's not the time for us to die yet," I replied.

The bombardment had softened the ground around our positions so that we bogged down easily. Not a single whole tree could be found anywhere on the hill. Only jumbled tree trunks were lying all over the place. Barkless tree roots could be seen here and there. The few tree stumps that we encountered were only one to two feet high, and all were marked by shell and bullet holes.

The depth of the entrenchments was about the height of a man; one could easily walk around in them without leaning over. Some soldiers were cleaning their weapons, others talking. Seeing us coming, they all stood up right away, promptly and correctly. Pairs of bright, piercing eyes manifesting emotion and determination were distinguishable in their dusty faces tarnished with gunpowder smoke. Each man was standing straight at attention. Even those whose injured head or arms were bandaged stood up with their backs straight. Having seen this, my heart was overflowing with emotions: these are our unmovable soldiers who are always able to make headway in spite of setbacks.

"Thank you all! Thank you, comrades!" I was unable to say anything else but could only shake their thick, calloused hands and touch their uniforms that were torn up by bomb and shell splinters. I just wanted to thank them, our soldiers. I did not propose to see their newest military invention until Li was finished with a speech.

The company's commander, whose name I cannot recall, was a comrade from Sichuan Province. He had a typical short, slight Sichuan stature and was well muscled. He led the way to the rear side of their positions.

Many bomb shelters had been dug alongside the cliffs behind the forward positions and were similar to what we call today "cat's ear" shelters. The company commander told me that each shelter allowed one person to sit. Some of them were paired up, forming a U-shape like a small tunnel—that was indeed the early form of the later tunnel fortifications—and thus allowed several people to hide. He told me that when the enemy started dropping bombs, our soldiers retreated into these shelters; once it stopped, they rushed back to their surface positions.

"Very good!" I admired this invention from the bottom of my heart and told the company commander, "You may calmly wait without opening fire until the enemy troops approach closer." He nodded assent at my suggestion. At this point, I could not help remembering the departure fortifications of the Shijiazhuang campaign. I asked him, "Can you dig the shelters even deeper? Let them be linked with each other. You can also dig a few holes for observation purposes and some others as embrasures. That would save you unnecessary climbing up and down, going back and forth, wouldn't it?" "That's right!" he cheered, clapping his hands. "We'll do it right away!"

The visit to the Sixty-fifth Army was really rewarding. As we returned to the Army Group Headquarters, reports arrived that the Sixty-fifth had linked several U-tunnels that could handle a squad, a platoon, or even a company of soldiers. Commanders and soldiers, all in high spirits, were digging toward the front line. I remember that Xiao told me about it by saying, "My Sixty-fifth Army was originally the Northern China Army Group, so there is a possibility that North China's tunnel warfare in the Anti-Japanese War would be transplanted here into the Korean War!"

I reported by telephone to Commander Peng what the army was doing. He was happy with the news: "This is a creation; I will never believe that the Americans can punch through the earth by bombing it!" He also told me that some other troops were doing the same. Peng asked us to sum up this experience in writing.

The next day, after we submitted our report on tunnel construction, Peng approved it over the telephone. He also wanted the experience to be put to use further in the entire Volunteers Force. Later on, when he proposed the new strategic principle of "fighting a protracted war and an active defense," he once again confirmed the concept of tunnel fortification by saying, "This is an expression of the combined excellent characteristics of our revolutionary army's political and combat capabilities, creating extremely favorable conditions for protracted warfare."

Since Peng advocated and encouraged the idea, the whole battlefield saw a great upsurge in building fortifications. In order to better carry through the instructions of the CPVF General Headquarters and to summarize the experience so as to facilitate further combat, in late October our army group convened a meeting of the divisional and higher level officers at Songnydong. The commanders were all in the same area and belonged to the same army group, and having a chance to get together in the smoke of the battleground created a joyful reunion.

At that time, most commanders of division and higher levels were in their thirties or even younger. The overwhelming wartime responsibility falling on their shoulders made them appear mature beyond their years and quite steadfast. Once together, they nevertheless displayed youthful vigor, liveliness, and sometimes an irreverent spirit, which made them even more delightful. I told the comrades working at the headquarters to entertain them well, for as field commanders these young men had hardly been able to have a good night's sleep. They deserved a couple of days of rest. I also had the comrades of the army group's performing arts troupe do a show for them.

Several of our commanders who were responsible for the army group went to their rooms every evening, though we were also seeing each other during the daytime meetings. Together we played cards, chess, and chatted about family matters or concerns about the troops. Those who wanted to dance were dancing with the troupe's members; those who did not know how were taught by the performers. The camaraderie among us at that time was so intimate that there were virtually no hierarchical barriers or differences in treatment of ranks. Everyone felt himself a member of the revolutionary ranks, like brothers and sisters of the same big family. If there happened to be anyone who harbored dark schemes or hidden thoughts, he would not deserve the title of our comrades-in-arms.

During the meetings, battlefield circumstances were reported and situations analyzed. Basing it on the actual circumstances, I also made my report to the party committee of the Nineteenth Army Group, focusing on the state of affairs and principles of tactics.

The current situation between us and the enemy had become a stalemate. The military strength of our adversaries amounted to more than 500,000 men coming from seventeen countries, large and small, who enjoyed superiority in equipment. They had established three strategic defense lines in South Korea. We had numerical superiority but inferior technical equipment. All our provisions needed to be shipped from China. Moreover, the fact that geographically Korea has a long and narrow shape and that the enemy's forces were well centralized made it difficult to eliminate them through large-scale mobile warfare. However, our enemy lacked the courage to make daring advances, due to several previous disastrous defeats.

Given this, it was determined that our future combat style should primarily be positional warfare (or positional attacks plus positional defense). Our strategic principles for combat should be based on the assumption of protracted warfare, and our tactical principle should follow the instructions of Comrade Mao Zedong "to eat sticky candy bit by bit"—that is, combine raids, ambushes, and counterattacks to inflict casualties on the enemy forces. That way we could turn many small victories into one big victory.

I proposed, under the principle of protracted warfare, some concrete points concerning troop management, teaching of tactics, cadre training, organization and discipline, and so forth. On the subject of teaching tactics, I focused on offense and defense and the use of small assault teams. Another point I emphasized was that when constructing fortifications, we should integrate defense works on mountaintops, slopes, and bases, coordinate those on plain and hill areas, and construct open shelters and tunnel embrasures. Further, to prevent the enemy from outflanking us, we should form positions into triangle constellations and later into "fish-scale" posture for mutual support.

Organization of small teams for night assault was another point on which I elaborated in my report. Night combat was a traditional warfare in which our army had excelled, an effective one that had in the past enabled us to defeat enemies with superior equipment. Small team night assaults combined night combat tactics and mobile warfare. It was, so to speak, a dagger forged over a long time by our army, a practice scarcely seen in other armies of the world. Making assaults at night means to hit and run—to give a punch on one side and a kick on the other. Just like the Monkey King [*Sun Wukong*] making trouble in the belly of the Princess of the Iron Fan,[3] we could turn the enemy upside down. This was indeed a trump card that we ought to use often during the positional defense period.

Those meetings were successful; one could sense it in the facial expressions and voices of the participating officers; confidence was abundant. If confidence is the stimulus for an advance, the military man's confidence will be the guarantee for victory on the battlefield.

Peng often said, "Combat mainly depends upon soldiers. Capable soldiers have always been the most important thing. Competent officers are nothing else but commanders whose interest meets that of the soldiers. A commander is comparable to the conductor of an orchestra; there is no good orchestra without a good conductor, and the reverse is also true." After the army group's meeting, the big orchestra composed of our soldiers and commanders played a new movement in constructing tunnel fortifications.

This approach means operating inside the mountains, dealing with rocks, sandy grit, and cave-ins. Lacking technology or advanced tools, we were depending largely on our hands. Pickaxes were worn down so that they ended up looking like rounded iron blocks about the size of a hammer. Since vehicles were unavailable, wheels were put on shell boxes to transport earth. Lacking lamps to light the tunnels, we burned pine resin instead. Broken glass and metal plaques were also used at tunnel entrances to reflect sunshine inside during the daytime. When their tools ran out, soldiers built blacksmith ovens themselves to forge new ones. They worked so hard that their palms blistered, then became thick and badly calloused.

During that time, anyone who happened to enter the mountainous area of our positions could hear the sound of earthwork. Arduous effort was made to overcome tremendous difficulties and hardships. Gradually, a defense system took shape. It was backed up by supporting points with tunnel fortifications as main structures. In this system, many "underground great walls" were created by our soldiers' hands. Here one could find all kinds of facilities, such as dorms, canteens, and latrines as well as defended fortifications, communications entrenchments, and crisscrossing main tunnels and branch lines. There was also what our soldiers called the "underground mansion," our club hall. Even a bathing facility was built in the tunnel system of the General Headquarters of the army group. Because of their simplicity and crudeness, these halls, galleries, rooms, and mansions were obviously incomparable to those bearing the same names in China, yet they reflected our revolutionary optimism and provided much better living conditions than when we were stationed in Tochongdong. Conditions were also much better than during the earlier period of our first entry into Korea when we had only "a handful of parched flour plus a handful of snow" for food. Even though the enemy continued dropping thousands of bombs that exploded on top of the mountains, our commanders were able to sit down and peacefully read books and newspapers or play cards and chess.

Later, statistics were released at the Exhibition on the War to Resist America and Aid Korea. During three years, the total length of the tunnels dug by our army was 1,250 kilometers, the equivalent of a stone tunnel from Lianyungang on the east coast of China, going through Jiangsu and Henan Provinces, and passing over the Yellow River up to Xi'an in Shanxi Province. The various kinds of entrenchment and communication lines that we dug amounted to a total length of 6,240 kilometers. That is roughly comparable to the length of the Great Wall, the greatest construction in the history of our country. Finally, the earthwork construction of more than 100,000 bunkers was equal to at least 60 million cubic meters. This amount of earth, if built in the form of a long dam one meter high and one meter wide, could encircle the globe one and a half times. These statistics expressed the great effort and wisdom of the soldiers and commanders of the Chinese People's Volunteers Force.

Chairman Mao highly appreciated the defense system, praising it in a talk he made in August 1952:

Whether we can defend our positions is a question that was resolved last year. The solution was to hide in grottos. We dug out a two-level fortification. We hid in the tunnels when the enemy came over. It operated like this: the enemy occupied the surface positions, but the underground level remained ours. Once the enemy entered the surface positions, we started counterattacks and inflicted heavy casualties on them. By this crude means we were able to seize and take away the equipment left by the enemy. The enemy was at the end of its tether.

The problem of food—that is, how to guarantee the provision lines—had been for long time a real question. We did not know, until last year, that digging up grottos for storing food was the solution. Now we are aware of it. Each of our divisions has enough food for three months. All have their storage and ceremonial halls. They are well off.[4]

Once they had fortifications and various resources stored, the troops began to send out small teams for military activities. This was not limited to reconnaissance squads or individual combat activities but consisted primarily of infantry teams backed up by artillery and reserve teams. The nature of their mission was not merely patrolling or reconnaissance but essentially ambushing, counterambushing, and raiding. In its initial stage, the nature of such activities was defensive, with the purpose of attacking the enemy's reconnaissance and disturbing their activities, protecting our fortifications, and thus providing security to our main positions. Later, when our defense system was established, we employed more offensive tactics, gradually dominating the no-man's-land between us and the enemy and taking over their exposed outposts as well as their company- and platoon-level supporting positions. The size of the forces we put into those activities increased over time so that they ended up being offensive in nature.

I can remember quite well three tactics that we frequently used. The first was named "grab a handful" and targeted difficult objectives not crucial for us to control. Hit-and-run tactics were used to inflict casualties on the enemy in such positions by means of fighting short battles requiring quick, adaptive decisions while taking full topographical advantage. The second one was named "squeeze out positions." It was aimed at medium zones where the enemy's most threatening front positions and squad and platoon supporting positions became the objects of our attack. What we wanted was to push the enemy forces from these positions by whatever means. It was obvious that they would not abandon them easily. Pitched battles therefore took place repeatedly over these important positions, which changed hands in a seesaw fashion. This provided us with opportunities to eliminate the enemy forces, and we took full advantage of it. The third tactic was "strike nails"— sending out small task teams at night to lay mines in the positions that the enemy wanted to occupy only in daytime. This had the effect of killing enemy forces when they reentered the positions the next day. Task teams were also sent out to go deep into the enemy's rear area, including artillery positions, to create disturbances.

Tagged "sniper battle," widespread, simultaneous sniping action was launched along the entire front line. No matter whether you were infantry or artillery, you were a sniper. Everyone tried all possible means: camouflaging, lying in ambush, then actively looking for any exposed enemy targets to fire upon. A great number of top marksmen and crack gunners emerged from the sniping action. In those days, wherever you went in the area of our positions, you could hear soldiers chanting to the accompaniment of bamboo clappers:

Battleground is our living shooting range,
Let's advocate sniping to kill foes.
Let's compete to see who's most skillful,
Let's see who's best in the art of war.
Strike then fire one by one,
Hell is where they will be gone.
For many a little makes a great deal,
On bulletin of merits I'll be a hero.

Our sniper shooting was so astute and precise that the enemy dared not make a rash move. Their arrogance eventually diminished. A journalist of the Associated Press wrote: "Creeping forward toward their positions, our brothers of the allied forces felt a cold shiver climbing their back, wondering if the enemy's shells would drop on them. Crossing themselves, they prayed for God's blessing to be able to safely get back to their bunkers." Yet bunkers could not protect them either, for our crack gunners quite often blew them up to the sky.

Moreover, mobile warfare was organized and random shelling conducted to attack the enemy's tanks and vehicles. We also destroyed their artillery positions in a planned and organized way.

According to incomplete statistics, from May through August 1952, 13,500 allied troops were casualties in sniper warfare. The figure does not include those killed in mobile artillery bombardment. The enemy's positional daytime activities were thus drastically reduced because of elimination of their forces. Vigorous task teams were often out at night to destroy supply depots, blow up artillery positions, and attack living quarters, or at least to take a few POWs. Taking full advantage of our strong points and keeping clear of weaknesses had always been the guiding principle of our army in conducting wars; thus we eventually turned passivity into an aggressive position. This principle was even more important when an army with inferior equipment faced a superiorly equipped one. Night fighting and mobile warfare exactly represented our strong points on the Korean battlefield. It goes without saying that night fighting in Korea differed with respect to what we had done formerly in China: it was used not only tactically but also extended to the campaign level, both in mobile and positional warfare. In fact, throughout the entire Korean War night fighting was employed. Hence, it became a major characteristic of the War to Resist America and Aid Korea.

The military situation had become stabilized after we took the battlefield initiative into our own hands. Before New Year's Day 1952, from the headquarters' staff to the troops, we were cheerfully getting ready to celebrate the first New Year's Day on Korean territory. A few days before, Comrade Zheng Weishan and I took a walk on the reservoir next to the headquarters of our army group when our security guard Guo Changrong ran out of breath toward us, shouting, "Commanders, your guests have come! Your guests have come!"

Guests? We stopped and looked into the distance; it was indeed *ajumoni* [a

Korean term for aunt], our landlord at Tokchongdong and her daughter, who had come to visit us. Zheng and I quickly stepped forward to greet them. The arrival of *ajumoni* and her daughter was a big event for the headquarters. They were received the same way as our relatives would have been and stayed with us to celebrate New Year's Day at Songnydong.

On New Year's Eve, the headquarters and the political division both held evening parties. Among our guests were fellow villagers of Songnydong and the Korean Workers Party's comrades from the local committee of Sokbyon-ri. The program was quite similar to what we used to have in China, except for the language differences. Yet we had a special feeling about the firm Chinese-Korean friendship that we had not felt at home.

Right after the New Year's celebration, the army group announced the main tasks for the year 1952. In accordance with the instructions from the CPVF's General Headquarters, they included striving for a peaceful settlement through a well-conducted war to resolve the problem of Korea; in the spirit of the instructions from the CCP Central Committee and CMC, conducting the movement toward administrative simplification and reorganization in the CPVF and the movement against the three evils (corruption, waste, and bureaucracy); and continuing to overcome difficulties and carry forward the hard work and brave fighting.

We were indeed psychologically prepared for the continued attacks from the enemy on both the battleground and at the negotiating table. However, we did not expect that the American imperialists, defying world opinion, would launch inhuman bacteriological warfare against the Korean and Chinese people.

FIGHTING BACTERIOLOGICAL WARFARE

On the evening of January 28, 1952, the CPVF General Headquarters informed us in a circular that enemy aircraft had dropped in the areas of Kumgok-ri, Oewonji, Ryongsangdong, and Ryongsudong, southeast of Ichon, three different kinds of insects.[5] The first kind looked like black flies, the second was a kind of flea, and the third was similar to both ticks and small spiders. The circular asked us to pay close attention, to have sanitary departments conduct tests, and at the same time to mobilize troops to eliminate these insects. On January 29, enemy airplanes came to drop another batch of flies and fleas over Ichon.

On February 11, four enemy airplanes flew over our headquarters, and a milky mucus was dropped on the sleeve of my uniform. Subsequently, a report arrived from Sokbyon-ri: batches of flies, milky mucus stuck on paper sheets, and graphic cards had been found in Songnydong and villages in the surrounding area. Our troops also reported similar finds. Tests by medical officers showed that those insects were carrying cholera and other types of germs. This was indeed critical information. We at once reported to the General Headquarters and simultaneously asked the sanitary department to apply emergency measures.

The General Headquarters informed us that they had also found insects such as fleas, flies, mosquitos, crickets, spiders, and sand flies, all dropped by enemy aircraft in the areas of Chorwon, Pyonggang, and Saknyong. Laboratory tests identified more than ten types of insect-borne germs and viruses that might cause diseases such as plague, cholera, typhoid, dysentery, meningitis, encephalitis, and so on. The General Headquarters asked us to take preventive measures and to exterminate the insects simultaneously. We were also asked to work on the morale of the troops, who under no circumstances must panic. Special attention had to be paid to the mood of the frontline troops whose combat strength must by no means be affected.

The American imperialists had launched against us a special weapon— bacteriological warfare![6]

We encountered many obstacles in the early stage of dealing with germ warfare. The main problem was our lack of psychological as well as material preparations, coupled with our lack of any experience in this type of warfare. Still, the party and the people of our motherland are always the resources for our strength and are our powerful supporting forces.

At the same time this germ warfare was going on in Korea, the American imperialists also dropped bacteriological bombs in northeastern China, including Fushun, Xinmin, Dandong, and on the coastal city of Qingdao. Premier and Foreign Minister Zhou Enlai made a declaration at once and solemnly pointed out that "the Chinese people will fight to the end with the people of the rest of the world to stop the American government from committing such a crazy crime!"

In late February 1952 we received successive instructions from the CMC: "All cadres working at all levels must give priority to epidemic prevention above any other work with troops and local residents. . . . Whether there is already a case of infection or not, we ought to conduct the preventive work quickly and firmly without any room for hesitation and wavering."

In March the CCP Central Committee founded the Central Commission of Epidemic Prevention, with eighteen national leaders and commanders as its members: Zhou Enlai, Chen Yun (Ch'en Yun), Guo Moruo, Li Dequan, He Cheng, Su Jinguan, Peng Zhen, Luo Ruiqing, Teng Daiyuan, Zhang Bojun, Lu Dingyi, Xie Juezai, Li Fucheng, Zhang Hanfu, Nie Rongzhen, Su Yu, Liu Lantao, and Xiao Hua. Zhou Enlai was the director; Guo Moruo and Nie Rongzhen were deputy directors. The commission called on local regions to establish prevention teams and to accelerate the pace in research, production, and distribution of vaccines and pesticides. Within one month the commission established 129 prevention teams with 20,000 members. In the first ten days of March, 5.8 million kits of vaccine were shipped to different areas in Korea, which basically met frontline needs.

In the meantime, our party and country sent a Voluntary Oversight Epidemic Prevention Team to Korea, which was composed of more than forty experts, including bacteriologists Yang Shuya, Fang Liang, Guo Chengzhou, and Xie Zhiru; parasitologist Wu Guang; entomologist Liu Zhiying; epidemiologist Yu Huanwen; pathologist Yan Jiagui; and technicians from Beijing, Shanghai, Tianjin, and

Hangzhou. They were divided into three teams, one of which was at work in our army group.

The American imperialists' inhuman atrocity inevitably incurred the wrath of the people of the whole world, including that of the American people themselves. The government of the People's Democratic Republic of Korea first declared a protest statement. Jean F. Joliot-Curie, president of the World Peace Council, then made his declaration condemning the criminal conduct of the American invaders by using germ warfare. Statements and declarations were successively made against the American imperialists by the World Federation of Labor Unions, representing 78 million union members; the International Federation of Democratic Women, representing 1,035,000,000 members of sixty-two countries; the World League of Democratic Youth, representing 72 million young men and women of eighty-four countries; and the International Students' Union, representing 5 million students of seventy-one countries; also included were several governments of the world, various social groups, and celebrities.

The International Association of Democratic Workers in Law organized an investigation team and sent it to Korea and northern China; they uncovered irrefutable evidence proving the American army's use of germ warfare and made the matter known to the public. They requested that the criminals be punished. The International Scientific Commission on the Investigation of Germ Warfare also conducted on-site investigations in Korea and northern China. In the final report, this group pointed out that "the people of Korea and northern China have become the objects of attack by germ weapons. The U.S. Army in various ways has used these germ weapons. Some of them seem to have been developed from germ warfare technology that the Japanese army had used in World War II."

The Red Cross of China, various social groups, and experts and scholars of different disciplines also made up an American Germ Warfare Crime Investigation Team. The results of their investigations were publicized worldwide. Beijing and Shenyang held exhibitions of objects and pictures revealing the American crime. The Xinhua News Agency successively issued public statements made by twenty-five American POW pilots concerning the employment of germ warfare by their army. Our Volunteers, together with the Korean people, were indeed fighting on three fronts: combat on the battlefield, negotiations, and fights against germ warfare. Victories were gained one after another.

During that period, a great number of writers and artists from the motherland came to visit the CPVF troops. Those who came to our Nineteenth Army Group included the famous writers Ba Jin and Wei Wei. The latter, a veteran of our army group and a former regimental political commissar in the Sixty-third Army, wrote *Who Are the Most Beloved People*. Comrades Li Zhimin, Zheng Weishan, and I had several talks with them, providing them with information and leads for future writing. They were greatly welcomed by the troops and actively participated in the fight against germ warfare. These writers reported what they saw with their own eyes in a co-signed article condemning the use of germ warfare by the American invaders. I once noted their names in my memorandum book: Ba Jin, Gu Yuan, Song Zhidi, Ge Luo, Bai Lang, Li Rui, Huang Guliu, Wang Xijian, Han Zi, Wang Xin, Luo Gongliu, Xin Mang, Xi Hong, Lu Pei, Yi Ming, Xi Ye, Gao Hong, Han Feng, Li Zhihua, Du Zhen, and Yang Shuo.

After almost a year's fighting, we finally defeated the UN/U.S. germ warfare in winter 1952. Our soldiers commented, "The American invaders can't defeat us on the battlefield, nor can they do so in the negotiations; what is the good of using some flies and mosquitos then?" In fact, germ warfare taught me at least two useful points.

First, bacteriological warfare proved that the American imperialists were no match for us either on the battlefield or at the negotiation table; its use caused them even more ignominious defeat in terms of political and moral support, since even some of their allied countries drifted away. Thus American imperialism became more isolated in the world. Second, this special warfare broadened our knowledge and enhanced our confidence in eventually besting the enemy. Our victory made it clear to the world that the Korean and Chinese people are not afraid of fighting, negotiation, or any kind of warfare, even bacteriological warfare. Neither bombs nor bacteria could save the invaders from the fate of losing.

ANTILANDING PREPARATIONS, WINTER 1952

Many events happen coincidentally in history, though their occurrence might be merely fortuitous.[7] I received a new appointment as the deputy commander of the CPVF from the CMC in July 1952. Two months earlier, in May, there had also been some changes in the top commanding officers of the American invading forces. Ridgway left after he had commanded the UN Forces for about one year. Our information showed that he would replace Dwight Eisenhower as the commander in chief of the North Atlantic Treaty Organization (NATO). His successor was Mark Clark, another American general.

I knew something about Clark before he took over as commander of the UN Forces. What impressed me most was that as the U.S. Army field training commander he had headed a group of American military experts who visited the Korean battleground in February 1951. He introduced new combat techniques into the training curriculum for new American recruits. It was said that he and MacArthur were old family friends. When he was a lieutenant, MacArthur often spent his holidays with Clark's family, since their fathers were both army officers. Clark was also a good friend of Ridgway's. After they became classmates [class of 1917] at West Point Military Academy, they maintained a close relationship in their careers as U.S. Army officers.

It was perfectly clear to us that Clark would make few changes in carrying out the basic policies of the American government. What we needed to consider was how to adjust to a new counterpart [on the battlefield].

After I arrived at the CPVF General Headquarters, Comrade Xie Fang came back from the Panmunjom truce talks and spent a couple of days with us. He gave a report to Comrades Deng Hua, Gan Siqi, Zhang Wenzhou, Du Ping, and me about the truce negotiations. Although I had not had a chance to work with Xie in the past, I had heard a great deal about his experience. Commander Peng, in particular, told me a lot about Xie after I came to Korea. I knew that Peng was extremely demanding of lower rank officers. Serving as Peng's chief of staff and being able to satisfy him was really a tough job. Xie, however, did it. I also heard that while making operational plans Peng often said, "Please let our Zhuge Liang give his ideas!"[8] Peng's Zhuge Liang was Xie. Speaking fluent English and Japanese, Xie was indeed one of the special and extraordinary generals in our army.

Xie reported on the Americans' unreasonable requests in the truce negotiations and on their brutal suppression and bloody slaughter of Chinese and North Korean POWs in the [UN/U.S.] camps. He predicted that the Americans would probably make some military moves when they could not get what they wanted from the truce talks. This was also my opinion after I came to the General Headquarters.

Apparently, the tactics of "eating sticky candy bite by bite" had proved wise and effective on the Korean battleground, given our repeated victories. But "all military tactics have always to consider many battlefield changes in defense and offense by both sides."[9] The international situation and domestic conditions were also changing all the time and inevitably had their impact on the Korean battleground and the truce talks. Although Clark could not differ fundamentally on American policy from his predecessors, he nonetheless had his own personal features and characteristics in field command. As the old Chinese saying goes, "A new official makes some changes [*xinguan shangren sanbahuo*]." Clark might be the case in point, even though he did not know this adage.

"Preparedness ensures success and unpreparedness spells failure." "Building dams ahead of time" was much better than "using earth to keep the water back when it rises."

After Xie returned to Panmunjom, I talked to Zhang Wenzhou, acting chief of staff, and to Wang Zhengzhu, deputy chief of staff, about my thoughts. I asked them to discuss our major concerns and necessary preparations with the comrades at the headquarters' General Office and Operational Department.

When Commander Peng worked at the General Headquarters, its General Office was also his personal office. Besides handling field communications, departmental coordination, and other headquarters' routines, however, the office had as one of its most important tasks the job of providing almost everything for Peng's studies and analyses of the military situation. Usually, Peng liked to hear information provided by the comrades in the General Office while he stood in front of the wall maps, considering possible operational plans himself. After he made up his mind, he passed his plans to the Operational Department for discussion and refinement. Then the department submitted final drafts for his approval.

As the new CPVF deputy commander for operations, I had my own different approach. Usually before a decision or a plan was made, I carefully read and studied telegrams and reports myself, repeatedly analyzing and considering our own and the enemy's situation. After I formed a clear idea about the situation and a preliminary plan for operations, I opened discussions with the comrades of the Operational Department and others in the headquarters. During the discussions, I absorbed their essential points, adding these to my ideas and formulating a plan. Then I gave my plan to the comrades for further discussion before a final decision was shaped. Despite different methods, the chief CPVF commanders had the same goal. My decision making or command approach, though it took more time, was accepted by the comrades in the General Headquarters.

Apart from my living quarters at the headquarters, I spent most of the time at the Operational Department. When I came to the General Headquarters, the offices of the Commanding Headquarters had already moved out of an old gold mine. A tunnel fortification in an S-shape had been constructed near the gold mine, and all the offices were built at the back of the tunnel. There was a small wooden house at the top of the tunnel with four large windows on both the front and back. This housed the Operational Department. In the middle of the room there was a rectangular table like a ping-pong table surrounded by many working desks for staff, secretaries, and communications personnel. Usually the chief of staff, director of the Operational Office, other commanding officers, and I sat around the table reading telegrams, studying intelligence reports on enemy moves, and discussing situations together. If I wanted to know something, I could ask them right there. Whenever they needed me to make a decision, I could do it right way. At that time, there was no bureaucratic paperwork traveling about as in some offices today. War does not allow you to circulate a document instead of making a decision.

One day as soon as I came to the Operational Department and sat down, Wang Zhengzhu handed over a batch of reports and said, "The enemy is likely to make a new move." The intelligence reports summarized the enemy's situation since that August. On August 12, Mark Clark, James Van Fleet [commander of the U.S. Eighth Army], the commanders of the U.S. I, IX, and X Army Corps, and the director of the Operational Department of the Far East Command Headquarters suddenly inspected the area where their Seventh [Infantry] Division was stationed. On August 15 the U.S. 187th Airborne Regiment was transferred from Koje Island to the front line, reinforcing the Seventh [Infantry] Division's defense. On August 17 Clark announced that the designations of all American military units in Korea would not be identified publicly thereafter. On August 20 Van Fleet and Syngman Rhee went to the Chorwon area and inspected the puppet Ninth Division. Meanwhile, the report continued, all American naval ships were supplied with large amounts of munitions. From August 9 to 22, the U.S. First Marine Division was busy with transportation. During the busiest day, its trucks made more than 800 round trips. Three U.S. Navy carriers were sailing toward the eastern and western coasts of Korea. The puppet agents were ordered to collect information on our troops stationed in the Yonan and Paechon areas, which was of apparent "importance that could change the war situation." Furthermore, according to prisoners' confessions, the report emphasized, the enemy was delaying the truce negotiations because they intended to take over Kaepung and Yonbaek Counties.

Since mid-August, the battlefront in Korea had been unusually quiet. My experience of many years told me that a big battle usually came after such a period of silence. I asked my staff to pass the report on the enemy's situation to CPVF Acting Commander Deng Hua, North Korean deputy commander in the CPVF–NKPA Joint Headquarters, CPVF Vice Political Commissar Gan Siqi, other CPVF commanding officers, and all the CPVF's armies. Meanwhile, on behalf of the CPVF General Headquarters, I issued Instructions on Watching Closely the Current Changes in the Enemy's Situation to all the CPVF's units:

> The enemy is seemingly preparing a major move according to the current changes in its situation. However, it is hard to make a conclusion as to whether the enemy intends to activate a landing operation or launch a local offensive campaign. Therefore, all the CPVF units must closely watch changes and developments of the enemy's troops facing your positions. You should conduct reconnaissance immediately and capture prisoners through small-scale combat. Especially, the 68th and 15th Armies must arrange reconnaissance combat at once so as to find out the new movements of the U.S. 1st Marine and 7th Infantry Divisions. The CPVF Western Coast Headquarters should strengthen your lookout posts for western coastal defense. It is very important that all the units report all information about the enemy to the headquarters as soon as available.

What kind of moves did the enemy intend to make? I talked to Deng Hua and decided to have a Joint Headquarters commanders' meeting to discuss the enemy's situation within two days. I also ordered the Intelligence Department to gather more information about the enemy while I myself fell into deep thinking.

At that time, the CPVF units had established a new command pattern: no longer were they limited by unit command or army group command. All the troops were under a regional command that divided command scope by geographic areas, operational needs, and military deployment. Such an arrangement enabled each army group normally to maintain one or two armies as reserves and to cope with any emergency situation within its own area.

Our armies consolidated their positions throughout that spring and summer. By fall, along the entire front line, which ran about 230 kilometers from east to west across the Korean peninsula, we had built up a strong defensive system. It had tunnel fortifications about twenty to thirty kilometers in depth as major defensive works with supporting points. The construction of core works along the third defense line was also begun. The frontal areas on the eastern and western coasts are open and flat, places not easy for constructing underground tunnels; for these key positions we began to build up steel-reinforced concrete defense works, which were to be completed by the end of November, according to our schedule. Thus, our entire defensive system became more consolidated and nearly perfect. Moreover, there was a big improvement in our transportation and logistical supplies. These advances strengthened our army's combat effectiveness in defense.

During the fall, our troops were fighting the antibacteriological assaults and were engaged in sniper combat with vigor and vitality. Their morale was really high. People need to be inspired by their success. An army needs to be recharged with victory. Our victories in the small-scale positional combat bolstered our commanders' and soldiers' spirits and further enhanced their confidence in the final victory. Although life in the tunnel was simple, our soldiers enriched and made it colorful. They created various sports and made musical instruments with their own hands, such as *Huqin*.[10] Its voice box was made by a tin can with a piece of snake's or frog's skin on it; its stick was from a branch of a tree; the strings were made from electric copper wires and a bow from the tail hairs of horses. One of our artillery regiments organized a good-sized band with forty of these. Their handmade percussion instruments were even more interesting. For example, our soldiers lined up different-sized bits of steel drill as a steel-drill-bits piano, hung up different-sized artillery shells as a shell organ, used worn-out shovels as gongs, and made drums out of broken wooden boxes. When I visited our troops, I quite often saw all kinds of entertaining activities and heard beautiful songs in the tunnels or in the bushes. "The foundation of our army is our soldiers."[11] With these brave, tough, and highly spirited soldiers who could turn hardship into enjoyment, what kind of enemy in the world could not be defeated by us?

The enemy troops, on the contrary, without enough manpower, had low morale, though they kept their superiority in weaponry and technology behind their defensive fortifications. Moreover, the superior firepower of their heavy artillery pieces and airplanes was ineffective against our strong, tunneled positions. When they launched attacks, they were always beaten back; when they conducted defense, they usually lost both their soldiers and positions.

Under such circumstances, we felt confident that we could smash any new move they made. Under the same circumstances, on the other hand, Clark would certainly make no move without careful thought. He would not simply repeat the old tricks his predecessors had used in their offensives, so we had to pay close attention to every move he would make. We needed to be prepared against not only his coastal but also his frontal offensive, or both.

At the Joint Headquarters commanders' meeting, I explained my thinking. Deng Hua agreed with me. He said:

Lao Mei [America] now is riding a tiger and finding it hard to get off. If it continues the war, it will lose in the battles all the time, and the people of the world, including the American people, blame it for the fighting in Korea. If the American government stops the war, it loses face. It is easier to start than to stop. It is also important that its munitions cannot be eaten as bread. That is why the Korean problem becomes one of the major issues in this presidential election in America. Eisenhower has to promise publicly and repeatedly that if he wins the election that he will come to Korea and end this war himself. It seems to me not that easy, even though Eisenhower said so. Every time I listen to these capitalist countries' presidential speeches, I always have the same feeling as when I used to listen to the talk by those who played dirty tricks or wanted to sell snake medicine in China's countryside just before they collected money. Both Clark and Eisenhower are Republicans. We now need to watch what kind of games Clark is going to play.

Vice Political Commissar Gan Siqi smiled and told Korean Deputy Commander of the Joint Headquarters Choi Yong Kyon, "We need to mobilize our Korean comrades in the printing shop immediately."

"For what?" Choi Yong Kyon did not get Gan's meaning. Neither did I.

"For printing more safety passes!" Gan answered.

All the commanders laughed. Choi said in his fluent Chinese, "No problem, leave it to me. Guaranteed supply."

Gan's joke was based on the fact that almost all the UN/U.S. soldiers captured by our troops kept a copy of our "safety pass" or "summons to surrender." Our policy of good treatment of the captives was printed on both documents in English, Chinese, and Korean, and printed on the back were instructions:

Chinese and North Korean commanders and soldiers:

You must politely receive this foreign soldier who comes to you with the pass. Whatever his nationality and rank is, you must guarantee the safety of his life and property—no killing, abusing, or insulting. Please escort him to the nearest headquarters or political department of your troops. Your careful observation [of these rules] is expected.

The CPVF–NKPA Joint Commanding Headquarters

Some of these papers also included a photo showing the happy life of the UN/U.S. soldiers detained in our POW camps.

One of the captured American soldiers told us, "We looked for a copy of the safety pass after we arrived in Korea. Your pass is working better than our 'amulet' from our bosses." As a veteran, he had participated in World War II and had come to Korea after our five offensive campaigns.

I did not know if the American commanders and soldiers received their "amulet" together with their uniform and weapons. Anyway, nine out of ten captured American soldiers had a copy of a Bible or a handwritten "amulet" in their pocket. There was a tale in the American army that during World War I a soldier put a Bible in his left pocket, which blocked a bullet and saved his life. Afterward, the Bible became the savior of the American soldiers. We also found the words on the amulet both funny and annoying, for example, "Whoever carries the amulet, God gives this person sacred power, with which he is not afraid of weapons and bullets, not afraid of enemies and murders, and will not be hurt or captured, Amen."

When their little spiritual dream was smashed numerous times, our safety pass became the only hope they could have. When I visited our POWs camps, an American captain held his safety pass and told me, "This is my real God. I am safer here than anywhere else in the world, as long as Ridgway does not send airplanes to bomb our camps." Thus our safety pass and summons to surrender, sent out by the CPVF's reconnaissance patrols and the NKPA's guerrillas, became the most welcomed "gifts" among the UN/U.S. troops.

At the commanders' meeting, we analyzed the information about the enemy. The participants agreed that they would probably launch another fall offensive campaign against key sectors so as to meet their political needs at home and to fulfill their bargains at the Panmunjom truce negotiations. They would most likely gather two divisions with air and naval assistance to initiate a landing on the Yonan peninsula. Then their landing forces could either outflank our army and proceed to our rear or occupy the Yonan-Paechon area to surround and threaten Kaesong. Meanwhile, in coordination with the landing campaign, they would probably attack our frontal positions to pin down our forces. Their frontal attack could be centered on the Pyonggang area.

Basing their plans on these calculations, the Joint Headquarters issued its Decision on Antilanding Preparations Around the Yonan Peninsula. According to this decision, dated August 28, the headquarters ordered the CPVF Nineteenth Army Group and the NKPA Twenty-first Brigade to make plans and be prepared to resist an enemy landing and to defend Kaesong. We ordered all the armies on the front line to conduct more reconnaissance and to be ready for firm resistance if the enemy launched attacks on the front. We also issued orders to our armies along the eastern and western coasts for necessary combat preparations. The same day we reported our decision to the CMC. The day after we issued our orders, we received antilanding operational plans from the Ninth Army Group and the Sixty-fourth Army, carefully designed and full of confidence for victory. They carried out our orders promptly.

At that time, the CPVF's rotations were still on the original schedule. In September and October, the Twenty-third, Twenty-fourth, and Forty-sixth Armies would enter Korea to replace the Twentieth, Twenty-seventh, and Forty-second Armies, which would return to China.

VICTORY IN THE FIRST PHASE OF
THE TACTICAL OFFENSIVE CAMPAIGN

In early September 1952 our frontline troops were ready like an arrow on the bowstring for enemy attacks.[12] The enemy, however, did not come. There were some changes in their situation: their troops in the center became active. In the Kumhwa area, for example, their planes dropped many smoke bombs in front of our Fifteenth Army's positions to conceal enemy land transportation. Their vehicles made

1,300 round-trips within one week to this area alone, doubling the numbers of the week before. The Fifteenth Army reported that according to its reconnaissance there were more than 1,000 enemy trucks and jeeps involved in transportation in front of its Forty-fifth Division's positions alone, including 100 trucks carrying fully armed American troops.

After double-checking the information, we concluded that the enemy had abandoned their attempts for a coastal landing to attack our flank because our preparations alarmed them. Instead, we predicted they would attack part of our frontal positions. Military strategists always believe that "he who strikes first gains the advantage" (*Xianxiashou Weiqiang*) and "strike where the enemy is unprepared, appear where he does not expect us" (*Gongqi Bubei, Chuqi Buyi*). We had to defeat the enemy's plan for a selective offensive at an early stage.

The CPVF–NKPA Joint Headquarters made a timely new decision and reported it to the top Chinese and Korean leaders. Our telegram to the CMC on September 10 was signed by CPVF Acting Commander Deng Hua, CPVF Vice Political Commissar Gan Siqi, the Korean Vice Political Commissar, and me:

> We are proposing tactical, continuous offensive campaigns in order to retain our initiative, smash the enemy's plans, and let newly arriving troops have more combat experience. Before this troop rotation, we will deploy the 39th, 12th, and 68th Armies as main forces in the campaigns. Each of them will choose three to five [UN/U.S.] outposts and eliminate part of [the] enemy forces during their offensives. They will eliminate more enemy troops through repeated counterattacks against the enemy. Each of the other armies will pick up one to two targets in order to cooperate with the three armies. We expect that the enemy will counterattack, or even retaliate with a selective offensive, all along the front after our offensives. Should the enemy attack, we will be in a better position to eliminate more enemy troops. We are planning to fight our battles between September 20 and October 20. The rotation will begin by the end of October. Please advise us as soon as possible whether the above plan is feasible so that all the CPVF armies can start their preparations.

Two days later we received a short but clear-cut telegram from the CMC: "Received your telegram of September 10. Agree to your three armies' rotation plan by the end of October and your tactical operations before the rotation."

The CMC's prompt reply and approval really excited all the leading commanders at the Joint Headquarters. After reading the telegram together, Deng, Zhang, and I came up with the same idea: act immediately! By 6:00 P.M. September 12, only one hour after we received the CMC's reply, we issued orders to the Twelfth, Thirty-ninth, and Sixty-eighth Armies.

At 11:20 P.M. on September 14, the Joint Headquarters issued an order to all armies to start tactical offensives between September 20 and October 20. Each army should make its own particular timetable, provided they were fully prepared for attacking each chosen target. Our orders urged the armies to attack enemy positions successfully and to eliminate enemy troops so as to inflict as many casualties as possible. It meant that after occupying an enemy position, our troops must be prepared to resist repeated counterattacks, in which our soldiers would eliminate more enemy troops during seesaw fights over the position. If our attack failed, we should withdraw immediately. We should not hesitate to leave the battle, our order emphasized.

Chairman Mao always taught us to fight no battle unprepared, to fight no battle we were not sure of winning. This campaign was the first all-out counteroffensive after the five offensive campaigns. Therefore, our orders made specific requirements: first, be fully prepared before launching attacks and do not attack in haste; second, using accurate information from repeated reconnaissance, make a detailed plan that coordinates infantry and artillery and creatively employs tanks in support of infantry; third, organize combat training and practice before attacks and construct tunnels and caves at launching-attack points in order to reduce casualties and to use surprise; fourth, concentrate forces and employ second-wave attacks in a timely way, according to the flow of battle in order to guarantee the victory of this campaign. After all, our tactic was either to attack and win or not to attack at all. We wanted the newly appointed Clark to "get acquainted with" the CPVF.

After issuing orders, we called each army group to check their preparations. Since the Thirty-ninth Army finished preparations ahead of time, our attacks started on September 18, two days earlier than scheduled.

After the Thirty-ninth Army began its attacks, other armies followed, attacking about twenty enemy points in front of our positions along a 180-kilometer front line. Given our fierce fire and attacks on all fronts, the enemy thought we had launched a general offensive. UNF Commander Clark flew to the front on September 24 and held an army commanders' meeting to discuss how to handle the situation. He transferred the reserve U.S. Forty-fifth Infantry Division to the front, taking over the puppet Eighth Division's position. Clark also moved forward the puppet First Division to reinforce the U.S. Third Infantry Division.

During this early phase of our offensive, it seemed that Clark could hardly retain his composure. In fact, this first phase was on a small scale; each army employed only one or two regiments. They used only a few companies to attack one enemy position manned by no more than four companies. But our attacks were indeed remarkable in strength and impetus. "There can never be too much deception in war [Bingbu Yanzha]." Our powerful and dynamic attacks caused panic among the enemy.

I remember telling Zhang Wenzhou with a smile in the Operational Department at that time, "It seems to me that this Clark has a lot to learn."

"We can't blame Clark himself. As I well know, the U.S. Army in World War II certainly fought fewer battles than we did in the Anti-Japanese War," Zhang continued.

"Well, let's forgive this general," Deng said.

The first phase of our tactical offensive campaign ended on October 5. Our armies occupied all enemy positions as expected in our operational plans, elimi-

nating and capturing a total of 8,300 enemy troops, including 2,000 American soldiers.[13] This part of the campaign provided us with some valuable lessons and good
study topics, though it had been but a short combat period. First, our combat organization was based on a principle of full preparation. The general plan did not
require each unit to start its attacks at the same time. Unit commanders could make
their own decisions and had full play in using their own intelligence, experience,
and creativity in commanding. The Twentieth Army Group, for example, commanded its Twelfth and Sixty-eighth Armies to launch attacks on five connected
enemy positions on September 28 in order to improve positions along the north
bank of the Han River. With the momentum of an avalanche, their attacks were so
successful that the enemy could not guard both ends.

Many years later when I talked to Comrade Zheng Weishan about the Twentieth Army Group's offensive, he said,

> My attacking time was ten days later than the other armies. These ten days,
> however, granted me three advantages. First, my armies had more preparation
> in logistical supplies and manpower maneuvers. Second, they had better psy-
> chological preparation. Having seen the other armies' successful attacks, the
> rank and file were bursting with energy. As soon as I gave the order, everyone
> rushed at the enemy like a hungry tiger at its prey. Third, I lowered the
> enemy's guard. When the fighting began in other areas, the enemy troops in
> front of our positions became alert for a while. Then, seeing I made no move,
> they relaxed. At this moment, I hit them like a thunderbolt so fast they couldn't
> cover their ears, attacking five of their positions at the same time. With such
> heavy surprise attacks, I got better results.

Second, in terms of our valuable experience in troop deployment, we reduced
the relative number of attacking troops (infantry) but increased the number of supporting troops (artillery). In this campaign, the ratio between our attacking troops
and enemy defensive troops was 2:1 or 1:1. However, our supporting troops were
at a much greater strength. On average, in attacking one enemy company's position, we employed eight to ten supporting artillery companies, including mountain
and field artillery, howitzer batteries, and mortar companies (a total of forty artillery
pieces). Without such heavy artillery firepower, we hardly could have destroyed the
enemy's strong fortifications and overcome enemy firepower around our targets.

Third, we reduced our casualties through fighting quick battles. Most of our
attacking troops took over enemy positions within thirty minutes, eliminating all
or most of the troops on guard. The average casualty rate between the enemy and
us in this part of the campaign was 4:1.[14]

Fourth, the enemy retaliated wherever they lost their positions. Our troops had
to repulse repeated counterattacks after we occupied every enemy position. We
could consolidate our occupation only after seesaw combat. For example, after one
unit of the Sixty-eighth Army captured Height 57.4, the enemy concentrated six
battalions and organized sixty-five counterattacks with the support of eighty-eight

airplanes, eighteen tanks, and many heavy artillery pieces. Having defeated their counterattacks and eliminated about 3,000 enemy troops, our unit eventually consolidated its occupation. During the first part of our campaign, our troops defeated 168 counterattacks of platoon to regiment size and eliminated a large number of enemy troops.

THE BATTLE OF SHANGGANLING: THE SECOND PHASE OF THE TACTICAL OFFENSIVE

After the first phase of our tactical offensive campaign, the enemy's situation did not change much except for Clark's transfer of two divisions to the front.[15] Thus we decided to start the second half of our tactical offensive to expand our victory.

For the second phase, we made a plan different from that of the first phase. This time, all armies would launch attacks simultaneously. Although some units were not fully prepared, they had to feign attacks to cooperate with the campaign so as to divert the enemy's manpower and firepower and deliver a heavier blow.

On the evening of October 6, we issued orders to seven armies on the front line. They employed numerous units with the fire support of 760 artillery pieces, attacking twenty-three enemy targets along the 180-kilometer front at the same time. Excited by this overwhelming offensive, our soldiers said, "The entire Korean peninsula seemed [to be] shaking under our feet."

After some serious battles, the result of our offensive was fruitful. Our troops occupied twenty-one enemy positions that night or the next morning, except for two targets that were not captured after repeated attacks. Our attacking troops continued their victorious offensive toward new targets. Based on this outcome, our armies could finish their offensive campaign by October 22 and then turn back to their normal defensive positions, continuing their rotations and taking turns for rest and reorganization, according to our original plan.

At the CPVF Headquarters, the leading commanders usually had meals together except in emergency situations. We were free and easy in exchanging information, discussing problems, and even making some important decisions at the dining table. During lunch on October 15, we discussed the enemy's situation and our next plan. We agreed that we should report our offensive's results to the CMC immediately and at the same time warn our armies to be on the alert and not to become unwary because of our victory. Our armies must promptly complete their winter preparations against the oncoming cold weather and pay special attention to possible enemy retaliation.

Before we finished lunch, our headquarters' office received a telegram from the Fifteenth Army, which was stationed at Osung Mountain. It reported that enemy air and artillery forces had been bombing our positions in the Shangganling area on Osung Mountain on October 12 and 13. At 3:00 A.M. on October 14, the enemy intensified its shelling of our positions for two hours. Around 5:00 A.M. the American and puppet armies launched fierce attacks from six different directions on two of our positions at Heights 597.9 and 537.7. The enemy attacking forces included seven battalions, supported by 300 heavy artillery pieces, 30 tanks, and 40 airplanes. Meanwhile, the enemy deployed four more battalions to attack our positions at Heights 391 and 419, intending to pin down our Forty-fourth and Twenty-ninth Divisions.

The telegram also reported that the enemy had been continuing its multi-directed charges, during the daytime of October 14, wave after wave, against Heights 597.9 and 537.7. Its artillery battery fired more than 300,000 shells, and its airplanes dropped more than 500 bombs on our positions. When the enemy started attacks in the morning, we had two companies of the 135th Regiment to defend our positions with only fifteen mountain guns and twelve mortars. By 1:00 P.M. most of our field defensive works had been destroyed, and most of our surface positions had been occupied by the enemy. Suffering heavy casualties, our troops had to move into underground tunnels to continue their defense. In the evening, before the enemy could get reorganized, we launched counterattacks and took back some of our positions. The telegram was sent and signed by the Fifteenth Army's commander Qin Jiwei and Political Commissar Gu Jingsheng.

After reading the telegram, I told Deng Hua, "You forgave Clark, but he doesn't forgive you."

"The enemy moves so fast, and its attacking points are so focused. Clark must have entertained the plan for a long time," Zhang Wenzhou said.

"Well, now he has delivered [his troops] to our door, we will take them," Deng said.

I realized at the moment that the American delegation had unilaterally adjourned the truce negotiations indefinitely at Panmunjom on October 8 so that Clark could launch his offensive at the front on October 14. Apparently, an integrated plan for this had been prepared for a long time.

We returned to the Operational Department before we could finish our lunch.

Shangganling is in the southern hills of Osung Mountain (north of Kumhwa) and totals 3.7 square kilometers. Its Heights 597.9 and 537.7[16] were two of the supporting points for our major defensive positions on the mountain. At the key point in the middle of our entire cross-peninsula defensive line, Osung Mountain is of great strategic importance, facing the Pyonggang Plains in the west and controlling the Kumhwa–Kumsong–Tongchon communications and transportation lines in the east. Like two fists on the mountain, our troops on the two heights had wedged into the enemy's positions, enabling us to watch them in the entire Kumhwa area and to threaten their transportation and communications north of Kumhwa.

Clearly, the main purpose of the enemy offensive against Shangganling was, first, to take over the two heights, and second, to occupy Osung Mountain so as to improve their defenses around the Kumhwa area and create a favorable situation for their further offensives in the areas north of Kumsong. The enemy also wanted to destroy our tunnel system and stop our ongoing offensive campaign.

When the enemy did come, we had to fight back and, of course, we had to win this battle. After discussions, the top CPVF commanders decided that our all-front tactical offensive would not stop by October 22 but continue to the end of the month in order to cooperate with the Fifteenth Army in defeating the enemy's attacks. We also decided that the Forty-fifth Division of the Fifteenth should change its original attacking plan and immediately move to Osung Mountain to reinforce our troops and defend our positions there.

The Fifteenth Army was under the command of the Third Army Group. Comrade Chen Geng had been its commander and political commissar. After Commander Peng went back to China, Chen also had a new assignment there, after he worked for a short period at the CPVF General Headquarters as the acting commander. The leading commanders of the Third Army Group at the front were now Deputy Commander Wang Jinshan, Vice Political Commissar Du Yide, Chief of Staff Wang Yunrui, and Director of the Political Division Liu Youguang.

I wanted to talk to the Third Army Group's commanders to ensure that the army group and the Fifteenth Army understood our decision and that ideas and information would be exchanged between them and the General Headquarters. I asked my staff on duty to call the Third Army Group's Headquarters. Wang Yunrui answered the phone and reported their arrangements to me. After the enemy started the attacks, the commands at four levels—the army group, army, division, and regiment—had all moved forward, he emphasized. After informing him of the decision made by the General Headquarters, I told him that although the battle had just begun, according to enemy troop deployment and the intensity of their attacks, this battle could be one of the toughest and most unusual in recent years. I asked him to tell the Fifteenth Army not only to work out every detail but also to get ready to pay a high price. Our positions on Osung Mountain constituted an important part in our overall defense. We had to defend it firmly. I said that the General Headquarters would fully support the front commanders.

Wang answered, "No problem, commander! Comrade Qin Jiwei has already launched an iron man movement in the Fifteenth Army. Our field commanders had pledged in the past: defend your position to the death. They're now saying that we must never lose one inch of our position. Both our positions and soldiers must definitely be protected."

I agreed with him from the bottom of my heart. This was a manifestation of heroism and unbeatable revolutionary spirit. We could defend any position firmly with these kinds of commanders and soldiers. Meanwhile, I also clearly realized that this defensive battle would be a tough one since Clark bet all on a single throw. The Third Army Group, especially its Fifteenth Army, would endure a serious and unprecedented trial.

The battle of Shangganling began on October 14 and ended on November 25 when we completely defeated the enemy's offensive. For forty-three days and nights, it developed from a tactical battle into the scale of a campaign. With its unique character and historical impact, and with our army's heroic deeds, the battle of Shangganling has been inscribed in the military history of the world.

Step One: Resisting the Enemy Offensive

The battle of Shangganling can be divided into three phases. The first part, from October 14 to 20, was to resist enemy attacks and continually carry on our counter-offensives. During the first day, the enemy employed seven battalions to attack our positions in an area of only 3.7 square kilometers. They bombed our frontal positions with 300,000 shells. The side position of Height 597.9 alone was hit by 45,000 shells that day. Our position on the frontal hill of the mountain received five to six shells every second for more than half an hour. Our surface defensive works were almost totally destroyed. Platoon- to battalion-sized enemy troops repeatedly charged our positions. Our defending troops fired back from their covert positions against these intensive attacks.

For example, to defend their position, platoon commander Sun Zhanyuan led his men in fierce fighting. After he lost both legs, Sun still commanded the platoon to resist repeated enemy charges. He fired two machine guns himself until he ran out of bullets. The enemy troops charged again and reached his position. He pulled out the last grenade and perished together with the enemy soldiers. His name will coexist with Osung Mountain forever. Sun was a role model for our Volunteers.

From October 15 to 18 the enemy deployed two more regiments and four more battalions and continued intensive assaults on Heights 597.9 and 537.7 with heavy fire support from the air and artillery forces. Our troops engaged in repeated and unusually tough combat in seesaw battles over our positions. We lost our positions during the daytime but took them back at night.

Qin Jiwei was a smart and decisive commander. Having adjusted his deployment promptly, he established a joint command headquarters of the 134th and 135th Regiments at Osung Mountain. The 133d Regiment's headquarters moved forward to Sangsak-ri. Their divisional headquarters also moved forward to Toksanhyon.

On October 18 two enemy battalions occupied our surface positions; the situation was serious. Qin, however, handled the tension calmly, halting his troops and waiting. That night he sent two companies of the 134th Regiment into the underground tunnels and moved two other companies to the northern bottom of Height 537.7, still asking them to wait for his orders but not to attack.

At 5:30 P.M. the next day, after our positions had been occupied by the enemy for forty-eight hours, Qin ordered his troops to launch a counterattack. The 209th Rocket Artillery Regiment and other artillery batteries fired heavily on the enemy's positions. The 134th Regiment's two companies launched a surprise attack from the tunnels on the hills, and the Sixth Company of the 135th Regiment attacked from the bottom of the hill. The enemy was suddenly surrounded. After fast and strong attacks, our troops took back three positions on Height 597.9 in a short period.

Before they could capture the entire height, the enemy troops in the last position increased defensive firepower, which stopped our attacking troops on the middle of the hill. Our troops suffered heavy casualties. The Sixth Company had just sixteen men; among them only nine were able to continue the charge. This was a crucial moment. If they could not capture the last position, their whole day's efforts would be in vain because the next morning the enemy would launch counterattacks from their fortified positions, and our troops could hardly defend our occupied positions.

The Fifteenth Army was capable and heroic, its commanders and soldiers totally dependable. At this critical moment, the battalion's chief of staff arrived with his signalman Huang Jiguang. They were only two men, but history has proved that they played a great role. The Sixth Company's commander and political instructor reported to the chief of staff that they had lost all but four of their men in front of the enemy's firing point, leaving only the two of them and their two signalmen. They were the only people who could try to blow up the enemy's firing point, and they asked to do it themselves. Before the chief of staff could answer them, Huang Jiguang, twenty-two years old, stepped up in front of the three commanders. He said only two words, "I go!" These two words sounded to the chief of staff, the company's commander, and the political instructor not like a request but like an order. The commander asked Huang to take the two signalmen with him. Huang took off the souvenir badge of the War to Resist America and Aid Korea and gave it to the chief of staff.

Later, I asked the comrades of the Fifteenth Army many times about what Huang Jiguang said at that moment. They told me that before Huang ran to the enemy's position, he said to the battalion's chief of staff, "Please tell our countrymen and tell the comrades in the condolences delegation to wait for the news of our victory!" He spoke these words calmly. The comrades of the 135th Regiment also told me that at the time they knew the second group of the motherland condolences delegation had already arrived in Korea, but they had not yet met any comrade from the delegation.

This three-man demolition team climbed up the hill and blew up two enemy firing points. But during their mission one of them was killed, and both Huang and another comrade were wounded. There was one more enemy pillbox up there, from which a machine gun fired fiercely; the grenades that Huang threw could not destroy it. Our attacking troops could not move one inch in front of the enemy fire. Huang stood up. Overcoming the pain of his wounds, he reached the pillbox from the side. Then he opened his arms without any hesitation and threw himself on the firing point, blocking the machine gun with his body. Comrade Huang Jiguang sacrificed his life in clearing the path for our attacking troops. Our soldiers ran up the hill, shouting aloud, "Avenge Comrade Huang Jiguang!" They eliminated all enemy defensive troops and recovered our positions on the height.

The enemy made a frenzied counterattack after we captured these positions. At 5:00 A.M. on October 20, the enemy concentrated two battalions, repeatedly charging our positions with the support of thirty airplanes and many artillery batteries. After a whole day's fighting, the enemy took over all the surface positions again except three positions on the northeastern side of the height. Our troops again retreated into the tunnels to continue their struggle. After this, we started our all-front tactical offensive as the second phase of the battle of Shangganling.

Step Two: Tunnel-based Defense and Small Counteroffensives

During the second phase, the enemy employed seventeen infantry battalions from seven different regiments. Our Forty-fifth Division employed twenty-one infantry companies from its three regiments. Both sides used unusually heavy artillery firepower. The enemy concentrated eighteen artillery battalions with 300 artillery pieces; our side concentrated forty-six heavy artillery pieces and twenty-four rocket artillery guns.

It became a combat pattern during this period that the enemy launched offensives in the daytime; we did counteroffensives at night. During the seven days of fighting, we launched seven nighttime counteroffensives on the height, reoccupying the entire height three times, capturing part of it four times, and eliminating more than 7,000 enemy troops. The prisoners confessed that among the seventeen enemy battalions engaged in the battle of Shangganling, each battalion and company had been rotated to make attacks at least two or three times. The U.S. Seventeenth Regiment lost half its men during the first day of fighting. One of its companies had only one second lieutenant left. Our twenty-one companies engaged in the battle also suffered heavy casualties. Most of the companies lost more than half their men. In one of our front tunnels, for instance, twenty-four soldiers who continued the fighting were from thirteen different companies. The fighting was truly heavy and tense. Because of continual fighting day and night, our troops in the tunnels ran out of water, food, and medicine. Most important, they needed munitions and weapons.

As soon as I knew of this situation, I called Gao Cunxin, commander of the CPVF Artillery Headquarters, asking him to support the Fifteenth Army with more artillery firepower. As a senior artillery commander with many years' experience, Gao had been the artillery commander in the Nineteenth Army Group. During our telephone conversation, he decided to reinforce the Fifteenth Army with one battalion from the Seventh Artillery Division and four companies and one antiaircraft artillery regiment from the Second Artillery Division.

Then I conferred with Deng Hua and decided to replenish the Forty-fifth Division with 1,200 new recruits. Meanwhile, we ordered the Twenty-ninth Division of the Fifteenth Army to engage in the battle and ordered the Twelfth Army, which was on its way back to China for rest and reorganization, to stop its northward journey and return to the front immediately. It would be under the command of the Third Army Group as a reserve. We also ordered all logistical depots near the Fifteenth Army to improve their transportation in order to guarantee supplies. At the same time, we decided that Deng would talk to the commanders and soldiers on the front by telephone on behalf of the CPVF General Headquarters, expressing our sincere concern in order to heighten the troops' combat morale.

On October 24 the CMC cabled a reply to our recent report on the all-front tactical offensive campaign. Chairman Mao drafted and signed this telegram himself:

> Our Volunteers with the Korean People's Army began the tactical offensive campaign against enemy positions on all fronts on September 18. Having eliminated more than 30,000 enemy troops within one month, your campaign has achieved a great victory. The CMC warmly congratulates you and all CPVF commanders and soldiers.
>
> During this campaign, concentrating our superior forces in number and firepower, you made surprise attacks on some selected, tactically important enemy positions in which whole units of enemy platoons, companies, and battalions were totally or largely eliminated during our offensives. Then, larger numbers of enemy troops were eliminated during their counteroffensives and repeated fights over these positions. Based upon the conditions of these captured positions, if possible, you defended some firmly; if not, you evacuated the others in order to keep your initiative and be prepared for further attacks. You may continue your operations in this way, which will have the enemy by the throat and definitely force the enemy to end the Korean War through making some compromises.
>
> Since last July when our armies adapted to trench warfare, enemy casualties have far exceeded those in our earlier mobile warfare. Meanwhile, our casualties have declined significantly. For the Volunteers, the monthly casualties in the past 15 months have decreased progressively, about two-thirds every month on average in comparison with those in the first eight months. It is the result of the above position-based combat method. This method deserves special attention because, from September 18 till now, it became more organized and has been expanded to all the fronts.
>
> While celebrating the second anniversary of the CPVF participation in the Korean War, we hope that you will study your experience, better your organizational structure, improve combat skills, and save munitions. You will further unite the Korean comrades and people closely in order to achieve a greater victory in your future operations.

This telegram, more than a simple reply to our request, is actually a summary of our previous operations from the CMC at a higher level. It recognized our achievements in the first phase of the campaign; it also set a higher and clearer requirement for our future strategic and tactical operations. Chairman Mao's great foresight added great strength to the CPVF. We circulated Beijing's telegram immediately among all the armies engaged in the all-front tactical offensive campaign and among all the commanders and soldiers who were fighting at Shangganling.

After handling the telegram, I led the CPVF delegation to Pyongyang on October 24 to participate in a celebration hosted by the Korean party and government to commemorate the second anniversary of the CPVF's entering Korea. We stayed for three days. When I returned to the General Headquarters, Deng had already left for Beijing to report on the war to Chairman Mao. Gan Siqi went with him. So the leading commanders remaining at the headquarters at that time were only Acting Chief of Staff Zhang Wenzhou, Assistant Chief of Staff Wang Zhengzhu, Director of the Political Department Du Ping, and I. Deputy Commander Hong Xuezhi was still based at Songchon-ri.

As a CPVF deputy commander in charge of the combat operations, I was primarily concerned about the battle of Shangganling at the time. Compared to the first phase, our fighting in the second phase became even more difficult. Our troops had to fight the enemy over the positions inch by inch to capture the heights piecemeal because both sides clearly understood that the one who occupied the heights would gain the initiative in launching a decisive offensive campaign later.

After seven days of fierce attacks, enemy troops suffered heavy casualties and did not accomplish their goal. The American invaders, however, did not want to give up their offensive. After October 21 they tried every possible means of destroying our troops stationed inside the underground tunnels while they continued attacking our surface positions. Meanwhile, they made some new deployments. The badly hurt U.S. Seventh Infantry Division moved westward to prevent our attacks against its right flank from the west of Hantan-chon and left its mission to the puppet Second Division, including guarding the area east of Hantanchon and attacking Height 597.9. The Second Division allotted part of its defense to the ROK Sixth Division, which was on its right side. The U.S. Third [Infantry] Division replaced the ROK Ninth Division in defending the Chorwon area, and the latter was transferred eastward to the Sachang-ri area south of Kumhwa as reserves.

By that time, our Twenty-ninth Division of the Fifteenth Army began to engage in the battle. It gradually replaced the Forty-fifth Division over all our positions at Shangganling except Heights 597.9 and 537.7. Thus, the Forty-fifth was able to concentrate its troops on these two heights. The main strength of our Twelfth Army had moved into the Osung and Changcha Mountain areas. And one artillery battalion from the Seventh Artillery Division and four artillery companies and one antiaircraft artillery regiment from the Second Artillery Division had already engaged in the battle.

During this period we operated tunnel-based defense and launched small-scale counterattacks, or squad attacks. After all our troops moved into tunnel defenses, we conducted 149 successful small-team attacks, with only nine unsuccessful, and eliminated 2,000 enemy troops. Although it was not a big number in the entire campaign, our squad attacks caused serious psychological panic among the enemy troops, who were kept worrying day and night. Because they held the surface positions and we were in the underground tunnels, they were uncertain of when and where they would be killed by the bullets coming from the underground or captured by the Volunteers, who could suddenly jump from the tunnels.

Clark hated our tunnel warfare like a thorn in his flesh. To consolidate its occupied surface positions, the enemy tried all possible means, such as blockading, shelling, demolishing, setting fires, poison-gas bombing, and stuffing up the entrances to our tunnels with mud—all to destroy our troops in the underground tunnels. These destructive methods, combined with powerful antipersonnel weapons, created brutality difficult to endure. Brave, intelligent, and unusually capable of withstanding difficulties, our soldiers firmly defended their tunnels and bore unbelievable hardship. At Height 597.9, for instance, one of the 133d Regiment's tunnels was bombed into several parts. The enemy used explosives to destroy all the entrances except one small hole. They dropped white phosphorous bombs into the hole and then filled it up with mud to suffocate our troops inside.

In Number Two Tunnel on Height 597.9, there were twenty-four officers and soldiers from sixteen companies, most of them wounded. Not knowing one another, some of them panicked. Some wanted to get out of the tunnel, some insisted in moving to other tunnels, and some wanted to wait. There was neither a united command nor an agreed-upon decision. At that moment, an older soldier with a broken arm stood up and introduced himself: "I am a Communist party member and a company quartermaster. I had been fighting [the civil war] for several years before I came to Korea. Here I am in charge now, all of you must be under my command." Asking Communist party and Youth League members to raise their hands, he organized them into two groups, a party member group and a league member group. He said, "We are the troops led by the Communist party. We are the sons of the People's Republic. We left our country and are fighting the War to Resist America and Aid Korea. We can never lose face before our motherland. The party members must be the role models here, and the party member group is our collective leadership. We will take good care of our wounded brothers and be well prepared for our army's counteroffensives." He organized nonwounded and lightly wounded comrades into a platoon to carry on the defense of their tunnel.

I was so touched by these reports that I wanted to go to Osung Mountain to visit the Fifteenth Army. It was of course impossible under the circumstances. So I called the headquarters of the Third Army Group. Comrade Wang Yunrui answered the phone and told me that the Fifteenth Army's commanders had held a command meeting on October 25. They planned to launch a decisive counteroffensive if the situation would permit because the enemy apparently could not do any more in the seesaw battles at Shangganling. The army commanders decided to concentrate their troops to recapture Height 597.9 first and then organize their forces to attack Height 537.7. According to their plan, the Twenty-ninth Division would employ five companies to recapture Height 597.9 and five other companies to recapture Height 537.7. The Ninety-first Regiment, Thirty-first Division, Twelfth Army, was to be used as the reserves. To ensure logistical support, the army and division logistical services were ordered to speed up supply transportation; the Fifteenth Army, in particular, employed three infantry battalions of the Twenty-ninth Division and much of its office staff to handle the fourteen-mile-long, cross-mountain battleline transportation.

After talking to Wang, I called Liu Juiying, commander of the front transportation headquarters. As an intellectual, Liu had a large responsibility to solve problems and often came up with excellent ideas. He had made a great contribution in establishing our unbreakable transportation line in the Korean War. I told him about the Fifteenth Army's plan to organize a force of human porters to cross the fourteen-mile long mountain path, and I asked him to arrange transportation and supplies beyond it.

Liu said, "No problem, commander. You still have my word: everything is for the front; everything is for our victory. I have already arranged two truck regiments to transport munitions and supplies to the Osung Mountain area." After telling me the number of trucks and their traveling routes, he said, "I had worried before about the mountain path as a bottleneck between our truck route and the front. Now the battleline transportation fleet solves this problem."

I asked him, "Do you have any other problems over there since it won't be long before we start our all-out counteroffensives?"

He said, "Logistical supplies will play a big role in our victory if they can be shipped promptly and safely to the front. It is necessary to have some troops to escort our supplies to the front."

"You are right!" I told him, "I will talk to Chief of Staff Zhang and Assistant Chief of Staff Wang about this. Whenever you need some troops, you can contact them directly."

Step Three: Launching Decisive Counteroffensives

The third phase of battle unfolded on October 30 when we launched decisive counteroffensives and completely smashed the enemy's offensive efforts.

At 2:00 A.M. on October 30 the three companies that had been firmly defending their underground tunnels attacked the enemy first. Then, outside the tunnels, five companies of the Forty-fifth Division and two companies of the Twenty-ninth Division engaged promptly and attacked from the other side. After five hours of continual attacks, they eliminated four defensive companies and defeated one battalion's repeated counterattacks. By the next morning, we had recaptured all the positions on Height 597.9.

Between October 31 and November 3, the enemy reinforced their troops at Shangganling. Among others, one regiment of the puppet Ninth Division, three battalions of the U.S. Seventh [Infantry] Division, the U.S. 187th Airborne Regiment, and the Ethiopian battalion engaged in the battle, one after another. The enemy used one to two regiments every day to sustain their counterattacks, with the support of strong air- and artillery firepower. On November 1 we ordered our reserve, the Ninety-first Regiment, to participate in the battle and moved nine more artillery companies to the front. The Fourth Squad, Eighth Company, Ninety-first Regiment fought bravely and smartly. It became a glorious example in our history: this one squad eliminated about 400 enemy soldiers at a cost of only three casualties.[17]

Our artillery troops fought gloriously and creatively in the battle of Shangganling. Certainly, they bore extreme hardships and experienced intensive fire. Promptly responding to the infantry troops' requests, they cooperated in both defense and offense with strong fire support anytime and anywhere. Because of close cooperation between the front and the rear, plus our artillery troops' accurate surveys and timely shellings, we destroyed the enemy's defensive works, artillery positions, and tank groups one by one. In the fall campaign, our artillery troops' engagement was widely heralded by our infantry.

Chairman Mao also highly praised our artillery troops' achievements in the fall campaign. In December 1952, when he analyzed the situation in Korea, Mao said, "During the fall campaign, we achieved a great victory. In addition to our brave infantry troops, strong fortifications, good leadership decisions, and sufficient supplies, another important reason for winning the battles is indeed our artillery troops' strong firepower and accurate shelling."

On November 5 we received a cable from the Third Army Group's Deputy Commander Wang Jinshan, Vice Political Commissar Du Yide, and Chief of Staff Wang Yunrui, the Report on Operational Plans at Osung Mountain. It made new arrangements for consolidating Height 597.9 and recapturing Height 537.7, according to new developments between the opposing armies. The army group decided to reinforce their operations on the two heights with three more regiments of the Thirty-first Division of the Twelfth Army. Two regiments of the Thirty-Fourth Division were used as reserves. The Forty-fifth Division of the Fifteenth Army withdrew from the engagement for rest and reorganization, except for its artillery, liaison, and logistical services troops. For more efficiency, Li Desheng, deputy commander of the Twelfth Army, organized an Osung Mountain Command Post at Toksanhyon as the central command for all engaged infantry troops in this area; and Yan Fu, commander of the Seventh Artillery Division, organized an artillery command post as the central command for all artillery troops. Both were directly under the Fifteenth Army's commander Qin Jiwei.

The Third Army Group also reported its decision on an operational guideline. "After our successful counteroffensives, we will firmly defend key positions on the main peak. As for the rest of the positions, we will only defend some of them, if to our advantage, or withdraw if not." If the enemy were to reoccupy some of the positions, "we [would] make counterattacks only after we are well-prepared. We will not make responsive attacks without full preparation. We will do it only with a good chance of success. Lacking such an opportunity, we must create favorable conditions." The report also set up clear guidelines for "cooperation between the inside and outside of the tunnels," "combination of small- and large-scale attacks," and other plans. The report continued, "All of our combat tactics and methods must not fall into certain patterns so as to keep the enemy in the darkness and nervous. The more panicked the enemy is, the more and better combat chances we will have." And the report emphasized, "We need to give more flexibility to the commanders at all levels, who will have the tactical initiatives."

Carefully designed and detailed, this workable and flexible report showed that the commanders of the Third Army Group had racked their brains over the battle of Shangganling. While passing their report to the CMC, I also submitted our report, Decisions and Arrangements on Strengthening the 15th Army's Operations.

We received the CMC's reply on November 7. It endorsed our decisions and arrangements on strengthening the Fifteenth Army's operations: "The battle around Osung Mountain has already escalated into a campaign scale in which you have made great achievements. Hope you will encourage the entire army to carry out the fighting and strive for the final victory."

On November 9 we received a citation telegram for the troops engaged at Shangganling from the CMC and the PLA General Staff. It also mentioned that Chairman Mao passed around the citation for the Fifteenth Army on November 8 to all the PLA military regions, all services, and military academies and institutes in China. On November 9 the CMC replenished our troops at Shangganling with 7,192 new recruits, who arrived at the Yangdok train station and moved to the front.

Exciting pieces of news came one right after another. We telegraphed the Third Army Group about the good news and asked its commanders "to encourage the engaged troops of the 15th and 12th Armies and the service troops to fight decisively and to strive to recapture all the positions so as to eliminate more enemy troops and achieve the final victory."

At 4:00 P.M. on November 11, two companies of the Ninety-second Regiment, Thirty-first Division, launched attacks in two directions, with direct supporting firepower of seventy artillery pieces, twenty mortars, and twenty-four rocket guns. By 5:00 P.M. they recaptured Height 537.7 and eliminated all the enemy's defensive troops. Meanwhile, in cooperation with the Ninety-second Regiment's attacks, the Ninety-third Regiment recovered the last position on Height 597.9. The next day the enemy used one regiment to counterattack our troops on Height 537.7; after intense fighting, they took over four positions there. Then both sides engaged in fierce seesaw battles over these positions. We reinforced the 106th Regiment of the Thirty-fourth Division in the battle. By November 25 our troops had defeated the enemy's counterattacks and consolidated the positions on the heights. Because of their heavy casualties, the puppet Second and Ninth Divisions had to withdraw. Their defensive positions were taken over by the U.S. Twenty-fifth [Infantry] Division. Then the enemy stopped their counterattacks. The battle of Shangganling had ended, with victory for our army.

The battle lasted for forty-three days. Both sides employed large numbers of forces and engaged in constant fierce battles in a small area of 3.7 square kilometers. The fighting was intense, especially the artillery firing; the concentration of shelling had hardly been seen even in World War II. The enemy had employed the U.S. Seventh [Infantry] Division, a U.S. airborne regiment, the puppet Second and

Ninth Divisions, an Ethiopian battalion, and a Colombian battalion for attacks that included eleven regiments and two battalions (plus 9,000 new recruits added during the battle). The enemy also employed eighteen artillery battalions, including 300 heavy artillery pieces; they used 170 tanks and flew 3,000 sorties. The total enemy troops engaged were about 60,000 men.

We employed the Forty-fifth and Twenty-fifth Divisions of the Fifteenth Army, the Thirty-first and Thirty-fourth Divisions of the Twelfth Army, the Second and Seventh Artillery Divisions, the 209th Rocket Regiment, the Sixtieth Army's Artillery Regiment, and part of the 601st and 610th Antiaircraft Artillery Regiments, with their 114 artillery pieces, 24 rocket launchers, and 47 antiaircraft artillery pieces. Our total troops engaged were about 40,000 men, including an engineering battalion and a stretcher-bearer battalion.

During this battle, the enemy fired a total of 1.9 million shells and dropped about 5,000 bombs. The heaviest attack occurred when they fired about 300,000 shells and dropped 500 bombs in one day. Some [Chinese] newspapers reported at the time that "the mountain was cut lower, and the tunnels were cut shorter." This language was not inflated. No tree, not even a single piece of grass could be found on the two heights. Both sides called them "burning hills."

According to our statistics, we repulsed 25 enemy attacks of battalion size and beat back 650 enemy attacks of smaller scale. Meanwhile, we launched several dozen counterattacks and finally defeated the enemy's offensives. We eliminated or captured 25,000 enemy troops, shot down and damaged 270 enemy airplanes, destroyed 61 heavy artillery pieces, and destroyed 14 tanks. The enemy recognized that their material and equipment losses were equal to what they had lost in the entire year of 1950.[18] I read a news release by the American Associated Press from the Korean front that reported, "At the beginning of this battle, the UN commanders predicted that, though a fierce battle, it would be but a typical limited mountainous attack. But later this battle became the Battle of Verdun in the Korean War."[19]

The battle of Shangganling was a serious test of our defensive system: tunnels with supporting points. Our victory further proved that it worked and played an important role in the Korean War. It added a new dimension to our army's defensive operations. Because we had tunnel-based positional defensive works, we could turn Clark's millions of artillery shells into scrap metal. Because we had strong, tunnel-based fortifications, we could make counterattacks and eliminate large numbers of enemy troops in the seesaw battles. In the repeated fighting, we had control of our surface positions as long as we kept our underground tunnels. Thus, each position became a place where our troops could eliminate enemy troops repeatedly, and tunnel warfare became one of the new tactics in our army's defensive operations. The battle of Shangganling provided extremely valuable experience for our new defensive tactics.

Shangganling became well known in the world, a symbol of the Korean War. Neither side can forget it.

After the battle, the American delegation returned to the table for talks at Panmunjom. Comrade Xie Fang told me that the American representatives did not mention it at all, as if it had never happened and as if there had been no such place in the world. It was understandable, I said. Nor did Clark make any more hasty moves, as he had at Shangganling when he faced his first challenge. We, however, knew that he would take other risks in new military operations. We were fully prepared.

8

The Korean Truce Negotiations

Major General (Ret.) Chai Chengwen

Editors' Note: Chai Chengwen served as chargé d'affaires of the People's Republic of China to the Democratic People's Republic of Korea from July 10 to August 12, 1950, when China opened its embassy at Pyongyang. Chai was then head of the PRC military mission to North Korea from August 1950 to January 1955. Between July 1951 and July 1953, he served in the Chinese–North Korean delegation to the Korean truce talks at Panmunjom as the secretary general and liaison officer of the Chinese People's Volunteers Force, holding a rank equivalent to colonel. He became a senior colonel in 1955 and a major general in 1961.

Born in Suiping County, Henan Province, in 1915, Chai (then using the name Chai Junwu) joined the Communist revolutionary movement in 1936 and the Eighth Route Army in the Anti-Japanese War. He became a CCP member in 1937. He received his degrees and English language training from Qinghua University in Beijing and the Military and Political Academy of the Anti-Japanese War in Yan'an. During the Asia-Pacific War, 1941–1945, Chai became a political instructor and officer in the Political Department at the Military and Political Academy. Then he served as an officer in the staff section of the Eighth Route Army's Headquarters and as a deputy director of the intelligence section of the Eighth Route Army's East China Regional Command. During the Chinese civil war he served as head of the staff department of the Central China Regional Military Command, its acting chief of staff, and head of the Intelligence Department of the PLA's Second Field Army. After the founding of the People's Republic of China, he served in North Korea from 1950 to 1955, then as envoy extraordinary and minister plenipotentiary of the PRC to Denmark from 1955 to 1956, as deputy chief of the Second Department (Intelligence Service) of the PLA General Staff in the 1950s, and as chief of the Foreign Affairs Bureau of the Ministry of Defense in the 1960s. Chai retired in 1982.

General Chai published his memoirs, Banmendian Tanpan [The Panmunjom negotiations], *coauthored with Zhao Yongtian (Beijing: PLA Press, 1989); in 1992, a second edition was printed. The translated selections here are from the second edition.*[1] *Excerpts from Chai's memoirs reveal Beijing's negotiating goals, strategy, and tactics in the Kaesong and Panmunjom talks. He provides important insights into how the Chinese delegates viewed their American counterparts in the negotiations, how they identified problems, and how they tried to cope with them.*

There is no single, authoritative account of the Kaesong-Panmunjom negotiations. The Chinese perspective may be found (but must be read carefully) in Chai Chengwen, Banmendian Tanpan *and in Yang Dezhi,* Weile Heping [For the sake of peace]. *The official history of the war by the Ministry of Defense, Republic of Korea,* Hanguk Chonchaengsa [The history of the Korean War], *has been revised and printed in Korean, and in English as* The Korean War *(Seoul: Korean Institute of Military History, 1999–2000). Volumes 2 and 3 of the English language version contain extensive accounts of the truce negotiations, written from American sources and from interviews with the South Korean participants. The only account that originates from a North Korean source and transcends political hyperbole is the memoir-biography of Maj. Gen. Lee Sang Cho, North Korean People's Army, Lee Ki Bong, ed.,* Chungon [Testimony]: Lee Sang Cho *(Seoul: Won Il Chong Bo, 1989). General Lee lived in exile in Russia until his death in 1996.*

Although the documentary archives in Beijing, Moscow, and Pyongyang may bulge with materials on the truce negotiations, only those in the United States are open to nongovernmental researchers. The entry points to the Department of State and the Department of Defense records are the documents published in the Foreign Relations of the United States *series, commonly abbreviated as* FRUS *and published in a multivolume series for each year, organized around both subject and geographical regions. The Korean War truce talks appear in* FRUS 1951, Volume 7, China and Korea *(two parts), published in 1983, and* FRUS, 1952–1954, Volume 15, Korea *(two parts), published in 1984. There was, however, a definite change in policy in handling the documentation for 1951 and for 1952–1953. The 1951 volume reprints much of the on-site documentation from Panmunjom, but the 1952–1954 volume excludes many local documents in the interest of space and to stress the interaction in Washington (bureaucratic and coalition) and among Washington, Tokyo and South Korea. The records of the negotiations may be found in both Record Groups 59 (the Decimal File, General Records of the Department of State) and Record Group 218 (Records of the Joint Chiefs of Staff) in the National Archives, with extensive files in the presidential libraries of Harry S. Truman (Independence, Missouri) and Dwight D. Eisenhower (Abilene, Kansas). Another critical location of documentary material is the Hoover Institution of War, Revolution, and Peace, which holds the files collected by Dr. William H. Vatcher Jr., an Army Reserve officer and political science professor, San Jose State University, California, who served as UN negotiation team historian. The two secretaries of state, Dean Acheson and John Foster Dulles, assembled extensive files on the negotiations in their private papers; Acheson's are housed at the Truman Library and Dulles's in a special collection at Princeton University.*

Many of the American officers who participated in the negotiations at the the-ater level left extensive papers: General Matthew B. Ridgway Papers *(Military History Institute, Carlisle Barracks, Pennsylvania)*, General Mark W. Clark Papers *(The Citadel, Charleston, South Carolina)*, Admiral C. Turner Joy Papers *(Hoover Institution on War, Revolution, and Peace)*, Lieutenant General William K. Harrison Jr. Papers *(Military History Institute)*, Admiral Arleigh A. Burke Papers *(Naval Historical Center), and* Vice Admiral Ruthven E. Libby Papers *(Naval Academy Library). These officers usually supplemented their papers with oral histories, col-located with their papers but with copies distributed to other presidential and mil-itary repositories.*

The key printed accounts based on this documentation are William H. Vatcher Jr., Panmunjom *(New York: Frederick A. Praeger, 1958); Rosemary Foot,* A Substitute for Victory: The Politics of Peacemaking at the Korean Armistice Talks *(Ithaca, NY: Cornell University Press, 1990); Allen E. Goodman, ed.,* Negotiating While Fighting: The Diary of Admiral C. Turner Joy at the Korean Armistice Conference *(Stanford: Hoover Institution Press, 1978); Admiral C. Turner Joy,* How Communists Negotiate *(New York: Macmillan, 1955); and Sydney Bailey,* The Korean Armistice *(New York: St. Martin's Press, 1992). A civilian adviser to the UN delegation left an extensive and critical account: Herbert Goldhammer,* The 1951 Korean Armistice Conference: A Personal Memoir *(Santa Monica: RAND Corporation, 1994). Another important source is the transcripts of the Princeton Seminars, 1953–1954, a series of conferences sponsored by Princeton University and Secretary Acheson to interview the principal policy makers of the foreign pol-icy establishment (most of them civilians) in the Truman administration, an exer-cise in ex post facto group-think designed to help Acheson start his memoirs. During the war Acheson had his personal office collect documents from through-out the government for reference purposes, a sort of Pentagon Papers collection of value to researchers and housed in the Truman Library.*

For the interaction between the negotiations and American domestic policies, see House Committee on Foreign Relations, U.S. Congress, U.S. Policy in the Far East, Part 1: The Korean War and Peace Negotiations *(Washington, DC: Govern-ment Printing Office, 1980).*

These primary and secondary sources in the United States are helpful to an understanding of the Chinese perspectives and interpretations in General Chai's memoirs.

THE BEGINNING OF THE TRUCE TALKS

A Difficult Agenda

According to an agreement between the CCP's and the KWP's Central Commit-tees, Li Kenong (Li K'e-nung) would lead the Chinese and North Korean delega-tion in the Korean truce talks at Kaesong,[2] and Qiao Guanhua (Ch'iao Kuan-hua) would assist him.³ For security reasons, both men would not make any public appearances. Following our own practices, we gave the code name "working team" to the delegation; Li became Captain Li, and Qiao Instructor Qiao.

For several days, Li worked so hard that he could not even take a short break. He had to become acquainted with every Chinese and Korean comrade in his delegation as soon as he could. Li chaired meetings on schedules and arrangements and had individual talks with delegation members. He was so busy that he had a recurrence of asthma and had to take medication all the time. Around ten o'clock the night before the truce talks [which began on July 10, 1951], Li called for a general meeting, including all the Chinese and Korean members of the delegation.

Qiao first briefed the delegation on meeting plans for the next day. Then Li explained some important issues regarding the overall situation in the truce talks. His speech was translated into Korean by a female Korean interpreter, An Choi Chaeng.

The whole world was watching our negotiation, Li said. We were prepared to put forward three principles as our first step toward solving the Korean problem peacefully. These principles were consistent with a hope for peace by the people of the whole world, including the Americans and the British. The other side had expressed a possible acceptance of our basic points. Our three principles were that both sides should stop fighting immediately, that both sides withdraw from the Thirty-eighth Parallel in order to establish a demilitarized zone, and that all foreign forces withdraw from the Korean peninsula. On the first two points, Li continued, though both sides had some disagreements, the basic goals were not unattainable. On the last point, the other side did not want to discuss it yet; however, they did agree to talk about "gradual withdrawal" in the future. Although both sides differed greatly on this last point, there was still room for discussion and a possibility for reaching an agreement. Nevertheless, it would be a formidable task for us to deal with the American imperialists. We needed to think about all possible difficulties. Therefore, our task required all the Chinese and Korean comrades to unite under the leadership of Chairman Mao Zedong and Premier Kim Il Sung and work with collective wisdom and concerted efforts for the best result.⁴

Then Li emphasized four points about the negotiation. First, he said, we should take a clear-cut stand in presenting our principles for peace before the people of the world. We would make our ideas powerful, demonstrating the power of our policy. Mao told us quite often that any policy we made should be able to inspire people and mobilize millions and millions to join our efforts to realize our goals. The three principles we had prepared should be a powerful weapon for such a purpose. Thus in the meetings we would avoid being tied up with minor problems. Our first priority was to try to make our principles well known in the world, making them a powerful slogan for peace-loving people and uniting all the peoples of the world to work together for peace.

Second, the truce talks would be held in an area under our control. On the one hand, this location was relatively more convenient and politically more favorable to us than the meeting place, a Danish hospital ship, proposed by the other side. On the other hand, however, the safety of our proposed location was a problem that worried us. However, since both sides agreed to meet at this location, enemy airplanes probably would not come to raid. Moreover, our site was one of our newly occupied areas. It had been administered by the Japanese imperialists for thirty-six years and occupied by the Americans and the Syngman Rhee regime for six years. Its social structure was complicated.[5] And it was located at the Thirty-eighth Parallel, where both sides had planted many mines before the Korean War broke out. It would not be easy to clean up these dangerous mines completely. We would be responsible for any safety problems during the meetings, no matter which delegation was involved. So safety was our first major concern. The CPVF's Forty-seventh Army and the NKPA I Corps, both stationed in the Kaesong area, should make sure that nothing happened to the delegations. Li asked Comrades Lee Sang Cho and Xie Fang to check carefully with our troops about our arrangements. We needed to be absolutely sure of security and never on any account be negligent, Li emphasized.

Third, Li continued, the negotiation was also "fighting." We were fighting a "political battle" rather than a military one. We should always define our political goals in a strategic context and strike only after the other side made moves over specific issues. Since the talks were so important, we had to defend every word we said; we could not go back on our word at the negotiation table. So we must be extremely cautious when we represented our position in public. On some important matters, we could wait a day rather than rush to speak too early. We would try to speak from preprepared notes as much as possible. Besides our basic notes, we would also prepare some supplemental notes in case of need. The situation at the talks was just like that on the battleground: once it started, anything could happen.

For the delegation members, it was impossible, Li said, to leave the table for private discussions in the middle of the meetings. Chai Chengwen could come back any time for briefing and guidance. If we were not sure about a certain issue, we should wait for the meeting's recess to discuss it rather than rush to make our point. As for our comrades, Li said, he did not worry about whether a member would depart from our correct stand in the talks. Instead, he was concerned that most of our members were so young and full of enthusiasm that they might react on a rash impulse to the other side's provocations.[6] Most of our comrades did not have any experience in dealing with the Americans. Thus all our participants must pay full attention to every detail at the meetings, carefully weighing the other delegation's words and closely watching their members' expressions in order to have a thorough and quick grasp of the other side's ways.

Fourth, as Li's last point, the truce talks could not be separated for even one second from the situation on the battleground. Li said that Xie should ask Comrade Li Shiqi, who was the CPVF liaison officer, to follow closely the development and changes on the battlefield and promptly inform the delegation. We could not possibly work out a truce agreement if we did not know what was going on at the front.

The meeting lasted until midnight.

Our American Counterparts and the First Day of the Negotiations

Before the Korean truce talks started, Truman had decided that the military officers would represent the United States at the Kaesong negotiations.[7] Truman asked the Departments of State and Defense to establish an interagency team responsible for drafting plans regarding the goals, objectives, and contents of the negotiations. According to [Secretary of State] Dean Acheson, all the guidance documents for the Korean truce talks had been examined and approved by the Joint Chiefs of Staff, [Secretary of Defense] Gen. George C. Marshall, Gen. Matthew B. Ridgway, and himself before the president signed them in person.[8]

In the afternoon of June 30, 1951, Ridgway appointed Vice Adm. C. Turner Joy, commander of the U.S. Naval Forces Far East, as his chief representative in the negotiations. Joy proved himself to be a steadfast man with a sure hand at the truce-talks table. His negotiating skills left a deep impression on several Chinese–North Korean delegation members. However, as a professional military officer, Joy could do no more than follow the instructions of Truman, Acheson, and Ridgway. It was quite obvious that at times his ideas differed from his superiors' intentions. The negotiations were broken off several times by the American delegation, not because of Joy's ideas but because of instructions that he received from his superiors.

After Joy accepted the appointment as the chief representative, he recommended his own deputy chief of staff, Rear Adm. Arleigh A. Burke, to be the [naval] representative at the talks. The commander of the U.S. Far East Air Forces recommended his deputy commander, Maj. Gen. Lawrence C. Craigie, as a representative. Among the others, Commander of the U.S. Eighth Army James Van Fleet recommended his deputy chief of staff, Maj. Gen. Henry I. Hodes, and the commander of the South Korean I Corps, Maj. Gen. Paik Sun Yup, as representatives. These nominations were all approved by General Ridgway.

General Craigie had good analytical skills and was eloquent. General Hodes, who was once assistant commander of the U.S. Seventh Infantry Division, was a rather plain and straightforward man, always with a cigar dangling from his lips. Admiral Burke was "very intelligent and talented," according to Joy. Yet we did not see these qualities during the process of the truce talks.

The American delegation also included a group of officers and civilian officials from the offices of the Joint Chiefs of Staff, State Department, and Ridgway's headquarters in Japan who made up a think tank for their negotiating team. Among them were naval Capt. Henry M. Briggs, an officer with a ready pen whom Joy transferred from the Headquarters of the U.S. Navy to the negotiations as the secretary of the American delegation. Col. Donald H. Galloway from the U.S. Army was responsible for its administrative work. Col. Andrew J. Kinney from the U.S. Air Force, Col. James C. Murray from the U.S. Marine Corps, and Lt. Col. Lee Soo Young of South Korea were the liaison officers.

During the later negotiations, Colonel Kinney seemed frivolous and arrogant and liked to make caustic remarks. Colonel Murray impressed us as being well educated and refined in his manners. There sometimes appeared to be several civilian officials sitting near the negotiation table who seemed to have come from the State Department. The high-ranking Korean officers, like Paik Sun Yup and Lee Hyun Gun, were young, with a training background in the U.S. Army. They, however, had merely an ornamental function in the delegation. For instance, Paik Sun Yup was sitting to the right of Joy who, nevertheless, often skipped over him to pass notes to Hodes for advice. Lee was even more ignored by the Americans.[9] It happened once that during a recess, he was left alone in our area by his fellow delegation members, which made him extremely nervous. The Chinese–North Korean delegation sent Comrade Bi Jilong to invite Lee to rest in our rooms and eat a meal with us. We had to call the other side and ask them to come over to pick him up.

In an apple orchard near Munsan, south of the Imjin River, the U.S. Eighth Army set up a tent camp for the American delegation. When the meetings were adjourned, they lived there unless the recess was very long. On the eve of the Korean truce negotiations, July 9, 1951, General Ridgway, commander of the UN Forces, flew from Tokyo to Seoul with the American delegation. On the morning of July 10, the delegation took helicopters to Munsan. Ridgway came to see the delegates off.

According to what we found out later, the Americans in the delegation expected early success in the truce discussions. In his memoirs, Joy admitted that he thought at the beginning of the talks that two months would be enough time to bring an end to the war. But even as the number one post–World War II power in the world, the United States had not won the war on the Korean battlefield. The American government had to send [Joy] to an area under our control to negotiate peace as the representative of the commander of the UN Forces. This fact itself put him and his delegation under heavy psychological pressure. Although Washington and Ridgway had given him detailed instructions, Joy had no idea what the adversary would look like, what kind of situations he would face, and how he could best deal with his counterparts at the talks. These circumstances made him uneasy, and he had to look carefully before taking each step. Just as Li Kenong had asked us, Joy asked his delegation members to "watch closely every move made by the other side's representatives."

Kaesong was an ancient capital of the Koryo Dynasty between 918 and 1329. The people on the Korean peninsula, who had suffered much in the whirlpool of the war, were now watching the truce negotiations there. The Chinese and American peoples, as well as the peace-loving peoples of the whole world, were also watching.

Kaesong had a lot of sunshine on July 10, something rare for the Korean summer season. Men and women, old and young, indeed the entire population of the town, revealed some joy in the midst of concerns and doubts. Roads and streets were cleaned up to receive the delegation from the other side.

The PRC–DPRK delegation set up a liaison station at Panmunjom, which is located outside Kaesong on the bank of the Sachon River. Our security officers, with some translators, were sent out by our delegation to receive the other delegation. Soldiers of the NKPA and the CPVF in charge of security had received rigorous instructions to guard their posts carefully in order to guarantee the safety of the representatives from the other side. All the participating members of the PRC–DPRK delegation gathered a half hour in advance. Delegates from the CPVF put on dark green uniforms. On the left side of their chests, red ribbons read in Korean and Chinese "Sino-Korean Delegation for Truce Negotiations."

At eight o'clock the motorcade of jeeps and trucks carrying some delegation members from the other side departed from Munsan. Following the designated roads across the Imjin River, they headed to the Panmunjom bridge on the Sachon River. From there our security officers led the way so they could rest in the white pavilion located on the outskirts of Kaesong. At 9:00 A.M. two helicopters carrying Vice Admiral Joy and some of his staff arrived on the landing site we had prepared.[10]

At 10:00 A.M. the two delegations from both sides met in the hall of Naebongjang [tea house]. Then both delegations walked into the meeting room, sat down, and exchanged certification papers for inspection. A rectangular table covered with green woolen cloth was set up at an east-west angle in the negotiating room. On the southern side were the five representatives from the other side: Joy sat in the middle, with Paik Sun Yup and Hodes on his right-hand side and with Craigie and Burke on his left-hand side. The PRC–DPRK representatives were sitting on the northern side of the table. Nam Il sat in the middle, with Deng Hua and Xie Fang on his right-hand side and with Lee Sang Cho and Chang Pyong San on his left. Behind the representatives of both sides were staff members, translators, and recording secretaries in roughly equivalent numbers.

According to international negotiating practice, the Chinese–North Korean side should have taken the floor first, since the truce talks were held in an area under our control and especially so given that the negotiations were based on equity, without a chairman. Joy, however, raced to take the floor without waiting for our representatives to have a say.

Having stressed the importance of the negotiations, Joy said that the Korean War would continue until a cease-fire agreement took effect and that any delay in reaching an agreement would mean prolonging the war and increasing casualties. These were plain words, yet they certainly carried a threatening connotation under these particular circumstances. Before ending his speech, Joy proposed, "What we are going to talk about will be confined to purely military matters regarding the Korean territory. If you agree with me on this proposal, please sign a document right now as the first agreement of our negotiations. Would you do that?" It was really disappointing that at the first meeting that attracted the world's attention, the other side was unable to make any substantial proposition.

We ignored Joy's request. General Nam Il as our chief representative made his speech next. He pointed out that the Korean people insisted, as they had before, on ending the war as quickly as possible. For this reason, he and the PRC–DPRK delegation supported the proposition made by Jacob Malik, Soviet ambassador to the United Nations, on June 23, 1951, calling for an immediate cease-fire by both sides and a withdrawal of all troops back from the Thirty-eighth Parallel.

Nam Il then officially stated three fundamental principles. First, on the basis of a mutual agreement, both sides should simultaneously order their troops to stop military actions. He stressed that a cease-fire by both sides would not only reduce the loss of human lives and property but would also contribute the first step toward putting out the fire of war in Korea.

Second, both sides should agree to establish the Thirty-eighth Parallel as the military demarcation line. All troops should retreat ten kilometers away from it. This area between both sides then should be considered as a demilitarized zone for a certain time period. The civil administration of the area would be restored to the same condition prior to June 25, 1950. At the same time, negotiations between both sides on exchanges of prisoners of war should be held as soon as possible.

Third, foreign troops must withdraw from Korea as early as possible so as to put an end to the conflict permanently and settle the Korean problem peacefully. Only the withdrawal of foreign troops could provide the fundamental basis for ending the war.

Nam Il also expressed a sincere wish that the negotiations at Kaesong reach an armistice at the earliest possible time, in order to meet the needs of the peace-loving people. After his talk, General Deng Hua, representative of the CPVF, made a speech in support of Nam's viewpoints. Deng said that an important step toward a peaceful solution of the Korean problem could be taken only after we met and talked about a cease-fire on fair and reasonable grounds. A cease-fire, a temporary military demarcation line along the Thirty-eighth Parallel, and the withdrawal of all foreign troops were the conditions that the Koreans, the Chinese, and the people of the world were wishing and waiting for. Nam's three principles were fully supported by the Chinese Volunteers, Deng emphasized.

The Chinese and North Korean governments had already made an agreement that Nam Il would be the key speaker representing the Chinese–North Korean side. Deng's speech was arranged specifically just for the first day, because the people of the entire world were fully aware that the Americans were expecting to hear China's position at the truce negotiations. If the representatives of the CPVF had articulated nothing, not only would the Americans not have confidence at Kaesong but also the peace-wishing people of the world would not be satisfied.

Originally, the PRC–DPRK delegation thought that it would save a lot of time in such urgent talks if both sides first put their cards on the table, found similarities in their positions, and then discussed their differences item by item. We had sufficient reasons for such an approach because there existed many common points and similar views in the speech made by George Kennan[11] and the declaration of Jacob Malik at the United Nations.[12]

Such, however, was not the case at Kaesong. After Nam's and Deng's speeches, the other side proposed nine items for immediate negotiations:

1. Pass an agenda for the talks.
2. Identify the locations of prisoners' camps on both sides. Give permission to the International Committee of the Red Cross to visit camps.
3. Limit discussions and negotiations at the talks only to military matters on the Korean territory.
4. Stop all hostile actions and military movements between both sides' armed forces. Discuss clauses to guarantee that no such military actions and movements would take place again in the future.
5. Determine a demilitarized zone in Korea.
6. Discuss the organization, authority, and responsibilities of a supervising commission for the truce in Korea.
7. Discuss principles for establishing a military observation group that would conduct observations in Korea under the supervising commission of the Korean Armistice.
8. Decide the organization and responsibilities of the above group.
9. Make arrangements for prisoners of the Korean War.

At the lunch recess, the members of the PRC–DPRK delegation studied the wording of the other side's proposals. It seemed to us that the first item concerned only the procedure of the negotiations. The second item seemed to be a needless, rigid insertion because there was no need to talk about POW camp visits by the Red Cross International Committee at the truce negotiations. The third item was evidently added unnecessarily. Regarding the scope of the talks, although Kennan had proposed [to Malik] that negotiations for an armistice be an independent issue, the mere definition of military matters would itself create endless debate in the negotiations.

Our guess about the real intention behind the proposal of these two items was that the Americans were afraid of getting involved in the debate concerning the question of Taiwan and the issue of a PRC seat in the UN, or perhaps they wanted to instigate conflict between the International Committee of the Red Cross and the PRC–DPRK delegation at the talks. Among the other proposals, the fourth and fifth items were actually at the core of the issue. However, the other side did not raise the real question about how to define a demilitarized zone. Without military boundaries, there would be no basis for determining such a zone. The sixth, seventh, and eighth items dealt with the supervision of an armistice, that is, how to guarantee that no more military actions would take place in the future. The last item was about the POWs.

In fact, the substance of the nine items was already included in the three principles proposed by Nam. To our regret, the other side did not mention even a word about withdrawing foreign troops, nor did it mention anything about retreating from the Thirty-eighth Parallel. Those were the key issues that needed discussion and solutions. It was apparent that the Americans had already modified their stand at the talks. Li Kenong said that the Americans no longer seemed to be in a hurry to reach an armistice as much as they had been when Kennan wanted to meet Malik.

Since the negotiations were based on equal status between both sides, it would have been inappropriate for us to oppose the other side's agenda for discussions. That afternoon the Chinese–North Korean side also proposed five items for discussion:

1. Pass the agenda for the negotiations.
2. Use the Thirty-eighth Parallel as the military demarcation line for the purpose of a cease-fire on both sides. Establish a nonmilitary zone. These measures are the basic foundation for the armistice.
3. Withdraw all foreign armed forces from Korea.
4. Define concrete, specific measures to enforce the cease-fire.
5. Make arrangements for the prisoners of war.

Each speech delivered at the meeting was translated into two languages—ours into Korean and English, theirs into Korean and Chinese. The two-language translations, in fact, worked toward the advantage of both sides, because the time required by the translations could be used to think and even discuss how to reply to the questions from the other side.

Nonetheless, on several occasions, possibly because of nervousness or negligence, after [the American delegation's interpreter] Richard Underwood translated Joy's words into Korean, the vice admiral kept going on with his speech without waiting for the Chinese translation by Kenneth Wu [in the American delegation]. This was corrected only after the PRC–DPRK delegation complained about it.[13]

There was no joint record-keeping or note-taking team. Each side took notes for itself. The other side was using a stenographic machine and thus seemed at some ease, while we, using pens, were pressured by haste. We tried to keep the records of the other side's speeches in English since Underwood did not speak Korean very well, nor did Wu speak Chinese well.

Underwood's father was an American missionary in Korea. Although Underwood grew up in South Korea, his Korean was imprecise, and he was not proficient enough as an interpreter for negotiations. However, he set high standards for himself. In the long and tense process of translation, Underwood even kept an accurate record of his smoking by jotting down in his pocket-size notebook the exact time he had a cigarette.

Kenneth Wu was a young and capable Chinese-American. He had a sense of justice. His language ability improved quickly during the process of the negotiations, and the Chinese–North Korean delegation members were well disposed toward him. Yet his Chinese was underqualified for the needs of the negotiations. For example, he once translated "running into someone" as "two cars run into each other on the road." Particularly when his speakers were logically inconsistent in the debates, Wu reluctantly did his job and then looked at the Chinese representatives with an expression of resignation.[14]

Beyond the Negotiating Table

The first day's meeting at the Kaesong negotiations adjourned.[15] Widespread media attention was given to the meeting, including detailed information from inside and outside the meeting room. Major world news agencies highlighted the three principles proposed by the PRC–DPRK delegation. Our stance gave hope to the people of the world and meanwhile made journalists pressure the other side because they thought that the American delegation provided far less information than the media had expected. This was the likely reason that Ridgway later made the reporters' news coverage a big issue and wanted to talk with us about it during the negotiations.

It was regrettable that in some reports made by Chinese and North Korean journalists there were words that really hurt the other delegation's feelings. One such example was "Joy comes to the meeting at Kaesong upholding a white flag," meaning that Joy came to the talks as a capitulator because of the white flag. This certainly made the generals and officers from the most powerful country in the world feel humiliated. They were even more unhappy when they mistakenly felt threatened by the maximum security along their travel route and around their rest areas. It was therefore no surprise when Ridgway instructed his representatives to "try to change the negotiating atmosphere at Kaesong" after the first day's meeting.

Carrying a white flag to the meetings was based on an agreement made between both sides. It was, in fact, initiated by Ridgway himself in a letter he addressed to Kim Il Sung and Peng Dehuai on July 3: "To insure efficient arrangements of the many details connected with the first meeting, I propose [that the motorcade follow the main road leading from Seoul to Kaesong]. Each vehicle will carry a large white flag."[16] Ridgway also said in the letter: "If you can inform us of the itinerary, time, and description of motorcade vehicles of the liaison officers of your side, such a motorcade will be given the guarantee not to be attacked on the way to and from the meeting." The next day, in a telegram to Ridgway, Kim and Peng clearly stated, "We agree with your proposition." Moreover, the vehicle that Li Kenong rode in from Pyongyang to Kaesong also had a white flag. At play here were the different cultural traditions and customs of the two sides.

After the first day's meeting there were two motions for an agenda at the negotiating table that were clearly diverse and differently focused. Discussions on the essential issues in the two proposals could not be avoided. From the very beginning, the Chinese–North Korean side proposed to list on the agenda the issue of withdrawing all foreign troops from Korea. The other side, however, said nothing about the substance of what was at stake in this matter in reply but unexpectedly made a case for "the issue concerning the journalists' coverage of the Korean truce negotiations." Joy asked us to allow twenty journalists to come to Kaesong for news coverage on July 12. In accordance with the principle that required the consent of both sides on issues concerning the meetings, the Chinese–North Korean delegation agreed to consider his request. At 5:45 A.M. on July 12, we informed the other side through liaison officers of the result of our considerations: we agreed that journalists from both sides should come to cover the news at an appropriate time. When the negotiations reached some agreement, we would welcome the journalists.

The other side, however, ignored our official reply and used coercion against us. Around 7:45 A.M. the American motorcade carrying sixty-five members of their delegation with twenty journalists arrived at our side's area at Panmunjom. Our liaison officers told the Americans at once that we could not let the journalists pass our garrison area because no agreement about the issue of news coverage had been reached. Then the whole motorcade turned back with the delegation and journalists. As the chief representative of the UN Forces, Joy wrote a letter the same day to Nam Il:

> (1) At 9:30 on the morning of July 12, 1951 the motorcade carrying our side's needed personnel for the meeting was refused passage by your armed guards at a lookout post along the Munsan-Kaesong road. (2) I have ordered our motorcade to turn back to the front positions of the U.N. Forces. (3) After I receive your notice that our personnel selected by myself, including those representing the media whom I believe necessary, will not be disturbed in our travel to the meeting site, then I will be ready with my delegation to resume the negotiations that recessed yesterday.[17]

On the morning of July 13, Nam Il wrote to Joy in reply:

> Your letter has been received. My reply is as follows: (1) Our side did not prevent your delegation from coming to the meeting at 7:45 in the morning of July 12. The journalists riding on the same motorcade naturally could not be admitted to visit the meeting site, simply because both sides have not yet reached an agreement on this issue. So there is no reason for your delegation not to come to the meeting because of this issue. (2) Regarding the issue of news coverage and interviews by journalists and media representatives at Panmunjom, our suggestion is that before both sides reach an agreement on the issue, no journalist or media representative of either side should be allowed to enter the negotiating area. (3) Thereby, I suggest that the meeting be resumed today at 9:00 in the morning (Pyongyang time).[18]

The PRC–DPRK delegation was not fully aware of how sensitive "the journalist issue" was. We simply thought that there was no need for the journalists to come when there was no mutual agreement yet and thus no results to speak of. In fact, since the Korean truce talks were the focus of the attention of the entire world, it was natural for major world news agencies to try everything they could to get information and pictures in their competition for news coverage. The value of their news depended on the timing of its release. Under such circumstances, it should be fully understandable that the media representatives pressured the American delegation about allowing the reporters to enter the Kaesong area.

There was another reason why the other side made a case of the "reporters issue." On the first day of the talks there was a photographer from the Chinese–North Korean side who entered the meeting room and shot some pictures. Even though our chief representative signaled for him to leave at once, the fact was that the Chinese and North Koreans took pictures and the other side did not. This rather sensitive matter angered the other delegation.

The other side hung on to this reporters issue and brought it up immediately to the top commanders of both sides by asking whether there was to be equal treatment at the meeting site. In a letter to Kim and Peng on July 13, Ridgway pointed out that on June 30 he had suggested that the talks be held on a Danish hospital ship where free access could be enjoyed equally by both sides' personnel and other people, such as reporters, from each side. He asserted that such a site would have created a totally neutral atmosphere and avoided a threatening impression by the presence of armed troops from either side. When he accepted Kaesong as the negotiating location, he said he thought that it should provide all these conditions. At the liaison officers' meeting on July 8, Ridgway continued, his officers proposed that a ten-mile-wide neutral zone along the Kumchon-Kaesong-Munsan road should be created for the negotiation meetings and that armed forces of both sides should withdraw from Kaesong. But unfortunately, Ridgway claimed, the proposals were rejected by the Chinese and North Korean liaison officers at the meeting.

Ridgway suggested at the end of his letter the creation of a circular area as the neutral zone, with Kaesong being the center and having a five-mile radius. The Panmunjom bridge would be the eastern boundary. No hostile actions should be allowed in the neutral zone during the talks, and no armed personnel would be stationed in it or along the road that the delegates would take to get to the meeting place. He also suggested that the maximum number of personnel from each side in the neutral zone would not exceed 150. Under these conditions, the organization and selections of each delegation should be completely decided by the commander in chief of each side. Ridgway concluded: "If you agree to these proposals, the present recess can be terminated and the conference resumed without delay and with some expectation of progress."

Kim and Peng wrote back the next day to the UNF commander in chief:

General Ridgway:

We have received your letter of July 13. In order to clear up some misunderstandings and disagreements on some side issues so that the peace talks can proceed smoothly, we agree with your proposition that Kaesong be established for the peace talks as a neutral zone where both sides will stop hostile actions and where all armed personnel will be excluded from that area as well as from the roads both delegations will use. We would like to propose to let the delegations decide the size of this neutral area and other related details during one meeting. The issue of reporters which caused the recess of the current negotiating meeting has nothing to do with establishing a neutral zone for the peace talks. The issue of a neutral zone was never mentioned by your delegation except only once when it was proposed by your liaison officers on July 8. The mission of liaison officers is to discuss details of the meeting, and they have no right to talk about issues of such importance as establishing a neutral zone.

The reporters issue leading to the recess of the peace talks is, in fact, a minor problem. It is not worth stopping the meeting, and it is not worth at all having a breakdown in the negotiations. Your delegation requested to have reporters at Panmunjom during the past meetings. The reason why our delegation did not agree with you on this point is that our delegation believed it unnecessary to have reporters come to Kaesong while nothing has been accomplished at the negotiations and not even the agenda has been agreed upon by both sides. We still believe the principle that resolution on any issue needs to be agreed upon by both sides before its implementation. We also maintain that this principle is a fair and indisputable one. Given that no agreement has been reached on the reporters issue, there is no reason for your side to execute the action of bringing in reporters unilaterally and forcibly.

To prevent the negotiating talks from a long-term recess or even breaking down, we now agree to your suggestion: we consider twenty reporters from your side as part of the personnel of your delegation. We have already ordered our delegation to provide your party with conveniences and facilities on this issue.

In retrospect, the process of determining Kaesong as the location for the Korean truce talks was quite simple. On June 30 Ridgway proposed that the talks could be held on a Danish hospital ship in Wonsan Harbor. On July 1 Kim and Peng suggested instead the Kaesong area on the Thirty-eighth Parallel. Ridgway wrote to them in reply on July 3 that he was ready to send his representatives to "meet your representatives at Kaesong." Thus an agreement on the meeting site was made. It was obvious that upon contact between both delegations, Ridgway regretted this agreement. In order to overturn the agreement, he created a string of incidents at the risk of breaking down the negotiations. As a result, the representatives of the two sides continued debating over these side issues until late October.[19]

Evidently the reporters issue as well as the neutral zone issue were used as pretexts by the Americans. Their real intention was revealed later by Joy in his memoirs:

Because reporters were involved, we concluded to point out that the key to the problem was freedom of speech. Although freedom of speech has an importance that can never be overestimated, its application here is not fully appropriate. These unexpected incidents were used to force a showdown with the Communists on the subject of equal treatment for both sides. This included the neutrality issue concerning the whole area surrounding the negotiation site, freedom of exits and entrances in that area, and whether or not the top commander of each side had the absolute authority on the makeup of his delegation. After a three-day recess, upon General Ridgway's request, the supreme command of the Communists made some simple pledges. The negotiating talks then were resumed.

At the time when the other side made cases of the reporters issue and the Kaesong-as-a-neutral-zone issue at the talks, Zhou Enlai sent instructions for the Chinese delegation. He was not happy that our delegation declined the other side's suggestion for a neutral corridor and a neutral zone for the negotiations during the preparatory meetings. Because our security arrangements were not carefully thought out, our delegation now experienced excessive pressure and responsibility for the security of both delegations. Nonetheless, the other side was responsible for using this as an excuse to interrupt the negotiations arbitrarily.

MAJOR PROBLEMS IN THE NEGOTIATIONS

The Issues at the Negotiating Table

Two of the most prominent items on the agenda were whether or not the Thirty-eighth Parallel should be regarded as the military demarcation line and the problem of withdrawing foreign troops.[20] On the first item, the other side did not elaborate on the substance of the issue but stated only that an agenda was concerned with what to talk about, not the substantive issues of the talks. The Chinese–North Korean side eventually accepted this viewpoint on the military demarcation line. Thus, the second item, whether the withdrawal of foreign troops should be on the agenda, became the focus of debate.

It should be noted that the item "withdrawal of all foreign troops," which was put forward by the Chinese and the North Koreans, really touched the Americans' sore spot. Since the end of World War II, the Truman administration had violated the agreement made by the three foreign ministers of the United States, the United Kingdom, and the Soviet Union at the Moscow Conference on December 12, 1945, which was aimed at "reconstructing Korea as a unified country." The Truman administration instead had established the South Korean government, which divided the Korean peninsula into two parts. Without the support of the American armed forces, Syngman Rhee could not have come to his presidency or stabilized his power after his long exile abroad.[21]

During September and October 1947, the Soviet government suggested several times that the American and Soviet armies withdraw simultaneously from Korea, but Truman rejected the idea. Rhee, in particular, was afraid of the withdrawal of the American troops. Before the Soviets made their suggestions, he had claimed he wanted to do away with "the military-administration regime supported by foreign troops." Once the Soviets made statements in favor of withdrawing foreign troops, Rhee turned around and called for an immediate withdrawal of the Soviet troops, a dismantling of the North Korean army, and the maintenance of American troops in South Korea until the strength of the South Korean army could be fully expanded. Under these circumstances, [Gen.] Albert Wedemeyer undertook an inspection mission to Korea on September 12, 1947, and thereafter made a "secret report" to Truman, suggesting that the American troops stay in South Korea.

Nevertheless, the Soviets' suggestion of withdrawing foreign troops struck such responsive chords in the hearts of the people that it was echoed everywhere in the world, especially wherever American troops were stationed. In those countries where democracy had a foundation, the cry "Yankees go home" was even raised, which put the American troops into embarrassing situations. The announcement made by the Soviet Union on December 25 that the Soviet armed forces had completely withdrawn from North Korea gave more momentum to the work for peace. Under the pressure, Truman had to take similar steps in South Korea, but he dragged out this action until June 30, 1949, when he announced a complete withdrawal of American troops. Truman once again lost the battle over withdrawing foreign troops.

In fact, Truman's policy toward the Korean peninsula had always been either reunification by the American forces or maintaining the long-term division of two Koreas.[22] Truman did not admit the failure of his reunification-by-force policy until MacArthur's Christmas campaign had been defeated. Truman now had to sit down to negotiate a settlement of the Korean problem. Rhee, however, would not accept this situation. When both sides were about to start their negotiations, Rhee made a statement on June 27 that he would not accept any armistice plan because he believed it would lead to a war of terror. On June 30 he elaborated on the South Korean government's position on a cease-fire in Korea: the Chinese Communist troops must withdraw from Korea completely; the [North Korean] People's Army must be disarmed; the UN should prevent any other third country from assisting North Korea; the international conference on the Korean problem must invite South Korea to attend; and his regime would oppose any decisions or plans that would lead to disputes over the sovereignty and integrity of Korea's territory.

After the three-day interruption, the truce negotiations resumed [July 15, 1951] to discuss the agenda for the meetings, the focus remaining on whether the withdrawal of foreign troops should be included. The Chinese–North Korean side said that withdrawal of foreign troops was a necessary condition to prevent war from breaking out again in Korea, since their presence had been the source of the war. The other side insisted that there were no foreign troops in Korea when the war broke out; when it started, the foreign troops had just withdrawn. Their argument could be refuted, because according to their own logic, only when the Neo-imperialists stationed their armies everywhere in the world would a war be prevented and peace be maintained. Being unable to further their arguments to justify themselves, the other side made another point, that withdrawal of foreign troops was a political issue. They said that the commander in chief of the UN Forces only had the power of commanding those troops but no authority to order any country to withdraw its own troops from Korea. This was obviously a pretext, and it was meaningless to pursue the debate at this point in the talks.

After a whole week of intense debate under these circumstances, the Chinese–North Korean delegation proposed a three-day recess for our side to discuss the matter. We took into account the fact that Kennan had once told Malik that there was no room for negotiations on complete withdrawal of foreign troops but that the question concerning progressive withdrawal could be discussed in the future.[23] On July 25 our delegation proposed to put on the agenda "items of concern to the two parties to be reported to their governments," in an attempt to take the issue to another meeting for resolution. Thus, five items were finally agreed upon by both sides on July 26:

1. Pass the agenda of the talks.
2. Determine the military demarcation line between the two sides in order to establish a nonmilitary zone. This will provide a foundation for the hostile actions in Korea to come to an end.
3. Arrange details for an effective cease-fire and armistice in Korea, including the organization, authority, and responsibilities of a committee supervising the implementation of the clauses concerning the cease-fire and armistice.
4. Exchange prisoners of war and civilian detainees.[24]
5. Propose items needed to be suggested to the governments related to the two parties.

The peace-loving people of the world were expecting and hoping that these items on the agenda, so difficult to obtain, would turn into reality.

New Instructions from Beijing

In late November 1951 the winter had already arrived in the central region of Korea, and the temperature fell rapidly at Kaesong.[25] On November 20 Li Kenong called a short meeting of the Chinese–North Korean delegation in the conference room at the Little Villa. Having had a relapse of his asthma, Li coughed severely when he talked. Bian Zhangwu [his assistant] sitting next to him made a cup of hot tea for him.[26]

Li's health had always been a problem. One night in November he had a heart attack and fell down on the floor. At that time our delegation had qualified, experienced medical doctors present. Without moving him, they administered oral emergency medicine for artery expansion and let him sleep on the floor for more than an hour. Eventually, Li recovered consciousness. Although Li did not want us to report his collapse to the CCP Central Committee, the Chinese delegation still telegraphed

Zhou Enlai about his illness. Thus the committee later sent Wu Xiuquan (Wu Hsiu-ch'uan) here to replace Li.[27] After Wu arrived, however, Li asked the committee to allow him to stay at Kaesong for the talks, reasoning that there should be "no changing commanders in the middle of a battle."

At this delegation meeting, Li reported on the current situation and our policy according to the CCP Central Committee's instructions. He described the situation in the first part of the truce talks by making two points:

> First of all, this negotiation is not one between winners and losers. Reasonably speaking, the talk is between two sides which have fought to a draw on the battlefield. Even so, the other side has refused to accept such a fact. America is the number one power in the world. It will hardly get down from its high horse. On the other hand, we are the people who have just achieved our own liberation. No power in the world can possibly overwhelm us. Here is the fact that the enemy wants to overpower you, but you do not want to accept his suppression. This fact has determined the protracted and complex nature of our mission at the truce talks. The other side's approach seems like this: he thinks about talks while fighting; when the talks cannot serve his goal, he wants to fight again. After he fails to win the fight, he comes back to the negotiating table. And then he plays all the games at the talks. After all, the other side does not intend to reach an agreement with us easily and quickly. Thus, comrades, we must guard against impetuosity. Your impatience does not help anything.
>
> Second, we must wage a tit-for-tat struggle. We are fighting for nothing but a peace, a peaceful solution for the Korean problem. All of the peace-loving people in the world support us. So we are capable of handling the enemy's pressure. He attacks us on the battlefield, we can fight back on the battlefield; he raises unreasonable issues during the talks, we explore and refute them at the meetings; and he makes deliberate provocations outside the meetings, we investigate and protest them one after another. Of course, when we talk about a tit-for-tat struggle, we do not mean no flexibility. The truce talks are a political battle, not a military battle. We cannot depend only on our bravery. We have long since realized there will not be an easy solution, that it is always diamond-cut-diamond when the two sides meet inside or outside the talks. But the problem for us now is how to turn this situation around. We thought panel discussions and staff meetings might relax the tense environment at the talks. In fact, however, both sides still confront the tough with toughness at these small meetings.
>
> I am worrying a lot about how to change this situation. Premier Zhou had talks with the Guomindang for many years [during the Anti-Japanese War and the Chinese civil war]. Although the Communists and the Nationalists squared off on issues in an argument, their delegations at the talks also had many per-

sonal contacts. Some tough problems which could not find any solution at the negotiation table were handled through meetings of individuals outside of the negotiation room. Even though today's rigid situation in the Korean truce talks is certainly caused by both sides, we should take a chance to change such a situation through our own "ways," if possible.

Li then analyzed the current situation. It was our victory, he said, through a tit-for-tat struggle on the battlefield as well as in the negotiations, to have resumed the truce talks on October 25. It was also a victory for the people of the world, including the American people, who wanted peace and opposed the war. America had difficulties, even more serious than those we encountered. The American people did not want a war. The people in the world did not want a war. The Second Plenary Meeting of the World Peace Council passed a resolution on the Korean question denouncing America's attempt to expand the conflict and delay the negotiations. This was a just voice from the people all over the world. Moreover, the UN General Assembly was totally different this year from last year; the nations allied with the United States had long since lost the interest in the Korean War that they had demonstrated last July and August. Even England's newspaper the *Times* [London] published articles asking for the establishment of a military demarcation line along the Thirty-eighth Parallel and an end to the Korean War. Though Andrei Y. Vishinsky's proposal could not be passed at the UN, it had a strong influence; that was why the Americans decided to talk to the Soviets about resuming the truce negotiations. The Americans said something entirely irrelevant, attempting to blame the Soviet Union for the postponed talks. In fact, America wanted to return to the negotiating table under the circumstances in order to save face. This proved that it had difficulties.

Li continued his analysis: "America resumes the truce talks because of domestic and international pressures. The resumed talks, in turn, will increase the domestic and international pressures on America for a peace. This follows [the] dialectics of situational development. Therefore, we can say that there is now an increasing possibility for an armistice treaty. This is a calculation made by both Chairman Mao and Premier Kim. We must seize this opportunity and make great efforts for reaching the armistice agreement within this year."

Since Bian Zhangwu, Qiao Guanhua, and Xie Fang had already read the instructions cabled by Mao Zedong, they showed confidence in "reaching an armistice agreement within this year." The other delegates at the meeting, however, half believed and half doubted that such a quick armistice was possible. The outspoken Shen Jiantu said, "It seems to me very difficult."

Li looked at him and continued:

As you said, it is certainly not an easy job. But we can make our efforts for it. Premier Zhou often tells us that a negotiation depends upon two things: the first is an opportunity, and the second is a condition. I have already discussed our good opportunity. Now let me talk a little bit about the present conditions in the talks. Regarding the truce line issue, we proposed the current frontal line as a military demarcation line during the truce period. We believed that this proposal could be accepted soon. After we made our proposal at the meeting, the other side was thrown into a panic. Though they gave up their request to draw a truce line deep in the rear of our army's position, they rushed to a counterproposal on November 8, putting on a good bluff and asking for the city of Kaesong. At that time I knew that they could not sustain their proposal because they did not have any justification for such a request. Just as I expected, they had to basically accept our proposal about the truce line on November 17.[28]

Qiao cut in at this moment: "Regarding the enemy's request of Kaesong, I have a feeling that it is Rhee's idea. Kaesong is an ancient capital of Korea. Rhee would not be able to politically justify his loss of the ancient capital after only one battle. So the Americans seem to have to cover up perfunctorily for his loss of Kaesong."

Li nodded and continued:

It is quite possible. That is why we firmly denounced their request, and we have made them withdraw [it]. While we need to fight back against unreasonable requests, we also need to make progress toward a truce. The issue of the truce line is a basic condition for the armistice. An agreement on this issue means that the most important problem in the armistice talks is solved. Of course, I do not mean by this that there is no problem with other items. When you are dealing with Americans, you can never imagine that there is no problem. The third item for the talks, for example, is about how to check on the cease-fire. According to a conventional way which the Americans have adopted for handling this kind of situation in the past, they may ask for unlimited checking, which is unacceptable to us. Before the war, we did not allow them to come to our side. After the cease-fire, how can we agree to let the enemy come to our rear areas for inspection or checking? Sovereignty is the life of a nation. So both sides may stick to this point. We have prepared a resolution to ask a neutral country to check the cease-fire in one or two rear port cities on both sides.

All the delegates at the meeting believed this a wise counsel. With such an approach we would not have major problems during the discussions over the third item.

Li continued. "There may be other problems or troubles during the discussions on this topic, such as nomination of the neutral countries. We can think about which countries we are going to choose as our candidates. We are not afraid of disagreement or argument over the nomination. As long as we set up the principle for a neutral country's visits, the nomination of neutral countries should not be an unsolvable problem."

Regarding the POWs, Li said that our position was to exchange all the prisoners on both sides. They were the less fortunate in the war. Exchange of POWs was not only a principle established by international code but also an issue of humanitarianism. To reach an agreement on this issue should not be too difficult.

Regarding the summit meeting following an armistice, Li said that the other side would be forced to accept discussions for a top leaders' international conference as part of the talks. The other side, he said, was most afraid of talking about withdrawing foreign troops from Korea and discussing the problems of the Far East. Yet, the results of discussions on these topics would only be the delegations' recommendations to the relevant governments of both sides. The outcome of such talks would include only certain agreements, such as holding a high-ranking governmental officials' meeting at a certain time to discuss withdrawal of all foreign troops and a peaceful solution of the Korean problem. Other details, such as where to have the meeting and who would attend it, would be left for later discussions after the truce treaty was signed.

Li then concluded:

The Central Committee has given us its bottom line. And a good opportunity is there for us. It is now up to us to carry out the plans and seize the opportunity. We should be firm with principles and flexible with tactics. We certainly could at most control half of the truce talks. But as long as we do our part right, the other side has to respond to us. If they don't, they will put themselves into an extremely disadvantageous position in front of the people of the world, including the American people. So we need to have two preparations. Through our work and our efforts, we will be prepared to welcome a truce agreement, but we will also be ready for having no agreement reached. With the two plans in readiness, we will benefit by the arrival of peace, and not worry about any delay. Neither do we have to worry about the battlefield. Commander Peng told us a long time ago, "The army must fight bravely, and the delegation must talk patiently." Our mission is to carry out the talks.

Li's lengthy speech greatly inspired the attendants at the meeting. During the midnight meal at the break, everybody looked happy. Nam Il joked with Qiao: "This [Li's speech] makes much easier your work as 'the instructor.'"

After the break, the meeting continued. Nam Il gave a talk first. He said that he fully supported the great decision made by Chairman Mao and Premier Kim. We had problems in the talks because the enemy was so cunningly knavish. Having been always inconsistent in their words and deeds, they created one obstacle after another. But the current conditions were favorable to us. On the battleground we forced the enemy into a military stalemate. At the talks we now had an overall plan. We should try our best at the talks, of course, for a truce agreement. But if the enemy wanted the talks to drag on, we were not afraid of any delay.

Then Xie Fang, Lee Sang Cho, and others also talked about their thoughts, one after another. Qiao gave his own opinion on the POW issue:

The Central Committee does not think there are major problems in an agreement about the POWs. I am, however, somewhat worried about this issue. A recent bad omen [November 14, 1951] is the statement made by [Col. James M.] Hanley, chief of the military law section in Van Fleet's Eighth Army Headquarters.[29] Hanley said that our army killed American prisoners. That is pure slander and certainly does not square with the facts. He said the CPVF 23d Regiment, 81st Division, did it. In fact, our army does not have any regiment [with such a number]. Even the U.S. Defense Department announced that Hanley's statement did not have a factual ground. Though Ridgway supported Hanley's statement, he did not allow Hanley to meet reporters. It is a surprise that Truman said the day after Hanley's statement that "the Chinese troops killed American prisoners of war in Korea. It is the most brutal action in the past 100 years." As the president of a major power in the world, Truman supported an army military-law section chief's statement which his own defense ministry refused to accept. This is an unusual situation. It signals that the American policy makers may want to do something with the POW issue. I am not sure, but I'd like to raise this question for our comrades' further discussions.

Qiao's suggestion showed his thoughtful, intellectual analysis and judgment as a diplomat. Before long, as Qiao predicted, the POW issue really became a major obstacle in reaching the armistice agreement.

The Cease-fire and the Third and Fifth Items

The truce negotiations proceeded with discussion of the third item on the agenda.[30] At that time, the battleground was relatively quiet except for the enemy's "mincing attacks" (*jiaoshazhan*). There was a favorable opportunity to make some progress in the talks both inside and outside the meeting room.

With regard to the issue of cease-fire inspections, the Chinese–North Korean delegations considered a military cease-fire merely a short transition period to the peaceful solution of the Korean problem. The so-called inspections [or supervision] were but a temporary military arrangement to help both sides prepare for a subsequent political summit meeting to discuss withdrawal of all foreign troops and to find a final and peaceful solution to the Korean problem. Only a complete solution could possibly guarantee that hostile conflict would never resume between both sides. The other side's point of view, however, was different from our understanding of this issue. They wanted to keep Korea divided for a long time. During the separation of North Korea from the South, the Americans intended to curtail the former's economic recovery and development as much as possible. For their purposes, therefore, they believed that the tougher the cease-fire supervision was, the better. They wanted to use cease-fire inspections to interfere in the internal affairs of North Korea. These different purposes revealed themselves at the negotiation table. Another round of serious struggle began.

On November 27, having agreed on the second item in the talks [on November 23], both sides started immediate discussions on the third item, including "detailed arrangements for realizing a cease-fire in Korea," "organization of cease-fire inspection teams," and "the teams' responsibilities and authority." The Chinese–North Korean delegation proposed at once five principles:

1. All the armed forces of both sides, including ground, naval, and air force regular troops and nonregular troops, should stop all hostile actions on the day that a cease-fire agreement is signed.
2. All the armed forces of both sides should withdraw from the nonmilitary zone within three days after the cease-fire agreement is signed.
3. All the armed forces of both sides should withdraw from the other side's rear areas, offshore islands, and coastal waters according to the military demarcation line within five days after the cease-fire agreement is signed. If one side does not withdraw its troops on time and offers no reason for their delayed withdrawal, the other side has the right to adopt any necessary measure to handle these troops in order to safeguard local security.
4. The armed forces of both sides will not enter the nonmilitary zone and will not conduct any military movement within the zone.
5. Both sides should appoint the same number of committee members to organize a cease-fire committee, which will work on detailed cease-fire arrangements and check on the cease-fire's implementation.

We thought the first four provisions, along with the last item concerning an oversight team's organization and function, were enough for us to ensure a smooth transition to the high-level political meeting. But the other side proposed seven countersuggestions. They changed the stance that they had had in the past: "Withdrawal of foreign troops is a political issue; political issues are not supposed to be discussed during a military truce negotiation." They now emphasized discussions on some general topics, such as "no increase of military forces" during the cease-fire period, which were obviously political issues related to both sides' internal affairs. They also insisted on "unlimited visits" to the other side's rear areas by air and land after the cease-fire began. The Chinese–North Korean delegation definitely could not accept these measures, which would entail interference in their internal affairs. Nevertheless, the Chinese and Koreans were not surprised by the Americans' suggestions, nor did we feel frustrated after we heard them. On the contrary, we felt confident that these knotty problems would be smoothly solved as soon as we used our "wise counsel" of neutral countries' checking on the cease-fire.

Meanwhile, we sped up our preparations for reaching a truce agreement by the end of the year. As Li had suggested, the Central Committee transferred a group of governmental officials and military commanders to Kaesong from China, from the CPVF Headquarters, and from CPVF army groups along the front in order to strengthen our delegation. For the next negotiation item, prisoners of war,

Li suggested including Du Ping, director of the CPVF's Political Department, in our delegation to prepare talks on POW problems. Our delegation thus was quickly strengthened. To enhance delegation members' psychological preparedness and political education, Li selected senior political officer Ding Guoyu, a CPVF army political director, to head the delegation's political task force.

Du had been in charge of POW work at the CPVF General Headquarters. As soon as he joined the delegation, he prepared two detailed POW lists, which met the requirements of the International Committee of the Red Cross. One listed the captured UN/U.S. prisoners, the other the Chinese and North Korean prisoners.

At the same time, the CPVF NKPA Joint Command Headquarters made new plans on the battleground to coordinate our efforts at the negotiation table. For example, the Joint Headquarters ordered the CPVF Fiftieth Army to launch four amphibious attacks on enemy-held offshore islands along the western coast between November 5 and 30, 1951. The continual offensive campaigns, which started from islands nearby and progressed to farther islands one after another, liberated the Taehwa, Sohwa, Ssuk-som, and Tan Islands and more than ten other ones. Although the amphibious attacks eliminated only about 570 enemy troops and special agents, our campaigns destroyed enemy intelligence bases on these islands. Our military efforts on the battleground compelled the other side to accept our terms at the negotiation table of "withdrawing all the armed forces from the other side's rear areas, offshore islands, and coastal waters according to the military demarcation line within five days after the cease-fire agreement is signed." These efforts also eliminated threats to the Chinese–North Korean rear and flank areas posed by the enemy troops and secret agents on the western offshore islands.[31]

After one week of heated debates at the negotiation table, we could tell that the other side was actually worrying that the Chinese and North Koreans would use the cease-fire to strengthen military forces. In order to relieve the other side's anxiety, on December 3 we added two more supplemental suggestions to our proposal, aimed at stopping the other side's making excuses and preventing one side from interfering with the other side's domestic affairs. Without changing anything in the first four principles, our additional suggestions modified the fifth item slightly to make it consistent with our new items. Then we added two more to the original five items, proposing altogether seven principles. Our new proposal included an important guarantee that "no military force, weapons, and munitions of both sides can enter into Korea from the outside under any excuse" after the cease-fire was in effect. We also divided the item on cease-fire checking into two parts: that the cease-fire committee would be directly responsible for monitoring within the nonmilitary zone, and that neutral countries' verification committees would be responsible for cease-fire monitoring in the rear areas outside the nonmilitary zone.

With these new suggestions, the Chinese–North Korean delegation had now formulated a seven-principle proposal (with no change in the first four items):

5. Both sides should appoint the same number of people to form a cease-fire committee, which will work on detailed cease-fire arrangements and check on all cease-fire implementations except the responsibilities defined by the sixth item.
6. To ensure military stability during the cease-fire so as to have a good political conference between both sides' leaders, both sides should promise not to transfer any military force, weapons, and munitions from the outside into Korean territory under any excuse.
7. In order to have strict inspection on the implementation of the sixth item, both sides agree to invite representatives from countries neutral during the Korean War to organize a monitoring committee. The committee should make necessary visits to rear areas' seaports outside the nonmilitary zone (both sides having agreed on which seaports) and then make reports to the cease-fire committee about the results.

The other side did not expect these proposals. Not knowing what to do, they suggested turning the meeting into panel discussions. They clearly needed time to report to and ask instructions from Washington's policy makers.

Unable to make any counterproposal, the other side temporized at the panel discussions for nine days. Apparently, they were unwilling to give up their attempt to visit the rear areas directly. Moreover, they had problems with complete "no entry" since they needed to rotate military personnel and supply their troops. A promise not to transfer "any military force, weapons, and munitions from the outside into Korean territory under any excuse" would result in tying themselves up. But without a better idea, they falsely accused the Chinese–North Korean delegation of attempting to employ a method to reduce their forces in order gradually to achieve the goal of kicking out all foreign troops. "No entering," according to their words, meant no entry, only withdrawal. As time passed, their troops would be drained off. In fact, they could not make out a good case even for themselves. This principle was to apply to both sides, so how could it reduce troops only on their own side?

Having idled away nine days, the other side put forth a counterproposal on December 12, reluctantly accepting our idea of neutral-country teams visiting seaports in rear areas. However, it insisted on transferring troops and supplying weapons and munitions in large numbers. More important, it proposed prohibiting all construction, repair, and improvement of airports and aviation facilities in Korean territory. This item became a big obstacle to reaching an agreement at the peace talks and was a serious issue of principle. Any sovereign country cannot tolerate such a prohibition on aviation construction within its own territory. The other side actually intended to cut off international air communication and transportation to North Korea. Among other things, they also wanted to keep their armed forces on some offshore islands and in the waters along the rear areas of North Korea.

The Chinese–North Korean delegation kept seeking for truth, accepting fair proposals and refusing unfair ones. Reasonably speaking, since the American troops were an overseas expedition, it was inevitable for them to be transferred and rotated. The invasion of Korea was not their decision. According to America's service system, a soldier should be transferred back home after he had served on the front for ten to twelve months. Troop rotation was an issue of humanitarianism and concerned thousands of families. We should give their suggestion of troop rotation some reasonable consideration.

Therefore, the Chinese–North Korean delegation worked out a new proposal on December 14, two days after the other side presented its counterproposal. We added a new paragraph to our sixth item. After "both sides should promise not to transfer any military force, weapons, and munitions from the outside into Korean territory under any excuse," we added, "if either side needs to transfer or replace its troops who are already in Korea, it must send its request to the cease-fire committee for permission. The maximum rotation of troops cannot exceed 5,000 men per month. These rotations should take place at rear area seaports agreed upon by both sides and examined by neutral-countries' cease-fire monitoring committees on the sites."

Moreover, during later discussions, the Chinese–North Korean delegation also accepted the other side's suggestion that "no reinforcement of military airplanes, armored vehicles, and combat munitions" should be allowed into Korea after the cease-fire became effective. In other words, this item meant that the American army could make necessary replacements or changes of their weapons and equipment as long as they were not sending in reinforcements.

In their counterproposal, the other side argued that visits and examinations conducted only within the demilitarized zone and seaports in the rear areas would not ensure the implementation of the truce agreement. To get rid of the excuse [for them to check all our rear areas], our new proposal suggested that neutral-countries' monitoring committees should examine the cease-fire "at the seaports in the rear areas and outside of the demilitarized zone, agreed upon by both sides, and at any location where a violation of the cease-fire takes place." By adding fourteen [Chinese] words here, "at any location where a violation of the cease-fire takes place," we extended the cease-fire examination by neutral countries to anywhere in Korea.

The other side, however, did not make any compromise after our concession. They put forward another counterproposal on December 23 that accepted our new points but still insisted on their attempts to [check the rear areas so as to] interfere in the internal affairs of another country. Their new excuse was that the repair and construction of airfields and aviation facilities must inevitably increase the military strength of the Chinese and North Koreans. To relieve their anxiety, on December 24 we made another change to our December 14 proposal and clearly pointed out that "no military aircraft should be allowed to enter Korea." Our proposal also agreed with the other side's idea that "when either side of the Cease-fire Committee requests an investigation of any violation of the cease-fire agreement, the neutral-countries' monitoring committees must conduct a visit and examination immediately."

Even though the Chinese and North Koreans made many efforts, there was no truce treaty to be signed by December 27. This very important day was wasted. A month earlier, on November 27, both sides had reached an agreement on the military demarcation line: "If a truce treaty is not signed within 30 days [by December 27], then the front line between the two sides at the time should be recognized by both sides as the military demarcation line." From that moment, all peoples of the world, including the American people, looked forward to a truce treaty to be signed within thirty days. The news from the negotiating table, however, crushed their hope.[32]

Who was responsible for this? Xie Fang, the Chinese–North Korean representative for the third item's panel discussions, said at the talks on December 27: "It is your side who plays around for so much time at the talks. Of course, you can continue postponing the truce negotiations. But we believe that we must put our contentious issues in front of the entire world. Let the peoples of the world know who is actually delaying the Korean truce negotiations." There was a reason for the deadlock in the negotiation of the third item: one side intended to interfere in the internal affairs of the other, and the other side refused to let it happen.

The Chinese–North Korean delegation said that it could not accept the proposal to prohibit airfield development because the internal affairs of our side could not be interfered with by others. It was another matter, however, if we decided to restore or resupply any equipment. The other side, however, said that they already were interfering in our internal affairs by using their military power. "Currently, we are interfering in your internal affairs. You are repairing airfields. After you finish them, we bomb and destroy them. You repair them again, we bomb them again."[33]

Xie got angry hearing this assertion. "This kind of bloody, overbearing explanation of your aggression is too preposterous and not worth refuting. You should know that you have no right to interfere in our internal affairs, even though you can bomb and destroy our side with military means. You just can't do whatever you want to. You simply cannot get what you want through military power in the war. Neither can you get it now through negotiations. I tell you the truth that you can never get from the negotiating table what you fail to get from the battleground."

The other side said that there was no absolute sovereignty in today's world. As complete sovereignty did not exist, why, they asked, did we try to square accounts in every detail and assume complete sovereignty and noninterference in domestic affairs?

We answered that the other side's point explicitly exposed the aggressive ambition of American imperialist rulers to seek hegemony in the world. Since they intended to invade other countries, they refused to recognize that all the nations in the world had their own sovereignty. They insisted on their point by saying that we should forget about meaningless terms like "sovereignty" and "internal affairs."

The Chinese–North Korean delegation made it clear that many countries had been dominated by America, which was why they did not have meaningful, complete sovereignty. But please do not forget, we stated, that your attempt to dominate the entire world has run into obstacles and has been foiled in many areas because there are not only countries with complete sovereignty but also countries that want to be armed to defend their own sovereignty and resist foreign interference. We also wanted to say that there were millions and millions of people in the world who were now fighting bravely for their countries' sovereignty and independence.

The American side said that, nevertheless, truce means to give up part of one's sovereignty. They argued that since we had suggested ensuring that no foreign military personnel, combat airplanes, armored vehicles, and weapons and munitions be allowed to enter Korea and had invited representatives of neutral countries to examine the rear areas' seaports, that, in fact, we had already accepted interference in one side's internal affairs by the other.

We said that their argument was an absurd inference that intentionally ignored the fact that our suggestion itself was actually aimed at stopping foreign interference in Korea through methods such as preventing any foreign military forces from entering and inviting neutral countries to conduct inspections, which had nothing to do with the Korean War. Our suggestion sharply distinguished between Korea's foreign relations and domestic affairs. It was the only possible resolution to stabilize a military truce as well as to avoid domestic problems on both sides.

At that time, we thought these ridiculous arguments from the other side were merely careless speeches by the American generals at the talks. They were at least not politicians. We should not wonder at their political naivete. Later, however, after I read Admiral Joy's diaries and memoirs, I knew that the "copyright" of these arguments belonged to the White House and the Department of State.

The Chinese Communists and Chinese government have always believed that there are two different kinds of war in the world. One is just, the other unjust. A just war is to employ military power to defend our country's sovereignty and territorial integrity and to safeguard our own internal affairs from foreign interference. Although a just war might fail once because of disparity in strength, the just struggle should continue until its final victory. Our belief reflects the interests and wishes of the peace-loving people in the world. Our purpose in the talks was to stop the war and pursue peace. How could we allow the other side to interfere in our internal affairs after the cease-fire? Even a "reduced interference" could never be tolerated; it was still an interference.

The panel discussions continued without any result until January 27, 1952.[34] Unable to advance any further arguments to justify themselves, the other side began to pester us endlessly, insisting on their proposed restriction of airport facilities. Since the discussions went nowhere, both sides agreed to adjourn them and hold staff meetings to talk over the details of what had been agreed to by both sides in principle.

The discussions on the fifth item of the talks at staff meetings reached an impasse over the issue of nominating neutral countries for cease-fire examination. At the beginning, both sides had already agreed on a definition of "neutral country," which meant "its armed forces did not participate in the Korean hostilities." But when we nominated the Soviet Union, Czechoslovakia, and Poland, the other side without any reason refused to accept the Soviet Union as a neutral country.[35]

The panel discussions on the fourth item, which started on December 11, 1951, also reached a deadlock. On January 31, 1952, the other side suggested starting another panel discussion on the fifth item on the agenda. The Chinese–North Korean delegation agreed and suggested holding a general meeting instead of a panel discussion in order to break the deadlock.

On February 6, 1952, a general meeting of the delegations began. Regarding the fifth item, the Chinese–North Korean delegation [Nam Il speaking] suggested that within three months after the truce treaty became effective, each side should appoint five representatives to prepare for a political conference. Its task would be to discuss withdrawal of all foreign troops from Korea, peaceful resolution of the Korean problem, and other issues related to Korea's peace.

Discussing our suggestion, the other side wanted to avoid an explicit announcement about a higher level political conference. They actually intended to make this item in the negotiation meaningless, saying, "The commanders of both sides should not examine various issues on a political solution of the Korean problem."

As everyone knew, the purpose of the truce negotiations was to stop hostile actions and create favorable conditions for withdrawing all foreign troops and for solving the Korean problem peacefully. How could they say that both sides' commanders should not examine the "various issues" of a political solution?

They countered, "After the truce treaty is signed, both delegations should suggest to their governments or concerned authorities that the governments make some further efforts at political meetings or through political means within three months to handle other problems in Korea." They were simply juggling words. In fact, the other side wanted to make no commitment to a political conference and attempted to replace the "political meeting" with "political means."[36] Regarding the conference agenda, the other side did not like our suggested third topic, "other issues related to Korea's peace." They changed it to "other Korean problems related to the peace."

On February 16, after more than ten days' discussions at the general meeting of both delegations, the Chinese–North Korean team put forth a revised proposal for the fifth item: "In order to insure a peaceful solution of the Korean question, the military commanders of both sides hereby recommend to all concerned governments [on both sides] that within three months after the armistice agreement is signed and becomes effective, a political conference of a higher level of both sides be held by representatives appointed respectively to settle through negotiations the questions of the withdrawal of all foreign forces from Korea, the peaceful settlement of the Korean question, and other issues." We added "and other issues" to the last sentence of our revised proposal. Our fighting for the one word "other" made it possible that the higher level political conference would be able to discuss "other issues related to Korea's peace."[37]

After more discussion on the fifth item, both sides finally reached an agreement on February 17.

THE POW ISSUES AND NEW EFFORTS

The Fourth Item in the Negotiations

Discussions proceeded on the fourth item—"arrangements for prisoners of war."[38] The Chinese–North Korean delegation thought it would not be a very difficult issue because by the time the Korean War ended there were many existing international regulations on POWs and so many precedents in the world that the exchange of prisoners already had become mandatory after an international conflict.

The *Geneva Joint Pledge* [Convention] *on POWs' Rights,* for example, passed in 1929 and revised on August 12, 1949, clearly states this issue in Article 118: "As soon as a war ends, prisoners of war must be released and repatriated without any delay." Article 7 also says that "prisoners of war must not give up part or all of the rights as agreed upon in this joint pledge."[39] Sixty-one countries signed the *Geneva Joint Pledge* in 1949. More countries joined them and signed thereafter. The United States was one of the signatories, but the People's Republic of China was not at that time; China announced its recognition of the pledge on July 13, 1952.[40]

Moreover, releasing prisoners of war is an issue of humanitarianism. After a soldier is captured in a foreign war, no matter which side he belongs to, his loved ones at home hope for his safe return and reunion with his family. What a prisoner wants [to go home] is understood and needs no further explanation. In the Korean War, the prisoners and their families had the same desire. The UN prisoners detained by the Chinese and North Korean armies had a Central Committee of American and British Prisoners Promoting Peace. Its Twelfth POW Camp Committee issued a letter, "To Peace-loving Peoples of the World," on December 20, 1951: "We want to go home. For many of us, this will be our second Christmas holiday since we became prisoners of the Korean War. Though the Chinese People's Volunteers treat us very well here, cooking good food and taking good care of us, we still miss our hometowns and families very badly. . . . The reason why we want to go home is very simple. We want to see our wives, children, and parents." The Chinese and North Korean prisoners in the American camps expressed even stronger requests to go back home. They used not only words and language to proclaim their eager desire but also their lives and blood to dramatize their longing.[41]

In early December 1951, when most discussions on the third item had been resolved, the other side suggested opening a new, parallel panel discussion on POW issues. The Chinese–North Korean delegation had been preparing the talks on these issues after our Little Villa meeting on November 20, 1951. A list of names of the UN prisoners in our camps was already completed, but the list of Chinese and North Korean POWs was not yet available since some of our armies were still fighting and unable to make their reports. Even so, we still considered the other side's proposal a good suggestion so that both the third and fourth items could be discussed at the same time, speeding up the talks. We immediately agreed with their suggestion.

The panel committee on the POW issues began to work on December 11, 1951. Lee Sang Cho and Chai Chengwen represented the Chinese–North Korean delegation, and U.S. Navy Rear Adm. [Ruthven E.] Libby and U.S. Army Col. [George W.] Hickman Jr. represented the other side. At the beginning of the panel discussion, we proposed the principle that all the prisoners of the Korean War should be repatriated promptly as soon as the truce became effective. Unexpected as it was, the other side refused to state clearly its stand on our suggested principle and instead insisted on exchanging each sides' list of POW names first.[42] On December 12, the second day of the meetings, we submitted a formal proposal in writing with five suggested topics on the fourth item for panel discussions:

1. Work out a principle [by which] all the prisoners of the Korean War currently detained by both sides should be released.
2. Discuss a schedule for the war prisoners' repatriation. Within the shortest possible period after the truce treaty is signed, both sides should complete their release and repatriation by groups of all the prisoners they detained during the war. Both sides should accept a principle that wounded and sick prisoners should be released and repatriated in the first group.
3. Suggest Panmunjom or Kaesong as the location for exchanging the war prisoners between both sides.
4. Suggest organizing a prisoners' repatriation committee under the Truce Negotiation Committee. Both sides would appoint the same number of members for the repatriation committee, which should be in charge of the prisoners' exchange, repatriation, and other matters according to this agreement.
5. Exchange the lists of names of all the current prisoners in the Korean War as soon as all the above suggestions are agreed upon and confirmed by both sides.

It would not have been very difficult to reach a prisoners' repatriation agreement based on these suggestions if the other side had been sincere about solving the POW problem as soon as possible. After our formal proposal, the other side still avoided responding to the principle of releasing and repatriating all the prisoners. Instead, they raised two new issues that brought up unnecessary ramifications: first, the International Committee of the Red Cross should send delegations to visit both sides' POW camps; second, the POW lists should be exchanged first.[43]

It was evidently proven later that the other side did not really intend to invite the Red Cross to visit the POW camps when it raised this issue. The Americans just wanted to cause trouble on our side since the Chinese and North Koreans had many difficulties in hosting such visits. At that time, making full use of their air superiority, enemy airplanes raided and bombed our positions and rear areas day and night. It would be extremely difficult for us to provide the Red Cross visitors with services, supplies, and transportation to the POW camps. And most important, we could hardly guarantee the prevention of accidents. If the Red Cross visitors had casualties during their visits in our areas, it would be too late to argue who was accountable. Thus our responsible and careful position in the talks was that we must be very cautious in the matter of the Red Cross visits.

For the Chinese–North Korean side, the exchange of POW lists was purely a technical issue at that point. In retrospect, this issue, like the Red Cross visits, was merely one of those cards the other side played in order to reduce pressures from world public opinion for a prompt agreement on the POW problems. The issues the UNC team raised were only shields to cover its POW proposal, which they dared not issue to the public early in the talks since it violated the *Geneva Joint Pledge*. Yet five days later, in order to remove the other side's excuses for delaying negotiations on the fourth item, the Chinese–North Korean side agreed to exchange POW lists first and did so on December 18.[44]

On January 2, 1952, the other side finally issued their so-called proposal for resolving the POW problems. It was indeed preposterous. Its principle for exchanging the POWs was based on a one-to-one exchange. If one side ran out of prisoners, or if it did not have enough detained prisoners to exchange for their soldiers captured by the other side, it could use civilian prisoners for exchange. If there were still not enough, those unexchanged prisoners could take the oath: "I will never participate in another war," and could then be released. The released prisoners could go wherever they were "willing" to go under strict control. The other side described it euphemistically as "voluntary repatriation."

At that time, all peoples of the world hoped that the Korean War could reach its end through a truce treaty in order to avoid more casualties and further disasters. The other side, however, issued its proposal on January 2, rejecting our proposal of repatriating all the prisoners after the truce, thus placing an insurmountable stumbling block in the way of reaching an agreement.

In the panel discussions, the Chinese–North Korean representatives firmly rejected the other side's proposal. Pounding the table and standing up, Lee Sang Cho criticized it: "You should know that POWs' release and repatriation is not a slave trade. The 20th century is not a brutal slavery era. . . . All the peoples of the world will swear against your proposal, and the American prisoners and their families will lay a curse upon your proposal because it is going to destroy the possibility of releasing and repatriating all the prisoners, and will block reaching a truce treaty promptly in the future."[45]

In the Chinese and North Korean camps, some of the American and British prisoners got very upset when they heard about this proposal [to exchange POWs one-to-one]. Their letters to the public pointed out that they hoped to return to their homes promptly and were totally disappointed by the American proposal. It also made their families more worried and pained, they believed: "Although we are in the middle of the 20th century, it seems to us that we the prisoners are still considered as commodities for selling and buying on top of an auction block."

During the panel discussions, the Chinese–North Korean representatives focused on criticizing the one-to-one exchange and "self-motivated repatriation."[46] We compared the one-to-one exchange to trafficking in human beings. The other side had nothing to say in reply and agreed to make a "compromise" by replacing "one-to-one exchange" with "exchange in the same number." The Chinese–North Korean side also pointed out that self-motivated repatriation killed any real self-determination the prisoners should have and interfered with their political beliefs. It bluntly violated the regulations of the *Geneva Joint Pledge on POWs' Rights*. Again, unable to find an answer, the other side agreed to make another compromise by changing "self-motivated repatriation" into "no forced repatriation."

We pointed out that observing the *Geneva Joint Pledge* closely was an obligation and responsibility of all the signatories, and we asked how they could bring the false charge of "forced repatriation" against our side. They said that releasing all the prisoners would mean enhancement of our military manpower. Our answer was that the Americans' argument showed that what they really were concerned with was not prisoners' rights and happiness but competition in combat forces and military power.

During these debates, the other side refused to promise to release and repatriate all the Chinese and North Korean prisoners they detained. At this point, they were impervious to reason. And on this point we could not make any compromise. The panel committee [on the POW issues] held more than fifty meetings. The more meetings we held, the more confrontations both sides were plunged into.

At the same time, the representatives from both sides of the panel committee on the third item also stood opposite one another on the issues of "restricting airport construction" and "nominating the neutral countries for cease-fire inspection." That committee therefore stopped its discussions and turned instead to staff meetings on January 27 to explore some details of what both sides had already agreed upon. Did this stalemate mean that the other side wanted to wait for a final showdown on both items? Whatever it might be, we had to make some progress in the ongoing panel discussions over the fourth item in order to break the deadlock in the truce negotiations.

After careful deliberations, the Chinese staff on the fourth item's panel discussion committee designed a new plan for our representatives. It was aimed at clearing away peripheral obstacles, emphasizing our main principles, and forcing the other side to make a concession on our POW repatriation principle. We added a new measure to our proposal stipulating that repatriated prisoners would promise not to participate in any military operation again in order to eliminate the other side's excuse that "releasing prisoners is equal to increasing military manpower." We also made an overall plan to help homeless civilian refugees return to their homes as soon as the truce became effective in order to foil the other side's attempt at using the "detained civilians" issue as a means of keeping prisoners detained. The Chinese staff worked out many feasible methods to deal with the problems of the fourth item, such as repatriating wounded and sick prisoners first, exchanging files of dead prisoners, inviting the Red Cross to arrange POW camp visits and to assist in the release and repatriation of prisoners, organizing a prisoners' repatriation committee and a committee for returning civilian refugees back home, and so forth. After all, we tried to find solutions for almost every problem we had [identified] in the panel discussions, and we accepted all reasonable ideas in the other side's proposal. After discussions, the Chinese delegation reported our new plan to Beijing. It was soon approved by Mao Zedong.

On February 3, Lee Sang Cho presented this new proposal at the fifty-fifth meeting of the committee:

1. Both sides agree to release and repatriate all the prisoners of the Korean War that each side detains as soon as the truce treaty is signed and becomes effective.

2. Both sides agree to guarantee that all repatriated prisoners on each side must return to their peacetime life and never again participate in any military operations.[47]

3. Both sides agree to release and repatriate seriously wounded and sick prisoners first. At the time when [these POWs] are released and repatriated, both sides should make possible arrangements to release and repatriate detained medical personnel in order to accompany and take care of these wounded and sick prisoners.

4. Both sides agree to release and repatriate all the prisoners detained by each side in groups, in addition to those who are released and repatriated earlier according to the third point, within a period of two months after the truce treaty is signed and becomes effective.

5. Both sides agree to repatriate the prisoners to and receive the prisoners from the other side at Panmunjom in the nonmilitary zone.

6. Both sides agree to appoint three military officers with the rank of major or lieutenant colonel or colonel from each side to establish a prisoners' repatriation committee as soon as the truce treaty is signed and becomes effective. Under the instruction and supervision of the Truce Treaty Committee, this committee is responsible for making detailed repatriation plans and examining both sides' performance in observing all the agreements

regarding the prisoners' release and repatriation included in the truce treaty. If the committee has difficulties in reaching an agreement itself on any of its assignments, it should report its problem to the Truce Treaty Committee for a final decision or solution. The prisoners' repatriation committee may be located near the Headquarters of the Armistice Agreement Committee.

7. Both sides agree to invite respectively the representatives from the Red Cross International Committee and the Red Cross of the DPRK and of the PRC to organize a joint visiting delegation as soon as the truce treaty is signed and becomes effective. This delegation will make site trips to visit the POW camps on both sides. It will also assist both sides with their release and repatriation tasks at the location where the exchange of prisoners will take place.

8. Both sides agree to provide the other side with all available documents of all prisoners who died during their detention, including their names, nationalities, rank, and other related information, as soon as possible or no later than ten days after the truce treaty is signed and becomes effective.

9. Both sides agree to assist civilian refugees who became homeless and victims in the war to return to their homes and resume their peacetime life after the truce treaty is signed and becomes effective. For this item, both sides agree:

    a. The UNF should allow and assist those civilians who had lived north of the current military demarcation line but are stranded south of the demarcation line because of the war to return to their homes in the north before the truce treaty is signed and becomes effective. The NKPA and the CPVF should allow and assist those civilians who had lived south of the current military demarcation line but are stranded north of the demarcation line because of the war to return to their homes in the south before the truce treaty is signed and becomes effective.

    b. The highest commanding officer of each side is responsible for publishing and widely spreading the above contents in this agreement in all the areas under his control. He shall authorize concerned civilian organizations to provide necessary guidance and assistance to all those who are willing to return to their homes among the above-mentioned civilians.

    c. Both sides agree to appoint two military officers with the ranks of major or lieutenant colonel or colonel from each side to establish a committee for assisting homeless civilians to return home as soon as the truce treaty is signed and becomes effective. Under the instruction and supervision of the Armistice Agreement Committee, the committee is responsible for handling and assisting the above-mentioned returning civilians to pass through the demilitarized zone and [in] other related matters. If the committee has difficulties in reaching an agreement itself on any of its assignments, it should report its problem to the Armistice Agreement Committee for a final decision or solution. The committee for assisting civilians to return home may be located near the Headquarters of the Armistice Agreement Committee.

Our new proposal removed all possible excuses the other side could have and gave a new hope to the truce negotiations. Many internationally well-known figures made supportive speeches, one after another. Many reporters wrote favorable comments on our proposal. All stated that this was an ideal proposal to make a breakthrough in the deadlock, which should not be delayed. Our counterpart in the panel discussions, Admiral Libby, seemed to learn from the negotiations and told reporters after the meeting in which we presented the new proposal: "[They] finally used cigarettes to fumigate a proposal." We then made a formal suggestion the next day that the panel discussions could change into staff meetings.[48]

On February 7, 1952, the staff from both sides began their meetings and discussions on the fourth item. In the twenty-two staff meetings that were held thereafter, the other side did not have any major problem with our suggestions except for the basic principle of releasing and repatriating all the prisoners. On this fundamental issue, the other side did not want to give in. Without any significant progress in the staff meetings, the talks on the fourth item had to return to the panel discussions.

Business Meetings During Talks on the Fourth Item

On February 29, [1952] the panel discussions resumed again. On the other side's suggestion, the talks became business meetings, starting on March 2.[49] Since business meetings did not release news, it was easier for both sides to look for some possible way of making the necessary concessions regarding unsolved problems. Thus the Chinese–North Korean representatives agreed with this suggestion.

At these business meetings, we made several suggestions to push the negotiations forward in order to reach an agreement on the fourth item as soon as possible. We suggested, for instance, on March 5, "based upon the current POW information which both sides had confirmed with one another, both sides should first recognize the principle of releasing and repatriating all the prisoners after the truce. 'All the prisoners' referred to those who are currently included in the lists of prisoners detained by both sides. In other words, both sides should accept the idea of releasing and repatriating all the prisoners on the lists." What we suggested, in essence, was to reach an agreement on first releasing and repatriating all the prisoners on the lists that were exchanged between both sides on December 18. Discussion of and solution for the rest of the prisoners' release and repatriation—about 40,000 detained Chinese and North Koreans who were not on the lists and categorized as civilians by the other side—could be postponed until an agreement was reached on the truce treaty.

The other side had a positive response to our exploratory suggestion. Then, on March 21, we proposed another principle: "After the truce treaty is signed and becomes effective, the Korean People's Army and the Chinese People's Volunteers Force will release and repatriate all 11,559 prisoners of war in their custody. The United Nations Command will release and repatriate all of the 132,474 prisoners in its custody. The lists of the names of the prisoners of war above shall be finally checked by staff officers of both sides." Seemingly, the other side was willing to solve the POW problems within a framework underlined by this principle. Thereafter, the panel discussion turned to staff meetings again.[50]

On March 25 the staff meetings changed to staff executive sessions. In the staff business meetings, the Chinese and North Korean representatives made further adjustments. Both sides detained some Korean civilians and POWs who had lived in the areas under the other side's control before the war. Since both sides had agreed to guarantee the repatriated prisoners' return to their homes, reunion with their families, and resumption of their peaceful lives as they wished after the truce treaty was signed, we agreed to make some adjustments on the ground that the Korean prisoners issue was a special, different case. Therefore, on March 27, the Chinese–North Korean representatives proposed a compromise on releasing and repatriating the prisoners: both sides should release and repatriate all the non-Korean and Korean prisoners [Chinese and North Korean soldiers] who did not live in the areas under the detaining side's control before the war. The Korean prisoners who had lived in the areas under the detaining side's control before the war could return to their homes themselves and resume their peaceful lives according to their own will and without formal repatriation. With this obviously responsible attitude, the Chinese–North Korean side worked hard to end the largest regional war since World War II as soon as possible.[51]

Our adjusted compromise proposal on March 27 was the most acceptable solution for all the parties. In light of the hopes of peace-loving peoples of the world and in consideration of the fundamental interests of the Chinese, Korean, American, and British people, the Chinese and North Korean decision makers worked out this excellent proposal, overcoming many difficulties and setbacks in a complicated and confused political arena created by America's ruling group. It was indeed a thoughtful, reasonable, and workable proposal, which enabled us to solve tough problems. It was regrettable that Truman lost this good opportunity. Worried about being accused of losing the Korean War in an election year, Truman added new obstacles and made the war one year and four months longer.[52] That was why the other side issued a revised principle for releasing and repatriating the prisoners on April 1. Unexpected by most people, their counterprinciple proposed that both sides in the war should release and repatriate all the prisoners who were detained when the armistice was signed and became effective. The release and repatriation would be based on the prisoner lists that had been examined and accepted by both sides before the truce agreement was signed. In their proposal, the other side had two so-called "understandings": first, all the POWs and civilian prisoners detained by each side who lived in areas controlled by the detaining side on June 25, 1950, should be released and repatriated, except for those who wished to stay where they had lived before; second, the rest of the POWs should be repatriated, "except [for] those who could not be repatriated without the application of force," who would be released by the detaining side and allowed to settle in a place of their choice.[53]

Apparent as it was, the other side's proposal retained the so-called "voluntary repatriation" principle without any modification. Moreover, their representatives contradicted themselves at the meeting. They announced first that the total number of Chinese and North Korean prisoners who would be repatriated to China and North Korea was 116,000 men, later they said the total number was 70,000.

During the business discussions at the staff meetings, the other side intentionally created an optimistic atmosphere concerning the POW problems. Meanwhile, they sped up their efforts in forcing war prisoners in their camps to say no to repatriation [to China and North Korea]. Under such circumstances, the Chinese–North Korean side announced the end of the staff business meeting on April 25. The other side then simply responded that the talks on the fourth item "adjourned *sine die*."[54]

From late March to early April 1952, the panel committee on the third item agreed on the location and scale of cease-fire checks in both sides' rear areas. The remaining two problems in the panel discussions were only the restrictions on airfield construction and the nomination of neutral countries. After April 11, however, the atmosphere changed at those meetings.

"Escaping Meetings" and "Adjourning *Sine Die*"

The other side's representative on the panel committee to discuss the third item was Maj. Gen. [William K.] Harrison [Jr.].[55] From April 11, Harrison began to obstruct normal negotiating procedures simply by showing up at the meetings and then suggesting that the talks adjourn.[56]

These meetings took place in one of the tents at Panmunjom that had two doors on opposite sides. The representatives from each side always used the same door on their own side entering or leaving the tent. Every day Harrison casually walked into the tent with file holders under his arm. As soon as he sat down, he suggested "that the meeting be adjourned." Then he stood up and left the tent. For the first couple of days the Chinese–North Korean representatives could still call him back to the table to listen to our responses to his suggestion. Later, he just ignored our requests and refused to come back. It seemed that he was trying to show a tough attitude by taking an immovable stance on principle. In fact, we merely considered this attitude as totally uneducated and uncivilized.

Consequently, the meetings were held only for a very short period. Sometimes the committee would meet for only two minutes. Later, the meetings became even shorter, lasting only one minute or a half-minute; the shortest meeting was held for only twenty-five seconds! In the history of international negotiations, General Harrison broke the record by finishing a meeting in twenty-five seconds.[57] With such a unique and creative method, Harrison delayed discussions on the third item and eventually stalemated the panel discussion, which was as bad as the situation in the panel discussions on the fourth item.

Around 7:00 P.M. on April 25 the other side suggested in the name of the chief representative of the UNC delegation to hold a general meeting of both sides' delegations at 11:00 A.M. on April 27. The Chinese–North Korean delegation accepted on April 26. On April 27, however, the other side suggested postponing the general meeting one more day. At the beginning of the plenary session on April 28, the other side proposed that this should be an executive session, a forum, they explained, best suited for the goal of this general meeting, which was to find solutions for all the unsolved problems.

In the general business meetings, the other side withdrew their unreasonable demand on restricting North Korean–Chinese airport construction. However, they still insisted on their proposals for nominating the neutral countries and for releasing and repatriating only 70,000 [Chinese and North Korean] prisoners. Their proposal was "solid, final, and unchangeable," they emphasized.[58] The Chinese–North Korean side rejected their proposal immediately.

At that time, Truman announced the replacement of Matthew Ridgway with [Mark W.] Clark as commander in chief of the UN forces. In April Gen. Dwight D. Eisenhower left Europe and returned to America for the presidential election race. Ridgway replaced Eisenhower as commander in chief of the NATO forces. There were some changes in both sides' delegations at that time. On the Chinese–North Korean side, Rear Adm. Kim Won Mu replaced Chung Tu Hwan [on May 25, 1953]. On the other side, Major General Levy replaced General Hodes.[59]

Ridgway issued a statement to strengthen the UN/U.S. position in the truce negotiations before his departure from Korea, saying that the American proposal would "not allow any substantial change. This is an extremely important point. Whatever difference the rival side may insist upon on some specific items, the proposal of the UNC Forces requires a total acceptance by the communist side."

Confronted by the other side's "solid, final, and unchangeable" proposal, the Chinese–North Korean delegation made a countersuggestion on May 2:

1. Regarding the neutral countries' nomination issue, we agree to make nominations only among the four countries which have been agreed upon by both sides. They are Poland, Czechoslovakia, Sweden, and Switzerland.
2. After the war ends, both sides are not restricted in their airport construction.
3. The solution of the POW problems should be based upon our revised and adjusted proposal of March 27 [the involuntary repatriation of all POWs].

Our suggestion was rejected by the other side.

Comparing the two new proposals from both sides, we could see that on the issues of nominating neutral countries and restricting airport construction, we had already reached some agreement. However, the obstacles toward solving the POW issue became even tougher and harder than before. As a result, the POW problems eventually deadlocked the Korean truce negotiations.

The Chinese–North Korean side could not tolerate the other side's unreasonable refusal to negotiate the remaining unsolved problems at the executive session, which was supposed to do the job. We had to expose to the public the other side's attempt to keep detained prisoners. On May 7 Nam Il pointed out at the plenary session that the American delegation had consistently adopted a nonnegotiable attitude at the executive sessions since we first started the meetings on April 28. Thus, the executive sessions could not function well at all. The American delegation used the meetings to conceal the truth in the talks from the people of the world. Our side always believed, Nam continued, that the solution to problems did not result from the form of the meeting but came from a sincere and cooperative attitude. We could negotiate and resolve problems in any kind of meeting as long as both sides were sincere, cooperative, and reasonable. Then Nam formally suggested stopping the executive session and beginning the plenary session.

We believed that world opinion needed to follow closely what was going on at the negotiations. The people who wanted an early end to the war should know where the obstacles really lay. Thus, on May 8, the news group for the Chinese–North Korean delegation published our proposals on the POW problems and the other side's responses. On May 9 the *People's Daily* in China printed the editorial, "Firmly Against America's Keeping Detained Prisoners."

On May 22, 1952, Harrison replaced Joy as the chief representative of the UN delegation at the truce talks. Our delegation members had greatly criticized him when he was the UNC representative of the third-item panel committee. We were especially disgusted by his record for the shortest meeting in the world.

Harrison only read written notes whenever he needed to talk at the meetings. Even for one-sentence statements such as, "I agree to adjourn the meeting," he still read it after it had been circulated and approved by his delegates. He seemed stiff and mechanical. Sometimes, however, showing his disdain for the Chinese–North Korean delegation, he even whistled at the meetings.

In the middle of the meeting on June 7, Harrison suggested adjourning the meeting for three days till June 11. He had made this kind of request to adjourn for three days many times before. It is acceptable for a party in the negotiations to ask to adjourn meetings for several days in order to prepare documents. However, there is a problem if that party has the same request and attitude all the time.[60]

So at this time Nam suggested continuing the meeting on June 8.

Harrison said, "Your side can surely come to the meeting tomorrow, but our side will not attend." Then, without listening to our response, he stood up and was ready to leave the table. Nam told him that his attitude was unacceptable and that he should observe necessary procedures at the talks. Without waiting for Nam to finish, Harrison turned around and walked out of the meeting room. We described Harrison's act as "running away from the meeting" or "escaping the meeting."

Perplexed by the attitude of the UNC delegation at the talks, Kim and Peng wrote to Clark on June 9, declaring that the only problem that prevented the delegations from reaching an agreement was the POW issue. Our side had already worked out a realistic and fair proposal in which all foreign prisoners should be released and repatriated; some of the Korean prisoners who had families on the detaining side could be released and returned to their local homes without being repatriated. The American side, however, insisted on the so-called "voluntary repatriation" and "discrimination." These demands were unreasonable and unfair. American representatives at the talks "refuse to negotiate, refuse to explain, and even refuse to come to the meetings." Such behavior, the letter continued, proved that the UNC delegation was afraid of the facts and the truth. In concluding, Kim and Peng asked Clark to order his representatives to attend the meetings on a regular schedule. In his letter of reply [approving walk-outs] on June 11, Clark gave some unreasonable explanations. Only one week later, Harrison performed his second "running away from the meeting" on June 17; ten days later he did it again for the third time.

Although there was slim hope for progress in the truce talks, the people of China, Korea, and the world still trusted that the Chinese–North Korean delegation would seize any opportunity and try their best. At the plenary session on July 1, for example, the other side expressed its willingness to end the bloodshed in Korea. They recognized that a proposal for the POW problems "must be a reasonable solution fitting both sides' needs." What did these words really mean? Could they be considered as an opportunity to make some changes? Both intellectual and wise, Nam Il suggested adjourning the meeting for one day on July 2 so that our delegation could have time for a good discussion. At the general meeting on July 3, Nam appreciated the other side's willingness for further executive and secret negotiations, which had been expressed in their talks July 4–13. The other side, however, did not want to have careful discussions. The only change they made on July 13 [19] was a new basic number: 83,000 prisoners could be repatriated. Again, they announced that this was their "final, solid, unchangeable" proposal. A couple of days later [August 3], they made a unilateral decision to adjourn the meeting for seven days. This was the first escalation of the "escaping the meeting" tactic.[61]

Two months later on September 28, the UNC delegation suggested another proposal, the so-called "one-out-of-three choices," regarding the POW problems. Their proposal still divided the prisoners into two categories: those willing to be repatriated and those "refusing to be repatriated." According to this approach, after the truce treaty became effective, all the prisoners would first be transported into the nonmilitary zone, and then would decide for themselves where they wanted to go; second, those "refusing to be repatriated" should be questioned in small groups by the neutral countries' representatives; third, the prisoners would be released thereafter in small groups.

The other side again said that their proposal of "one-out-of-three choices" was "final, confirmed, and unchangeable." Then they made a unilateral announcement to adjourn the meeting for ten days [the Communists agreed]. This was the second escalation of their "adjourning the meeting" game.

This proposal was apparently of a fraudulent nature. Our prisoners detained by the other side could not express their real desire to be repatriated since they were under the control of American, Chinese Nationalist, and South Korean secret agents.[62]

The Chinese–North Korean delegation made a counterproposal. After the truce was effective, we suggested, both sides should transport all the detained prisoners to the demilitarized zone and turn them over to the other side. Then the prisoners would be questioned, categorized by their nationalities and birthplaces, and repatriated. However, the other side refused to discuss this proposal. Moreover, they then announced without our consent on October 8 [7], 1952, to adjourn the meeting *sine die*.

People were indignant over Harrison's and Clark's unreasonable obstruction of the truce negotiations. Certainly their escaping the meetings and adjourning them *sine die* proved they were under instructions from Washington. As early as June 6, the U.S. Joint Chiefs of Staff indeed had issued orders to Harrison with Truman's approval to adjourn the meeting for three or four days to pressure our negotiating team.

Our New Proposal

Viewing the entire world situation, strategically speaking the United States could hardly get out of a stalemated situation in Korea except by ending the war.[63] And the Americans could find no other way to do so except by returning to the negotiating table at Panmunjom. Could we provide another chance for them to save face by letting the Chinese–North Korean delegation initially request resumption of the talks? Zhou Enlai asked Qiao Guanhua and other comrades to study such a possibility and to come up with their suggestions. On February 19, 1953, Qiao and the others submitted their analysis:

1. According to the recent situation, we are sure that America has nothing new to play with on the Korean battlefield. Its so-called "ending the neutralization of Taiwan"[64] is only a poor game which tries to deceive others only to end up in deceiving itself. It cannot organize a coastal blockade against China, and [a U.S.] landing in China would encounter even more difficulties. Eisenhower intended to use a landing threat to scare us, but he does not realize that it is he, not we, who are scared away by these policies. Since he has already made these hostile policies, however, it is not easy for him to turn around immediately. We need to wait and see whether these policies work or not, especially his policy of employing Asian people to fight against Asians.

2. The UN General Assembly has not yet dealt with our [rejection] of India's proposal.[65] But America's action of deneutralizing Taiwan has provoked

many neutral nations to anger, more or less counteracting the unfavorable impact caused by our [rejection] of India's proposal. After the General Assembly meeting begins, it will be very likely that this case will remain unresolved until next year's meeting.

3. America has stopped the talks at Panmunjom and now turns to the United Nations. It intends to use the UN to put pressure on us. The UN, in fact, could not overwhelm us. Meanwhile, America does not have any new tricks to play on the battlefield. In actuality, it could return to the negotiations at Panmunjom. But America is not reconciled to its defeat at the UN and has not lost all hopes for the battlefield. Thus, America is not willing to return to Panmunjom to resume the talks today, even though some of the nations have suggested that America do so.

4. If we send a formal notice to the American delegation at Panmunjom asking [to resume] the talks without any condition, our request will very likely be rejected. America would then have the following options: A) ignore our request; B) refuse us by saying that we have neither new proposals nor a willingness to accept American proposals; C) make a counterrequest that resuming talks has to be based on India's proposal; D) insist on her own way for resolving the POW problems by demanding that prisoners should not be forced to repatriate. B and C are most likely. If we send a letter signed by Peng and Kim, the other side will probably think that we have lost our patience and interpret this as a sign of our weakness, and will have some wrong ideas about our positions.

The conclusion is that waiting is better than initiating a move. Let the current situation continue until America is willing to make compromises and make the first move.[66]

Mao Zedong and Zhou Enlai agreed with the analysis. Mao said that the Americans would very likely turn to the Soviets again for help.

VICTORY AT THE NEGOTIATIONS

Punishment for Syngman Rhee

On February 22, 1953, after the negotiations at Panmunjom had been adjourned for four and a half months, Clark sent a letter to the Chinese–North Korean delegation and suggested that both sides should first exchange their wounded and sick POWs before the truce agreement.[67] This was an important signal that showed the Americans' willingness to return to Panmunjom. "Waiting is better than initiating a move. Let the current situation continue until America is willing to make compromises and make the first move."[68] Here came the opportunity [to make our moves].

It had been the fixed principle of the Chinese–North Korean delegation to reach a truce agreement as soon as possible and under fair and reasonable conditions.

Since there was now an opportunity, we should take it, push the negotiations toward the truce agreement, and end this unfortunate war, which the entire world wanted stopped. However, America was the number one superpower, and it was unwilling to make any embarrassing compromises. To make the world's dream for peace come true, we needed to give America more room for compromise by making adjustments on the POW issue, which had blocked the negotiations for so long.

This was an important development [in the talks]. China, North Korea, and the Soviet Union had joint, intensive discussions. At this critical moment, however, Stalin passed away, and his funeral delayed the decisions and actions. From March 8 to March 17 Zhou Enlai led the Chinese party and government delegation to Moscow for Stalin's funeral. Then from March 17 to March 20 he led the Chinese delegation to Prague for the funeral of Klement Gottwald, president of Czechoslovakia. Not until March 28 did China, North Korea, and the Soviet Union begin to make their new and dramatic moves to push the negotiations toward a truce agreement.[69]

Through mutual effort, the liaison meeting of the truce negotiations resumed on April 6. General Lee Sang Cho attended as chief of the Chinese–North Korean liaison team, and Rear Adm. [John C.] Daniel attended as the other side's chief. The negotiations on repatriating the wounded and sick POWs broke the deadlock in the talks; on April 11 both sides signed an agreement to exchange them.

On April 18 the Seventh UN Assembly passed the resolution proposed by Brazil: "[The UN] hope to see a prompt and smooth exchange of the wounded and sick prisoners, and hope that the further negotiations at Panmunjom will lead to an early truce in Korea, which is based upon the UN principles and spirits." The discussions on the Korean issues officially returned from the UN to Panmunjom again.

The agreement on the wounded and sick POWs' repatriation led to the resumption of the truce negotiations. On April 26 more than 100 reporters from all over the world gathered outside the negotiating tent at Panmunjom. At 11:00 A.M. the representatives from both delegations walked into the tent again. The negotiating talks restarted after a break of six months and eighteen days. The Chinese People's Volunteers Force had changed some of its delegates. Ding Guoyu replaced Bian Zhangwu, and Chai Chengwen replaced Xie Fang as the CPVF representatives.

The unpredictable talks at Panmunjom finally produced an agreement on POW repatriation, the only major obstacle in the truce negotiations for more than one year. On June 8, 1953, the document "The Duties and Responsibilities of the Neutral Countries' Repatriation Committee" was signed.

By then, all the other items in the negotiations had been settled. The delegation meetings were adjourned on June 10. Both sides had only regular staff meetings, which were divided into two groups. One group worked on the details of the demilitarization line, and the other on editing the truce agreement word by word.

June 8 is an unforgettable day for everybody who participated in the talks.

That evening, Zhou Enlai called Li Kenong and asked him to congratulate all the comrades in our delegation. Many of those who had been working so hard for the truce negotiations day and night were moved to tears.

The officers selected from the CPVF armies as the "truce inspection team" members arrived in the Kaesong area, as well as new staff members for our delegation, workers from China's Red Cross, and reporters from foreign countries. The Chinese government chartered two big, Hungarian-made buses and sent them over from Shenyang. Everything for the signing ceremony of the Korean Armistice agreement was prepared. Peng Dehuai, CPVF commander and political commissar, was in Beijing but he planned to leave for Kaesong on June 19 to sign the agreement.

On June 18, just before both sides were about to sign the truce, something suddenly happened. Syngman Rhee, who hated peace and opposed the agreement, released more than 27,000 NKPA prisoners in South Korea, in order to keep them in the South.

Peng did not change his travel plans, however. He shook hands and said goodbye to the Chinese party, government, and military leaders who saw him off at Beijing's Qianmen train station on June 19; then he boarded the international train to Pyongyang. Peng discussed Korea's situation with his staff on the train. He believed that if Rhee were to be let go without a military punishment, he would cause more troubles and further delay the truce agreement; then there would be no real truce on the Korean peninsula and no guarantee for world peace.

The train crossed the Yalu River and arrived at Pyongyang in the afternoon on June 20. Peng immediately called the Chinese–North Korean delegation at Kaesong. Li Kenong, head of the delegation, reported to Peng about Rhee's action and its consequence. Li said that the enemy was in a tight corner; Rhee and hawkish Americans did not have mass support. Li hoped that Peng could still make his trip to Kaesong. Peng promised him, "I am sure to come." Then Peng called the CPVF General Headquarters directly and talked to Deng Hua, CPVF acting commander, and Yang Dezhi, CPVF deputy commander. Deng and Yang briefed Peng on the CPVF's recent counterattack operations and told him that they were working on a plan to attack Rhee's army again. After putting down the telephone, Peng said, "Rhee can't tell good from bad. It is definitely necessary to teach him another lesson."

By then, Peng knew what was going on at the negotiations and also knew the CPVF Headquarters' operational plans. But he did not rush to a conclusion and issue his order to the CPVF at once. He was still thinking.

At 10:00 P.M. [on June 20], Peng drafted a telegram at Pyongyang and sent it to Mao Zedong. Peng suggested postponing the date for signing the truce in order to have time to punish Rhee and to inflict 15,000 more casualties on his troops. Mao agreed that signing the truce must be postponed. The right time to sign depended on the development of the situation. It was extremely necessary to eliminate at least 10,000 more of Rhee's troops.

Politically, it was a favorable moment for China and North Korea to deliver a heavy blow to Rhee as retaliation. Militarily, the CPVF and NKPA had an advantageous position at the front. After the CPVF's consecutive victories in its two most recent counterattacks, the position of four enemy [ROK] divisions formed a salient in the area south of Kumsong and east of the Han River. Moreover, the Volunteers enjoyed high morale, sufficient stores of supplies, and much-improved transportation lines. The CPVF had already concentrated four armies and more than 400 heavy artillery pieces in this area, and with such a strong force, it could launch a much larger offensive than in the two previous counterattacks.

The CPVF commanders issued their orders to the army groups [after Mao's telegram], ordering them to get ready immediately. On June 25 the offensive operation began along a 200-kilometer-wide front.[70]

The delegation meeting did not resume until July 10 [because of the newly developed military situation]. Harrison knew how much weight he bore at that moment. His habit of whistling at the meetings disappeared, and his magisterial and arrogant attitude changed. He listened carefully to the Chinese–North Korean delegation's questions. He wrote down his answers on a notepad word by word after careful thinking; then he passed his written notes to his delegates. After the delegates read and agreed to them, Harrison read his answers line by line. The delegation meetings continued for six sessions and adjourned on July 16.

On July 19, Nam Il published the other side's promises that Harrison as its chief representative had made. Even though the victorious CPVF troops could have pressed on for a bigger victory at that moment, the Chinese–North Korean delegation accepted Harrison's request to sign the truce agreement in order to end the war as soon as possible, acknowledging the other side's promises and the world's hope for peace.

Signing the Truce Agreement

The date for signing the truce agreement approached. For the past two years, the entire staff of our Chinese delegation had worked hard under tremendous difficulties. Heated debates at the meetings and an overload of work requirements between the meetings totally occupied everybody's daily life. Every morning, as soon as we got up, we read the Central Committee's instruction telegram[s]. Then [we had to] double-check that day's negotiating notes, especially for the major speeches. All the notes were prepared the night before in order to cope with all kinds of potential situations at the next day's meetings. If the Central Committee had agreed with our reports and suggestions sent [to Beijing] the night before, the staff members could eat breakfast peacefully. If not, they had to change the notes [according to the Central Committee's instructions], translate them into English and Korean, edit the final drafts, and retype all the new notes. All of this had to be done during breakfast. Then they got into the jeeps and rushed to Panmunjom. Right after each day's meetings, the staff needed to check the minutes and draft the reports. Next, they attended the staff meetings to analyze that day's negotiating developments, discuss what was probably going to happen the next day and how to deal with it, and prepare the next day's negotiating notes accordingly. Usually, Qiao Guanhua chaired the staff meetings, which lasted for two or three hours; sometimes, however, they lasted until midnight.

During these days, Li Kenong grew more gray hairs. Qiao lost a lot of weight. Ding Ming, a staff member, died of a stomach perforation; he was overworked, and medicine could not save his life. Dr. Pu Shan, praised as the "people's donkey," also suffered from failing health. The staff members, secretaries, interpreters, shorthand clerks, telegram translators, operators, typists, security guards, drivers, and cooks made their contributions to our victorious struggle for the truce. Comrade Shi Peixi was driving on the road between Kaesong and Pyongyang with the yellow flag on his jeep, the delegation vehicle sign that was agreed on by both sides, when it was strafed by enemy airplanes. He and two comrades were seriously wounded. Two messengers from Beijing were killed by an air bombardment before they got to Kaesong. Yet nobody on the staff ever asked for special consideration or requested any compensation. They thought about nothing but world peace, Korea's security, and their motherland's safety. The truce in Korea was the first step toward achieving peace in the Far East. Although it had not come easily, the date for signing finally arrived.

When all of us were ready to celebrate the victory, Li Kenong called for a meeting. He told us that Syngman Rhee deeply hated the truce. Rhee's acceptance of the agreement resulted merely from the CPVF–NKPA attacks and the American government's persuasion. Was he really willing to give up? Could he cause any more problems? If Rhee wanted to make trouble, nothing would be worse than a terrorist act at the signing ceremony, for instance, an assassination of any of the leading commanders from either side. It would cause more serious consequences than Rhee's release of the prisoners, and it would force both sides to start fighting again.

After careful discussion, the consensus was that there were two methods to solve this problem. The first was to persuade the UN/U.S. delegation not to allow anyone from Rhee's side to enter the neutral area at Panmunjom, and meanwhile not to allow any reporters from Taiwan to attend the signing ceremony. It was possible to get the other side to agree to ban the Taiwanese reporters but difficult for them to prohibit South Korea's personnel from entering the neutral area. The second method was to change the previous arrangement, which was for both sides' chief commanders to come to the meeting place to sign the agreement. It could instead be signed first by both sides' chief representatives, with the truce becoming effective immediately. Thereafter, the chief representatives would take the truce agreement to their own commanders for their signatures, and then the representatives would exchange the signed documents.

This plan was so important that [we] had to report it [to the Central Committee] and ask for instructions. In fact, Beijing had already thought about this problem. At

4:00 P.M. on July 26, 1953, the joint liaison meeting agreed to issue to the public the date and the method of signing the truce agreement. Both sides' liaison officers did not try to hide their relaxed and hearty smiles about their arrangement. At the end of their meeting, the officers from each side greeted the others, talked socially, and waved to one another. Nothing like this had ever happened before. The same day, the Chinese–North Korean delegation issued a statement:

> Both sides in the truce negotiations have completely reached the Korean Armistice Agreement. Both sides also agreed that the Truce Agreement will be signed first by our delegation's chief representative General Nam Il and the other delegation's chief representative Lieutenant General Harrison at ten o'clock (local time) in the morning of July 27 at Panmunjom, Korea. Then, they will send the Truce Agreement respectively to Marshal Kim Il Sung, NKPA supreme commander, General Peng Dehuai, CPVF commander, and General Clark, UN commander, for their signatures.

The same day [July 27], Nam Il went to Pyongyang with the original document of the armistice.[71] At 10:00 P.M. Marshal Kim Il Sung signed the Korean Armistice at the premier's mansion.

That afternoon, accompanied by Deputy Marshal Choi Yong Kyon, the NKPA deputy commander, Peng Dehuai arrived at Kaesong. He attended a welcome reception given by the CPVF and NKPA troops stationed there and then a grand banquet hosted by the Chinese–North Korean delegation to celebrate the truce agreement.

At 9:30 A.M. on July 28, Peng Dehuai signed the Korean Armistice in the CPVF delegation's newly built meeting room. After signing the agreement, he gave a speech to the commanders and officers representing the CPVF and the NKPA at the ceremony. Later, he wrote in his autobiography about his feelings at that moment: "When I signed the armistice, I was thinking that we had already created a precedent for many others that would exist for years to come. This [cease-fire] sounded very laudable to the peoples [of the world]. I, however, felt a bit disappointed because we had just become so well organized for combat. We had not fully used our might to deliver bigger blows to the enemy."

Peng Dehuai's words clearly indicated that the Chinese people love peace, and the Chinese government appreciated peace. From among the many choices the Chinese and Korean peoples and governments had, they chose peace as their first priority.

Appendix 1

CHINESE LEADERS' AND CPVF COMMANDERS' NAMES

Pinyin	Wade-Giles
Chai Chengwen	Tsai Cheng-wen
Chen Geng	Ch'en Geng
Chen Yi	Ch'en I
Chen Yun	Ch'en Yun
Deng Hua	Teng Hua
Deng Xiaoping	Deng Shiao-ping
Du Ping	Tu Ping
Gan Siqi	Gan Tsi-ch'i
Gao Gang	Kao Kang
Han Xianchu	Han Hsian-ch'u
Hong Xuezhi	Hong Hsue-ch'i
Huang Yongsheng	Huang Rong-sh'eng
Jiang Jieshi	Chiang Kai-shek
Lai Chuanzhu	Lai Ch'uan-ch'u
Li Juikui	Li Ch'ui-k'uei
Li Kenong	Li K'e-nung
Li Zhimin	Li Ch'i-min
Lin Biao	Lin Piao
Liu Shaoqi	Liu Shao-ch'i
Mao Zedong	Mao Tse-tung
Nie Rongzhen	Nieh Jung-ch'en
Peng Dehuai	P'eng Teh-h'uai
Qiao Guanhua	Ch'iao Kuan-hua

Qin Jiwei	Ch'in Chi-wei
Song Shilun	Sung Shin-lun
Wu Xiuquan	Wu Hsiu-ch'uan
Xiao Jinguang	Hsiao Ch'in-kuang
Xie Fang	Hsieh Fang
Xie Peiran (Xie Fang)	Hsieh Pei-lan
Xu Shiyou	Hsu Shih-yu
Xu Xiangqian	Hsu Hsiang-ch'ian
Yang Dezhi	Yang The-ch'i
Yang Lisan	Yang Li-s'an
Ye Jianying	Ye Ch'ien-ying
Zheng Weishan	Ch'eng Wei-shan
Zhou Enlai	Chou En-lai
Zhu De	Chu Teh

Appendix 2

MAPS OF THE CHINESE PARTICIPATION IN THE KOREAN WAR,
1950–1953

The maps in this appendix display in broad but comprehensive terms the terrain of
the Korean battlefields, the deployment and movement of the armies of the Chinese People's Volunteers Force, and the location and movement of the corps and
some divisions of the U.S. Eighth Army, the ground force of United Nations Command. The maps are new composites drawn from two sources: the maps used in
the teaching materials produced by the department of history, U.S. Military Academy, for student use in the Korean War segment in West Point's basic military history course and the maps produced as an appendix to the People's Liberation
Army's official history of the Korean War: the Chinese Academy of Military Sciences, *Zhongguo Renmin Zhiyuanjun Kangemi Yuanchao Zhan Shi* [*The history of
the Chinese People's Volunteers Force in the War to Resist America and Aid Korea*]
(Beijing, PRC: Military Science Press, 1988). The composite maps are used with
the permission of the department of history, U.S. Military Academy, West Point,
New York, which will use the maps in subsequent editions of its student cartographic workbook.

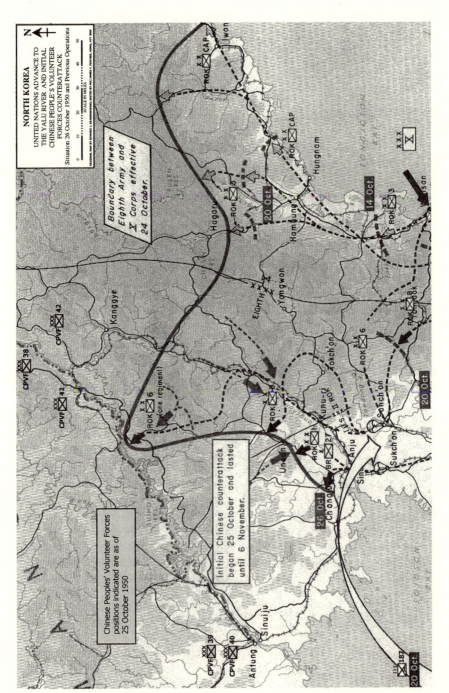

The First Chinese Offensive, October–November 1950

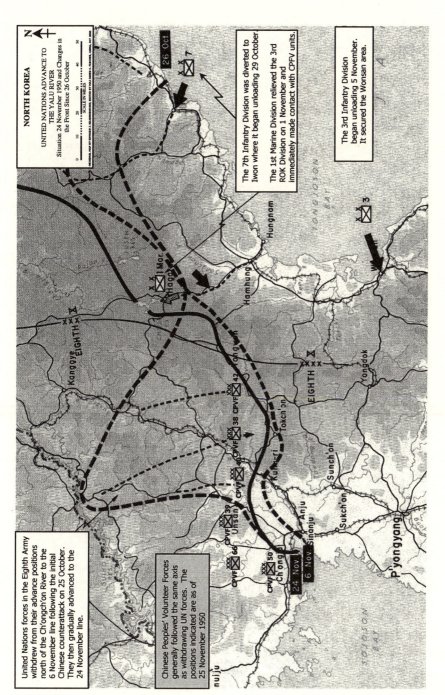

NORTH KOREA

UNITED NATIONS ADVANCE TO
THE YALU RIVER
Situation 24 November 1950 and Changes in
the Front Since 26 October

0   10   20   30   40   50
SCALE IN MILES

The 7th Infantry Division was diverted to
Iwon where it began unloading 29 October.

The 1st Marine Division relieved the 3rd
ROK Division on 1 November and
immediately made contact with CPFV units.

The 3rd Infantry Division
began unloading 5 November.
It secured the Wonsan area.

United Nations forces in the Eighth Army
withdrew from their advance positions
north of the Ch'ongch'on River to the
6 November line following the initial
Chinese counterattack on 25 October.
They then gradually advanced to the
24 November line.

Chinese Peoples' Volunteer Forces
generally followed the same axis
as withdrawing UN forces. The
positions indicated are as of
25 November 1950

The Second Chinese Offensive, November–December 1950

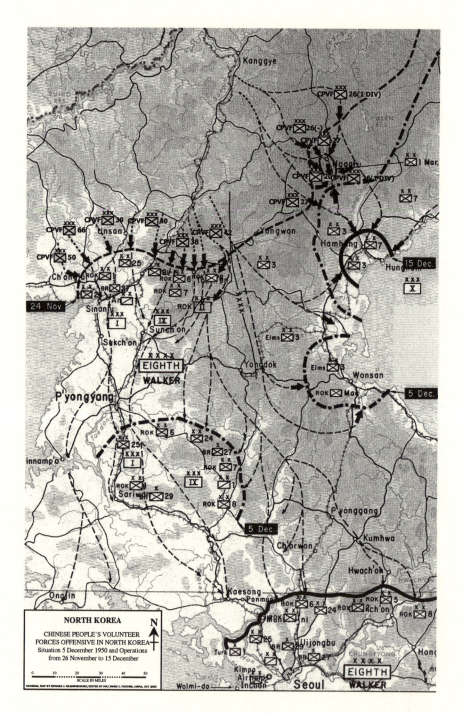

The Second Chinese Offensive

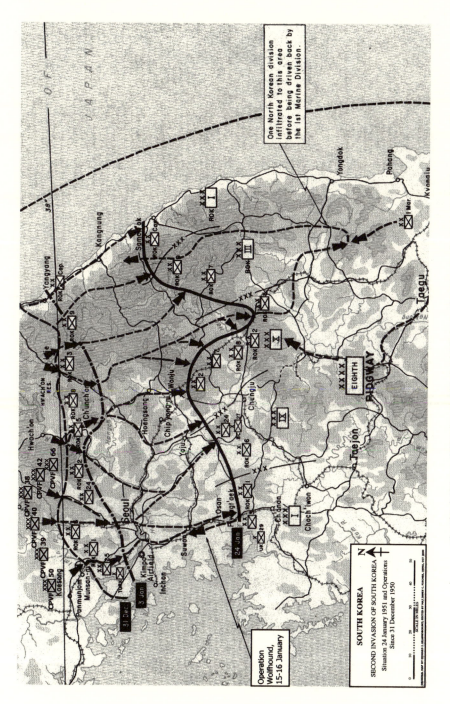

The Third Chinese Offensive and Limited 8th Army Counterattacks, January 1951

One North Korean division infiltrated to this area before being driven back by the 1st Marine Division.

Operation Wolfhound, 15-16 January

SOUTH KOREA

SECOND INVASION OF SOUTH KOREA

Situation 24 January 1951 and Operations Since 31 December 1950

N

SCALE IN MILES

0 10 20 30 40 50

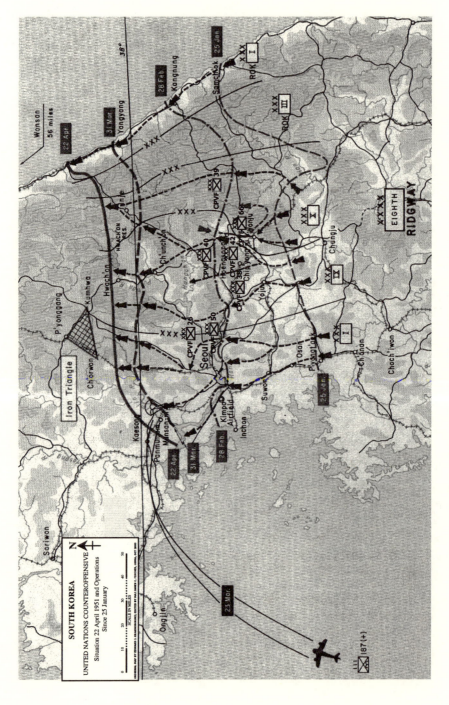

United Nations Command Counteroffensive and Chinese Fourth Counteroffensive, January–April 1950

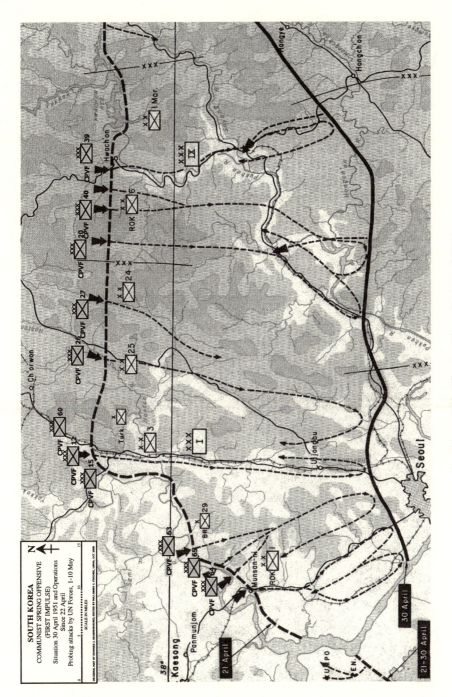

The Chinese Fifth Offensive (Phase One), April 1951

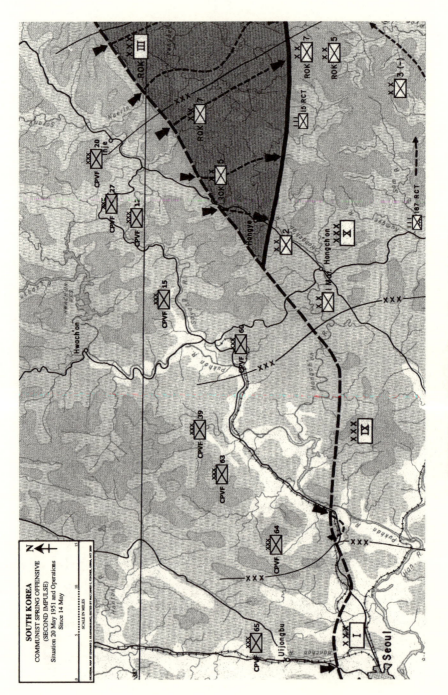

The Fifth Chinese Offensive (Second Phase), May 1951

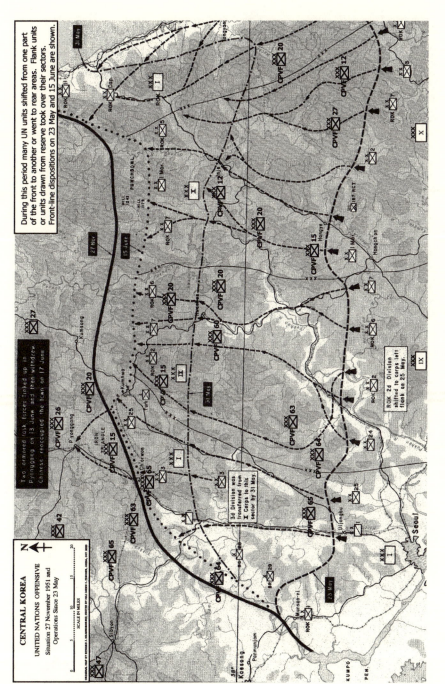

United Nations Command Counteroffensive, May–June 1951

The Stabilized Front, 1951–1953

Notes

INTRODUCTION

1. Chai Chengwen and Zhao Yongtian, *Banmendian Tanpan* [*Panmunjom negotiations*] (Beijing: PLA Press, 1992), 330.

2. Document 12, telegram, Mao to Stalin via Ambassador N. V. Roschin, Beijing, dated October 2, 1950, and received in Moscow, 12:15 P.M. October 3, 1950, reprinted in Alexandere Y. Mansourov, "Stalin, Mao, Kim and China's Decision to Enter the Korean War, September 16–October 5, 15, 1950: Evidence from the Russian Archives," *Bulletin of the Cold War International History Project* 6–7 (winter 1995–1996): 94–119. The draft telegram, probably not released, is Mao to Stalin, October 2, 1950, reprinted in vol. 1 of Mao, *Jianguo Yilai Mao Zedong Wengao* [*Mao's manuscripts since the founding of the PRC*] (Beijing: CCP Central Archives and Manuscripts Press, 1987), 539–41. This telegram, which begins, "We have decided to send a portion of our troops . . . to Korea," is often quoted as definitive proof of Mao's commitment to the war, but whether it represented a consensus of the CCP Central Committee Politburo on October 2 is questionable. The closest analysis of this issue is in Shen Zhihua, with Chen Jian (trans.), "The Discrepancy Between the Russian and Chinese Versions of Mao's October 2 Message to Stalin on Chinese Entry into the Korean War: A Chinese Scholar's Reply," *Bulletin of the Cold War International History Project* 8–9 (winter 1996–1997): 237–42. Shen is director of the Center for Oriental History Studies, Beijing, and the author of two books on the Korean War. For an account that assumes that the prowar telegram was sent, see Chen Jian, *China's Road to the Korean War: The Making of the Sino-American Confrontation* (New York: Columbia University Press, 1994), 158–209.

3. Shu Guang Zhang, *Mao's Military Romanticism: China and the Korean War, 1950–1953* (Lawrence: University Press of Kansas, 1995). The best single English-language source for Russian participation is in Mark A. O'Neill, "The Other Side of the Yalu: Soviet Pilots in the Korean War, November 1950–July 1951" (Ph.D. diss., Florida State University, 1996).

245

4. The Chinese statistics are from Xu Yan, "Chinese Forces and Their Casualties in the Korean War," trans. Xiaobing Li, *Chinese Historians* 2 (fall 1993): 51–54. The research article is based on Chinese military archival materials in Beijing.

5. *Renminbi* is the name of the Chinese currency.

6. Chinese statistics on war-related casualties and expenses vary widely among the Chinese sources. See Shenyang Military Regional Headquarters, *Zhongguo Renmin Zhiyuanjun Zhanshi* [*Military history of the Chinese People's Volunteers Force*] and *Zhongguo Junshi Baike Quanshu* [*Encyclopedia of Chinese Military Affairs*] (Beijing: Military Academy Press, 1993). The UNC intelligence statisticians put Chinese losses far higher: 1.5 million casualties in all categories, including killed in action, died of wounds and disease, missing in action, and wounded in action. Critics of Western intervention, including media sources, have put the dead alone at 1 to 3 million. Historically, American order-of-battle experts have overestimated enemy losses by a factor of 10 to 15 percent, largely because of the difficulty of handling the claims of aviators. The official Chinese sources may be low and the UNC estimates too high. The likely range is probably at 600,000 to 800,000 total casualties with around 300,000 to 400,000 Chinese dead. In 1953, the UNC processed 20,905 Chinese POWs.

1. WHAT CHINA LEARNED FROM ITS "FORGOTTEN WAR" IN KOREA

1. Sergei N. Goncharov, John W. Lewis, and Xue Litai, *Uncertain Partners: Stalin, Mao, and the Korean War* (Stanford: Stanford University Press, 1993); Chen Jian, *China's Road to the Korean War: The Making of the Sino-American Confrontation* (New York: Columbia University Press, 1994); William Stueck, *The Korean War: An International History* (Princeton: Princeton University Press, 1995). The author is grateful to Professors Allan R. Millett (colonel, USMCR) of Ohio State University and Jiang Chungliang (senior colonel) of the Chinese Academy of Military Sciences for their valuable comments on the original draft of this article. Special thanks also go to the Mershon Center of Ohio State University and to my research assistants, Deepa Samuel and Serge Thomas. The original version appeared in *Strategic Review,* U.S. Strategic Institute (summer 1998); it is revised and reprinted here in part with their permission.

2. According to Sheng Zhihua, an independent historian/scholar who has extensively examined the newly declassified Russian archives and the growing available information in China, Stalin reversed his prudent policy toward the Korean peninsula after yielding to China the Russian "interests" in the Far East (Port Arthur and the Manchuria Railroad), following three months of hard bargaining before the Sino-Soviet Alliance Treaty was signed on February 4, 1950. By "unleashing" North Korea, the Soviets would win a major ally in a unified Korea if Kim Il Sung won and could stand clear if he lost. Indeed, Mao was not informed about Kim's plan until May 1950, and Kim sent a field officer to Beijing to brief the Chinese only two days after the outbreak of the war. Mao, therefore, was "forced" into a conflict that he and his colleagues did not want to get involved with in the first place. Shen even argues that Stalin supported the use of force in Korea in order to prevent China's conquest of Taiwan, thus leading to the rise of a more powerful Communist neighbor in the south. For details, see Shen Zhihua, *Mao Zedong, Sidalin, yu Hanzhan: Zhongsu Zuigao Jimi Tangan* [*Mao Zedong, Stalin, and the Korean War: The Chinese and Soviet top secret documents*] (Hong Kong: Cosmos Books, 1998); see also Shen Zhi-

hua,"China Sends Troops to Korea: Beijing's Policy-Making Process," in *China and the United States: A New Cold War History,* ed. Xiaobing Li and Hongshan Li (Lanham, MD: University Press of America, 1998), 13–47. On July 2, 1950, a week after the outbreak of the Korean War, Premier Zhou Enlai met with N. V. Roshchin, Soviet ambassador to Beijing, and expressed China's strong displeasure regarding the "negative" impact of the war on Mao's planned attack on Taiwan. Zhou even handed Roshchin a Chinese summary of reactions to the Korean War from around the world, including a statement by a British diplomat that the Soviets "encouraged the North [to] attack in order to prevent PRC's unification with Taiwan" (*Shijie Ribao* [*World journal*], December 7, 1997, 2).

3. Shu Guang Zhang's work offers the most comprehensive treatment of the subject. It nonetheless exaggerates the role of Chinese culture in conflict behavior. See Zhang, *Mao's Military Romanticism: China and the Korean War, 1950–1953* (Lawrence: University Press of Kansas, 1995).

4. Chen Zhonglong, ed., *Lun Kangmei Yuanchao Zhan-zheng* [*On the War to Resist America and Aid Korea*] (Nanjing: Nanjing Daxue Chubanshe [University of Nanjing Press], 1991).

5. Zhang, *Mao's Military Romanticism,* 259.

6. Chen argues that the PRC's Communist ideology dictates an expansionist foreign policy to restructure the existing international system in Asia, hence the decision to intervene (Chen, *China's Road to the Korean War,* 1–30).

7. Such a "military romanticism" is said to be based on a "cultural" paradigm consisting of Communist ideology and Chinese traditional and political culture. As a result, China "chose to act aggressively, regardless of the calculated high risk and cost" (Zhang, *Mao's Military Romanticism,* 9–10).

8. Allen Whiting, *China Crosses the Yalu: The Decision to Enter the Korean War* (New York: Macmillan, 1960).

9. For a list of those pro-Beijing scholars, see Zhang, *Mao's Military Romanticism,* 2–4.

10. Mao was very dissatisfied with this and later confided that "they [North Koreans] are our next door neighbor, but they did not consult with us about the outbreak of the war." See Li Haiwen, "Zhonggong Zhongyang Jiujing Heshi Jueding Zhiyuanjun Chuguo Zuozhan?" [When did the CCP Central Committee decide to send the volunteers to fight abroad?] *Dang de Wenxian* [*Party Literature*] 5 (1993): 85, cited from Shen, "China Sends Troops to Korea," 20.

11. The 5.4 million PLA was being reduced by half, and Zhou Enlai, despite his staff's suggestion to reverse the demobilization, ordered at the end of June to continue to implement the cut. See Lei Yingfu, "Kangme Yuanchao Zhanzheng Jige Zhongda Juece de Huiyi" [Recall of several major policy decisions in the War to Resist America and Aid Korea], *Dang de Wenxian* [*Party Literature*] 6 (1993): 76, cited from Shen, "China Sends Troops to Korea," 22.

12. Shen, "China Sends Troops to Korea," 23–24.

13. According to Marshal Nie Rongzhen, PLA's acting chief of staff in 1950, the "majority's opinion" of top Chinese civilian and military leaders in their meeting on October 4, 1950 was that "unless absolutely necessary, the war should not be fought." See Nie Rongzhen, *Nie Rongzhen Huiyilu* [*Nie Rongzhen's memoirs*] (Beijing: PLA Press, 1984), 2:735.

14. Wang et al., *Peng Dehuai Zhuan* [*Biography of Peng Dehuai*] (Beijing: Dangdai

Zhongguo Chubanshe [China Today Press], 1993), 400. Yang Fengan and Wang Tiancheng, *Jiayu Chaoxian Zhanzheng de Ren* [*Those who commanded the Korean War*] (Beijing: Zhongyang Dangxiao Chubanshe [CCP Central Academy Press], 1993), 65 and 80–82; Xu Yan, *Diyi Ci Jiaoliang: Kangmei Yuanchao Zhanzheng Lishi Huigu yu Fansi* [*The first trial of strength: historical retrospection and a review of the War to Resist America and Aid Korea*] (Beijing: Zhongguo Guangbo Dianshi Chubanshe [China Radio and Television Press], 1990), 23–24.

15. Xie Lifu, *Chaoxian Zhanzheng Shilu* [*True stories of the Korean War*], 2 vols. (Beijing: Shijie Zhishi Chubanshe [World Affairs Press], 1994), 159–62.

16. Mao Zedong, *Jianguo Yilai Mao Zedong Wengao Diyi Ce (1949.9–1950.12)* [*Mao Zedong's manuscripts since the founding of the republic,* vol. 1, September 1949 December 1950] (Beijing: CCP Central Archives Press, 1987), 539–41.

17. Goncharov et al., *Uncertain Partners,* 179.

18. Xu, *Diyi Ci Jiaoliang,* 27.

19. Peng, *Peng Dehuai Junshi Wenxuan* [*Peng Dehuai's manuscript on military affairs*] (Beijing: Zhongyang Dangan Chubanshe [Central Archives Press], 1988), 322.

20. Mao sent Zhou Enlai and Lin Biao to Moscow to clarify the issue. Stalin nonetheless would not budge, due to his concern about a direct conflict with the U.S. forces and a possible "world war." See Xie, *Chaoxian Zhanzheng Jishi,* 178–82, and Goncharov et al., *Uncertain Partners,* 176–99. It is not convincing to conclude that Mao was not concerned about U.S. military superiority and "was too anxious to face down the 'arrogant' Americans to call off the operation" after Stalin refused to provide the Chinese with air cover. Similarly, it is doubtful that such a major decision by Mao was motivated by only one "grand" factor, such as Communist ideology or culture, and that he was blind to many other elements at work. See Chen, *China's Road to the Korean War,* 9–30, and Zhang, *Mao's Military Romanticism,* 9–10, 85, and 247–61.

21. Xie, *Chaoxian Zhanzheng Shilu,* 189–90; Yang and Wang, *Jiayu Chaoxian Zhanzheng de Ren,* 100–104.

22. *Nie Rongzhen Memoirs,* 935; Wang et al., eds., *Peng Dehuai Zhuan,* 405–6; Xie, *Chaoxian Zhanzheng Shilu,* 19 and 181–83.

23. Top Chinese civilian and military leaders came to the conclusion on August 23, 1950, the same day General MacArthur decided to land at Inchon on September 15, that U.S. forces would try to land behind the North Korean forces (Xu, *Diyi Ci Jiaoliang,* 18–19).

24. Ibid., 18.

25. Du Ping, *Zai Zhiyuanjun Zongbu* [*At the CPVF Headquarters: Memoirs of Du Ping*] (Beijing: Jiefangjun Chubanshe [PLA Press], 1989), 23–24; Xie, *Chaoxian Zhanzheng Shilu,* 184–85.

26. See Xu, *Diyi Ci Jiaoliang,* 22.

27. Ibid., 18.

28. This thinking and the behavior of the CPVF commanders run contrary to Zhang's claim that those officers "consistently favored military intervention" and "exaggerated the strength of the Chinese infantrymen, who had had no experience in modern warfare" (Zhang, *Mao's Military Romanticism,* 75 and 85). In the Chinese decision-making process, nominal or symbolic agreement with top leaders is perhaps less important than further bargaining and twisting of decisions later during the implementation stage. See Du Ping, *Memoirs,* 21–22; Xu, *Diyi Ci Jiaoliang,* 25.

29. See Stueck, *The Korean War,* 111–12; Xu, *Diyi Ci Jiaoliang,* 42.

30. Xie, *Chaoxian Zhanzheng Shilu*, 203–5; Chinese Academy of Military Science, *Zhongguo Renmin Zhiyuanjun Kangmei Yuanchao Zhanshi* [*The history of the Chinese People's Volunteers in the War to Resist America and Aid Korea*] (Beijing: Junshi Kexue Chubanshe [Military Science Press], 1988), 27.

31. Xu, *Diyi Ci Jiaoliang*, 45.

32. Zhao Yi-hong, *Saitshiba jun chuanqi* [*The story of the Thirty-eighth Army*] (Lanzhou: Dunhuang Yishu Chubanshe [Dun Huang Arts Publishing Company], 1994), 270–87.

33. Xie, *Chaoxian Zhanzheng Shilu*, 212 and 229–30; Du Ping, *Memoirs*, 68–70.

34. Wang et al., *Peng Dehuai Zhuan*, 423–24.

35. Xu, *Diyi Ci Jiaoliang*, 46–48.

36. Wang et al., *Peng Dehuai Zhuan*, 426–27; Xie, *Chaoxian Zhanzheng Shilu*, 243–56; Xu, *Diyi Ci Jiaoliang*, 49–52.

37. The U.S. account of this battle is somewhat different. The Second Infantry Division (less the Twenty-third Infantry Regiment) was ruined in the Gauntlet, but the Twenty-fifth Infantry Division (although hurt) got out on another road to the west but not to the coast. See Billy C. Mossman, *United States Army in the Korean War: Ebb and Flow, November 1950–July 1951* (Washington, DC: Center for Military History, 1990), 105–27.

38. Xie, *Chaoxian Zhanzheng Shilu*, 267–82; Yang and Wang, *Jiayu Chaoxian Zhanzheng de Ren*, 166–80; Du Ping, *Memoirs*, 101–26; Chinese Military Academy, *History of CPVF*, 52–67; Xu, *Diyi Ci Jiaoliang*, 55–57; Zhao Yi-hong, *Saitshiba jun chuanqi*, 297–319.

39. Zhang, *Mao's Military Romanticism*, 9.

40. According to the CPVF's account, the UN suffered 36,000 casualties and POWs, including 24,000 Americans, compared to 30,700 losses for the CPVF, a ratio of 1:0.85. The PLA's officially published casualty figures for the entire war both of the UN (718,477) and its own (360,000), however, are inaccurate at best. See Chinese Military Academy, *History of CPVF*, 2–3, and Table 1, appendix 3; Chen Yan et al., eds., *Zhongguo Junshi Baike Quanshu: Zhongguo Renmin Zhiyuanjun Zhanshi Fence* [*Chinese Military Encyclopedia: Battle History of the Chinese People's Volunteers*] (Beijing: Junshi Kexue Chubanshe [Military Science Press], 1993), 10. Some Chinese military historians have begun to question these figures recently. Ye Yumeng discusses the tendency of CPVF units to inflate the figures of the UN casualties while lowering their own casualty figures. The battlefield confusion also contributed to the inaccuracy. One problem was that the CPVF units could get fresh troops several times during one campaign. As a result, it was almost impossible to keep track of the actual number of men thrown into the same units. See Ye Yumeng, *Xue Yu* [Bloody rain] (Jinan: Shandong Renmin Chubanshe [Shandong People's Press], 1994), 265–67. The same accounting problem may also exist on the UN side. One case is the long-held 10:1 kill ratio of air combat between the United States and Chinese air forces during the war. The ratio has been recently contested by various sources (one version is 3:1 by *Aviation Week* in the early 1990s); see also *Far Eastern Economic Review*, April 22, 1993, 16–18. Chinese military historians, however, still argue that the figure is somewhat inflated by the United States (according to my interviews with some Chinese sources in 1994 and 1995). The total casualty figure of the UN forces, including the ROK forces, was 1,474,269, according to the Associated Press on October 23, 1953, and 1,168,160, according to the South Korean Defense Department's Korean War History (1976) (cited from Military Academy, *History of CPVF*, Table 1, appendix 3).

41. Yang and Wang, *Jiayu Chaoxian Zhanzheng de Ren,* 185–87; Xie, *Chaoxian Zhanzheng Shilu,* 282–92; Du Ping, *Memoirs,* 120–26; Military Academy, *History of CPVF,* 63–66; Xu, *Diyi Ci Jiaoliang,* 46–60.

42. The U.S. side lists one battalion of sixty tanks and three regimental tank platoons of fifteen tanks for the marines. See Lynn Montross and Capt. Nicholas A. Canzona, USMCR, *United States Marine Operations in Korea, 1950–1953,* vol. 3, *The Chosin Reservoir Campaign* (Washington, DC: HQMC, 1957), 365–71.

43. Xu, *Diyi Ci Jiaoliang,* 57–59.

44. Military Academy, *History of CPVF,* 71.

45. Wang et al., *Peng Dehuai Zhuan,* 437–38; Yang and Wang, *Jiayu Chaoxian Zhanzheng de Ren,* 200–201; Du Ping, *Memoirs,* 140–42; Xu, *Diyi Ci Jiaoliang,* 61–62.

46. Xie, *Chaoxian Zhanzheng Shilu,* 353; Xu, *Diyi Ci Jiaoliang,* 63 and 338.

47. Du Ping, *Memoirs,* 143–53; Xu, *Diyi Ci Jiaoliang,* 62; Military Academy, *History of CPVF,* 77–78, 88–89.

48. This finding differs from Zhang's conclusion that top CPVF commanders, including Peng, never doubted that Mao's military thought would work in Korea (see *Mao's Military Romanticism,* 255).

49. Xu, *Diyi Ci Jiaoliang,* 64; Xie, *Chaoxian Zhanzheng Shilu,* 399–403; Military Academy, *History of CPVF,* 88.

50. Du Ping, *Memoirs,* 186–91; Xu, *Diyi Ci Jiaoliang,* 71; Yang and Wang, *Jiayu Chaoxian Zhanzheng de Ren,* 221–22.

51. Wang et al., *Peng Dehuai Zhuan,* 444; Xie, *Chaoxian Zhanzheng Shilu,* 399–401.

52. Xie, *Chaoxian Zhanzheng Jishi,* 402–3.

53. Wang et al., *Peng Dehuai Zhuan,* 443; Xie, *Chaoxian Zhanzheng Shilu,* 404; Du Ping, *Memoirs,* 207; Xu, *Diyi Ci Jiaoliang,* 67–68.

54. Xu, *Diyi Ci Jiaoliang,* 70.

55. Ibid., 69 and 71; Military Academy, *History of CPVF,* 92–93; Du Ping, *Memoirs,* 192.

56. Views were obtained through author's interviews with the veterans. Also see Xu, *Diyi Ci Jiaoliang,* 70. These arguments in hindsight may not make too much sense, considering the immediate UN counterattacks, which surprised many CPVF officers. Given the huge gap between the UN and CPVF in terms of firepower, logistics, and maneuverability, as well as the gradual learning curve by UN forces, the CPVF was already in a more difficult situation.

57. Military Academy, *History of CPVF,* 98 and 102–3; Xu, *Diyi Ci Jiaoliang,* 72–73; Xie, *Chaoxian Zhanzheng Shilu,* 426–28.

58. The CPVF commanders mistakenly believed that UN forces in the area numbered only 3,000 and were underprepared. In fact, there were 6,000 well-entrenched UN forces. See Xu, *Diyi Ci Jiaoliang,* 77–78; Du Ping, *Memoirs,* 200–202.

59. Xu, *Diyi Ci Jiaoliang,* 72–74; Military Academy, *History of CPVF,* 120–21; Du Ping, *Memoirs,* 204.

60. Mao's directive was "neng susheiw ze susheng, buneng susheng ze huansheng" (win quickly if possible; if not, win with a delay), Wang et al., *Peng Dehuai Zhuan,* 452–53; Xu, *Diyi Ci Jiaoliang,* 81.

61. Military Academy, *History of CPVF,* 126–27; Du Ping, *Memoirs,* 218–19.

62. Xie, *Chaoxian Zhanzheng Shilu,* 456–58; Yang and Wang, *Jiayu Chaoxian Zhanzheng de Ren,* 252–61; Du Ping, *Memoirs,* 218–22.

63. Peng's other three mistakes were the 1932 attack on Nationalist forces in Ganzhou City, Jiangxi Province, the 1940 "Hundred-regiment Battle" against the Japanese, and the 1948 Xifu campaign against the Nationalists. See Xie, *Chaoxian Zhanzheng Shilu,* 456–58; Yang and Wang, *Jiayu Chaoxian Zhanzheng de Ren,* 252–61; Du Ping, *Memoirs,* 218–22, 101–4, 207–9, and 355–63.

64. The increasingly difficult supply situation caused many, sometimes nearly half, of the rank and file to lose their eyesight because of vitamin deficiencies. See Xu, *Diyi Ci Jiaoliang,* 190.

65. Ibid., 99–100.

66. Ibid., 159–94.

67. Ibid., 46.

68. Zhang claims that the Chinese military leaders somehow failed to see the challenge of the limited nature of the Korean War to their traditional thinking, and they "made little attempt to correct the crude images they had of themselves and the enemy" (*Mao's Military Romanticism,* 256).

69. Ibid., 326.

70. This phrase is borrowed from Thomas Christensen, *Useful Adversaries: Grand Strategy, Domestic Mobilization, and Sino-American Conflict, 1947–1958* (Princeton: Princeton University Press, 1996).

71. Du Ping, *Memoirs,* 593–603; Xu, *Diyi Ci Jiaoliang,* 145–48.

72. Current exchange rate is U.S.$1 = 8.27 yuan.

73. Xu, *Diyi Ci Jiaoliang,* 32; Wang et al., *Peng Dehuai Zhuan,* 501.

74. China bitterly complained that it had to pay for most of its arms from Russia even after losing hundreds of thousands of men in Korea.

75. Dan Bo, "*Zhonggong de Qingzhi ji Waishi Yanjiu Jigo* [The Intelligence and Foreign Affairs institutions of the Chinese Communists]," *Cheng Ming* [Hong Kong], September 30, 1996.

76. During his 1975 visit to China, Kim Il Sung sounded as if he was ready to use force to unify the country, as North Vietnam had just done. In his speech at the welcoming dinner, Kim said, "If revolution takes place in South Korea, we, as one and the same nation, will not just look at it with folded arms but will strongly support the South Korean people. If the enemy ignites war recklessly, we shall resolutely answer it with war and completely destroy the aggressors. In this war we will only lose the Military Demarcation Line and will gain the country's reunification." Mao apparently persuaded Kim not to do so. The militant rhetoric was dropped in Kim's farewell speech, and he instead stressed "peaceful" effort to unify the country. See *Peking Review,* April 25 and May 2, 1975.

77. China's reinterpretation of the Korean War apparently has led to considerable displeasure in North Korea. Since the opening of China's Korean War Museum in Dandong in July 1993, only one North Korean official delegation ever visited it. The North Koreans were "shocked" to see China's rewording of the cause of the war and the exhibition of Kim Il Sung's letter of October 1, 1950, pleading for help. It is ironic that most Koreans who have visited the museum are from the South.

78. See *People's Daily,* July 12, 1996.

79. Liang Ming and Guo Hongjun, "Military Confrontation in the Korean Peninsula Expected to Relax," *Liao Wang [Outlook],* May 12, 2000.

80. In 1999, both Koreas adopted more pragmatic and flexible policies toward each other and other countries. The South's "sunshine" policy by the Kim Dae Jung administra-

tion and its decision not to join the U.S.–led Theater Missile Defense (TMD) were reciprocated by Kim Jung Il, who has so far pursued an active and omnidirectional foreign policy that has seldom been seen in the country's history. In his June 1999 visit to China, North Korea's number two leader Kim Yong-nam publicly expressed his support for China's reform and open-up policy. Such a move to embrace China's market-oriented reform was publicly endorsed by Kim Jung Il himself during his secret visit to Beijing, May 29–31, 2000. This was unprecedented in that North Korea had been skeptical of China's economic reform. See *People's Daily,* June 1, 2000. See also Howard French, "North Korea Shyly Courts Capitalism," *New York Times,* April 30, 2000.

81. Zhang, *Mao's Military Romanticism,* conclusion, 247–61.

82. This was eight years before World War II started in Europe in 1939 when Hitler attacked Poland and ten years before the United States joined the Pacific War following the attack on Pearl Harbor in 1941.

83. *People's Daily,* July 7, 1997.

84. For "China threat" views, see Richard Bernstein and Ross H. Munro, "The Coming Conflict with America," *Foreign Affairs* (March/April 1997): 18–32. For a different view, see Robert Ross, "Beijing as a Conservative Power," *Foreign Affairs* (March/April 1997): 33–44; Andrew J. Nathan and Robert S. Ross, *The Great Wall and the Empty Fortress: China's Search for Security* (New York: W. W. Norton, 1997). See also John Schulz, "China As a Strategic Threat: Myths and Verities," and Stephen Aubin, "China: Yes, Worry About the Future," both in *Strategic Review* (winter 1998): 5–16 and 17–20. An entire issue of the journal *Issues and Studies* 36, 1 (January/February 2000) is devoted to the "China threat" debate.

85. The Korean War is somewhat of a "forgotten war" for the Americans also. President Truman, for example, defined it as a "police action." A memorial for the Korean War veterans was not constructed until years after the one for veterans of the Vietnam War.

2. MY STORY OF THE KOREAN WAR

1. In September 1955 the PLA for the first and only time in history awarded the rank of marshal to ten of its top commanders.

2. The translated chapters are renumbered by the translators with a note of their original page numbers in the Chinese version. This section comes from chapter 14's Part 1, "*Chubing Yuanchao*" [Despatching our troops to assist Korea], 257–58.

3. *Zhongnanhai* (the Middle and Southern Seas), a palace of the emperors and empresses within the Forbidden City in the center of Beijing, became the home of Mao, Zhou, and other top Communist leaders after the founding of the PRC in 1949. Most of the important top CCP, PRC, and PLA meetings, such as those of the Politburo, were and still are held here.

4. This section is from chapter 14's Part 2, "*Diyici Zhanyi*" [The First Campaign], 258–59.

5. Only small patrols from two UN Command divisions, one South Korean and the other American, reached the Yalu River.

6. The CPVF broke off its first attacks at Unsan on November 2, 1950.

7. The units Peng mentioned here were three battalions of the U.S. First Cavalry Division.

8. This section is from chapter 14's Part 3, *"Dierci Zhanyi"* [The second campaign], 259–60.

9. Actually, the UNC offensive took place on November 24.

10. Peng's figures do not coincide with the UN Command's own loss accounting, which attributes about 1,000 major equipment losses to the Chinese attack, nevertheless a serious setback.

11. This section is from chapter 14's Part 4, *"Disanci Zhanyi"* [The third campaign], 260–61.

12. Although the U.S. Eighth Army replaced the casualties caused by the Chinese intervention, it did not add any additional divisions to the UNC ground army or transfer troops from Europe.

13. Peng provided no firm casualty estimates, but half his force in January 1951 would have been around 200,000 men or more.

14. This section is from chapter 14's Part 5, *"Disici Zhanyi"* [The fourth campaign], 261.

15. Actually, it was February 1–11, 1951.

16. Peng's description of the battles of the Twin Tunnels, Chipyong-ni and Hoeng-song, does not catch the operational reality. The U.S. Second Division and the ROK First Division survived the battles and inflicted an estimated 40,000 casualties on the CPVF. The ROK Third, Fifth, and Eighth Divisions, however, suffered an estimated 10,000 casualties at Hoengsong; UNC casualties were around 14,000. The European troops included a French battalion, a Belgian-Luxembourg battalion, and a Dutch battalion. The "lost U.S. Army battalion" was either Company L, Third Battalion, Fifth Cavalry Regiment, which did, in fact, suffer serious casualties as part of Task Force Crombez, or Second Battalion, Thirty-eighth Infantry Regiment, which fought south with heavy losses to Hoengsong.

17. This section is from chapter 14's Part 6, *"Diwuci Zhanyi"* [The fifth campaign], 262–64.

18. The entire UNC land forces (ROK, U.S., and allies) numbered 683,000 in April 1951.

19. Presumably, Peng means the destruction of much of the U.S. Second Infantry Division in the Gauntlet, Pugwon-Kunu-ri, a true disaster for the Eighth Army. It lost 5,000 of 19,000 soldiers.

20. "Eliminated" is too strong a description of the losses in the ROK II Corps in the battle of the Kumsong salient, but its initial defeat and withdrawal of about twenty miles was serious enough for the UNC. UNC losses for July 1953 were almost 30,000; UNC estimated CPVF/NKPA losses were at 72,000.

3. BEIJING'S DECISION TO INTERVENE

1. In September 1955 the PLA for the first and only time created ten marshals from its top commanders. In May 1992 Nie, the last PLA marshal, died. The highest military rank in China now is full general. By the end of 1999, the PLA had forty-two full generals. The U.S. Army has thirteen full generals, and the other American services twenty-three.

2. This section comes from chapter 23's Part 1, *"Panduan yu Juexin"* [Calculations and decisions], 733–39.

3. Nie's use of the word "occupation" is misleading since the U.S. military response

was to send the Seventh Fleet to patrol the Taiwan Straits. A joint American military advisory group arrived in 1951.

4. Deng Hua was the commander of the Thirteenth Army Group, the core of the Northeast Border Defense Army, activated on July 13, 1950. When the Chinese forces entered the Korean War, he was the first deputy commander of the Chinese People's Volunteers Force and later its acting commander and political commissar. By the end of the war, Deng was de facto commander of the Chinese expeditionary force in Korea. On his return, he served as the deputy chief of the PLA General Staff. He became a full general in 1955.

5. Zhou also served as the chief of the PLA General Staff at the time.

6. This decision was contained in a letter from Mao to Stalin on October 2, 1950, requesting Moscow's assistance in the Chinese intervention.

7. Marshal Lin Biao was one of the top Chinese military leaders. At the outbreak of the Korean War, he was the vice chairman of the CCP Central Military Commission and the Chinese People's Revolutionary Military Committee and commander of the Fourth Field Army. He became one of the ten marshals in 1955.

8. The translation of the place is based on *Korea and South Korea Diming Suoyin* [*Index and translations of Korean places into Chinese and English*] (Beijing: China Atlas Publishing, 1984), 2. It is different from the English translation in America, which is Chonggo-dong, south of Sinuiju.

9. Nie apparently means only those UN Command forces then deployed in North Korea and confronting the Chinese, which were four U.S. divisions, six ROK divisions, and a British Commonwealth Brigade.

10. From mid-October (October 17) to early November, China sent its first group of the CPVF to Korea, including eighteen infantry divisions, three artillery divisions, and some logistical troops, totaling 300,000 men. Most of these CPVF infantry divisions originally came from the Fourth Field Army, the largest army in the PLA. Each of the divisions consisted of 13,000 to 15,000 men at that time.

11. The statistics do not differentiate between the U.S. and non–U.S. casualties in the UN forces, nor do they separate dead from wounded.

12. Even if one accepts the Chinese official statistics for combat deaths (152,400), this statement is incorrect since American deaths were 36,916, and U.S. total losses were 140,200. U.S. and ROK combined deaths were 293,916 (ROK estimated at 250,000).

13. This section comes from chapter 23's Part 2, "*Gongzuo Zhongdian Yixiang Kangmei Yuanchao*" [Our focal point shifts to the War to Resist America and Aid Korea], 739–47.

14. They were the U.S. Second Infantry Division and the ROK Sixth and Eighth Divisions.

15. The Chinese 180th Division, Sixtieth Army, CPVF, was surrounded by the UNF during its retreat, May 26–28. Most of its soldiers, estimated at 9,000, became prisoners.

16. Nie's estimates for the period between June and December 1951 seem much too high.

17. The new evidence based on Russian documents now shows the Chinese charges of biological warfare were fabricated.

18. Shangganling is one of the hills on the Osung Mountain, known in the West as Old Baldy—Capital Hill and White Horse Mountain.

19. Nie seems to accept exaggerated CPVF estimates of UNC casualties; in this case, largely ROK casualties were 50,000 in all categories.

20. The dual rail-highway bridges between Andong (Manchuria, China) and Sinuiju (North Korea).

21. This was true for the railway bridge only.

22. This section is from chapter 23's Part 3, "*Kangmei Yuanchao Zhongde Houqin Gongzhuo*" [Logistical task in the War to Resist America and Aid Korea], 747–61.

23. On April 8, 1951, the UNC airplanes bombed the CPVF warehouses at Samdung train station and destroyed eighty-four railroad cars loaded with supplies. Among other war materiel burned during the air raid were 2,780,000 *jins* of grain, 330,000 *jins* of cooking oil, 408,000 sets of uniforms, and 190,000 pairs of shoes.

24. Yang Liandi was the head of a platoon in the First Company, First Bridge Engineering Regiment, First Railroad Engineering Division, CPVF, in the war. Yang made a great contribution in repairing the Chongchon River bridge and keeping the cross-river traffic going during intensive air raids in 1951.

25. Nie's charge seems unsubstantiated.

26. Eisenhower made no such pledge, but his October 24, 1952 speech in Detroit was widely interpreted as a promise to end the war. He had no plan and actually promised only "to go to Korea."

4. POLITICAL MOBILIZATION AND CONTROL

1. In September 1955, the PLA for the first time in its history granted military ranks to its commanders, including 10 marshals, 10 chief generals, 57 full generals, 175 lieutenant generals, and 800 major generals. Before 1965, there were 2 more lieutenant generals and 560 more major generals appointed in the Chinese army.

2. This section is from chapter 1's Part 3, "*Shenyang Huiyi*" [The Shenyang meeting], 17–22; the subtitles have been added by the editors.

3. On July 7, 1950, the CCP Central Military Commission held a meeting to discuss the crisis brought about by the outbreak of the Korean War. It was decided that four armies of the Thirteenth Army Group, the Fourth Field Army, and three artillery divisions would be transferred to the Chinese-Korean border area by the end of July, that they would be organized as the Northeastern Border Defense Army, and that necessary logistical preparations and political mobilization should begin immediately.

4. Gao Gang was then also the secretary of the CCP Northeastern Bureau and a member of the CCP Central Committee Politburo.

5. Xiao Jinguang was the commander of the newly established PLA navy. He was selected by the CMC as the deputy commander of NEBDA. Xiao Hua, then the deputy director of the PLA Political Department, was selected as the vice political commissar of NEBDA. Neither assumed the positions because, as they claimed, they were so tied up with their duties that they could not accept new positions.

6. Hong Xuezhi was then deputy commander of the Thirteenth Army Group and was later appointed as deputy commander of the CPVF. Xie Fang was then chief of staff of the Thirteenth Army Group and was later chief of staff of the CPVF.

7. In fact, MacArthur employed about 50,000 UNC troops for the Inchon landing.

8. This section is from chapter 1's Part 4, "*Jianzai Xianshang*" [Arrow on the bowstring], 23–29.

9. The Liberation War, or the Chinese civil war, was fought between the Chinese Communist Party and the Nationalist government from 1946 to 1949. It resulted in a Communist takeover of mainland China and a Nationalist retreat to Taiwan and some smaller offshore islands.

10. The Chinese People's Volunteers Force was in fact part of the Chinese People's Liberation Army. The CPVF was the PLA in the Korean War, and the Volunteers were in fact the PLA soldiers in Korea.

11. Han Xianchu was then deputy commander of the Thirteenth Army Group and was later appointed deputy commander of the CPVF.

12. This section is from chapter 2's Part 3, "*Zhengzhi Dongyuanling*" [Political mobilization order], 55–57.

13. The Agrarian Revolutionary War, or the Second Chinese Revolutionary War, joined by poor and landless farmers and led by the CCP, fought against big landowners and the GMD regime from 1927 to 1937.

14. This is from chapter 2's Part 7, "*Dayudong Huiyi*" [The Taeyudong meeting], 71–77.

15. At Unsan, the CPVF troops first engaged the UN/U.S. forces on October 25, 1950, opening the Volunteers' first phase of their offensive campaign.

16. This section is from chapter 3's Part 2, "*Shoushi Zhanfu*" [The first release of the prisoners of war], 82–91.

17. The Jinggangshan period is one phase of the CCP's struggles between 1927 and 1934, also known as the Land Reform period, Agrarian Revolution, or First Revolutionary Civil War. Jinggangshan, Jiangxi Province, was the capital of the CCP's controlled areas.

18. These were the PLA's offensive campaigns against GMD forces in the Liaonan-Shenyang and Peiping-Tienjin areas during the Chinese civil war.

19. This description fits the conditions of part of the U.S. Second Infantry Division in the Gauntlet north of Kunu-ri.

20. There were no Turkish soldiers in this POW group from Task Force Drysdale, captured in part on November 30, 1950, north of Koto-ri on the road to the Changjin Reservoir. Du may have three different episodes compressed into one.

21. Actually, the GIs were part of the Third Battalion, Twenty-fourth Infantry Regiment.

22. "*Kang*" is a heatable brick bed, popular in Northeast China and North Korea.

23. This section is from chapter 3's Part 3, "*Zongbu Beizha*" [The General Headquarters bombed], 91–93.

24. Mao Anying was one of Mao Zedong's two sons.

25. This section is from chapter 3's Part 7, "*Zhengzhi Xunling*" [The political directive], 127–30.

26. This is from chapter 4's Part 4, "*Zhiyuanjun Bao*" [The Volunteers newspaper], 167–73.

27. This section is from chapter 5's Part 1, "*Yongzheng Aimin*" [Supporting the government and cherishing the people], 174–85.

28. The Three Main Rules of Discipline and the Eight Points for Attention were laid down by Mao for the Chinese Red Army in the 1920s, with some modifications and adjustments later on. The Three Main Rules of Discipline are (1) obey orders in all your actions; (2) don't take anything, not even a single needle or piece of thread, from the masses; and (3) turn in everything captured. The Eight Points for Attention are (1) speak politely; (2) pay fairly for what you buy; (3) return everything you borrowed; (4) pay for anything you

damaged; (5) don't hit or swear at people; (6) don't damage crops; (7) don't take liberties with women; and (8) don't ill-treat captives.

29. *Ri* and *dong* mean "village" or "township" in Korean; they are usually used after a place name, such as Taeyu-dong or Sangpaek-ri.

30. This section is from chapter 8's Part 1, *"Guangrong Jinjing"* [Visiting Beijing with glory], 300–304.

31. The cease-fire negotiations were held at Kaesong. Deng and Xie were the CPVF official representatives.

5. THE CPVF'S COMBAT AND LOGISTICS

1. This section is from chapter 1, *"Fengyun Tubian"* [A sudden change in the situation], 1–12.

2. American troops (Task Force Smith) did not land in Pusan, South Korea, until July 1 and engaged the North Korean troops on July 5 near Osan. Truman committed ground troops on June 30.

3. Reconnaissance flights crossed the border, but there is no evidence of raids into China's territory.

4. Pak's position in the North Korean government was not second only to Kim Il Sung, but his military service in the PLA (the Yan'an group) made him an excellent emissary to the Chinese.

5. The date of this meeting is probably October 1, 1950. North Korea's official letter, signed by Kim Il Sung himself, to plead for China's help was dated October 1. The original letter is now kept at the Korean War Museum in Dandong (Andong), China.

6. The UNC soldiers certainly had difficulty with Korean potable water, but the U.S. Eighth Army established many water purification points in Korea. Nevertheless, dehydration was a major problem for American soldiers.

7. This section is part of chapter 6, *"Youdi Shenru, Chuqi Zhisheng"* [Luring the enemy deep and attacking it with surprise], 75–79; the subtitle has been added by the translators.

8. Mao Anying, Mao Zedong's older son (Mao had two sons), was Peng's Russian interpreter and secretary at the CPVF General Headquarters.

9. This is chapter 10, *"Houfang Qinwu Silingbu Chengli"* [The establishment of the CPVF Logistics Department], 170–78; the subtitle here has been added by the translators.

10. The actual operational strength of the UNC air forces was around 500 frontline combat aircraft, according to the records of Headquarters, Far East Air Forces.

11. *Li* is a unit of length used in China; one *li* is equal to 0.5 kilometer or 0.31 mile.

12. This section is part of chapter 10, *"Houfang Qinwu Silingbu Chengli"* [The establishment of the CPVF Logistics Department], 170–86.

6. THE PURCHASE OF ARMS FROM MOSCOW

1. This section is from chapter 22's Part 1, *"Moscow Zhixing"* [My trip to Moscow], 797–895.

2. The five-starred Red flag became the national flag of the People's Republic of China on October 1, 1949, when the republic was founded.

3. At that time, Marshal He was the commander of the Southwest Military Region; Marshal Luo the political commissar of the Fourth Field Army; Marshal Nie the deputy chief of the General Staff; and Marshal Ye the commander and political commissar of the Guangdong Military Region.

4. Li, one of the CCP's senior leaders, was then minister of the CCP United Front Department.

5. The Soviet Union's Antifascist War refers to the Russo-German War, or the Great Patriotic War, 1941–1945.

6. Yugoslavia became one of the Communist countries at the end of World War II. However, its leader, Tito, resolutely opposed Soviet dominance of Eastern Europe, and hence he was regarded by the Soviet leaders as a traitor to the international Communist movement.

7. Current estimates put Soviet deaths, including both military and civilian, at closer to 30 million.

8. *Jiaozi* is a traditional Chinese food for special occasions such as the Chinese New Year or a family reunion. It is called "dumpling" or "pot sticker" in some Western countries.

9. The Guandong Army contained the best troops in Japan's Imperial Army at the beginning of World War II. Between 1931 and 1945, it was stationed in Manchuria along the Chinese-Russian borders. After the Soviet Union declared war on Japan in August 1945, the Red Army entered China and forced the Guandong Army in Northeast China to surrender.

10. Dr. Fu Lianzhang, then minister of the Public Health Ministry, had for a long time supervised the health of the CCP's top leaders, including Mao and Zhou.

7. COMMAND EXPERIENCE IN KOREA

1. This section is part of chapter 5, "*Zhadan yu Xijun*" [Bombs and germs], 89–101; the subtitle has been added by the translators.

2. The Shijiazhuang campaign was a major offensive that the PLA undertook during the Chinese Civil War. It is remembered as the first PLA attack against fortified positions.

3. This refers to a long-remembered rebel figure in the tale *Xiyouji* [*The journey to the West*], one of the best known folktales in traditional Chinese literature. Also known as *Pilgrimage to the West,* or *The Monkey,* it is a mythological novel dated from the mid-Ming Dynasty. Its main part is a series of episodes relating the adventures of the Tang Dynasty monk Xuanzang (commonly referred to as Tripitaka) on a pilgrimage to the Western Region (i.e., India) in search of Buddhist scriptures. He is accompanied by several mythological figures led by the real hero of the novel, Sun Wukong (the Monkey). In one of his adventures, Sun Wukong defeats the Princess of the Iron Fan by getting into her stomach.

4. Yang's note: Mao, *Mao Zedong Xuanji* [*Selected works of Mao Zedong*], 5:67.

5. This section is part of chapter 5, "*Zhadan yu Xijun*" [Bombs and germs], 101–5; the subtitle has been added by the translators.

6. No documentary evidence or personal testimony in the West has ever conclusively proved that the UNC conducted germ warfare. But recent Russian disclosures suggest an elaborate Russian–North Korean hoax. See Milton Leitenberg, *The Korean War Biological Warfare Allegations Resolved* (Stockholm, Sweden: Center for Pacific Asia Studies, May 1998).

7. This section is part of chapter 7, "*Qiuji de Shengli*" [Victories in the fall], 120–29; the subtitle has been added by the translators.

8. Zhuge Liang (A.D. 181–234) is one of the most famous statesmen and strategists in Chinese history. He was the prime minister of the Kingdom of Shu in the period of the Three Kingdoms (A.D. 220–265) and became a symbol of resourcefulness and wisdom in Chinese folklore.

9. Yang's note: He Shoufa (Ming Dynasty), *Toubi Futan* [*Writings on important topics*], vol. 2, article 8, "*Bing Ji*" [operational opportunities].

10. *Huqin* is a general term for certain two-stringed, bowed Chinese traditional musical instruments, which were and still are popular in China.

11. Yang's note: Mao, *Mao Zedong Xuanji* [*Selected works of Mao Zedong*], 2:500.

12. This section is part of chapter 7, "*Qiuji de Shengli*" [Victories in the fall], 129–33; the subtitle has been added by the translators.

13. The total UNC losses for October 1952 are 20,000, so General Yang's total of 8,300 for the period between September 24 and October 5 seems high.

14. These figures are clearly in error as to loss ratios. UNC calculations reverse the 4:1 estimate.

15. This section is part of chapter 7, "*Qiuji de Shengli*" [Victories in the fall], 133–56; the subtitle has been added by the translators. *Shangganling* is known in the West as Triangle Hill or Pike's Peak.

16. These Heights are known as Triangle Hill.

17. There is no UNC evidence of this improbable event.

18. The UNC certainly did not recognize such losses, since those of 1950 were much higher.

19. Yang's note: Verdun is an important town and key military fort in northeastern France. During World War I, French and German armies fought a major battle there from February to December 1916. On February 21 the Germans launched an attack on the French. By the end of the year the French occupied substantially the positions from which they had been routed in February. The losses on both sides were high, the French admitting to nearly 350,000 casualties and the Germans to 330,000.

8. THE KOREAN TRUCE NEGOTIATIONS

1. The first section comes from part of chapter 11, "*Yicheng Nanchan*" [Difficult agenda in the talks], 124–26; the subtitle has been added by the translators.

2. In 1951 Li (1898–1962) was the executive vice minister of the PRC Foreign Affairs Ministry, director of the CMC Intelligence Department, and member of the CCP Central Committee. Highly experienced in negotiations with the Nationalist and American representatives during the Chinese civil war, he was a successful political operative with close ties to Mao and Zhou.

3. In 1951 Qiao (1912–1983) served in the Ministry of Foreign Affairs as the director of the International News Bureau and as deputy director of the Policy Planning Committee. As a member of the CCP Central Committee, he was known as a knowledgeable and skillful diplomat and negotiator in the party, with a long working experience with Zhou. In summer 1951 he had just returned from the UN conference as the assistant to

China's representative Wu Xiuquan. From 1951 to 1953 Qiao served in the Chinese–North Korean delegation to the Korean truce talks at Panmunjom as the assistant to the chief of the Chinese delegation, deputy chief, and then acting chief. After his return to China, he became vice foreign minister and then foreign minister.

4. Although the UNC position had already been announced, Chai omits the prisoner-of-war issue at this point. The exchange of prisoners was already a UNC agenda item. See William H. Vatcher Jr., *Panmunjom: The Story of the Korean Military Armistice Negotiations* (New York: Praeger, 1958), 20–34. See also the note on sources at the end of this selection.

5. Kaesong was a center of Protestant missionary activity and anticommunist partisan resistance; thus the Chinese did not want full responsibility for security.

6. Li's remarks may have been directed at the three North Korean generals in the delegation. In July 1951, Nam Il was thirty-seven years old, Lee Sang Cho was thirty, and Chang Pyong San was thirty-two. The two Chinese generals in the delegation were slightly older; Deng Hua was forty-one, and Xie Fang forty-seven.

7. This section is part of chapter 11, "*Yicheng Nanchan*" [Difficult agenda in the talks], 126–32; the subtitle has been added by the translators.

8. This applies only to 1951 when Marshall was still the secretary of defense and Ridgway CINC FECOM/UNC. Acheson left office in January 1953 and was succeeded by John Foster Dulles. The basic working group included State Department officials, members of the Joint Staff, and the intelligence community.

9. Actually, Lee Hyun Gun was much appreciated by U.S. Army generals, but he was far more reserved than Paik Sun Yup. Generals Paik and Lee could do little since President Syngman Rhee did not support the negotiations and agreed to provide a representative only with the assumption that there would be no truce.

10. Chai's description refers to later meetings at Panmunjom, not the meetings on July 7 and 10. The CPVF–NKPA escort vehicles joined the column just outside Kaesong to give the impression that the UNC commanders had come to capitulate. See Col. James C. Murray, USMC, "The Korean Truce Talks: The First Phase," U.S. Naval Institute *Proceedings* 79 (September 1953): 980–89.

11. George Kennan, although serving as a U.S. State Department intermediary with Jacob Malik, held no official position and made no UN speech. In June 1951, Kennan had taken leave to work at the Institute for Advanced Study, Princeton, New Jersey. He did conduct Acheson-approved discussions on truce talks with Malik in New York City.

12. Jacob Malik made his declaration in a UN–sponsored radio broadcast, "The Price of Peace," on June 23, 1951.

13. There were two Underwood brothers who served as Korean language interpreters for the U.S. delegation. The reference is to 1st Lt. Richard Underwood, USA. At Richard's urging, his brother, Lt. (SG) Horace G. Underwood, USNR, joined the delegation later. A Japanese-language officer in World War II, Horace G. Underwood had more formal Asian language training than his younger brother, a CIC agent in Korea in 1945 and 1946 and an interrogator-interpreter in 1950 and 1951. Warrant Officer Kenneth Wu, now Lt. Col. Kenneth Wu, USA (Ret.), was the U.S. Chinese interpreter.

14. Colonel Wu recalls no such problem but admits that his south Chinese dialect caused problems for the Chinese delegates, all northerners. Nor does Richard Underwood recall his cigarette-counting (comments to Allan R. Millett on draft of this chapter, June 1999).

15. This is from chapter 11, *"Yicheng Nanchan"* [Difficult agenda in the talks], 133–37; the subtitle has been added by the translators.

16. Eighty-five words of the original message are omitted before Ridgway came to the question of vehicles. In fact, he preferred to use helicopters. The second paragraph begins: "In the event of bad weather, these officers will proceed in a convoy of 3 unarmed 1-quarter ton trucks, commonly known as jeeps, along the main road from Seoul to Kaesong. Each vehicle will bear a large white flag." Reprinted in *FRUS, 1951: Korea and China,* vol. 7, part 1 (1988), 616.

17. The original letter (in English) to Nam Il is different from Chai's version (in Chinese). Ridgway "instructed Admiral Joy to dispatch the following message to the Senior Communist delegate by Liaison Officer [July 12, 1951]: (1) At 0930, 12 July 1951, my motor convoy, proceeding along the Munsan-Kaesong Road, bearing personnel desired by me at the conference site, was refused passage past your control point by your armed guards at that point. (2) I have ordered this convoy to return to the United Nations lines. (3) I am prepared to return with my delegation and continue the discussions which were recessed yesterday, upon notification from you that my convoy, bearing the personnel of my choosing, including such press representation as I consider necessary, will be cleared to the conference site. The Liaison Officer carrying this message arrived Kaesong at 1104, July 12 and has not yet returned. (4) Message contained in Para. 3 above has been released to press." Reprinted in *FRUS, 1951: Korea and China,* vol. 7, part 1, 664–65.

18. Actually, General Chai (then a lieutenant colonel and liaison officer) intervened and, rebuffing Gen. Lee Sang Cho's objections to his action, read a more conciliatory note written in Chinese but read in English: "Both sides must agree to respect the delegations, including newsmen. We are prepared for the matter of newsmen with your delegates on the basis of that principle. We suggest a meeting at 1300 on July 13 since 0900 is now past."

19. It may have seemed so to Chai, but the issue at the time was the location of the cease-fire line, either on the Thirty-eighth Parallel (PRC–DPRK) or on the front when the firing ceased (UNC). Ridgway was adamant that UNC ground advances in May and June be preserved (Vatcher, *Panmunjom,* 69–86).

20. This section is from chapter 11, *"Yicheng Nanchan"* [Difficult agenda in the talks], 139–41; the subtitle has been added by the translators.

21. Born in 1875, Syngman Rhee was educated at George Washington University, Harvard University, and Princeton University. From 1919 to 1945, Rhee was head of the Korean Commission based in Washington, D.C., while his country was under Japanese rule. In 1945, after the Asia-Pacific War, he returned home and was elected president of the Republic of Korea (South Korea) in 1948.

22. That unification by U.S. military action was Truman's policy is without foundation until after June 25, 1950, but a divided Korea was certainly preferable to a Communist Korea. The ideal state for Korea before June 25 as Truman and Acheson saw it was unification and neutralization on the Austrian model. See "National Security Council (NSC)–8" (April 2, 1948), "NSC–8/1" (March 22, 1949), and "NSC–8/2" (March 23, 1949), all entitled "Position of the United States with Respect to Korea," available in complete text from the National Security Archives, Washington, DC.

23. This is Chai's interpretation of the Kennan-Malik talks of May 31, 1951, as reported by Kennan to the State Department the same day. Reprinted in *FRUS, 1951: Korea and China,* vol. 7, part 1, 483–86.

24. Chai does not include item four, the disposition of prisoners of war, which became the major unresolved issue from late 1952 until 1953. His item four became item five. The UNC negotiators believed there was agreement on July 20 (Vatcher, *Panmunjom,* 39–43).

25. This section is from chapter 15, "*Jiekai Xuwei de Miansha*" [Lift the covering mask], 179–83; the subtitle has been added by the translators.

26. The negotiations actually began again on October 25, 1951, at the new site at Panmunjom, and included a mix of plenary and subdelegation meetings on item two (the creation of the truce line) and item four (disposition of POWs).

27. Wu, as the PRC's representative to the UN from 1950 to 1954, made his trip to the UN meetings, China's first participation in UN proceedings, in November–December 1950. He visited Korea briefly in 1951 since Li refused to give up his post as head of the Chinese delegation.

28. Admiral Joy actually made the DMZ proposal (line of contact, 4-kilometer buffer zone) on November 17, which the Chinese–North Korean delegation accepted with minor changes on November 27 (See Vatcher, *Panmunjom,* 69–86).

29. Colonel Hanley was chief of the War Crimes Section, Judge Advocate General's Office, Headquarters, U.S. Eighth Army. General Chai has the story confused. The Defense Department did not discredit Hanley's statement, only his statistics, and General Collins had Ridgway issue a press release that charged "the Communists" with murdering POWs, perhaps as many as 3,545 Americans. Hanley estimated the murdered U.S. servicemen at 5,500. The Defense Department did say the Hanley affair was not a ploy to break off negotiations. See James M. Hanley, *A Matter of Honor* (New York: Vantage Press, 1995), 107–20, which includes a copy of Hanley's news release. Hanley's statistics proved too high since they included POWs who had died of disease and wounds. See War Crimes Section, Judge Advocate Division, Korean Communications Zone, "Final Historical and Operational Report," May 31, 1954, copy U.S. Army Center of Military History.

30. This section is from chapter 15, "*Jiekai Xuwei de Miansha*" [Lift the covering mask], 183–91 and 194–95; the subtitle here has been added by the translators.

31. Although a Chinese–North Korean expeditionary force caused UNC intelligence and special operations forces to withdraw from two small offshore island groups, UNC air and naval attacks stopped the CPVF's November operations as well as another amphibious offensive in February 1952. UN forces evacuated twelve island groups after the armistice but retained five others offshore from the DPRK below the Thirty-eighth Parallel (Ongjin peninsula). The retained islands are listed by name in the armistice agreement, printed in full in the Department of State, *Bulletin,* August 3, 1953. See Frederick W. Cleaver et al., *UN Partisan Forces in Korea, 1951–1954* (Baltimore, MD: Johns Hopkins University Press, 1964).

32. The UNC delegation did not accept this proposal of November 27, so there was no agreement.

33. This quote is an imaginative rephrasing of the rebuttal by Maj. Gen. Howard McM. Turner, USAF, who argued that airfield development in North Korea would pose an unacceptable threat to South Korea (Turner's words quoted in Vatcher, *Panmunjom,* 96–97).

34. It should be January 25, 1952.

35. Russian pilots and air defense forces had fought in the war along the Yalu, a matter of common knowledge within the UNC. Soviet military personnel actively engaged in late 1952 probably numbered 12,000.

36. This interpretation misrepresents the UNC position, which had endorsed the concept of a postarmistice conference from July 1951, provided the ROK participated, but this was unacceptable to the Communists.

37. The phrase "and other issues" does not appear in the final 1953 armistice agreement but instead reads "etc."

38. This section is part of chapter 16, "*Jincheng Zhongde Banjiaoshi*" [Insurmountable stumbling block in the negotiations], 196–98 and 205–9; the subtitle has been added by the translators.

39. This is a paraphrase of Article 118 and Article 7, also dealing with repatriation as a POW's right. For example, the actual text says "may," not "must," thus providing choice for a POW but not for a detaining power.

40. The DPRK announced it would follow the Geneva Convention in a message to the UN on July 13, 1950, when it was winning the war, but had already violated it by killing POWs. The Chinese thus were in violation by July 1952 and remained so in their treatment of captured airmen.

41. The CPVF included many impressed soldiers (some Nationalist army former officers and soldiers), and even without UNC encouragement, they did not want to return to the PRC. Another group of Chinese nonrepatriates were Christians. The nonrepatriates were equally dogged in their desire not to return, which meant war in the UNC–administered POW camps. Of the 20,905 Chinese in UN custody, 14,235 refused repatriation. See Col. Howard S. Levie, USA (Ret.), "The Korean Armistice Agreement and Its Aftermath," *Naval Legal Review* 41 (1993): 115–33. Colonel Levie was chief counsel for the UN delegation.

42. In fact, Admiral Libby proposed "the early regulated exchange of prisoners of war on a fair and equitable basis," with an emphasis on humanitarianism (Vatcher, *Panmunjom,* 120–25).

43. Both proposals were in accordance with the Geneva Convention [Articles 79 and 88] and sought a full accounting of the POWs in Chinese and North Korean hands. At the time, the Communists had released the names of fewer than 2,000 POWs released or still held. The UNC carried an estimated 80,000 soldiers of its own of all nationalities as missing in action (see Levie, "The Korean Armistice," 123–27, who admits that the Communists held a stronger legal position).

44. The first exchange of names produced surprise and anxiety for both sides. The exact names, of course, contained many errors, but the numbers alone were shocking. The UNC held 132,474 Chinese and North Koreans, far more than anyone thought. The Communists claimed to hold only 11,559 UNC POWs, only half the Americans thought to be POWs and one-tenth the ROK soldiers captured. More than 1,000 names already released by the Communists did not appear on the December 18 lists. The Geneva Convention formula is "all for all" in repatriating POWs.

45. Lee also argued that the "missing" POWs, mostly South Korean soldiers, had been "released at the front." Some had been released by the Chinese but most had been impressed into the NKPA (where some had been subsequently captured by the UNC), executed, or shipped off to labor camps in Manchuria, where they died. Five ROK POWs escaped as late as 1996 and 1999.

46. Chai refers to the UNC proposal of January 2, 1951, that POWs be given a choice to be repatriated or not.

47. The traditional term for such status is parole, but parolees may return to military status through further negotiation.

48. The Communists had still not accepted the critical principle of voluntary repatriation, but the UNC negotiators agreed to use staff negotiators to develop these proposals on February 4, to which the Communists agreed on February 6.

49. This section is from chapter 16, "*Jincheng Zhongde Banjiaoshi*" [Insurmountable stumbling block in the negotiations], 209–18; the subtitle has been added by the translators.

50. The UNC made no such offer but only agreed to keep discussing some sort of exchange (Vatcher, *Panmunjom,* 139–42).

51. Chai correctly calls this concept a breakthrough since it implies that South Koreans impressed into or recruited for the NKPA, former guerrillas, or other civilian internees might refuse repatriation.

52. The Communists still demanded complete repatriation of their regular soldiers, a position rejected by President Truman himself in December 1951.

53. In April 1952 the UNC estimated that only 21,102 of 51,491 NKPA POWs from North Korea would choose repatriation, although it had not processed another 52,000 Koreans (mostly hard-core Communist resisters). Almost all the 20,720 Chinese POWs had been screened and only 3,500 wanted to return to China.

54. The first and second figures in this paragraph do not reflect screening for voluntary repatriation and do reflect some loose counting. The next paragraph in the Chinese version is omitted here. (At that moment, an authoritative military strategist commented that when the other side came up with the total number of 70,000 as would-be repatriated prisoners, all the concessions the Chinese–North Korean side had made then vanished.) Its source is unclear (probably Hanson Baldwin's comments in the *New York Times*), and it adds nothing to the discussions. See CINC UNC, "To the Department of the Army, April 19, 1952," *FRUS, 1952–1954: Korea,* vol. 15, part 1, 160–63.

55. This section is from chapter 16, "*Jincheng Zhongde Banjiaoshi*" [Insurmountable stumbling block in the negotiations], 209–18; the subtitle has been added by the translators.

56. General Harrison replaced Admiral Joy as head of the UN delegation on May 22, 1952. Harrison, U.S. Eighth Army Deputy Commander, was promoted to lieutenant general on September 6, 1952.

57. Harrison staged the first UNC walk outs, which disconcerted the Chinese and North Korean negotiators. His calculated style represented an agreement in the UN delegation to dramatize a new unwillingness to listen to prepared Communist speeches.

58. The UNC position was, in fact, that it would not make any concessions that were not matched by some Communist concessions.

59. General Chai has the succession confused. Maj. Gen. Claude B. Ferenbaugh, USA, replaced General Hodes on December 17, 1951. When General Harrison became chief delegate, his army slot went to Brig. Gen. Frank C. McConnell, USA. "General Levy" is probably Lt. Col. Howard S. Levie, JAG, USA, a staff member for legal matters and subcommittee negotiator.

60. Harrison's confrontational, no-nonsense style perplexed the Communists, who expected his tacit collaboration in their propaganda "events." Harrison's behavior reflected his personal contempt for the Communists, but he received Ridgway's approval (Lt. Gen. William K. Harrison Jr., *Oral Memoir* [1981], 422–56, Oral History Collection, U.S. Army Military History Institute, Carlisle Barracks, PA).

61. In the meantime, organized Communist resistance to repatriation screening had turned the Cheju-do and Koje-do POW camps into battlefields.

62. During the Korean War, although Washington declined the Chinese Nationalist

offer to participate in the ground war, the UN Command did incorporate a group of Chinese Nationalist agents and interrogators in the POW camps. See Military Intelligence Section, General Staff, Headquarters of UNC and FECOM, "The Communist War in POW Camps," January 28, 1953, General James Van Fleet Papers, George C. Marshall Library, and P. W. Marshall to Ambassador J. Muccio (ROK), March 14, 1952, *FRUS, 1952–1954: Korea,* vol. 15, part 1, 98–99.

63. This section is from chapter 18, *"Banmendian Huichang Lenglengqingqing"* [Stalemate at the Panmunjom Truce Negotiations], 249–50; the subtitle has been added by the translators.

64. The reference is to the "unleashing Jiang" policy announcement of the Eisenhower administration on February 2, 1953.

65. On November 17, 1952, the Indian delegation proposed a resolution to the UN Political Committee assembly addressing the POW problems in the Korean Truce Negotiations: establish a repatriation committee to handle prisoners in the Korean War. The committee would consist of four neutral countries; one of them, recommended by the others as the arbitrator, would decide all disputed problems, and so forth.

66. Chai does not date this meeting, but it probably occurred in February 1953, i.e., before Stalin's death on March 28. Presumably, the "first move" was Clark's February 22 proposal to exchange sick and wounded POWs who volunteered for repatriation. On March 28 the Chinese–North Korean delegation accepted the proposal, which became "Little Switch," and offered to revisit the terms of a postarmistice POW exchange.

67. This section is from chapters 19 and 20, *"Chengfa Li Chengwan"* [Punish Syngman Rhee] and *"Heping Xieshang zhi Shengli"* [Victory at the armistice negotiations], 251–53, 259–61, 263–64, 267–68, 270–72, and 274–75.

68. This quote is from Qiao Guanhua's report to Mao and Zhou on February 19, 1953.

69. On March 28, Kim and Peng issued their reply to Clark, agreeing to exchange wounded and sick prisoners. On March 30 Zhou Enlai made an official statement on the Korean truce negotiations, suggesting that "both sides in the negotiations should promise to repatriate all the detained prisoners who firmly insisted on their repatriation right after the truce, and turn over the rest of the prisoners to the neutral countries, in order to guarantee a fair solution for the POWs." On March 31 Kim echoed Zhou's new suggestion. On April 1 Molotov, Soviet foreign minister, made an announcement in support of both Chinese and North Korean statements. Chai believed that Zhou's suggestion removed the major obstacle in the negotiations over the POW problem and won international support for the Chinese–North Korean side.

70. General Chai next describes the Kumsong offensive campaign, the CPVF's last battle in the Korean War and a victory over Rhee's army. The ROK Army's losses were 30,000, the CPVF's estimated 66,000.

71. As both sides agreed, Nam Il and Harrison had already signed the Korean Armistice agreement at Panmunjom at 10:00 A.M. on July 27, 1953, and the truce became effective.

Selected Bibliography

CHINESE PARTY AND MILITARY PAPERS AND ARCHIVES

CCP Central Archives. *Zhonggong Zhongyang Wenjian Xuanji* [*Selected documents of the CCP Central Committee*]. 14 vols. Internal edition. Beijing: CCP Central Academy Press, 1983–1987.

———. *Zhonggong Zhongyang Wenjian Xuanji* [*Selected documents of the CCP Central Committee*]. 18 vols. Beijing: CCP Central Archives and Manuscripts Press, 1989–1992.

Central Institute of CCP Historical Documents, ed. *Jianguo Yilai Zhongyao Wenxian Xuanbian, 1949–1950* [*Selected important documents since the founding of the PRC*]. Beijing: CCP Central Press of Historical Documents, 1991.

Chaoxian Wenti Wenjian Huibian [*Selected documents of the Korean problem*]. Beijing: People's Press, 1954.

Chen Yun. *Chen Yun Wengao Xuanbian: 1949–1956* [*Selected manuscripts of Chen Yun: 1949–1956*]. Beijing: People's Press, 1984.

———. *Chen Yun Wenxuan: 1949–1956* [*Selected works of Chen Yun: 1949–1956*]. Jiangsu: People's Press, 1984.

CPVF Political Department. *Zhongguo Renmin Zhiyuanjun Kangmei Yuanchao Zhanzheng Zhengzhi Gongzuo Zongjie* [*A summary of the CPVF political work in the War to Resist America and Aid Korea*]. Beijing: PLA Press, 1989.

Division of Central Archives and Manuscripts, CCP Central Committee. *Zhonggong Dangshi Fengyun Lu* [*Records of the winds and clouds of the CCP history*]. Beijing: People's Press, 1990.

Documents and Commentaries on the Cease-Fire and Armistice Negotiations in Korea. 2 vols. Beijing: Foreign Languages Press, 1953.

Li Weihan. *Huiyi yu Yanjiu* [*Recollections and analyses*]. 2 vols. Vol. 2. Beijing: CCP Central Press of Historical Documents, 1986.

Li Xiannian. *Li Xiannian Wenxuan, 1935–1988* [*Selected works of Li Xiannian: 1935–1988*]. Beijing: People's Press, 1989.

Liu Shaoqi. *Liu Shaoqi Xuanji* [*Selected works of Liu Shaoqi*]. 2 vols. Vol. 2. Beijing: People's Press, 1985.

Liu Wusheng et al. *Gongheguo Zouguo de Lu: Jianguo yilai Zhongyao Wenxian Zhuanti Xuanji* [*The Path the Republic has walked through: A selected collection of important historical documents since the founding of the PRC, 1949–1952*]. 2 vols. Beijing: CCP Central Press of Historical Documents, 1991.

"Mao Informs Stalin of China's Decision to Enter the Korean War, 1950," trans. Xiaobing Li and Chen Jian. In *Major Problems in American Foreign Relations*, vol. 2, *Since 1914*, ed. Dennis Merrill and Thomas Paterson. New York: Houghton Mifflin, 2000.

"Mao's Dispatch of Chinese Troops to Korea: Forty-Six Telegrams, July–October 1950," trans. and ed. Xiaobing Li, Wang Xi, and Chen Jian. *Chinese Historians* 5, no. 1 (spring 1992).

"Mao's Forty-Nine Telegrams During the Korean War, October–December 1950," trans. and ed. Xiaobing Li and Glenn Tracy. *Chinese Historians* 5, no. 2 (fall 1992).

Mao Zedong. *Jianguo Yilai Mao Zedong Wengao* [*Mao Zedong's manuscripts since the founding of the PRC*]. Vols. 1–4: 1949–1954. Beijing: CCP Central Archives and Manuscripts Press, 1987–1993.

———. *Mao Zedong Junshi Wenji* [*A collection of Mao Zedong's military papers*]. 6 vols. Vols. 5–6. Beijing: Military Science Press and Central Press of Historical Documents, 1993.

———. *Mao Zedong Junshi Wenxuan—Neibuban* [*Selected military works of Mao Zedong—internal edition*]. Beijing: PLA Soldiers' Press, 1981.

———. *Mao Zedong Shuxin Xuanji* [*Selected correspondences of Mao Zedong*]. Beijing: People's Press, 1983.

———. *Mao Zedong Xuanji* [*Selected works of Mao Zedong*]. 5 vols. Vol. 5. Beijing: People's Press, 1978.

———. *Selected Military Writings of Mao Tsetung*. Beijing: Foreign Languages Press, 1967.

Shipping Advice Files (Captured CPVF documents), no. 2018, box 2,115, Washington, DC National Records Center, Suitland, Maryland.

Wang Jiaxiang. *Wang Jiaxiang Xuanji* [*Selected works of Wang Jiaxiang*]. Beijing: People's Press, 1989.

Zhang Shu Guang and Chen Jian, eds. *Chinese Communist Foreign Policy and the Cold War in Asia: New Documentary Evidence, 1944–1950*. Chicago: Imprint, 1996.

Zhonggong Danshi Jiaoxue Cankao Ziliao [*Reference sources for teaching CCP history*]. 21 vols. Vols. 18–19, 1945–1953. Beijing: National Defense University Press, 1986.

Zhongmei Guanxi Ziliao Huibian [*A collection of materials concerning Chinese-American relations*]. Beijing: World Knowledge Press, 1957.

Zhou Enlai. *Zhou Enlai Shuxin Xuanji* [*Selected telegrams and letters of Zhou Enlai*]. Beijing: CCP Central Archives and Manuscripts Press, 1988.

———. *Zhou Enlai Xuanji* [*Selected works of Zhou Enlai*]. 2 vols. Vol. 2. Beijing: CCP Central Archives and Manuscripts Press, 1984.

GENERALS' MEMOIRS AND WORKS

Chai Chengwen and Zhao Yongtian. *Banmendian Tanpan* [*The Panmunjom negotiations*]. Beijing: PLA Press, 1989; 2d ed., 1992.

————. *Kangmei Yuanchao Jishi* [*A chronicle of the War to Resist America and Aid Korea*]. Beijing: CCP Central Press of Historical Documents, 1987.

Chen Geng. *Chen Geng Riji (Xu)* [*Chen Geng's diary (continued)*]. Beijing: PLA Soldiers' Press, 1984.

Cheng Zihua. *Cheng Zihua Huiyilu* [*Memoirs of Cheng Zihua*]. Beijing: PLA Press, 1987.

"Chinese Generals Recall the Korean War," trans. and ed. Xiaobing Li and Donald Duffy. *Chinese Historians* 13–14 (1994).

Cui Lun. "Recollections of the Days Working as Chief Peng's Communication Officer in the Initial Stage of the War to Resist America and Aid Korea." *Junshi Lishi* [*Military History*] 4 (1989).

Deng Hua. *Lun Kangmei Yuanchao Zhanzheng Zuozhan Zhidao* [*On combat organization and operations in the War to Resist America and Aid Korea*]. Internal edition. Beijing: Military Science Press, 1989.

Deng Hua, Li Zhimin, and Hong Xuezhi. "We Remember Comrade Peng Dehuai's Brilliant Leadership of the CPVF." In *Hengdao Lima Peng Jiangjun* [*Marshal Peng is on the battle steed*]. Beijing: People's Press, 1979.

Dong Qiwu. *Rongma Chunqiu* [*Years of my military career*]. Beijing: Central Press of the CCP History, 1986.

Du Ping. *Zai Zhiyuanjun Zongbu* [*At the CPVF Headquarters: Memoirs of Du Ping*]. Beijing: PLA Press, 1989.

Gan Siqi and Li Zhimin, eds. *Zhongguo Renmin Zhiyuanjun Kangmei Yuanchao Zhanzheng Zhengzhi Gongzuo Zongjie* [*A summary of the CPVF political work in the War to Resist America and Aid Korea*]. Beijing: PLA Press, 1985.

Geng Biao. *Geng Biao Huiyilu* [*Geng Biao's memoirs*]. Beijing: PLA Press, 1991.

He Changgong. *He Changgong Huiyilu* [*He Changgong's memoirs*]. Beijing: PLA Press, 1987.

He Long. *He Long Junshi Wenxuan* [*Selected military papers of Marshal He Long*]. Beijing: PLA Press, 1989.

Hong Xuezhi. *Kangmei Yuanchao Zhanzheng Huiyi* [*Recollections of the War to Resist America and Aid Korea*]. Beijing: PLA Literature Press, 1990.

————. "The Logistic Affairs in the War to Resist America and Aid Korea." *Junshi Lishi* [*Military History*] 1 (1987).

Hua Shan. *Chaoxian Zhanchang Riji* [*Diaries of the Korean battlefield*]. Chongqing: New China Press, 1986.

Lei Yingfu. "My Recollection of the Decision Making on Several Crucial Issues During the War to Resist America and Aid Korea." *Dang de Wenxian* [*Party's Archives and Materials*] 6 (1993).

Li Jukui. *Li Jukui Huiyilu* [*Memoirs of Li Jukui*]. Beijing: PLA Press, 1986.

————. "March Forward in the Face of Difficulties: Recalling the CPVF's Logistic Affairs Before the Fifth Campaign." *Xinghuo Liaoyuan* 5 (1985).

Li Yimin. *Li Yimin Huiyilu* [*Memoirs of Li Yimin*]. Changsha: Hunan People's Press, 1986.

Li Zhimin, ed. *Zhadan yu Xianhua* [*Bombs and flowers*]. Beijing: PLA Press, 1985.

Liu Bocheng. *Liu Bocheng Huiyilu,* 3 vols. [*Memoirs of Liu Bocheng*]. Vol. 3. Shanghai: People's Press, 1988.

Liu Zhen. *Liu Zhen Huiyilu* [*Memoirs of Liu Zhen*]. Beijing: PLA Press, 1990.

Lu Zhengcao. *Lu Zhengcao Huiyilu* [*Memoirs of Lu Zhengcao*]. Beijing: PLA Press, 1988.

Nie Rongzhen. *Inside the Red Star: The Memoirs of Marshal Nie Rongzhen,* trans. Zhong Renyi. Beijing: New World Press, 1988.

———. *Nie Rongzhen Huiyilu* [*Memoirs of Nie Rongzhen*]. 3 vols. Vol. 2. Beijing: PLA Press, 1984.

———. *Nie Rongzhen Junshi Wenxuan* [*Selected military writings of Nie Rongzhen*]. Beijing: CCP Central Archives and Manuscripts Press, 1992.

Peng Dehuai. *Memoirs of a Chinese Marshal: The Autobiographical Notes of Peng Dehuai, 1898–1974*, trans. Zheng Longpu. Beijing: Foreign Languages Press, 1984.

———. *Peng Dehuai Junshi Wenxuan* [*Selected military works of Peng Dehuai*]. Beijing: CCP Central Archives and Manuscripts Press, 1988.

———. *Peng Dehuai Zishu* [*Autobiography of Peng Dehuai*]. Beijing: People's Press, 1981.

Song Shilun. *Xuexi Mao Zedong Zhidao Zhanzheng de Weida Shijian* [*Study of the invaluable experience of how Mao Zedong directed wars*]. Beijing: PLA Soldiers' Press, 1983.

Su Yu. *Su Yu Zhanzheng Huiyilu* [*Su Yu's war memoirs*]. Beijing: PLA Press, 1988.

Wang Dongxing. *Wang Dongxing Riji* [*Wang Dongxing's diaries*]. Beijing: Social Sciences Press, 1993.

Wang Yazhi. "Peng Dehuai and Nie Rongzhen During the War to Resist America and Aid Korea: A Recollection of a Staff Member." *Junshi Shilin* [*Studies of Military History*] 1 (1994).

Wu Ruilin. "Report to Chairman Mao on the Accomplishment of the Engineering Corps [During the Korean War]." *Junshi Shilin* [*Studies of Military History*] 6 (1993).

———. *Wu Ruilin Huiyilu* [*Wu Ruilin's memoirs*]. Beijing: CCP Central Archives and Manuscripts Press, 1995.

Wu Xiuquan. *Huiyi yu Huainian* [*Remembering and cherishing the memory*]. Beijing: CCP Central Academy Press, 1991.

Xiao Hua. *Jianku Suiyue* [*Those difficult years*]. Beijing: PLA Literature Press, 1983.

Xiao Jinguang. *Xiao Jinguang Huiyilu* [*Memoirs of Xiao Jinguang*]. 2 vols. Beijing: PLA Press, 1988 and 1989.

Xie Fang. *Kangmei Yuanchao Zhanzheng Houqin Jingyan Zongjie* [*Summaries of the experiences of logistical affairs during the War to Resist America and Aid Korea*]. 5 vols. Beijing: Golden Shield Press, 1987.

Xu Xiangqian. *Lishi de Huigu* [*History in retrospect*]. Vol. 2. Beijing: PLA Press, 1988.

Yang Chengwu. "A Call on Chairman Mao." *Dangshi Yanjiu yu Jiaoxue* [*Research and Teaching of Party History*] 5 (1990).

———. "The Entry of the 66th Army into the Korean War." *Dangshi Yanjiu yu Jiaoxue* [*Research and Teaching of Party History*] 2 (1990).

———. "On the Eve and After the Tianjin Conference." *Dangshi Yanjiu yu Jiaoxue* [*Research and Teaching of Party History*] 3 (1990).

———. "Preparing for Going to Battle." *Dangshi Yanjiu yu Jiaoxue* [*Research and Teaching of Party History*] 4 (1990).

———. *Xin de Shiming* [*A new mission*]. Beijing: Zhuoyue Press, 1989.

———. *Yang Chengwu Huiyilu* [*Yang Chengwu's memoirs*]. 2 vols. Beijing: PLA Press, 1987 and 1990.

Yang Dezhi. *Weile Heping* [*For the sake of peace*]. Beijing: Long March Press, 1987.

———. *Yang Dezhi Huiyilu* [*Memoirs of Yang Dezhi*]. Beijing: PLA Press, 1992.

Yang Di. *Zai Zhiyuanjun Silingbu de Suiyueli; Xianwei Renzhi de Zhenqing Shikuang* [*My years at the CPVF General Headquarters: Untold stories and facts*]. Beijing: PLA Press, 1998.

Yao Xu. *Cong Yalujiang dao Banmendian* [*From the Yalu River to Panmunjom*]. Beijing: People's Press, 1985.

Zeng Keling. *Rongma Shengya de Huiyi* [*Recollections of my military service*]. Beijing: PLA Press, 1992.

Zeng Sheng. *Zeng Sheng Huiyilu* [*Zeng Sheng's memoirs*]. Beijing: PLA Press, 1991.

Zhu De. *Zhu De Xuanji* [*Selected works of Zhu De*]. Anhui: People's Press, 1983.

RECOLLECTIONS AND BIOGRAPHIES

Ba Jin. "Our Conversation with Comrade Peng Dehuai." *Renmin Ribao* [*People's Daily*], April 9, 1952.

Bo Yibo. *Ruogan Zhongda Juece yu Shijian de Huigu* [*My recollections of decision making on several important policies and events*]. 2 vols. Vols. 1–2. Beijing: CCP Central Archives and Manuscripts Press, 1991 and 1993.

China Today Series. *Peng Dehuai Zhuan* [*Biography of Peng Dehuai*]. Beijing: China Today Press, 1993.

Chinese Academy of Military Science. *Ye Jianying Zhuanlue* [*Biography of Ye Jianying*]. Beijing: Military Science Press, 1987.

Cui Xianghua and Chen Dapeng. *Tao Yong Jiangjun Zhuan* [*Biography of General Tao Yong*]. Beijing: PLA Press, 1993.

Division of Central Archives and Manuscripts, CCP Central Committee. *Zhou Enlai Nianpu* [*The chronicle of Zhou Enlai*]. Beijing: CCP Central Archives and Manuscripts Press, 1989.

———. *Zhou Enlai Zhuan* [*Biography of Zhou Enlai*]. Beijing: People's Press, 1988.

———. *Zhu De Nianpu* [*The chronicle of Zhu De*]. Beijing: People's Press, 1986.

Dong Fanghe. *Zhang Aiping Zhuan* [*Biography of Zhang Aiping*]. Beijing: People's Press, 2000.

Fan Shuo and Ding Jiaqi. *Ye Jianying Zhuan* [*Biography of Ye Jianying*]. Beijing: China Today Press, 1995.

He Xiaolu. *Yuanshuai Waijiaojia* [*A marshal and a diplomat*]. Beijing: PLA Press, 1985.

Hu Jiamuo. "A Factual Record of General Peng's Leading Troops to Korea." *Mingren Zhuanji* [*Biographies of historical figures*] 10 (1990).

Hu Shiyan et al. *Chen Yi Zhuan* [*Biography of Marshal Chen Yi*]. Beijing: China Today Press, 1991.

Huang Yao. *Sanci Danan Busi de Luo Ruiqing Dajiang* [*General Luo Ruiqing—Survivor of three major crises*]. Beijing: CCP Central Academy Press, 1994.

Huang Yi. "Peng Dehuai's Great Contribution to the Logistic Affairs During the War to Resist America and Aid Korea." *Junshi Shilin* [*Studies of Military History*] 1 (1989).

Jiang Feng. *Yang Yong Jiangjun Zhuan* [*Biography of General Yang Yong*]. Beijing: PLA Press, 1991.

Jing Xizhen. *Gensui Peng Zong* [*Working for Commander in Chief Peng*]. Shenyang: Liaoning People's Press, 1984.

———. *Zai Peng Zong Shenbian: Jingwei Canmou de Huiyi* [*With Commander Peng: Recollections of a staff member*]. Chengdu: Sichuan People's Press, 1979.

Li Yinqiao. *Zai Mao Zhuxi Shenbian Shiwunian* [*With Chairman Mao for fifteen years*]. Shijiazhuang: Hebei People's Press, 1991.

Lin Qinshan. *Lin Biao Zhuan [Biography of Lin Biao]*. 2 vols. Beijing: Knowledge Press, 1988.

Liu Han. *Luo Ronghuan Yuanshuai [Marshal Luo Ronghuan]*. Beijing: PLA Press, 1987.

Luo Yinwen. "Realistically Putting Forward New Ideas: A Few Facts About General Deng Hua." *Ren Wu [Biographical Studies]* 5 (1985).

Meng Yunzeng. *Peng Zong zai Zhongnanhai [Commander Peng in Zhongnanhai]*. Changsha: Hunan Youth Press, 1983.

Mu Xin. *Chen Geng Dajiang [Senior General Chen Geng]*. Beijing: New China Press, 1985.

National Military Museum of Chinese People's Revolutions. *Peng Dehuai Yuanshuai Fengbei Yongcun [The remarkable achievement of Marshal Peng Dehuai remembered forever]*. Shanghai: People's Press, 1985.

Peng Dehuai Zhuanji Bianxiezu. *Yige Zhenzheng de Ren: Peng Dehuai [A real man: Peng Dehuai]*. Beijing: People's Press, 1994.

Qi Dexue. "Zhou Enlai's Important Contribution to the Command of the War to Resist America and Aid Korea." *Junshi Lishi [Military History]* 1 (1992).

Qi Pengfei and Wang Jin. *Mao Zedong yu Gongheguo Jiangshuai [Mao Zedong and China's marshals and generals]*. Beijing: Red Flag Press, 1995.

Shi Zhe. *Zai Lishi Juren Shengbian: Shi Zhe Huiyilu [Together with historical giants: Shi Zhe's memoirs]*. Beijing: CCP Central Archives and Manuscripts Press, 1991.

Sun Yaoshen. "General Xie Fang in the War to Resist America and Aid Korea." *Junshi Lishi [Military History]* 4 (1990).

Sun Yaoshen and Cui Jingshan. "Winning Victory Not Just on the Battlefield: General Xie Fang in Korea." *Ren Wu [Biographical Studies]* 1 (1991).

Wang Bo. *Peng Dehuai Ruchao Zuozhan Jishi [A factual account of Peng Dehuai's leading troops to fight in Korea]*. Shijiazhuang: Huashan Literature Press, 1992.

Xu Peilan and Zheng Pengfei. *Chen Geng Jiangjun Zhuan [Biography of General Chen Geng]*. Beijing: PLA Press, 1988.

Yang Wanqing. "Liu Yalou: The First Commander of the PLA Air Force." *Zhonggong Danshi Ziliao [Sources of CCP History]* 42 (1992).

Yao Xu. "Comrade Deng Hua in the War to Resist America and Aid Korea." *Hunan Danshi Tongxun [Party History Studies in Hunan]* 3–4 (1985).

———. "Peng Dehuai's Contribution to the War to Resist America and Aid Korea." *Danshi Yanjiu Ziliao [Sources for Party History Research]* 1 (1982).

Zhang Pingkai. *Peng Dehuai Shuaishi Yuanchao [Peng Dehuai led the troops in the War to Aid Korea]*. Shenyang: Liaoning People's Press, 1989.

Zhang Xi. *Peng Dehuai Shouming Shuaishi Kangmei Yuanchao de Qianqian Houhou [The complete history of Peng Dehuai's appointment to lead the War to Resist America and Aid Korea]*. Beijing: CCP Central Archives and Manuscripts Press, 1989.

Zhang Yunsheng. *Maojiawan Jishi: Lin Biao Mishu Huiyilu [Maojiawan account: The memoirs of Lin Biao's secretary]*. Beijing: Chunqiu Press, 1988.

Zhu Shiliang. *Peng Dehuai zai Chaoxian Zhanchang [Peng Dehuai at the Korean battlefield]*. Shenyang: Liaoning People's Press, 1996.

THE CPVF HISTORY

Bao Mingrong. "When Was the Strategy of Mobile Warfare in Korea Made?" *Dangshi Yanjiu Ziliao [Sources for Party History Research]* 7 (1988).

Bao Mingrong and Hu Guangzheng. "Several Problems Concerning the Application and Development of Mao Zedong's Military Thought During the War to Resist America and Aid Korea." *Dangshi Yanjiu* [*Studies of Party History*] 6 (1983).

Cai Tianfu. "Major Lessons of the Fifth-Phase Offensive in the War to Resist America and Aid Korea." *Junshi Lishi* [*Military History*] 5 (1990).

Cao Yihong. *Sanshibajun Juanzi: Liang Xingchu yu "Wansuijun" Zhengzhan Jishi* [*The Thirty-eighth Army: Military history of General Liang Xingchu and the "Long-Live Army"*]. Lanzhou: Dunhuang Literature Press, 1994.

Chen Zhongnong, ed. *Zhongguo Renmin Zhiyuanjun Renwu Zhi* [*The chronicles of the Chinese People's Volunteers Force*]. Vol. 1. Nanjing: Jiangsu People's Press, 1990.

China Today Series. *Kangmei Yuanchao Zhanzheng* [*The War to Resist America and Aid Korea*]. Beijing: Social Sciences Press, 1990.

Chinese Academy of Military Science. *Zhongguo Renmin Zhiyuanjun Kangmei Yuanchao Zhanshi* [*The history of the CPVF in the War to Resist America and Aid Korea*]. Beijing: Military Science Press, 1988.

Da Wan. "Miraculous Forces from the Sky: The First Battle After Chief Peng Entered Korea." *Ren Wu* [*Biographical Studies*] 5 (1990).

Da Ying. *Zhiyuanjun Zhanfu Jishi* [*Voices from the CPVF POWs*]. Beijing: Kunlun Press, 1987.
———. *Zhiyuanjun Zhanfu Jishi, Xuji* [*Voices from the CPVF POWs (continued)*]. Beijing: China's Youth Press, 1993.

Eight Years of the Chinese People's Volunteers Forces in the War to Resist America and Aid Korea. Beijing: Foreign Languages Press, 1958.

Feng Jinhui. *Chaozhong Zhanfu Qianfan Neimu* [*Inside story of the repatriation of CPVF–NKPA POWs*]. Beijing: Huayi Press, 1990.

Guo Baohen and Hu Zhiyuan. *Chicheng Hanjiang Nanbei: Sishierjun zai Chaoxian* [*Fighting over the Han River: The Forty-second Army in Korea*]. Shenyang: Liaoning People's Press, 1996.

Huang Yi. "Major Lessons and Problems Concerning the CPVF Logistics Work in the State of Mobile Warfare in the War to Resist America and Aid Korea." *Junshi Shilin* [*Studies of Military History*] 5 (1990).

Hu Guangzheng. "On the Decision to Send Troops Participating in the War to Resist America and Aid Korea." *Dangshi Yanjiu* [*Studies of Party History*] 1 (1983).

Hu Guangzheng and Bao Mingrong. "Corrections of Some Historical Facts in 'On the Decision to Send Troops Participating in the War to Resist America and Aid Korea.'" *Dangshi Yanjiu* [*Studies of Party History*] 3 (1981).

Hu Guangzheng and Ma Shanying, eds. *Zhongguo Renmin Zhiyuanjun Xulie* [*The CPVF order of battles: October 1950–July 1953*]. Beijing: PLA Press, 1987.

Jiang Yonghui. *Sanshibajun zai Chaoxian* [*The Thirty-eighth Army in Korea*]. Shenyang: Liaoning People's Press, 1989.

Jing Yu. "The Military Experience of Our Troops During the Korean War." *Junshi Shilin* [*Studies of Military History*] 5 (1988).

Kangmei Yuanchao Zhanzheng Houqin Jingyan Zongjie—Houqin Zhanli Xuanbian [*A summary of the CPVF logistical service experience in the War to Resist America and Aid Korea—Selected cases*]. Beijing: Golden Shield Press, 1986.

Kangmei Yuanchao Zhanzheng Houqin Jingyan Zongjie—Jiben Jingyan [*A summary of the CPVF logistical service experience in the War to Resist America and Aid Korea—Basic lessons*]. Beijing: Golden Shield Press, 1987.

Kangmei Yuanchao Zhanzheng Houqin Jingyan Zongjie—Zhuanye Qinwu [*A summary of the CPVF logistical service experience in the War to Resist America and Aid Korea— Special work*]. 2 vols. Beijing: Golden Shield Press, 1987.

Korean War Series. *Chaoxian Zhanzheng: Zhonggongjun Canzhan ji Lianhejun Congxin Fangong* [*The Korean War: Intervention of the Chinese forces and counteroffensive of the U.S./UN forces*]. Vol. 1. Internal edition. Heilongjiang: Korean Minority Press, n.d.

———. *Chaoxian Zhanzheng: Zhanxian Dongdang Shiqi* [*The Korean War: The turbulent period*]. Vol. 2. Internal edition. Heilongjiang: Korean Minority Press, n.d.

———. *Chaoxian Zhanzheng: Duishi Chuqi* [*The Korean War: The initial stage of the stale-mated war*]. Vol. 3. Internal edition. Heilongjiang: Korean Minority Press, n.d.

———. *Chaoxian Zhanzheng: Duishi Zhongqi* [*The Korean War: The middle stage of the stalemated war*]. Vol. 4. Internal edition. Heilongjiang: Korean Minority Press, n.d.

———. *Chaoxian Zhanzheng: Duishi Huoqi* [*The Korean War: The last stage of the stale-mated war*]. Vol. 5. Internal edition. Heilongjiang: Korean Minority Press, n.d.

Li Hui. "Some Lessons from the CPVF Defensive Battles During the War to Resist Amer-ica and Aid Korea." *Junshi Lishi* [*Military History*] 3 (1994).

Li Hui and Jian Shihua. "A Short Story About the CPVF's Withdrawal from Korea in 1958." *Junshi Lishi* [*Military History*] 2 (1994).

Li Ying et al. *Jiekai Zhanzheng Xumu de Xianfeng: Sishijun zai Chaoxian* [*The Vanguard Army engaged first in the war: The Fortieth Army in Korea*]. Shenyang: Liaoning Peo-ple's Press, 1996.

National Military Museum of Chinese People's Revolutions. *Kangmei Yuanchao Zhanzheng Fengyunlu* [*Records of the War to Resist America and Aid Korea*]. Guangzhou: Huacheng Press, 1999.

Nie Jifeng. "The Bloody Battle at Mount Shanggan." *Junshi Shilin* [*Studies of Military His-tory*] 2 (1994).

Qi Dexue. "Important Decision Making in the Chinese People's Volunteers Force." *Danshi Yanjiu Ziliao* [*Sources for Party History Research*] 3 (1987).

———. *Chaoxian Zhanzheng Juece Neimu* [*Inside stories of decision making in the Korean War*]. Shenyang: Liaoning University Press, 1991.

———. "On Some Key Issues Concerning the Decision Making for Entering the Korean War." *Junshi Lishi* [*Military History*] 2 (1993).

Shi ling. *Jiaoshazhan de Kexing: Gongan Budui Fangkongshao* [*Heroes of the Korean War: Anti-air watchers of the (CPVF) Security Force*]. Shenyang: Liaoning People's Press, 1996.

Song Yijun. "One Challenge and One Progress: On the Cost and Benefit of the Fifth-phase Offensive in the War to Resist America and Aid Korea." *Junshi Shilin* [*Studies of Mil-itary History*] 5 (1990).

Sun Qitai. "A Brief Summary of the War to Resist America and Aid Korea." *Zhonggong Dangshi Ziliao* [*Sources of CCP History*] 36 (1990).

Tan Zheng. *Zhongguo Renmin Zhiyuanjun Renwulu* [*Biographical records of the CPVF members*]. Beijing: Central Press of the CCP History, 1992.

University of National Defense. *Kangmei Yuanchao Zhanzheng Jingyan Huibian* [*A col-lection on combat experiences in the War to Resist America and Aid Korea*]. Internal edition. Beijing: National Defense University Press, 1956.

———. *Zhongguo Renmin Zhiyuanjun Zhanshi Jianbian* [*A short military history of the*

Chinese People's Volunteers Force]. Beijing: National Defense University Press, 1986.

Wang Suhong and Wang Yubin. *Kongzhan zai Chaoxian [Air war in Korea*]. Beijing: PLA Literature Press, 1992.

Wu Ruilin. *Kangmei Yuanchao zhongde Sishierjun [The Forty-second Army in the War to Resist America and Aid Korea*]. Beijing: Golden City Press, 1995.

Wu Xinquan. *Chaoxian Zhanchang 1000 Tian: Sanshijiujun zai Chaoxian [One thousand days on the Korean battlefield: The Thirty-ninth Army in Korea*]. Shenyang: Liaoning People's Press, 1996.

Xu Chen. *Xueran de Jindalai: Chebing Chaoxian Jishi [Bloody tulips: True story of the CPVF withdrawal from Korea*]. Beijing: China Social Press, 1992.

Xu Qingyue. *Jichu Jiluo Sanbaxian: Kangmei Yuanchao Jishi [Fighting over the Thirty-eighth Parallel: History of the War to Resist America and Aid Korea*]. Beijing: Military Science Press, 1995.

Xu Yan. "Chinese Forces and Their Casualties in the Korean War: Facts and Statistics," trans. Xiaobing Li. *Chinese Historians* 2 (fall 1993).

———. *Diyici Jiaoliang: Kangmei Yuanchao Zhanzheng de Lishi Huigu yu Fansi [The first trial: A historical retrospective and review of the War to Resist America and Aid Korea*]. Beijing: China Radio and Television Press, 1990.

———. "The Tortuous Process of Making the Final Decision to Enter the Korean War." *Dangshi Yanjiu Ziliao [Sources for Party History Research]* 4 (1991).

Xu Yipeng. *Zhihu—Chaoxian Tingzhan Gaoceng Juedoulu [Straight curve—Story of the top-level struggle for the Korean Armistice*]. Nanjing: Jiangsu People's Press, 1997.

Xue Qi. "An Important Strategic Decision of the CPVF Command." *Dangshi Yanjiu [Studies of Party History]* 5 (1985).

Yan Shixin. "A Glorious Example of Patriotism and Internationalism: New Development of Political Work in the War to Resist America and Aid Korea." *Dangshi Yanjiu [Studies of Party History]* 6 (1984).

Yang Fengan and Wang Tiancheng. *Jiayu Chaoxian Zhanzheng de Ren [The people who controlled the Korean War*]. Beijing: CCP Central Academy Press, 1993.

Yao Xu. "Wise Decision Making in the War to Resist America and Aid Korea." *Dangshi Yanjiu [Studies of Party History]* 5 (1980).

———. *Cong Yalujiang dao Banmendian [From the Yalu River to Panmunjom*]. Beijing: People's Press, 1985.

Ye Yumeng. *Chubing Chaoxian: Kangmei Yuanchao Lishi Jishi [Entering the Korean War: A true story of the War to Resist America and Aid Korea*]. Beijing: October Literature Press, 1990.

Zhang Xi. "The Sudden Cancellation of the CPVF's Movement on the Eve of Its Entry into Korea." *Danshi Yanjiu Ziliao [Sources for Party History Research]* 1 (1993).

Zhang Yongmei. *Meijun Baiyu Woshou; Chaoxian Zhanzheng Jishi [How the American army lost to us: History of the Korean War*]. Beijing: PLA Press, 1995.

Zhang Zeshi. *Meijun Jizhongying Qinliji [Personal stories of the (CPVF) POWs in American camps*]. Beijing: History and Literature Press, 1996.

Zhao Yihong. *Nie Fengzhi yu Ershiqijun Zhengzhan Jishi [Military history of Nie Fengzhi and the Twenty-seventh Army*]. Changchun: Jilin People's Press, 1995.

Zhiyuanjun Yingxiong Zhuan [The chronicle of the CPVF heroes]. Vol. 1. Beijing: People's Literature Press, 1956.

Zhou Zhong, ed. *Kangmei Yuanchao Zhanzheng Houqinshi Jianbianben* [*Short history of the logistical affairs in the War to Resist America and Aid Korea*]. Beijing: Golden Shield Press, 1994.

OTHER CHINESE LITERATURE ON THE CPVF

Chen Yan, ed. *Kangmei Yuanchao Lunwenji* [*Essays on the War to Resist America and Aid Korea*]. Shenyang: Liaoning People's Press, 1988.
China Today Series. *Dangdai Zhongguo Haijun* [*China Today: The PLA navy*]. Beijing: Social Sciences Press, 1987.
———. *Dangdai Zhongguo Jundui de Junshi Gongzuo* [*China Today: The military affairs of the Chinese army*]. 2 vols. Beijing: Social Sciences Press, 1989.
———. *Dangdai Zhongguo Jundui de Qunzhong Gongzuo* [*China Today: Mass work of the Chinese military*]. Beijing: Social Sciences Press, 1988.
———. *Dangdai Zhongguo Kongjun* [*China Today: The PLA air force*]. Beijing: Social Sciences Press, 1989.
Chinese Academy of Military Science. *Zhongguo Renmin Jiefangjun Liushinian Dashiji: 1927–1987* [*Records of important PLA events from 1927 to 1987*]. Beijing: Military Science Press, 1988.
———. *Zhongguo Renmin Jiefangjun Zhanshi* [*The military history of the People's Liberation Army*]. Vol. 3. Beijing: Military Science Press, 1987.
Deng Lifeng. *Xin Zhongguo Junshi Huodong Jishi, 1949–1959* [*A factual record of China's military affairs*]. Beijing: CCP Central Press of Historical Documents, 1989.
Han Qiufeng and Li Qinyang. "Mao Zedong Inherited and Developed the Traditional Strategists' Thoughts on Military Spirit." *Mao Zedong Sixiang Yanjiu* [*Studies of Mao Zedong Thought*] 4 (1989).
Hu Changshui. "The Formation of the Concept That Imperialism Is a Paper Tiger." *Dangshi Yanjiu Ziliao* [*Sources for Party History Research*] 7 (1988).
Hu Hua et al. *Zhonggong Dangshi Renwu Zhuan* [*A collection of biographies of CCP historical figures*]. 50 vols. Xi'an: Shanxi People's Press, 1979–1991.
Hu Qinghe. *Chaoxian Zhanzheng zhong de Niuren* [*Women in the Korean War*]. Jinan: Yellow River Press, 1992.
Huang Yuzhang, ed. *Jubu Zhanzheng de Zuotian Jintian Mingtian* [*Limited wars: Past, present, and future*]. Beijing: National Defense University Press, 1988.
Huang Zhenxia. *Zhonggong Junren Zhi* [*Annals of the Chinese Communist soldiers*]. Hong Kong: Institute of Contemporary History, 1968.
Jiang Siyi, ed. *Zhongguo Renmin Jiefangjun Zhengzhi Gongzuoshi* [*History of the PLA's political work*]. Beijing: PLA Political Institute Press, 1984.
Kongjun Shi [*History of the PLA air force*]. Beijing: PLA Press, 1987.
Li Cheng, ed. *Jianguo Yilai Junshi Baizhuang Dashi* [*A hundred major events in military history since the founding of the PRC*]. Beijing: Knowledge Press, 1992.
Lin Boye. *Junshi Bianzhengfa Sixiang Shi* [*History of theoretic development of military dialectics*]. Beijing: PLA Press, 1989.
———. *Xuexi Mao Zedong Junshi Zhuzuo zhong de Zhexue Sixiang* [*The philosophical points contained in Mao Zedong's military writings*]. Tianjin: People's Press, 1982.

Liu Hongxuan. "A Summary of the Theoretical Symposium on the Fortieth Anniversary of the War to Resist America and Aid Korea." *Junshi Shilin* [*Studies of Military History*] 6 (1990).

Liu Huajing and Shan Xufa. *Mao Zedong Junshi Bianzhengfa Yanjiu* [*A study of Mao Zedong's military dialectics*]. Wuhan: Hubei People's Press, 1984.

Liu Zhiquan. *Zhidaoyuan Gongzuo Yishu* [*The art of political work of company political instructors*]. Beijing: PLA Press, 1990.

Lu Liping. *Tongtian Zhilu* [*The path to the sky*]. Beijing: PLA Press, 1989.

Ma Jinhai, ed. *Zhonggong Hujiang yu Mingzhan* [*China's great generals and their famous battles*]. Beijing: Social Sciences Press, 1995.

Meng Zhaohui. "The Application and Development of Mao Zedong's Military Thought in the War to Resist America and Aid Korea." *Junshi Lishi* [*Military History*] 1 (1991).

———. "Mao Zedong's Strategic Decisions [on the Korean] War Show Great Foresight." *Junshi Lishi* [*Military History*] 6 (1993).

The Military Library of the Chinese Academy of Military Science, ed. *Zhongguo Renmin Jiefangjun Zuzhi he Geji Lingdao Chengyuan Minglu* [*A list of the historical evolution of organizations and leading members of the PLA*]. 3 vols. Beijing: Military Science Press, 1987.

Pak Toufu. *Zhonggong Canjia Hanzhan Yuanyin zhi Yanjiu* [*An examination of why the CCP decided to participate in the Korean War*]. Taipei: Numin Cultural Service, 1975.

Ruan Jiaxin. "The War to Resist America and Aid Korea and the Rise of the New China." *Junshi Shilin* [*Studies of Military History*] 6 (1993).

Shang Jinsuo. *Luelun yi Lie Shengyou* [*On how a weak nation can defeat a strong enemy*]. Beijing: PLA Press, 1990.

Shen Zhihua. *Chaoxian Zhanzheng Jiemi* [*Secrets of the Korean War*]. Hong Kong: Cosmos Books, 1995.

———. *Mao Zedong, Sidalin, yu Hanzhan: Zhongsu Zuigao Jimi Tangan* [*Mao Zedong, Stalin, and the Korean War: The Chinese and Soviet top secret documents*]. Hong Kong: Cosmos Books, 1998.

Sun Ke. "On the New Development of Mao Zedong's Idea of People's War in the War to Resist America and Aid Korea." *Junshi Lishi* [*Military History*] 5 (1990).

Sun Yuqi. *Yalujiang Gaosu Ni* [*Story told by the Yalu River*]. Beijing: People's Literature Press, 1995.

University of National Defense. *Zhongguo Renmin Jiefangjun Zhengzhi Gongzuo Shi* [*History of the PLA's political work*]. Beijing: National Defense University Press, 1989.

Wang Funian. "A Summary of the Negotiations on the Korean Cease-fire." *Dangshi Yanjiu Ziliao* [*Sources for Party History Research*] 6 (1983).

Wei Bai. *Siye Shida Zhuli Chuanqi* [*The ten main formations in the Fourth Field Army*]. Jinan: Yellow River Press, 1996.

Wei Daizong. "Three Important Suggestions During the War to Resist America and Aid Korea." *Junshi Lishi* [*Military History*] 3 (1994).

Xia Zhennan. "On the Relationship Between War and Politics." *Mao Zedong Sixiang Yanjiu* [*Studies of Mao Zedong's Thought*] 3 (1987).

Xie Lifu. *Chaoxian Zhanzheng Shilu* [*True history of the Korean War*]. 2 vols. Beijing: World Affairs Press, 1993.

Xinghuo Liaoyuan, Editorial Division. *Jiefangjun Jiangling Zhuan* [*The chronicle of PLA senior generals*]. Vol. 1. Beijing: PLA Press, 1984.

———. *Jiefangjun Jiangling Zhuan* [*The chronicle of PLA senior generals*]. Vol. 3. Beijing: PLA Press, 1986.

———. *Jiefangjun Jiangling Zhuan* [*The chronicle of PLA senior generals*]. Vol. 7. Beijing: PLA Press, 1988.

Xiong Huayuan. "Zhou Enlai's Secret Visit to the Soviet Union Right Before China's Entry in the War to Resist America and Aid Korea." *Dang de Wenxian* [*CCP Documents and Materials*] 3 (1994).

Ye Yumeng. *Hanjiang Xue* [*The blood of the Han River*]. Beijing: Daily Economy Press, 1990.

———. *Heixue: Chubing Chaoxian Kangmei Yuanchao Lishi Jishi* [*The black snow: Historical records of Chinese military intervention in Korea*]. Beijing: Writer's Press, 1989.

Yi Yun. "When Was the PLA Air Force Established?" *Junshi Lishi* [*Military History*] 1 (1990).

Zhang Ding and Zhang Bing. *Lingxiu Shenbian de Junshi Gaocan* [*The senior staff by the leaders' side*]. Chengdu: University of Electronic Science Press, 1993.

Zhang Zhenglong. *Xuebai Xuehong* [*White snow and red blood*]. Beijing: PLA Press, 1989.

ENGLISH LITERATURE

Appleman, Roy E. *Disaster in Korea: The Chinese Confront MacArthur*. College Station: Texas A & M University Press, 1989.

Avakian, Bob. *Mao Tsetung's Immortal Contributions*. Chicago: RCP Publications, 1979.

Barnett, A. Doak. *China and the Major Powers in East Asia*. Washington, DC: Brookings Institution, 1977.

Chang, Gordon H. *Friends and Enemies: The United States, China, and the Soviet Union, 1948–1972*. Stanford: Stanford University Press, 1990.

Chen Jian. "China's Changing Aims During the Korean War." *Journal of American–East Asian Relations* 1 (spring 1992).

———. *China's Road to the Korean War: The Making of the Sino-American Confrontation*. New York: Columbia University Press, 1994.

———. "The Sino-Soviet Alliance and China's Entry into the Korean War." Working paper no. 1. *Cold War International History Project,* Woodrow Wilson International Center, Washington, DC, 1992.

Christensen, Thomas. "Threats, Assurances, and the Last Chance for Peace: The Lessons of Mao's Korean War Telegrams." *International Security* 17 (summer 1992).

———. *Useful Adversaries: Grand Strategy, Domestic Mobilization, and Sino-American Conflict, 1947–1958*. Princeton: Princeton University Press, 1996.

Cohen, Warren I. *America's Response to China: An Interpretive History of Sino-American Relations*. 3d ed. New York: Columbia University Press, 1990.

———. "Conversations with Chinese Friends: Zhou Enlai's Associates Reflect on Chinese-American Relations in the 1940s and the Korean War." *Diplomatic History* 11, no. 2 (1987).

Cumings, Bruce. *The Origins of the Korean War*. 2 vols. Princeton: Princeton University Press, 1981 and 1990.

Domes, Jurgen. *Peng Te-huai: The Man and the Image*. Stanford: Stanford University Press, 1985.

Farrar-Hockley, Anthony. "A Reminiscence of the Chinese People's Volunteers in the Korean War." *China Quarterly* 98 (June 1984).

Foot, Rosemary. "Make the Unknown War Known: Policy Analysis of the Korean Conflict in the Last Decade." *Diplomatic History* 15, no. 3 (1991).

————. *A Substitute for Victory: The Politics of Peacemaking at the Korean Armistice Talks.* Ithaca, NY: Cornell University Press, 1990.

George, Alexander L. *The Chinese Communist Army in Action: The Korean War and Its Aftermath.* New York: Columbia University Press, 1967.

Gittings, John. *The Role of the Chinese Army.* New York: Oxford University Press, 1967.

Godwin, Paul. *The Chinese Communist Armed Forces.* Maxwell, AL: Air Force University Press, 1988.

Goldstein, Steven M., and He Di. "New Chinese Sources on the History of the Cold War." *Cold War International History Bulletin* 1, Woodrow Wilson International Center (spring 1992).

Goncharov, Sergei N., John W. Lewis, and Xue Litai. *Uncertain Partners: Stalin, Mao, and the Korean War.* Stanford: Stanford University Press, 1993.

Hanrahan, Gene Z., and Edward L. Katzenbach Jr. "The Revolutionary Strategy of Mao Tse-tung." In *Modern Guerrilla Warfare,* ed. Franklin Mark Osanka. New York: Free Press of Glencoe, 1969.

Hao Yufan and Zhai Zhihai. "China's Decision to Enter the Korean War: History Revisited." *China Quarterly* 121 (March 1990).

Harding, Harry, and Yuan Ming, eds. *Sino-American Relations, 1945–1955: A Joint Reassessment of a Critical Decade.* Wilmington, DE: Scholarly Resources, 1989.

Holliday, Jon. "Air Operations in Korea: The Soviet Side of the Story." In *A Revolutionary War: Korea and the Transformation of the Postwar World,* ed. William J. Williams. Chicago: Imprint, 1993.

Hoyt, Edwin P. *The Day the Chinese Attacked Korea, 1950.* New York: McGraw-Hill, 1990.

Hunt, Michael H. "Beijing and the Korean Crisis, June 1950–June 1951." *Political Science Quarterly* 107 (1992): no. 3.

Hunt, Michael H., and Odd Arne Westad. "The Chinese Communist Party and International Affairs: A Field Report on New Historical Sources and Old Research Problems." *China Quarterly* 122 (1990).

Joffe, Ellis. *Party and Army: Professionalism and Political Control in the Chinese Officer Corps, 1948–1964.* Cambridge: Harvard University Press, 1967.

Kalicki, J. H. *The Pattern of Sino-American Crises: Political-Military Interactions in the 1950s.* New York: Cambridge University Press, 1975.

Kau, Michael Y. M., and John K. Leung, eds. *The Writings of Mao Zedong, 1946–1976,* vol. 1, *September 1949–October 1955.* Armonk, NY: M. E. Sharpe, 1986.

Khrushchev, Nikita S. "Truth About the Korean War." *Far Eastern Affairs* [Moscow] 1 (1990).

Kim, Chullbaum, ed. *The Truth About the Korean War: Testimony Forty Years Later.* Seoul: Eulyoo Publishing Company, 1991.

Kim, Chum-kon. *The Korean War, 1950–1953.* Seoul: Kwangmyong Publishing, 1980.

Lewis, John Wilson, and Xue Litai. *China Builds the Bomb.* Stanford: Stanford University Press, 1988.

Li Haiwen. "How and When Did China Decide to Enter the Korean War?" trans. Chen Jian. *Korea and World Affairs* 18, no. 1 (spring 1994).

MacFarquhar, Roderick, ed. *Sino-American Relations, 1949–1971*. New York: Praeger, 1972.

Matray, James I., ed. *Historical Dictionary of the Korean War*. Westport, CT: Greenwood Press, 1991.

Millett, Allan R. "Understanding Is Better Than Remembering: The Korean War, 1945–1954." In *The Seventh Eisenhower Lecture in Military History*. Manhattan: Kansas State University Press, 1997.

Pollack, Jonathan D. "The Korean War and Sino-American Relations." In Harding and Ming, eds., *Sino-American Relations, 1945–1955*.

Ryan, Mark A. *Chinese Attitude Toward Nuclear Weapons: China and the United States During the Korean War*. Armonk, NY: M. E. Sharpe, 1989.

Schram, Stuart. *The Thought of Mao Tse-tung*. New York: Cambridge University Press, 1989.

Scobell, Andrew. "Soldiers, Statesmen, Strategic Culture and China's 1950 Intervention in Korea." *Journal of Contemporary China* 22, no. 8 (1999).

Segal, Gerald. *Defending China*. New York: Oxford University Press, 1955.

Shambaugh, David. "China's Military in Transition: Politics, Professionalism, Procurement, and Power Projection." *China Quarterly* 146 (June 1996).

Shen, Zhihua. "China Sends Troops to Korea: Beijing's Policy-Making Process." In *China and the United States: A New Cold War History,* ed. Xiaobing Li and Hongshan Li. Lanham, MD: University Press of America, 1998.

Sheng, Michael M. "Beijing's Decision to Enter the Korean War: A Reappraisal and New Documentation." *Korea and World Affairs* 19, no. 2 (summer 1995).

Simmon, Robert R. *The Strained Alliance: Peking, Pyongyang, and the Politics of the Korean Civil War*. New York: Free Press, 1975.

Spurr, Russell. *Enter the Dragon: China's Undeclared War Against the U.S. in Korea*. New York: New Market Press, 1988.

Stueck, William. *The Korean War: An International History*. Princeton: Princeton University Press, 1995.

Teiwes, Frederick C. "Peng Dehuai and Mao Zedong." *Australian Journal of Chinese Affairs* 16 (July 1986).

Tucker, Nancy Bernkopf. *Patterns in the Dust: Chinese-American Relations and the Recognition Controversy, 1949–1950*. New York: Columbia University Press, 1983.

Tuchman, Barbara. "If Mao Had Come to Washington: An Essay in Alternatives." *Foreign Affairs* 51, no. 1 (1971).

Usov, Victor. "Who Sent the Chinese Volunteers?" *Far Eastern Affairs* [Moscow] 1 (1991).

Vatcher, William H. Jr. *Panmunjom: The Story of the Korean Military Armistice Negotiations*. New York: Praeger, 1958.

War Memorial Service–Korea. *The Historical Reillumination of the Korean War*. Seoul: Korean War Research Conference Committee, 1990.

Weathersby, Kathryn. "Soviet Aim in Korea and the Origins of the Korean War, 1949–1950: New Evidence from Russian Archives." Working paper no. 8. *Cold War International History Project,* Woodrow Wilson International Center, Washington, DC, 1993.

Weiss, Lawrence S. "Storm Around the Cradle: The Korean War and the Early Years of the People's Republic of China, 1949–1953." Ph.D. dissertation, Columbia University, 1981.

West, Philip. "Confronting the West: China as David and Goliath in the Korean War." *Journal of American–East Asian Relations* 2 (spring 1993).

Whiting, Allen S. *China Crosses the Yalu: The Decision to Enter the Korean War*. New York: Macmillan, 1960.

————. *The Chinese Calculus of Deterrence.* Ann Arbor: University of Michigan Press, 1975.

————. "The Sino-Soviet Split." In *The Cambridge History of China,* vol. 14, *The Emergence of Revolutionary China, 1949–1965,* ed. R. MacFarquhar and J. K. Fairbank. Cambridge: Cambridge University Press, 1987.

Whitson, William W. *The Chinese High Command: A History of Communist Military Politics, 1927–1971.* New York: Praeger, 1973.

Yu, Bin. "Sino-American and Sino-Soviet Relations." In *The Modernization of China's Diplomacy,* ed. Jianwei Wang and Zhinmin Lin. Armonk, NY: M. E. Sharpe, 1997.

————. "What China Learned from Its 'Forgotten War' in Korea." *Strategic Review* (summer 1998).

Zaloga, Steven J. "The Russians in MIG Alley." *Air Force Magazine* 74 (February 1991).

Zelman, Walter A. *Chinese Intervention in the Korean War: A Bilateral Failure of Deterrence.* Los Angeles: University of California Press, 1967.

Zhang, Shu Guang. *Deterrence and Strategic Culture: Chinese-American Confrontations, 1949–1958.* Ithaca, NY: Cornell University Press, 1992.

————. *Mao's Military Romanticism: China and the Korean War, 1950–1953.* Lawrence: University Press of Kansas, 1995.

————. "Preparedness Eliminates Mishap: The CCP's Security Concerns in 1949–1950 and the Origins of Sino-American Confrontation." *Journal of American–East Asian Relations* 1, no. 1 (1992).

Zhang Xi. "Peng Dehuai and China's Entry into the Korean War," trans. Chen Jian. *Chinese Historians* 6, no. 1 (1993).

Zhu, Fang. *Gun Barrel Politics: Party-Army Relations in Mao's China.* Boulder, CO: Westview Press, 1998.

Index